鳥 山 明

To be honest, I'm always struggling to come up with something to write about here. If you're busy working on a weekly serial, then there shouldn't be anything all that special happening in your life to write about. What's even more painful is coming up with the "What's happening this issue" promo text for the table of contents in **Weekly Shonen Jump** magazine. This is a secret, but more than half of the comments made on that page are actually written by my editor, Mr. Kondo. He always asks me, "Did anything interesting happen this week?" Nothing really did…

—*Akira Toriyama, 1991*

Artist/writer Akira Toriyama burst onto the manga scene in 1980 with the wildly popular **Dr. Slump**, a science fiction comedy about the adventures of a mad scientist and his android "daughter." In 1984 he created his hit series **Dragon Ball**, which ran until 1995 in Shueisha's best-selling magazine **Weekly Shonen Jump**, and was translated into foreign languages around the world. Since **Dragon Ball**, he has worked on a variety of short series, including **Cowa!**, **Kajika**, **Sand Land**, and **Neko Majin**, as well as a children's book, **Toccio the Angel**. He is also known for his design work on video games, particularly the **Dragon Warrior** RPG series. He lives with his family in Japan.

DRAGON BALL Z VOL. 11
The SHONEN JUMP Manga Edition

This graphic novel is number 27 in a series of 42.

STORY AND ART BY
AKIRA TORIYAMA

ENGLISH ADAPTATION BY
GERARD JONES

Translation/Lillian Olsen
Touch-Up Art & Lettering/Wayne Truman
Cover Design/Sean Lee & Dan Ziegler
Graphics & Design/Sean Lee
Senior Editor/Jason Thompson

Editor in Chief, Books/Alvin Lu
Editor in Chief, Magazines/Marc Weidenbaum
VP of Publishing Licensing/Rika Inouye
VP of Sales/Gonzalo Ferreyra
Sr. VP of Marketing/Liza Coppola
Publisher/Hyoe Narita

Printed in the U.S.A.

In the original Japanese edition, DRAGON BALL and DRAGON BALL Z
are known collectively as the 42-volume series DRAGON BALL. The
English DRAGON BALL Z was originally volumes 17-42 of the Japanese
DRAGON BALL.

Published by VIZ Media, LLC
P.O. Box 77010 • San Francisco, CA 94107

The SHONEN JUMP Manga Edition
10 9 8 7 6
First printing, May 2003
Sixth printing, March 2008

PARENTAL ADVISORY
DRAGON BALL Z is rated A for all ages
and is suitable for any age group.
Contains fantasy violence.
ratings.viz.com

www.viz.com

THE WORLD'S
MOST POPULAR MANGA

www.shonenjump.com

SHONEN JUMP MANGA

DRAGON BALL Z

Vol. 11

DB: 27 of 42

STORY AND ART BY
AKIRA TORIYAMA

THE MAIN CHARACTERS

Bulma

Goku's oldest friend, Bulma is a scientific genius. She met Goku while on a quest for the seven magical Dragon Balls which, when gathered together, can grant any wish.

Son Goku

The greatest martial artist on Earth, he owes his strength to the training of Kame-Sen'nin and Kaiô-sama, and the fact that he's an alien Saiyan. To get even stronger, he has trained under 100 times Earth's gravity.

Kaiô-sama

The "Lord of Worlds," he is Kami-sama's superior in the heavenly bureaucracy. He taught Goku the *kaiô-ken* and other amazing martial arts techniques.

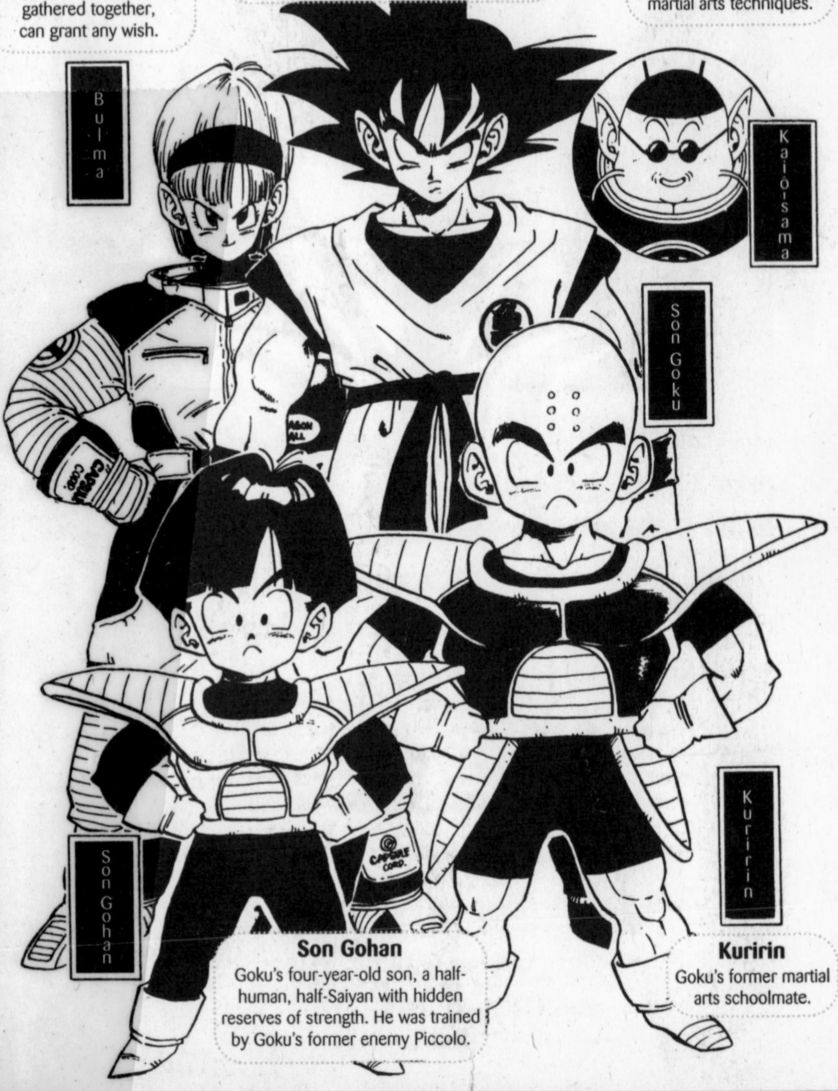
Bulma
Kaiôsama
Son Goku
Kuririn
Son Gohan

Son Gohan

Goku's four-year-old son, a half-human, half-Saiyan with hidden reserves of strength. He was trained by Goku's former enemy Piccolo.

Kuririn

Goku's former martial arts schoolmate.

Vegeta

Piccolo

Freeza

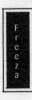

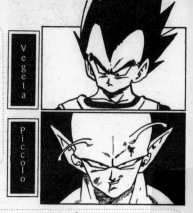

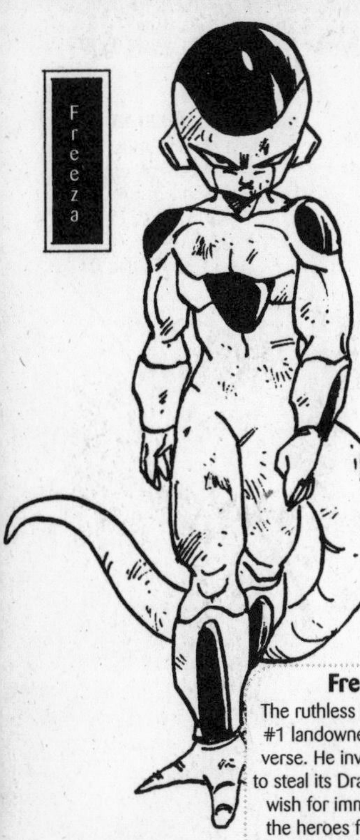

Vegeta

The evil Prince of the Saiyans. He hoped to become the legendary "Super Saiyan"—the strongest being in existence—and defeat Freeza, so he could rule the universe himself. He teamed up with the heroes out of convenience, but in the end Freeza killed him.

Piccolo

Goku's former arch-enemy, the Namekian Piccolo is the darker half of Kami-sama, the deity who created Earth's Dragon Balls. If Piccolo dies, Kami-sama dies too, and if Kami-sama dies, Earth's Dragon Balls will vanish. (In a similar way, Namek's Dragon Balls were tied to the life force of the dead Great Elder of Namek.)

Dende

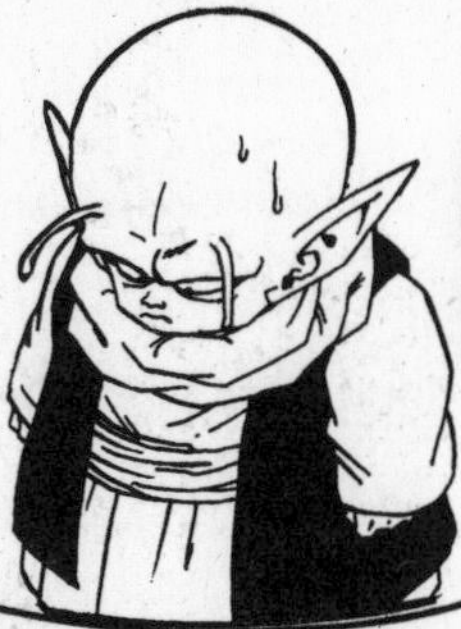

Dende

A young Namekian with healing powers. He was killed by Freeza.

Freeza

The ruthless emperor and #1 landowner of the universe. He invaded Namek to steal its Dragon Balls and wish for immortality, but the heroes fouled up his plans. Now he has sworn to destroy them all.

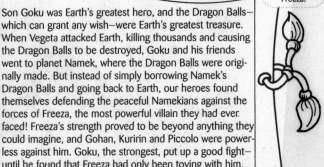

Son Goku was Earth's greatest hero, and the Dragon Balls—which can grant any wish—were Earth's greatest treasure. When Vegeta attacked Earth, killing thousands and causing the Dragon Balls to be destroyed, Goku and his friends went to planet Namek, where the Dragon Balls were originally made. But instead of simply borrowing Namek's Dragon Balls and going back to Earth, our heroes found themselves defending the peaceful Namekians against the forces of Freeza, the most powerful villain they had ever faced! Freeza's strength proved to be beyond anything they could imagine, and Gohan, Kuririn and Piccolo were powerless against him. Goku, the strongest, put up a good fight—until he found that Freeza had only been toying with him, not even using half of his full power...

DRAGON BALL Z 11

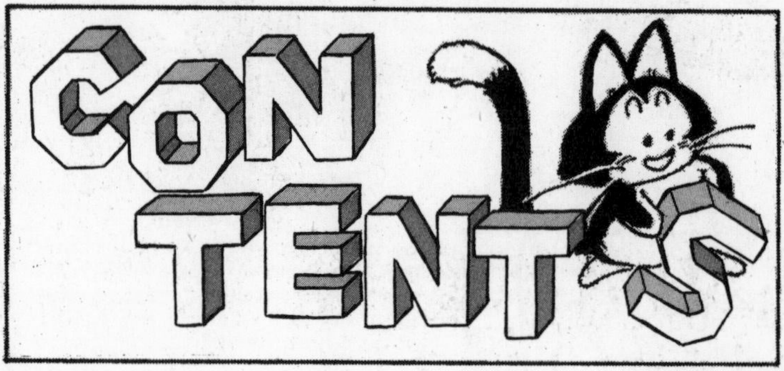
CON
TENTS

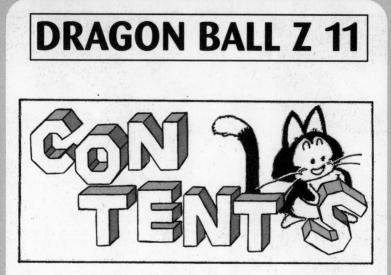

DRAGON BALL

DBZ:120 • The Great Genki-Dama

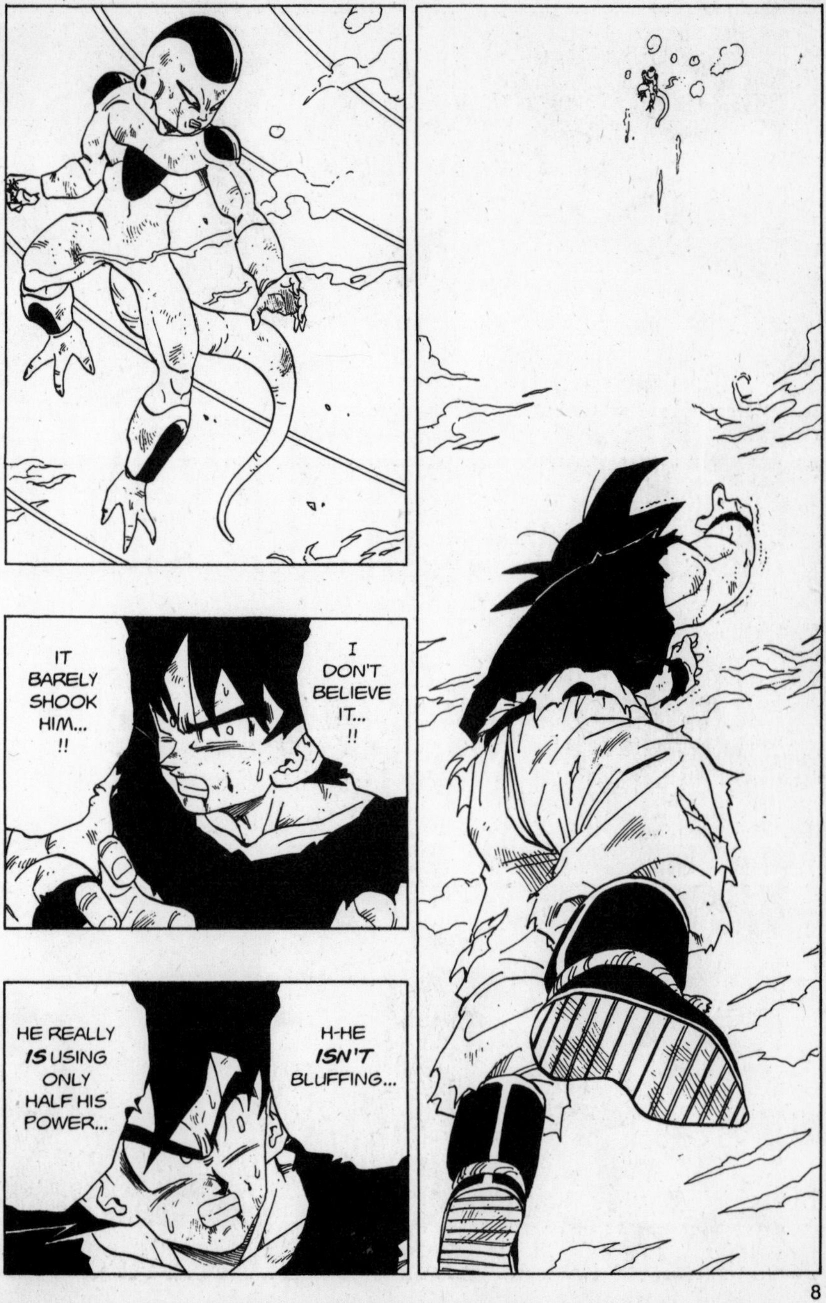
I DON'T BELIEVE IT... !!
IT BARELY SHOOK HIM... !!
H-HE *ISN'T* BLUFFING...
HE REALLY *IS* USING ONLY HALF HIS POWER...

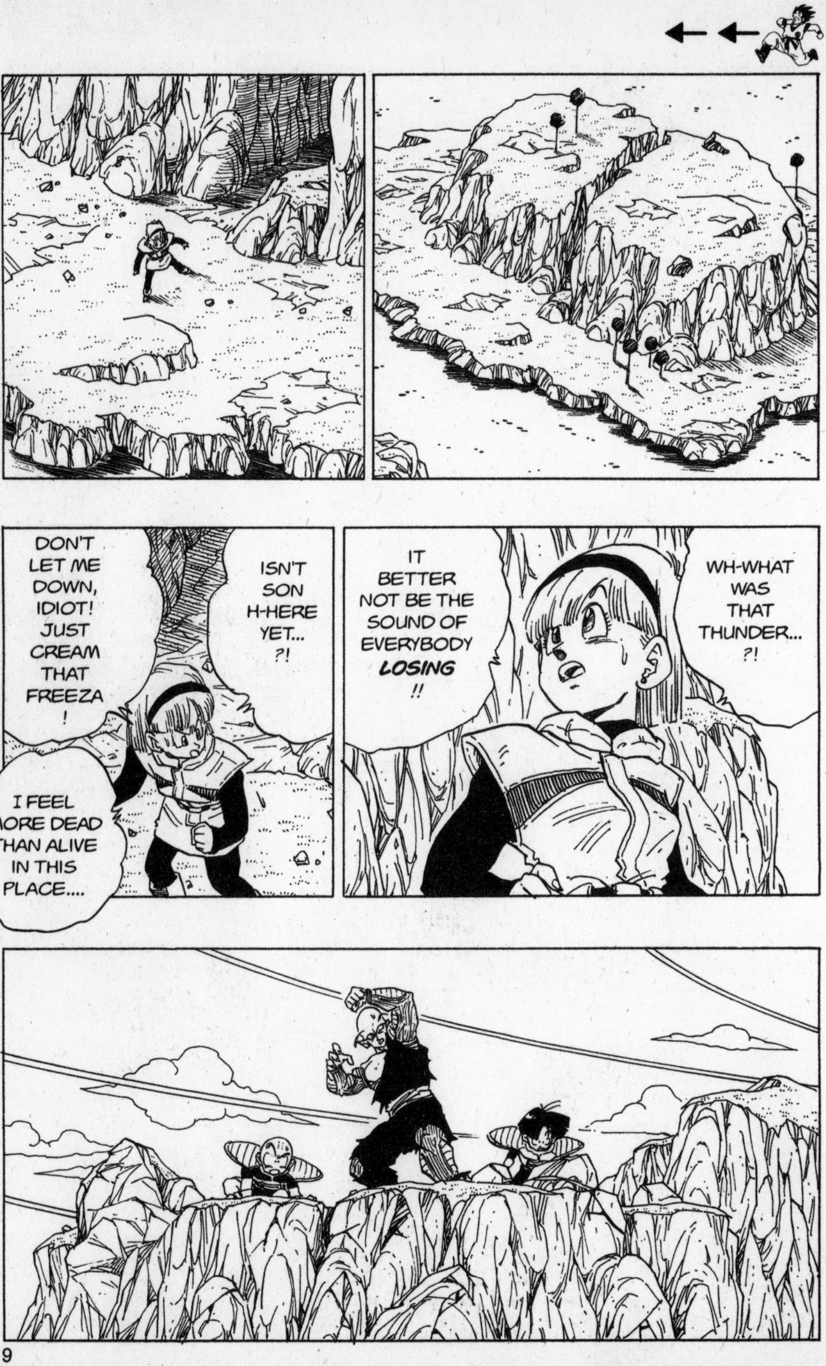
WH-WHAT WAS THAT THUNDER... ?!
IT BETTER NOT BE THE SOUND OF EVERYBODY *LOSING* !!
ISN'T SON H-HERE YET... ?!
DON'T LET ME DOWN, IDIOT! JUST CREAM THAT FREEZA !
I FEEL MORE DEAD THAN ALIVE IN THIS PLACE....

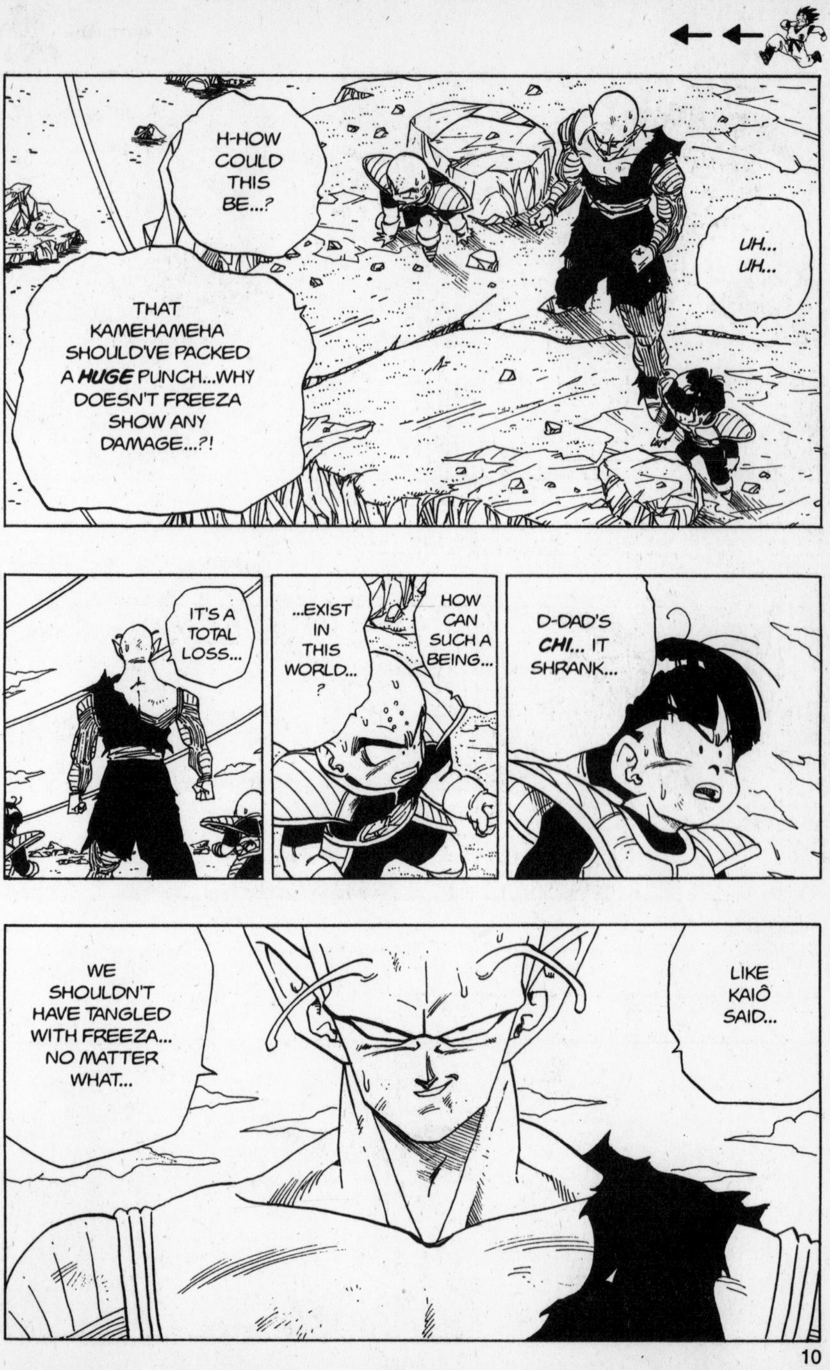
UH... UH...
H-HOW COULD THIS BE...?
THAT KAMEHAMEHA SHOULD'VE PACKED A **HUGE** PUNCH...WHY DOESN'T FREEZA SHOW ANY DAMAGE...?!
D-DAD'S **CHI**... IT SHRANK...
HOW CAN SUCH A BEING...
...EXIST IN THIS WORLD...?
IT'S A TOTAL LOSS...
LIKE KAIÔ SAID...
WE SHOULDN'T HAVE TANGLED WITH FREEZA... NO MATTER WHAT...

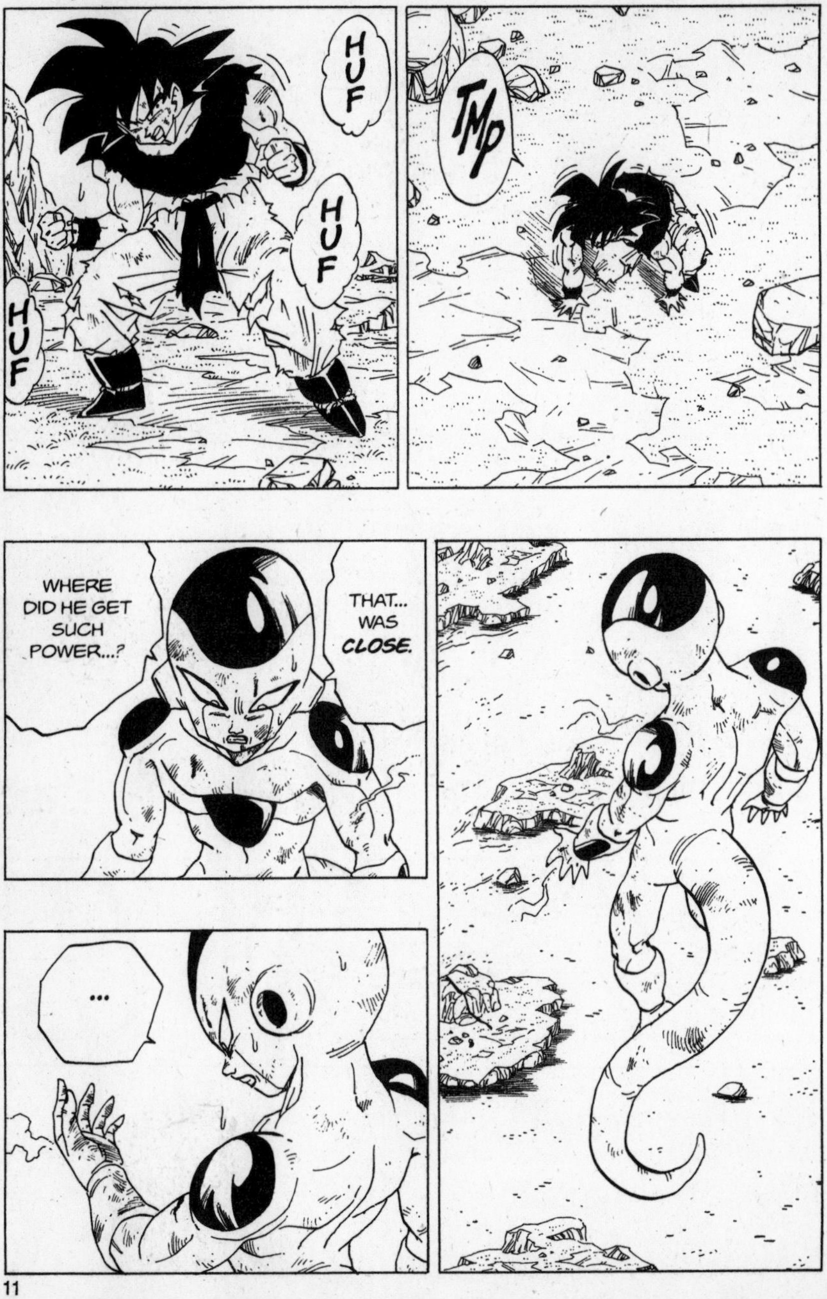
TMP
HUF
HUF
HUF
THAT... WAS CLOSE.
WHERE DID HE GET SUCH POWER...?
...

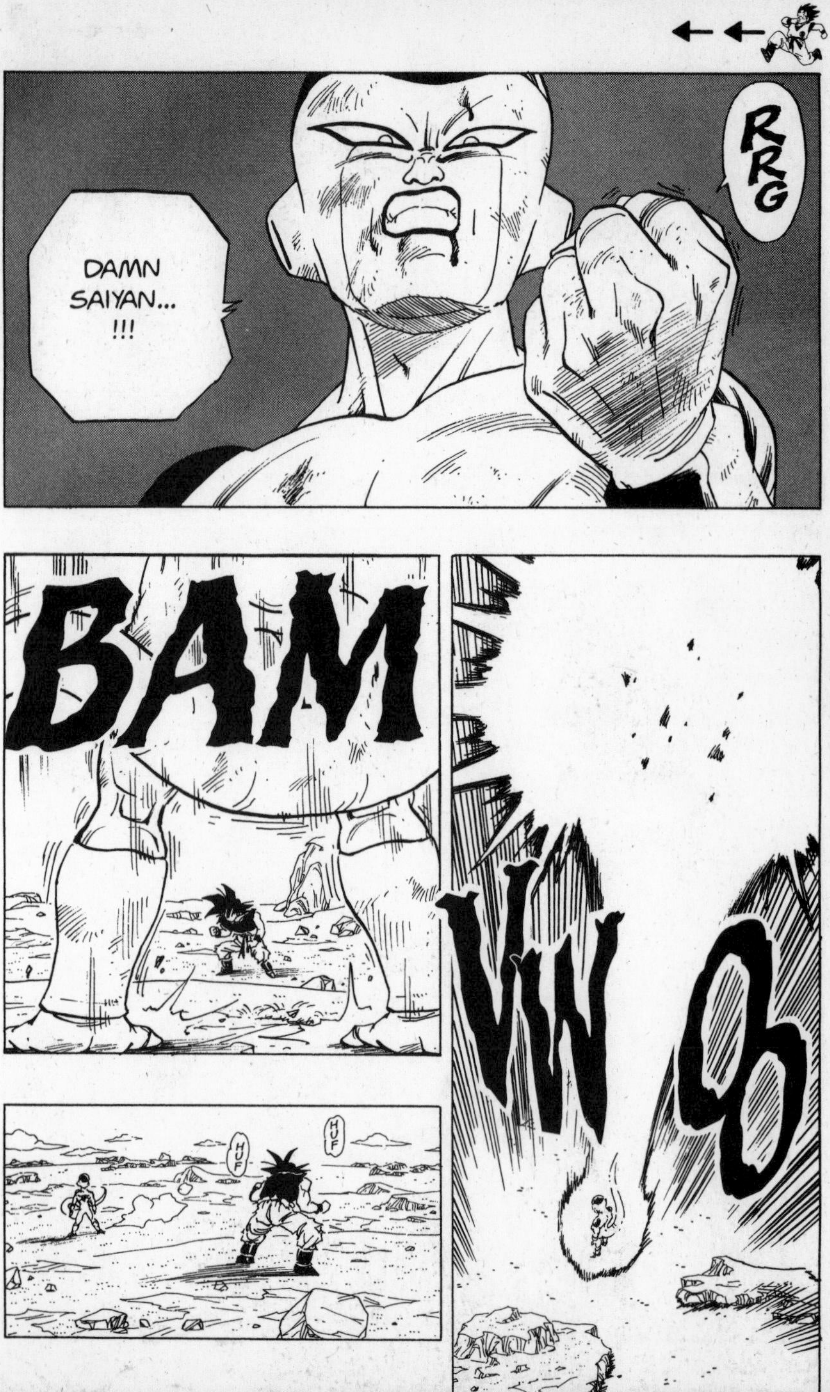
RRG
DAMN SAIYAN... !!!
BAM
HUF
HUF

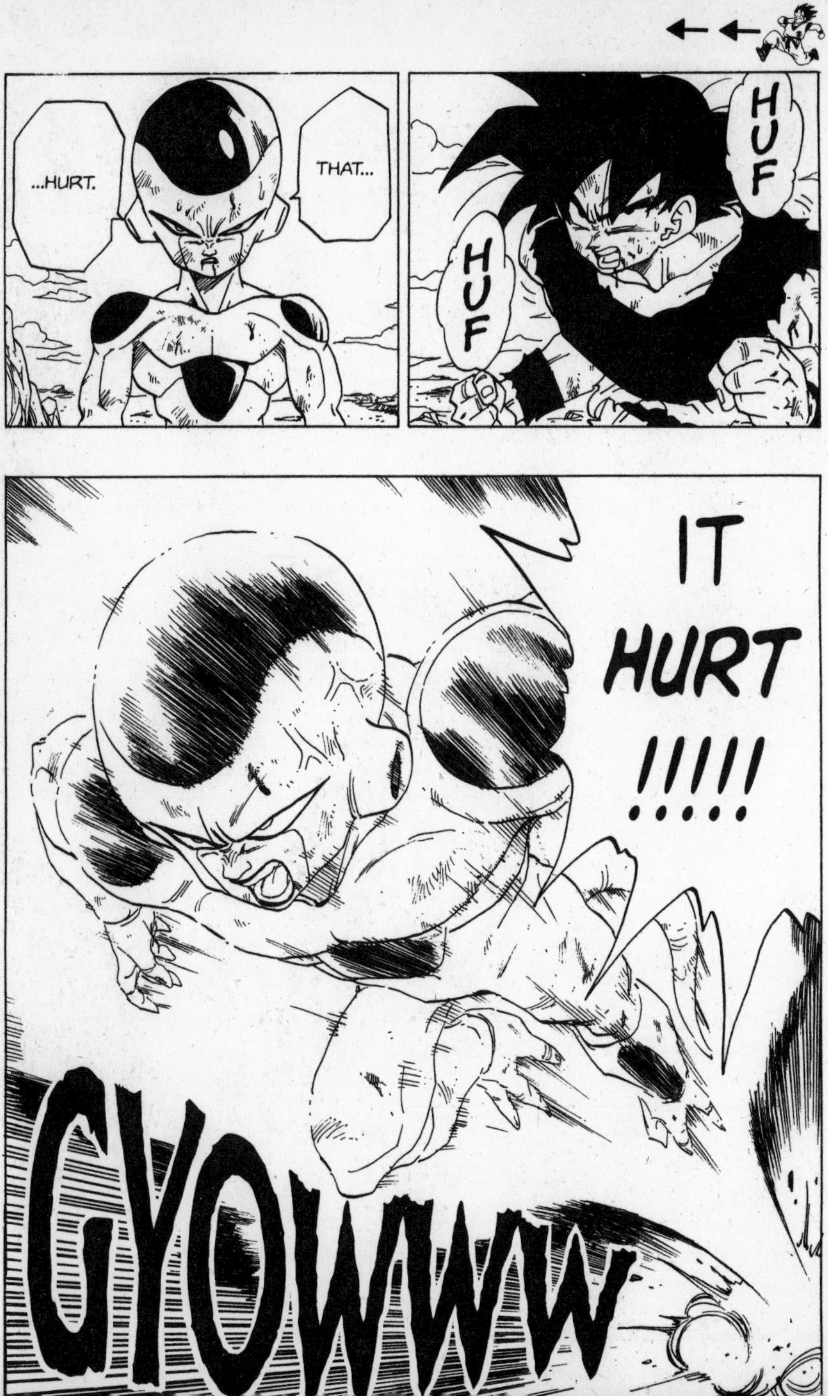
HUF
HUF
THAT...
...HURT.
IT HURT!!!!!
GYOWWW

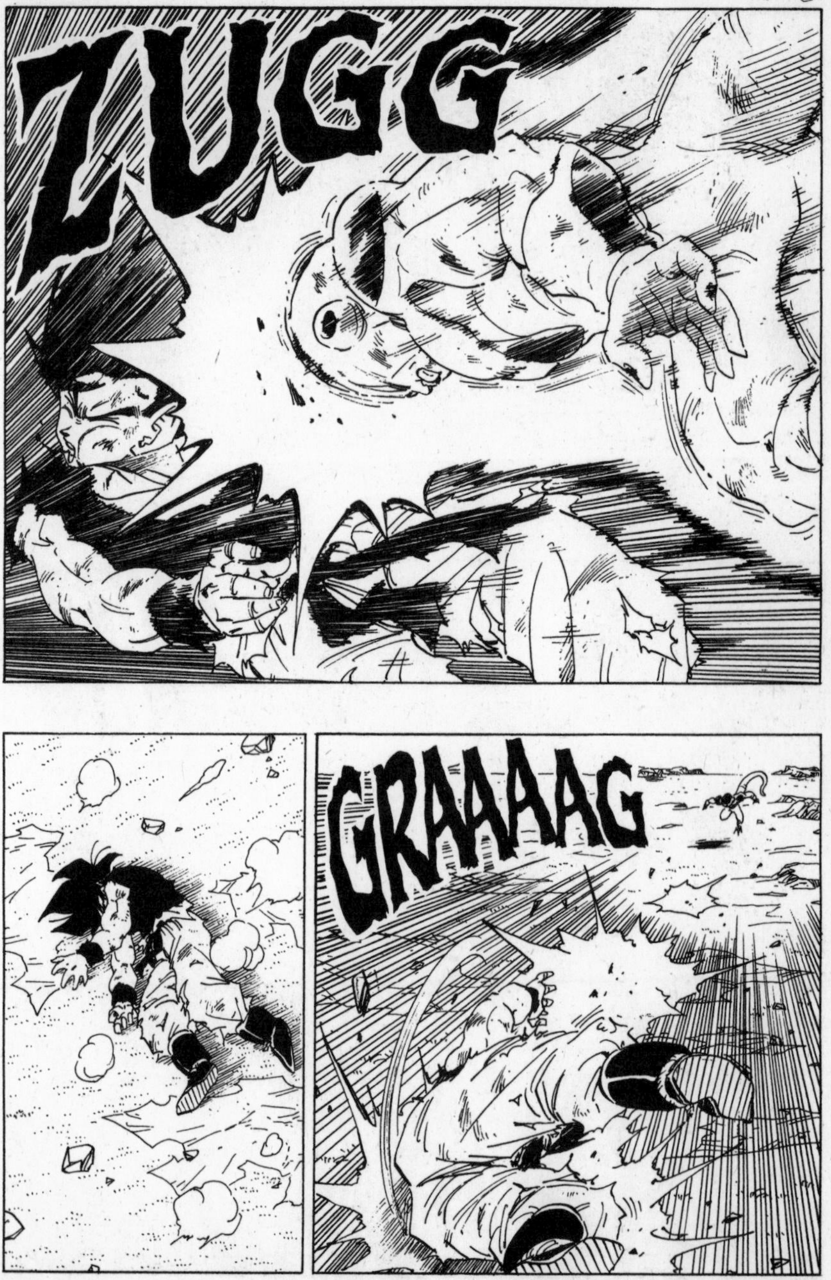
ZUGG
GRAAAG

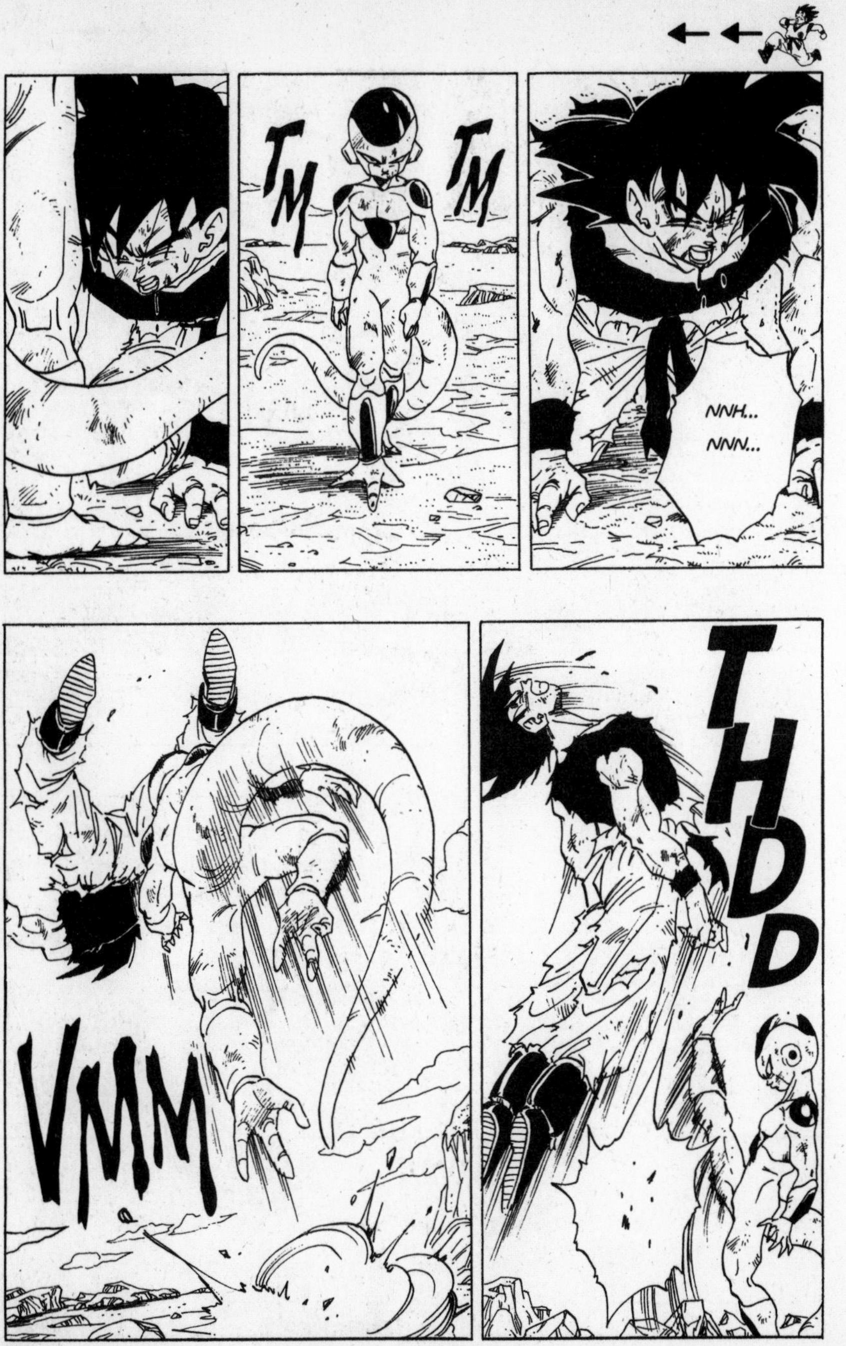
NNH...
NNN...
TM
TM
THDD
VMM

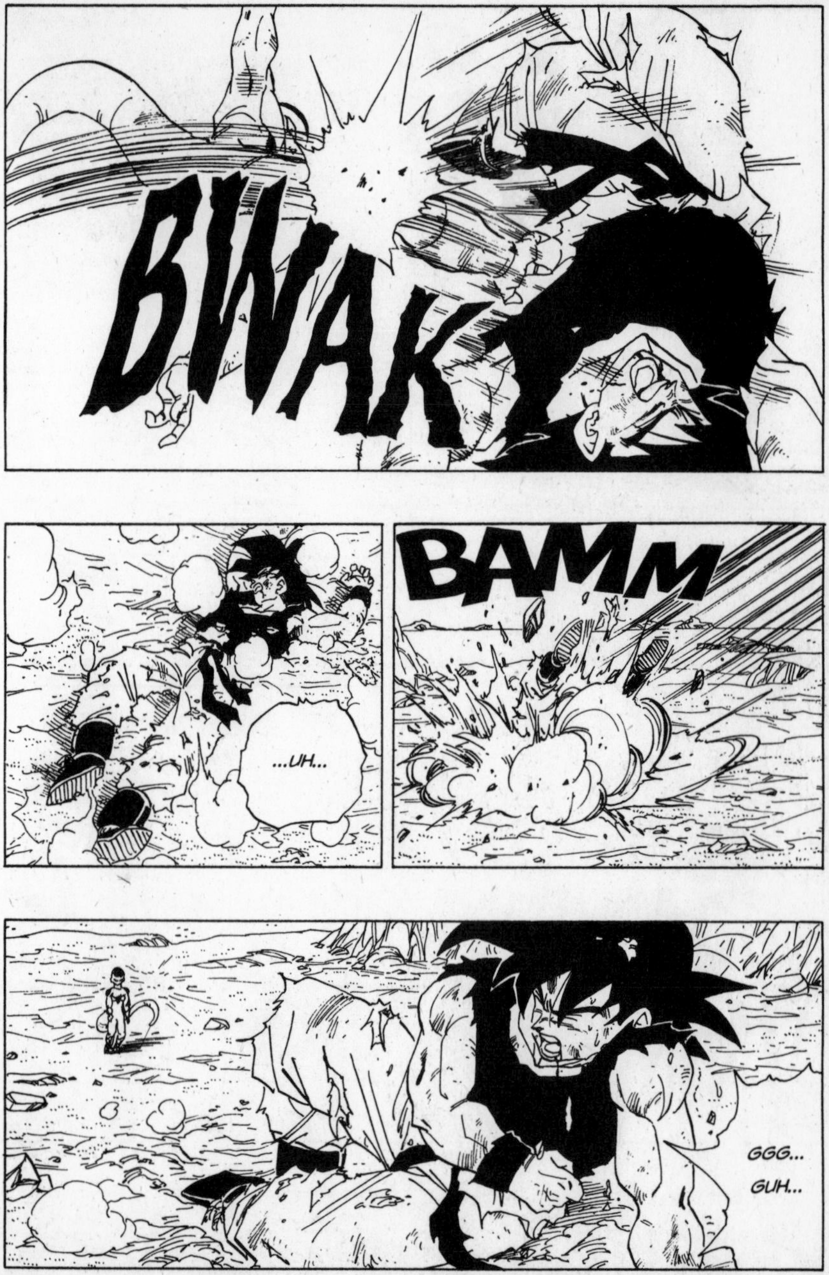
BWAK
BAMM
...UH...
GGG...
GUH...

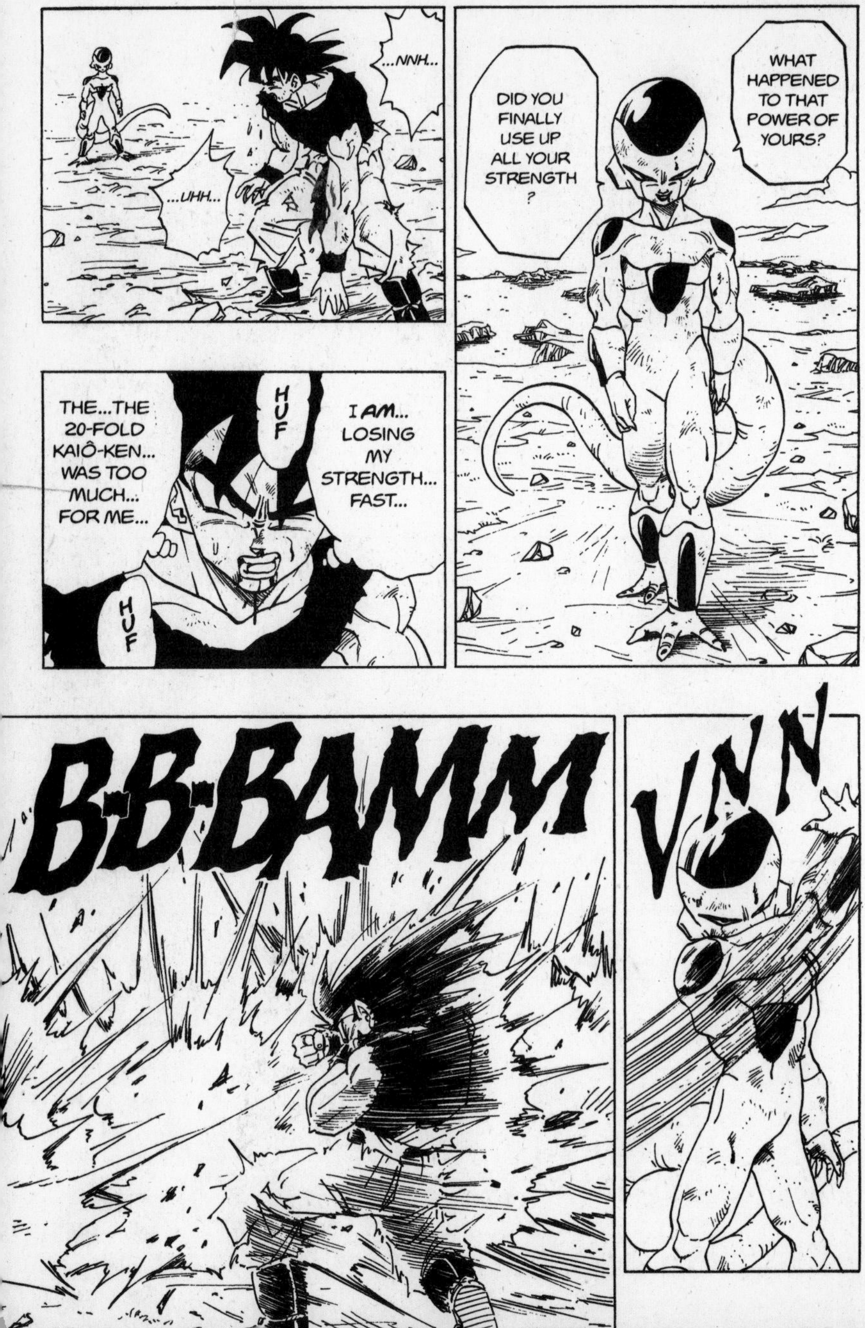
WHAT HAPPENED TO THAT POWER OF YOURS?
DID YOU FINALLY USE UP ALL YOUR STRENGTH ?
...NNH...
...UHH...
HUF
I AM... LOSING MY STRENGTH... FAST...
THE...THE 20-FOLD KAIÔ-KEN... WAS TOO MUCH... FOR ME...
HUF
VNN
B-B-BAMM

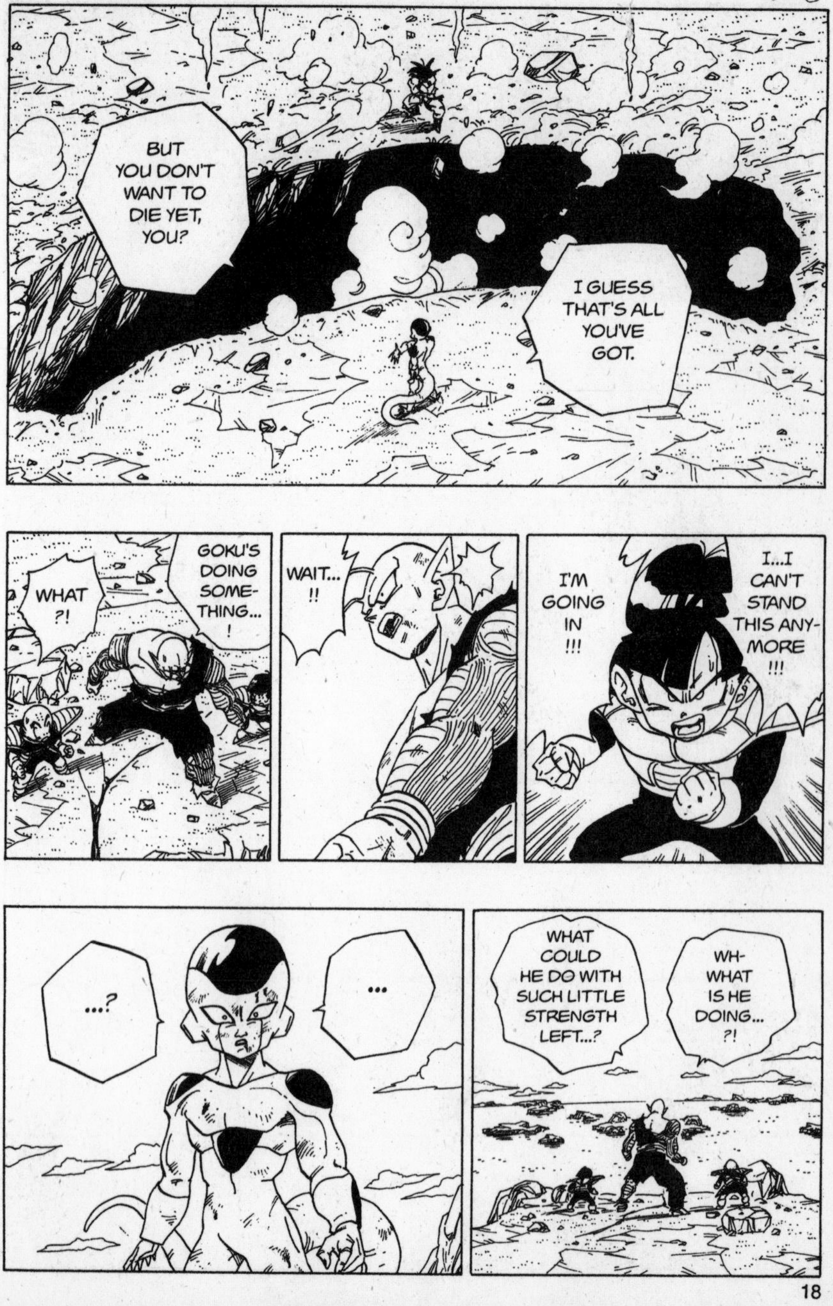
I GUESS THAT'S ALL YOU'VE GOT.
BUT YOU DON'T WANT TO DIE YET, YOU?
I...I CAN'T STAND THIS ANY-MORE!!!
I'M GOING IN!!!
WAIT...!!
GOKU'S DOING SOME-THING...!
WHAT?!
WH-WHAT IS HE DOING...?!
WHAT COULD HE DO WITH SUCH LITTLE STRENGTH LEFT...?
...
...?

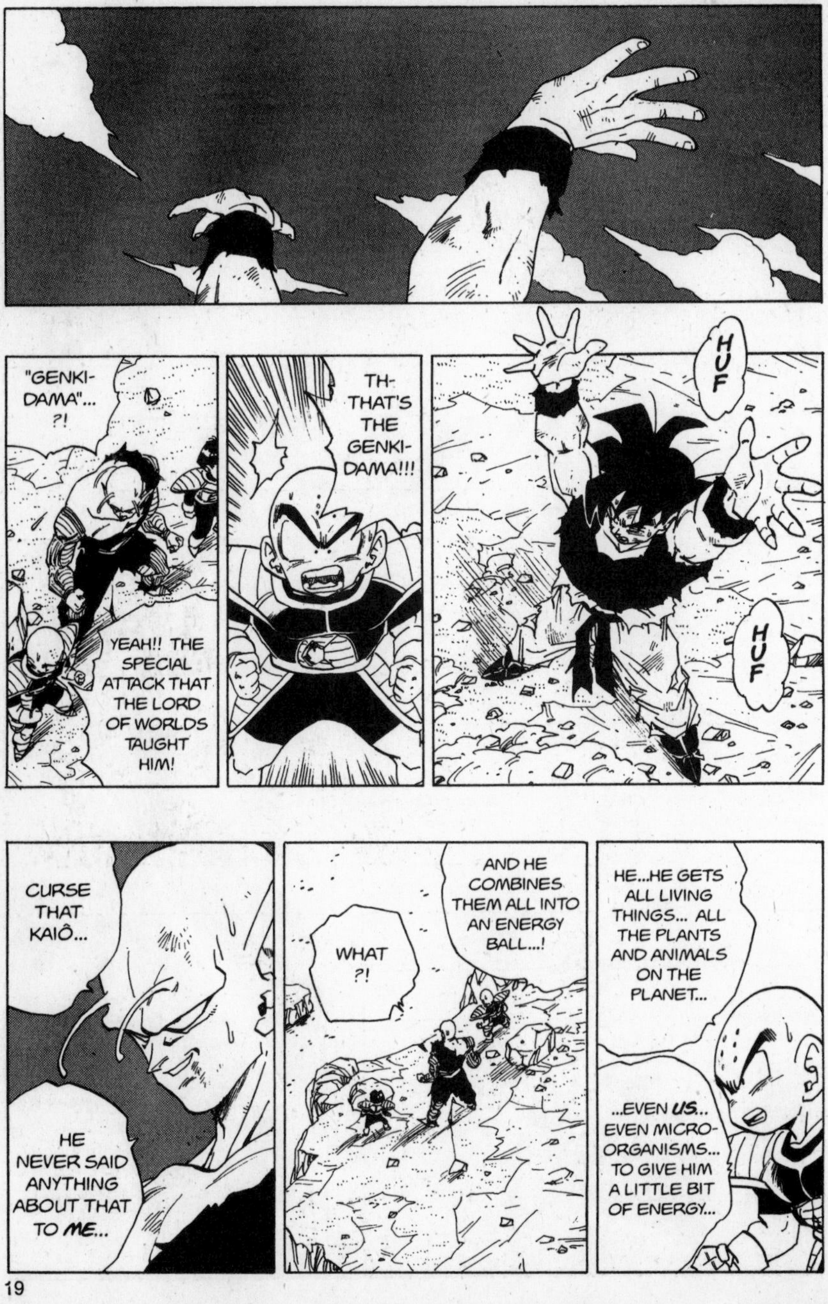
HUF
HUF
TH-THAT'S THE GENKI-DAMA!!!
"GENKI-DAMA"...?!
YEAH!! THE SPECIAL ATTACK THAT THE LORD OF WORLDS TAUGHT HIM!
HE...HE GETS ALL LIVING THINGS... ALL THE PLANTS AND ANIMALS ON THE PLANET...
...EVEN *US*... EVEN MICRO-ORGANISMS... TO GIVE HIM A LITTLE BIT OF ENERGY...
AND HE COMBINES THEM ALL INTO AN ENERGY BALL...!
WHAT?!
CURSE THAT KAIÔ...
HE NEVER SAID ANYTHING ABOUT THAT TO *ME*...

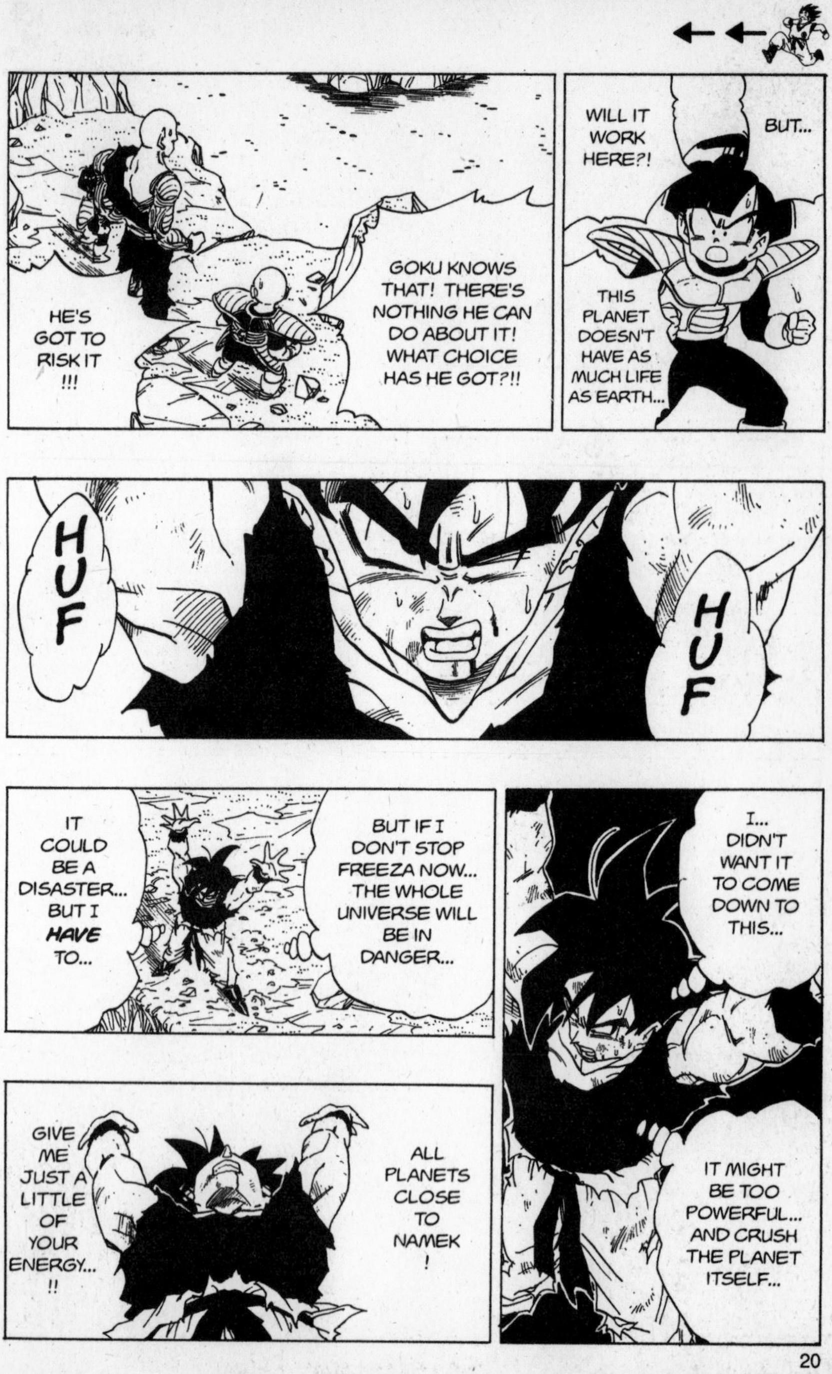
BUT...
WILL IT WORK HERE?!
THIS PLANET DOESN'T HAVE AS MUCH LIFE AS EARTH...
GOKU KNOWS THAT! THERE'S NOTHING HE CAN DO ABOUT IT! WHAT CHOICE HAS HE GOT?!!
HE'S GOT TO RISK IT !!!
HUF
HUF
I... DIDN'T WANT IT TO COME DOWN TO THIS...
IT MIGHT BE TOO POWERFUL... AND CRUSH THE PLANET ITSELF...
BUT IF I DON'T STOP FREEZA NOW... THE WHOLE UNIVERSE WILL BE IN DANGER...
IT COULD BE A DISASTER... BUT I HAVE TO...
ALL PLANETS CLOSE TO NAMEK !
GIVE ME JUST A LITTLE OF YOUR ENERGY... !!

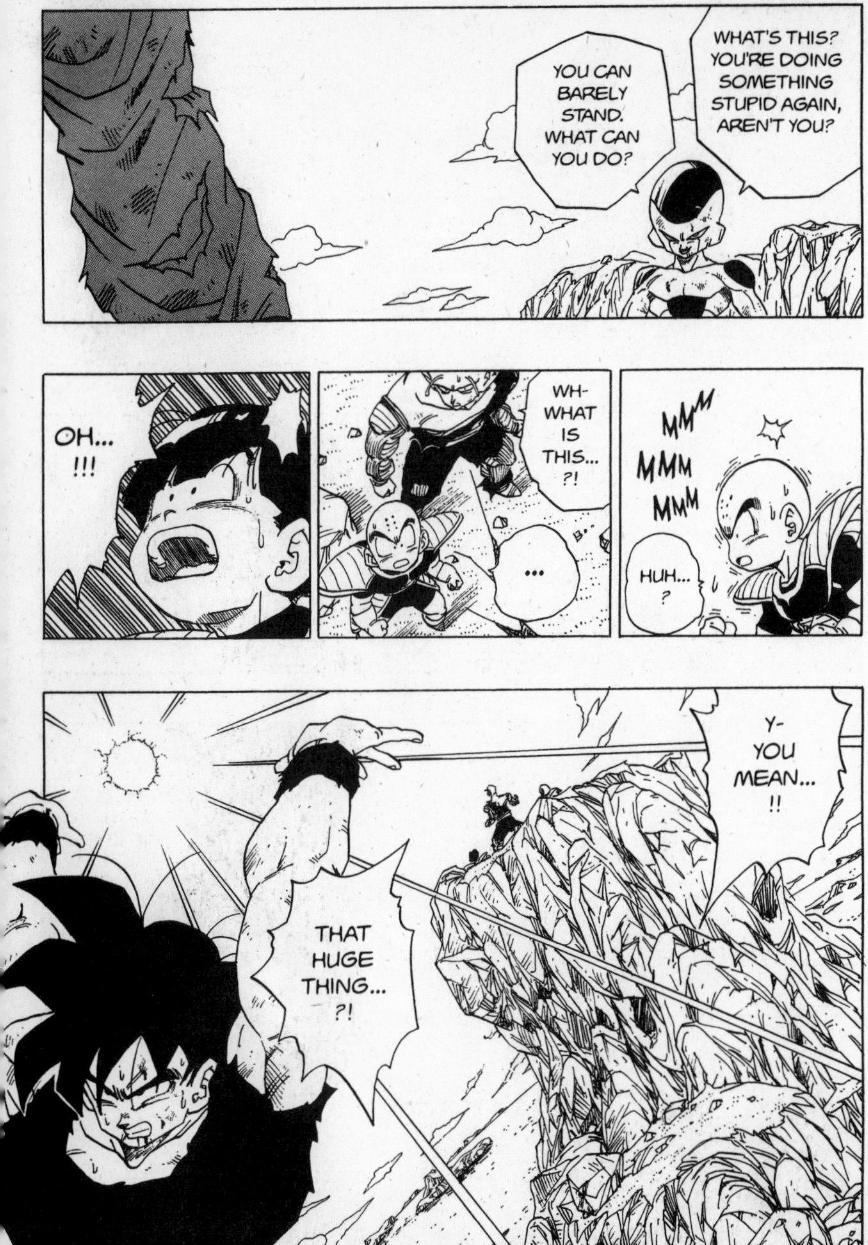
WHAT'S THIS? YOU'RE DOING SOMETHING STUPID AGAIN, AREN'T YOU?
YOU CAN BARELY STAND. WHAT CAN YOU DO?
MMMM MMM MMM
HUH...?
WH- WHAT IS THIS...?!
...
OH...!!!
Y- YOU MEAN...!!
THAT HUGE THING...?!

NEXT: Stalling for Time

DBZ:121 • The Last Chance

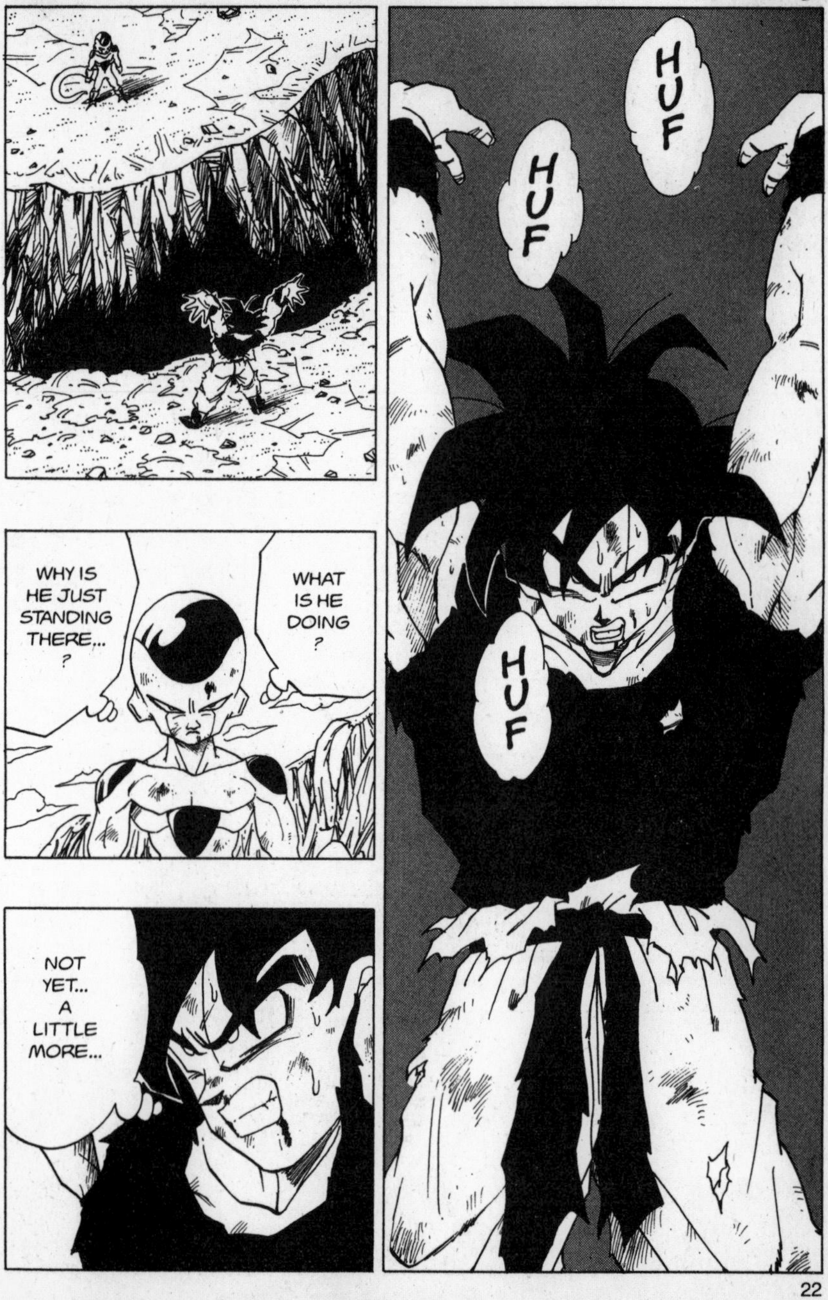
HUF HUF
HUF HUF
HUF HUF
WHAT IS HE DOING?
WHY IS HE JUST STANDING THERE...?
NOT YET... A LITTLE MORE...

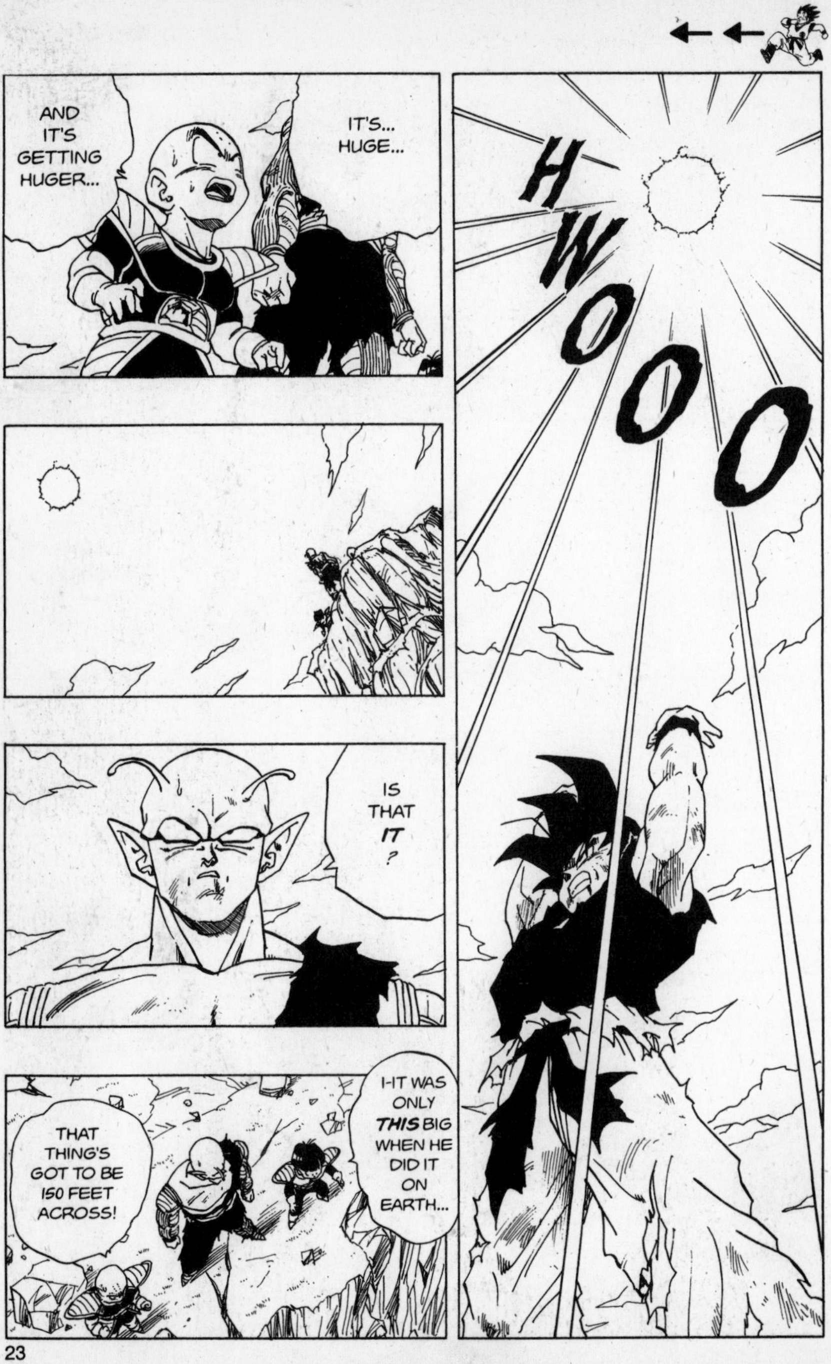
HWOOOO
IT'S... HUGE...
AND IT'S GETTING HUGER...
IS THAT IT?
I-IT WAS ONLY THIS BIG WHEN HE DID IT ON EARTH...
THAT THING'S GOT TO BE 150 FEET ACROSS!

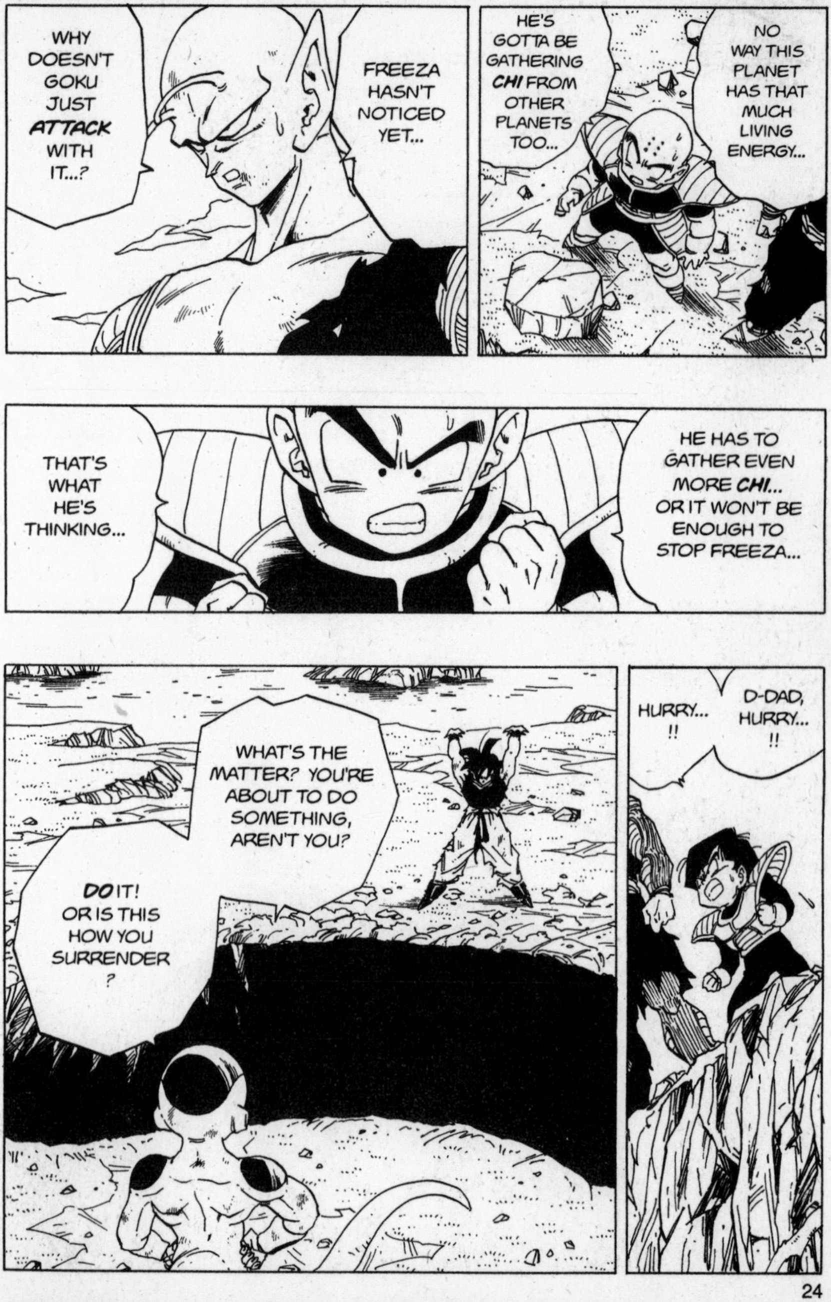
NO WAY THIS PLANET HAS THAT MUCH LIVING ENERGY...
HE'S GOTTA BE GATHERING CHI FROM OTHER PLANETS TOO...
FREEZA HASN'T NOTICED YET...
WHY DOESN'T GOKU JUST ATTACK WITH IT...?
HE HAS TO GATHER EVEN MORE CHI... OR IT WON'T BE ENOUGH TO STOP FREEZA...
THAT'S WHAT HE'S THINKING...
D-DAD, HURRY...!!
HURRY...!!
WHAT'S THE MATTER? YOU'RE ABOUT TO DO SOMETHING, AREN'T YOU?
DO IT! OR IS THIS HOW YOU SURRENDER?

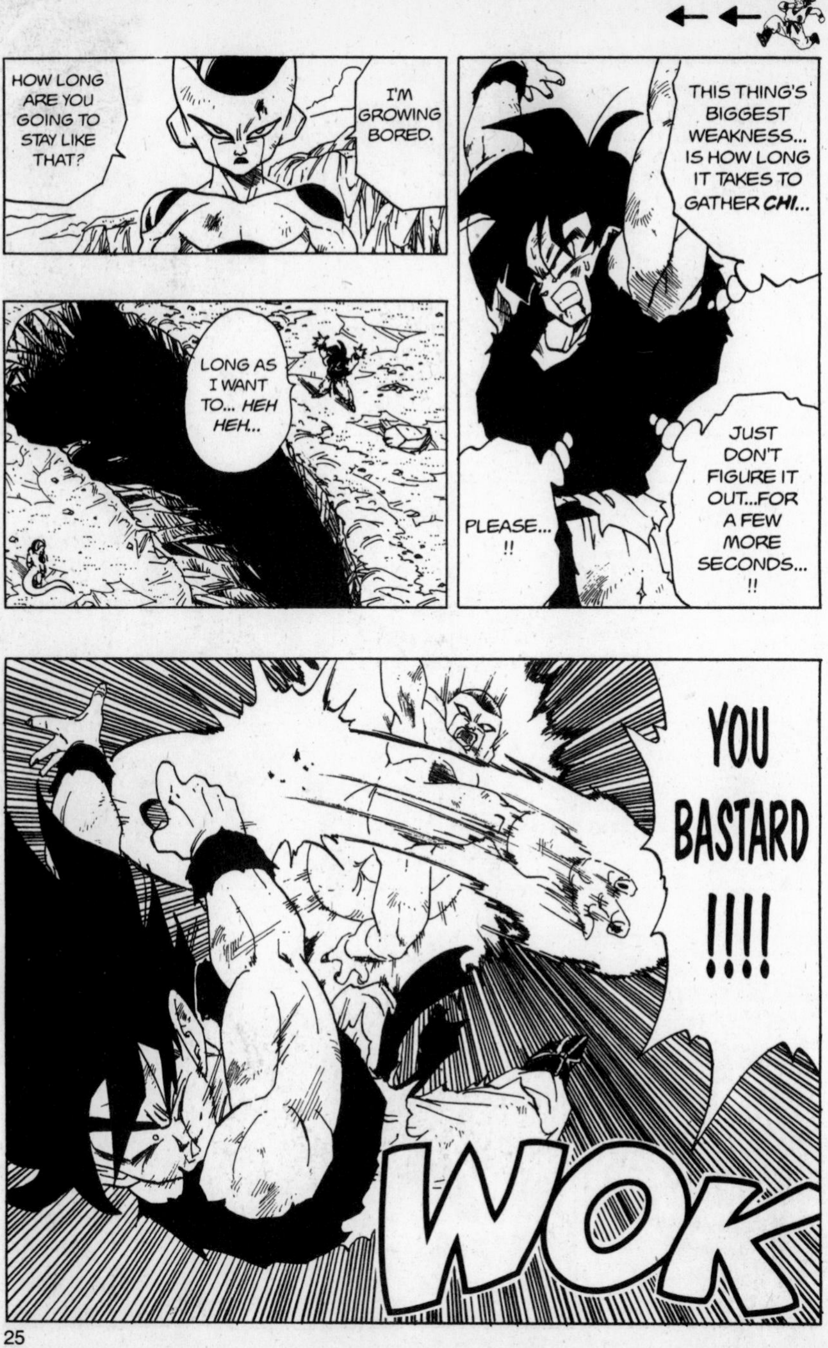
THIS THING'S BIGGEST WEAKNESS... IS HOW LONG IT TAKES TO GATHER **CHI**...
JUST DON'T FIGURE IT OUT...FOR A FEW MORE SECONDS... !!
PLEASE... !!
HOW LONG ARE YOU GOING TO STAY LIKE THAT?
I'M GROWING BORED.
LONG AS I WANT TO... *HEH HEH*...
YOU BASTARD !!!!
WOK

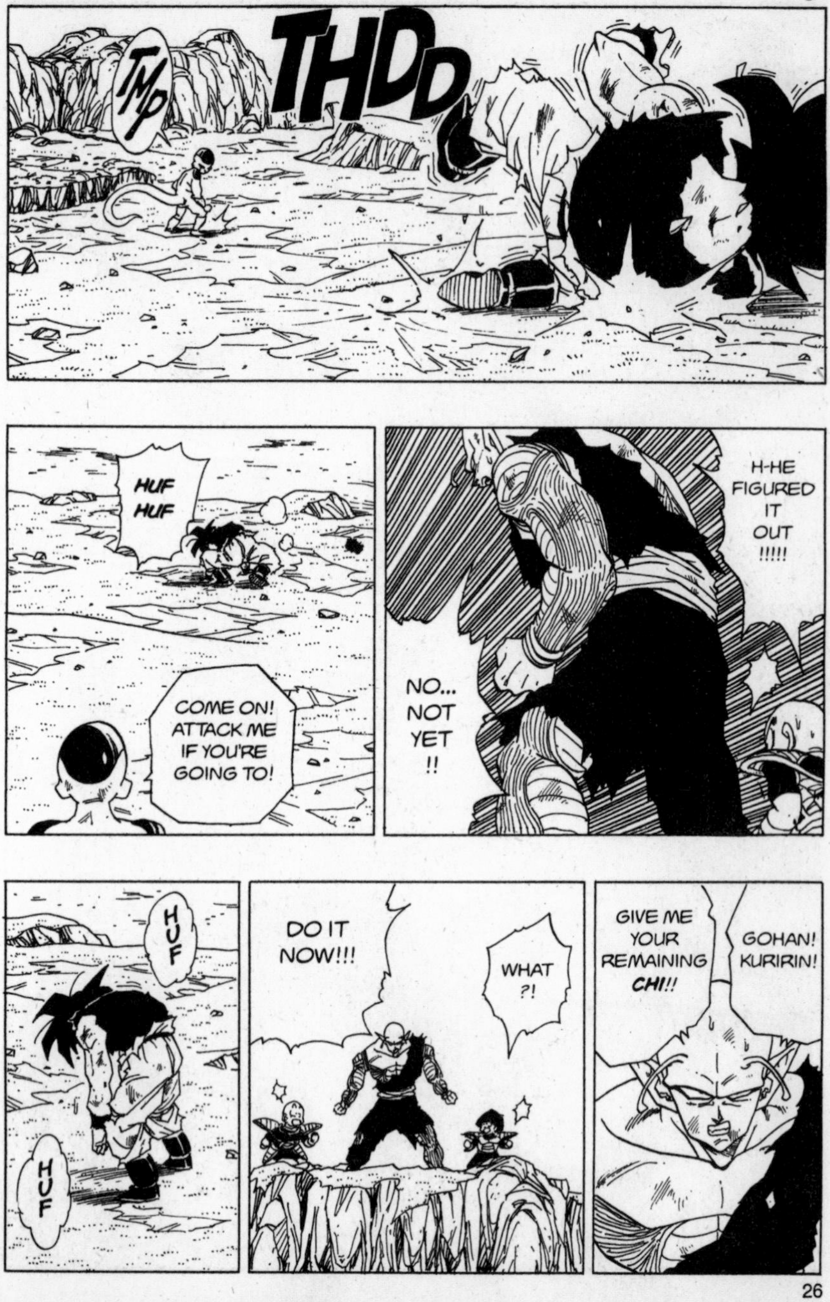
THDD
TMP
H-HE FIGURED IT OUT !!!!!
NO... NOT YET !!
HUF HUF
COME ON! ATTACK ME IF YOU'RE GOING TO!
GOHAN! KURIRIN!
GIVE ME YOUR REMAINING CHI!!
WHAT ?!
DO IT NOW!!!
HUF
HUF

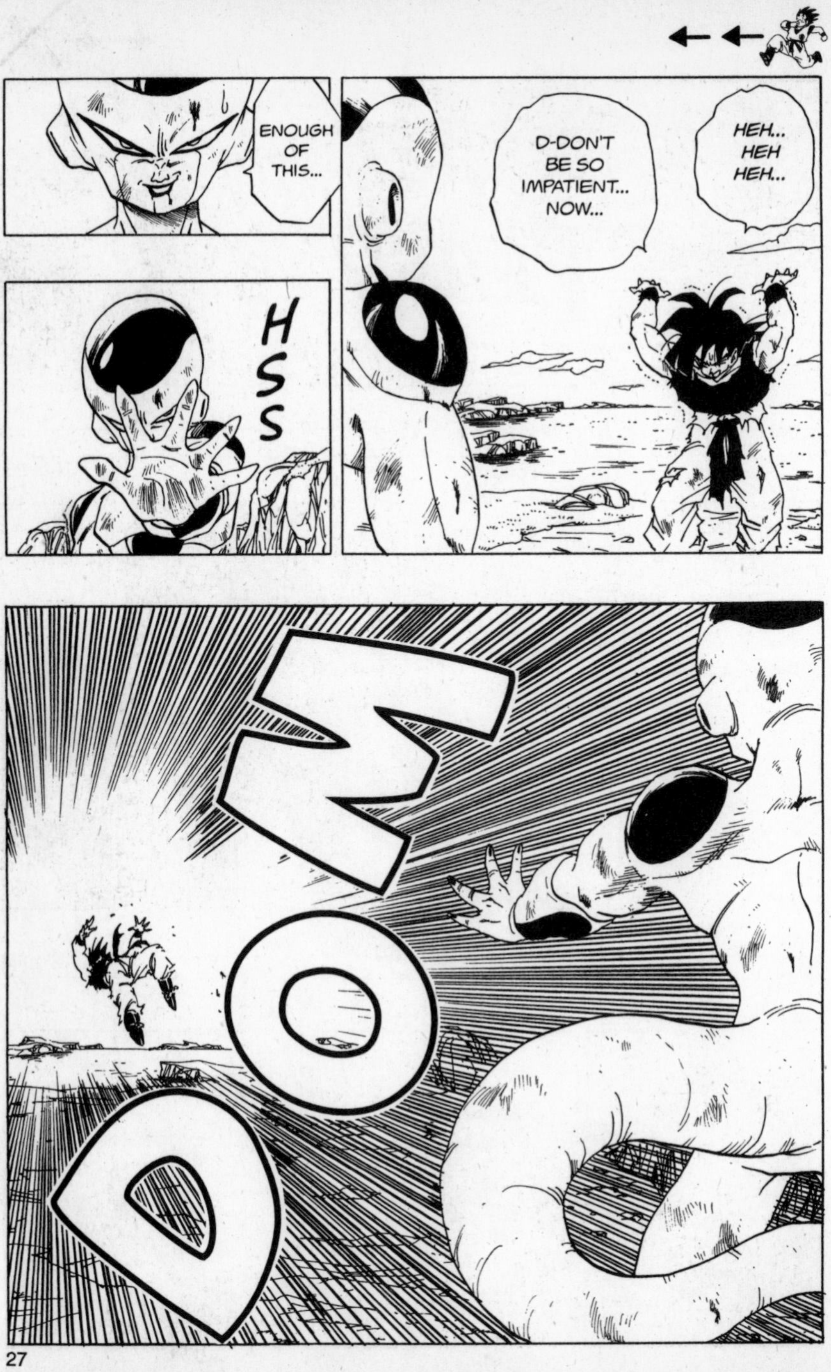
HEH... HEH HEH...
D-DON'T BE SO IMPATIENT... NOW...
ENOUGH OF THIS...
HSS
DOM

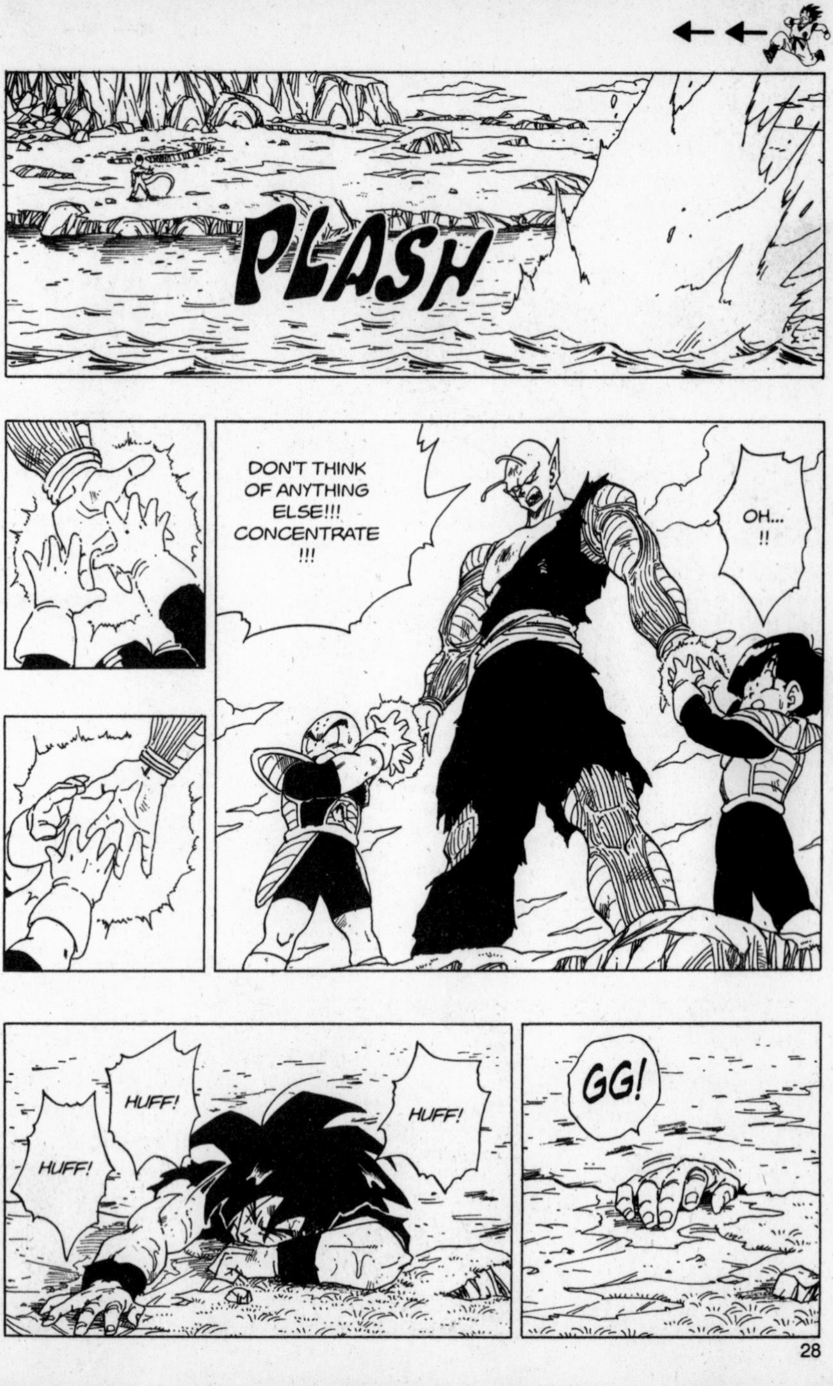
PLASH
OH... !!
DON'T THINK OF ANYTHING ELSE!!! CONCENTRATE !!!
GG!
HUFF!
HUFF!
HUFF!

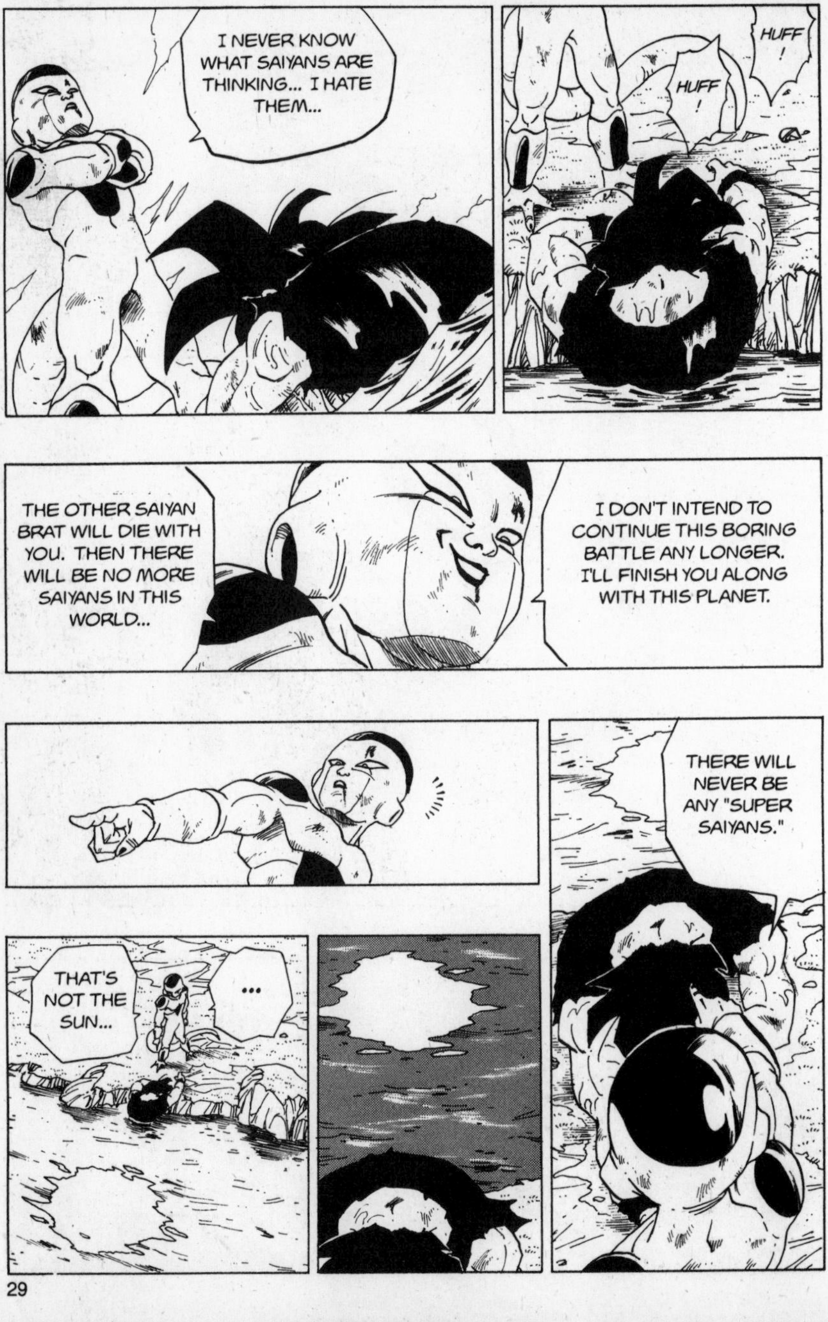
HUFF!
HUFF!
I NEVER KNOW WHAT SAIYANS ARE THINKING... I HATE THEM...
I DON'T INTEND TO CONTINUE THIS BORING BATTLE ANY LONGER. I'LL FINISH YOU ALONG WITH THIS PLANET.
THE OTHER SAIYAN BRAT WILL DIE WITH YOU. THEN THERE WILL BE NO MORE SAIYANS IN THIS WORLD...
THERE WILL NEVER BE ANY "SUPER SAIYANS."
...
THAT'S NOT THE SUN...

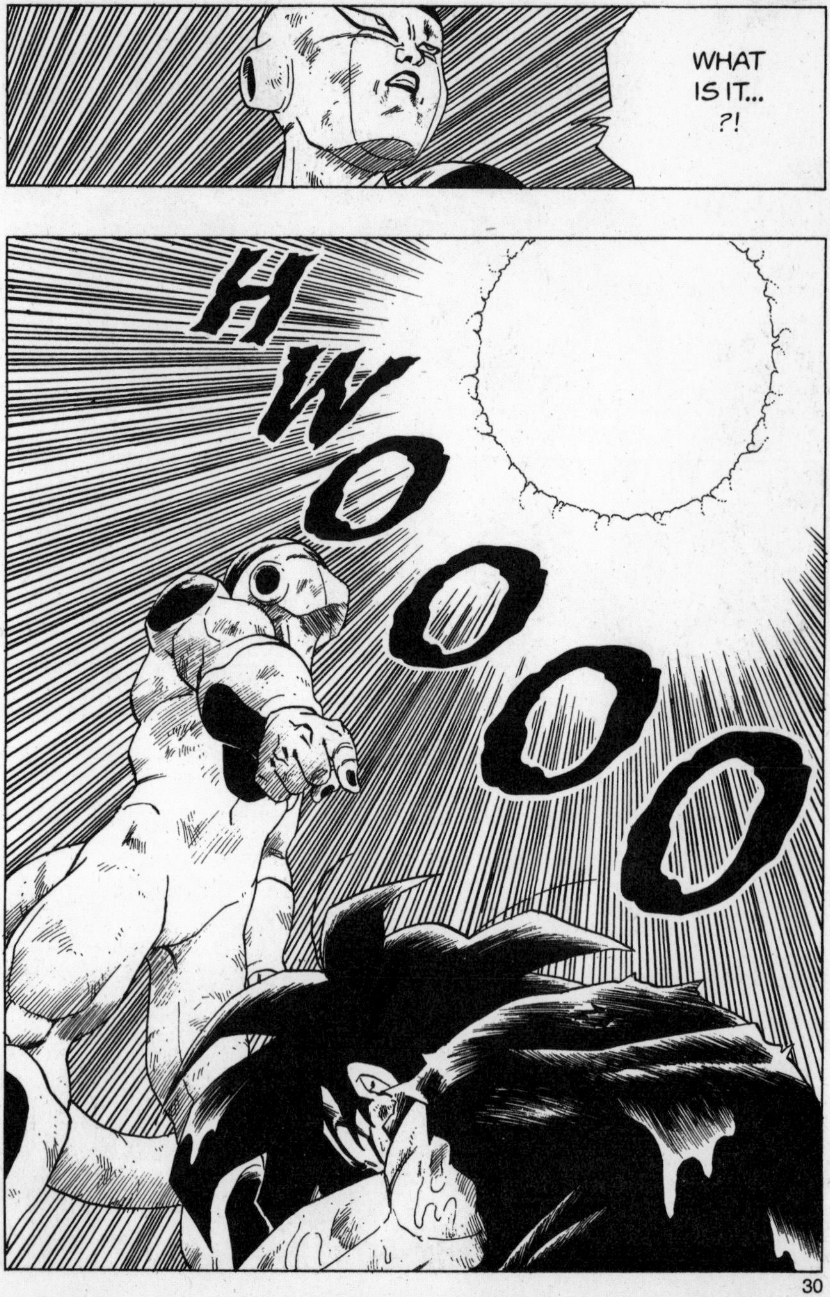
WHAT IS IT... ?!
HWOOOOOO

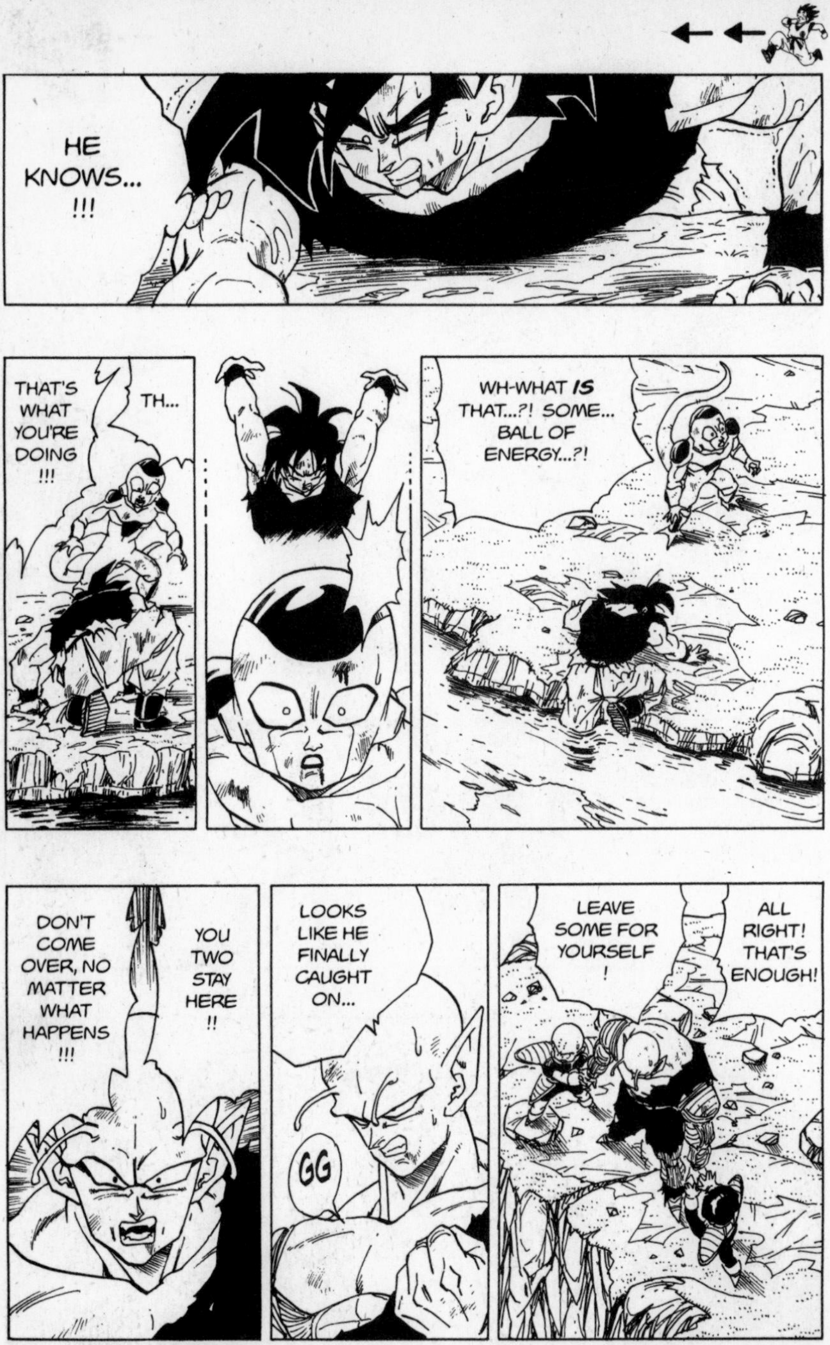
HE KNOWS... !!!
WH-WHAT **IS** THAT...?! SOME... BALL OF ENERGY...?!
TH...
THAT'S WHAT YOU'RE DOING !!!
ALL RIGHT! THAT'S ENOUGH!
LEAVE SOME FOR YOURSELF !
LOOKS LIKE HE FINALLY CAUGHT ON...
GG
YOU TWO STAY HERE !!
DON'T COME OVER, NO MATTER WHAT HAPPENS !!!

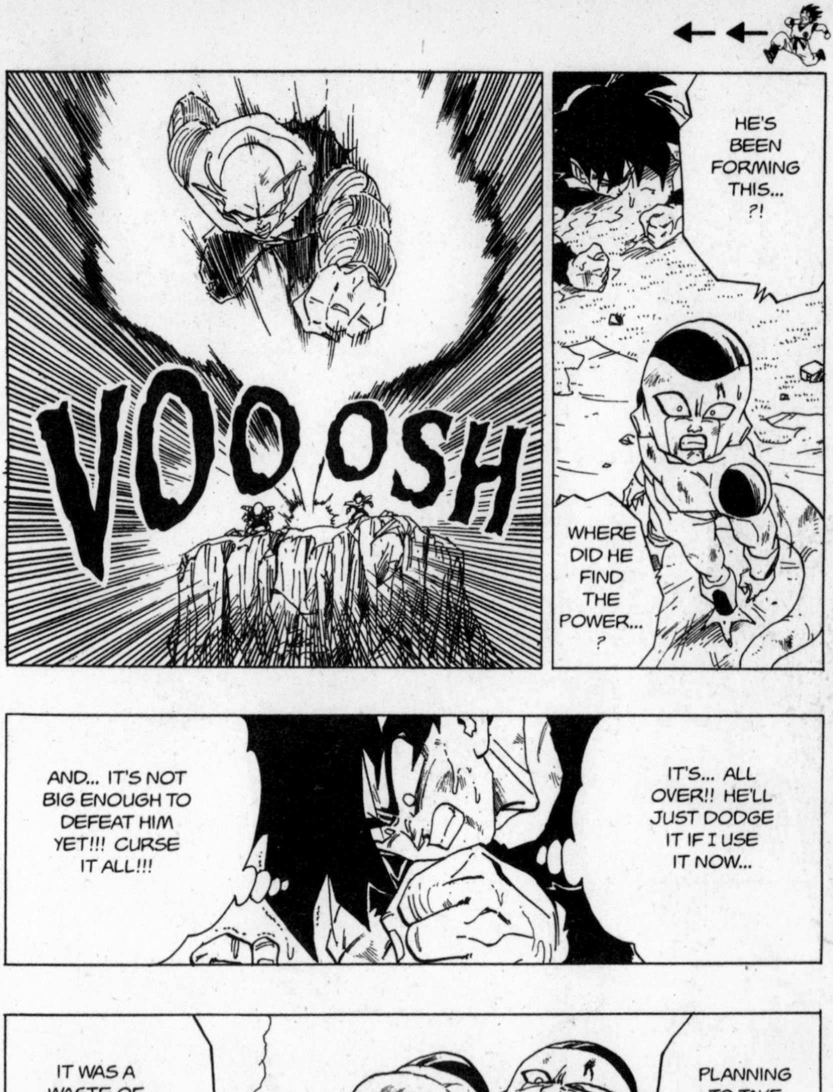
HE'S BEEN FORMING THIS... ?!
WHERE DID HE FIND THE POWER... ?
VOOOSH
IT'S... ALL OVER!! HE'LL JUST DODGE IT IF I USE IT NOW...
AND... IT'S NOT BIG ENOUGH TO DEFEAT HIM YET!!! CURSE IT ALL!!!
PLANNING TO TAKE ME BY SURPRISE, EH? YOU PATHETIC FOOL!
IT WAS A WASTE OF YOUR FINAL MOMENTS...

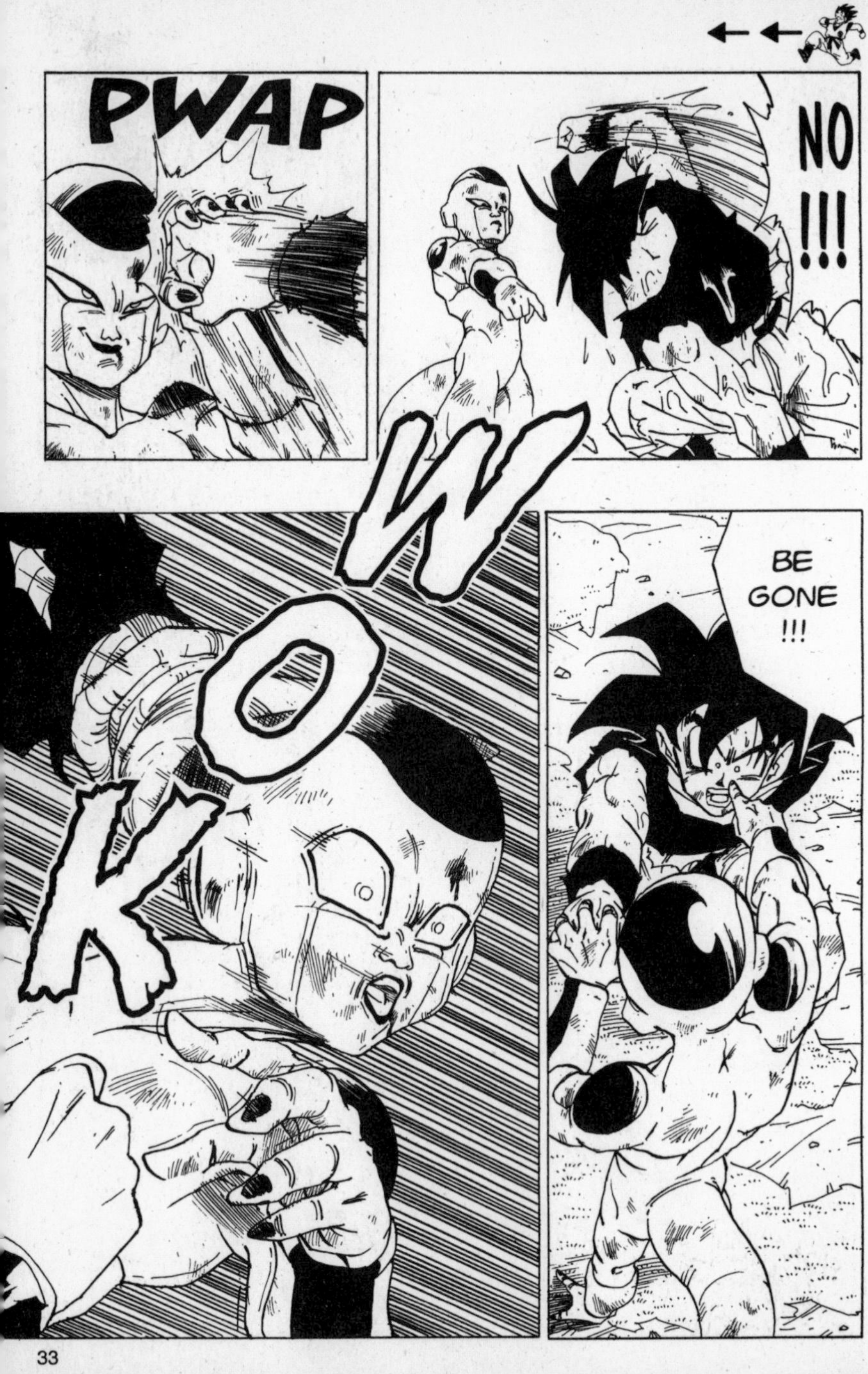
NO !!!
PWAP
BE GONE !!!
KOW

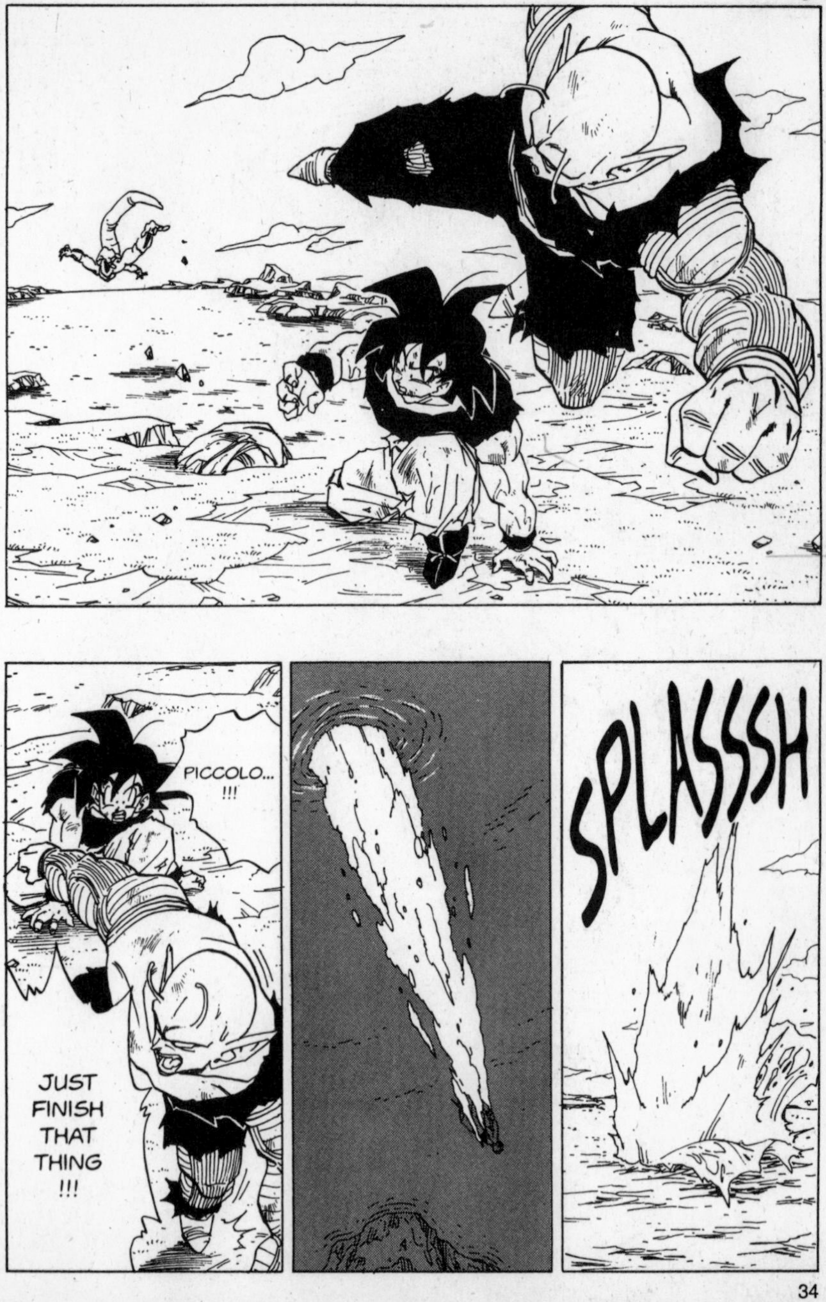
SPLASSSH
PICCOLO... !!!
JUST FINISH THAT THING !!!

DBZ:122 • The Galaxy Strikes Back!

FREEZA'S GETTING *ANGRY*, GOKU----

USE THE GENKI-DAMA *NOW*-- OR *NEVER* !!

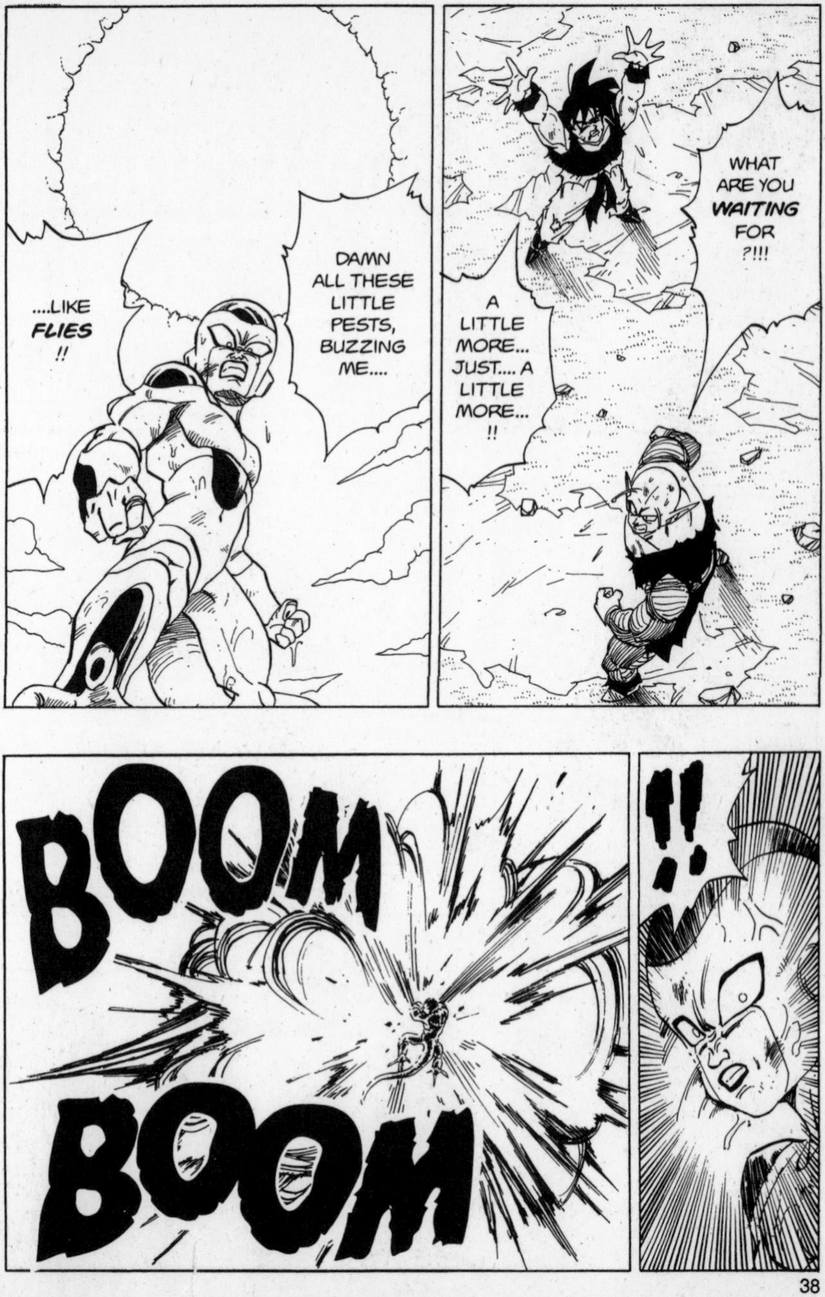
WHAT ARE YOU WAITING FOR ?!!!
A LITTLE MORE... JUST.... A LITTLE MORE... !!
DAMN ALL THESE LITTLE PESTS, BUZZING ME....
...LIKE FLIES !!
!!
BOOM
BOOM

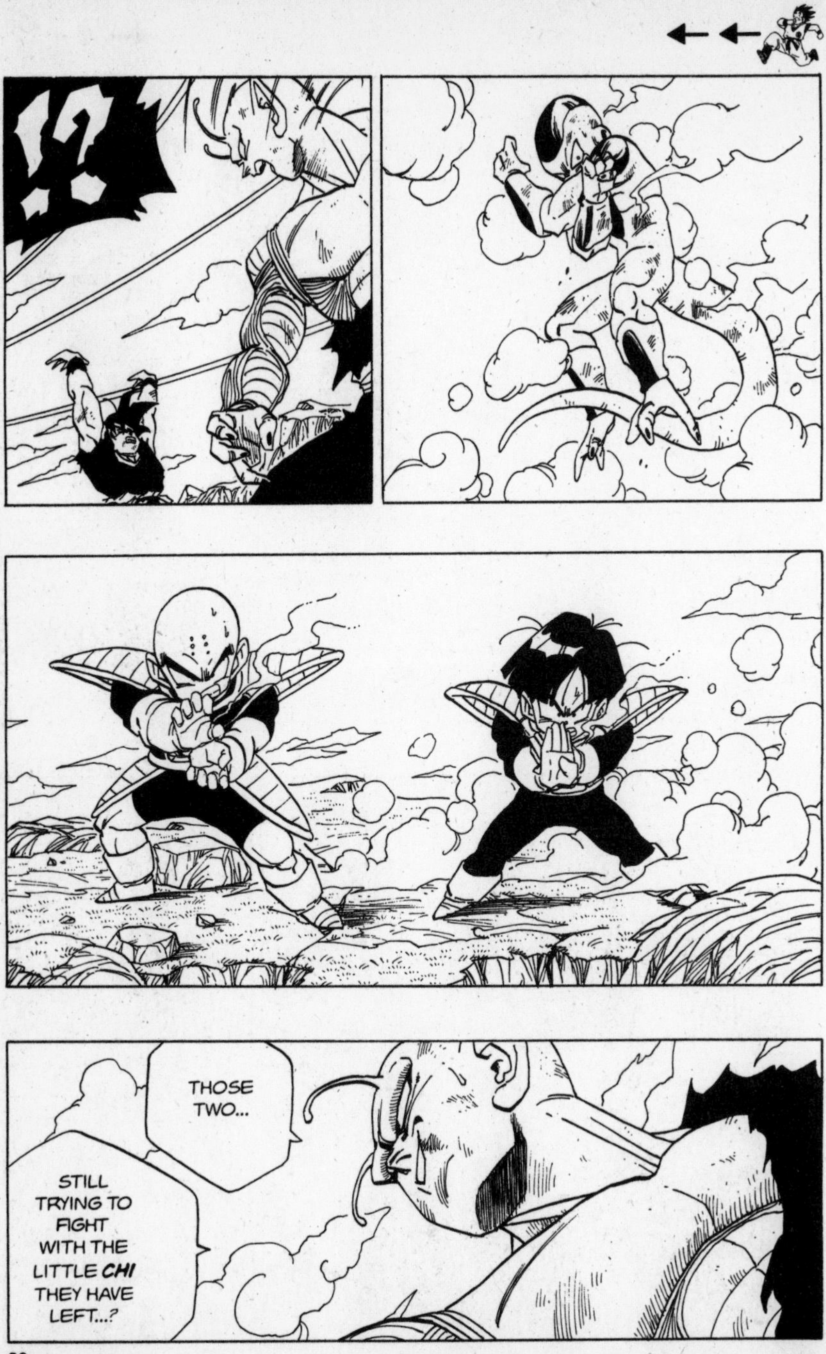
!?
THOSE TWO...
STILL TRYING TO FIGHT WITH THE LITTLE CHI THEY HAVE LEFT...?

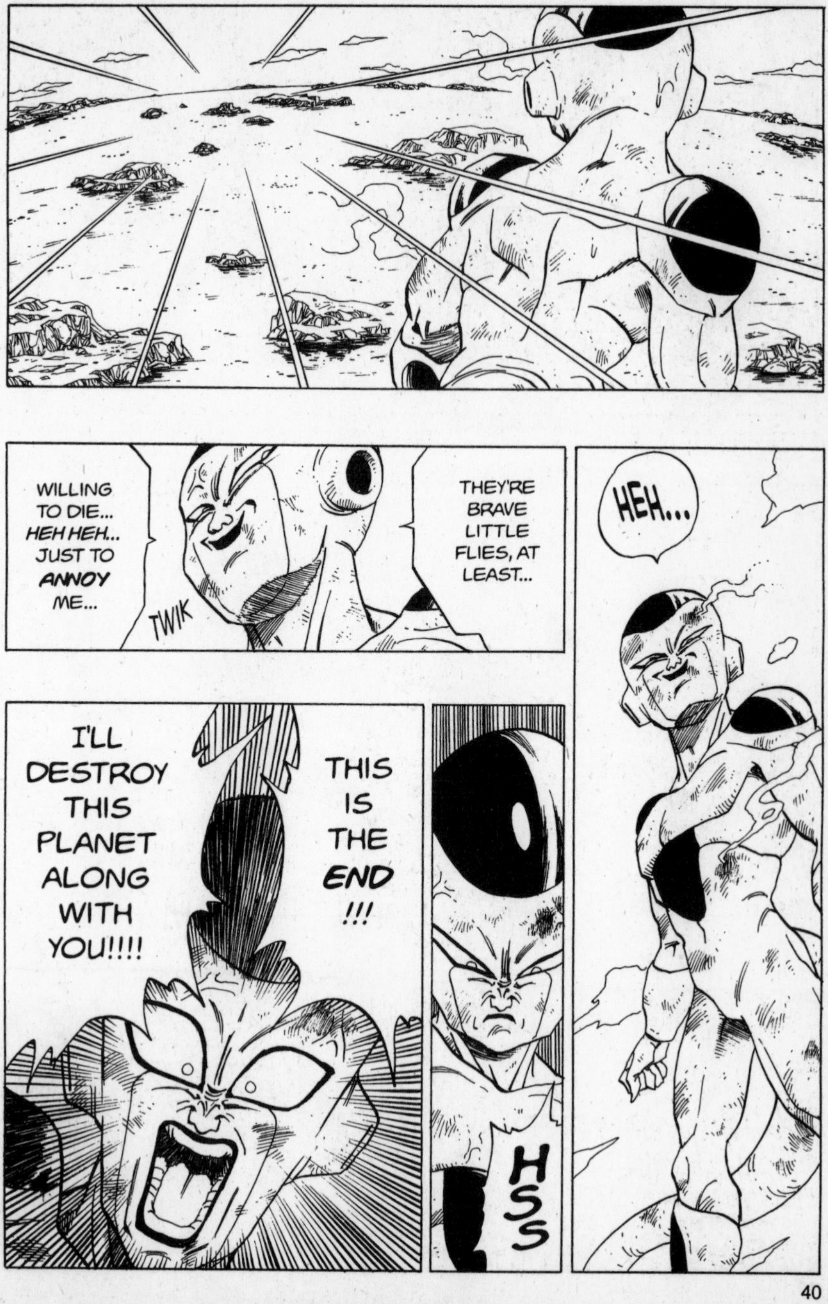
HEH...
THEY'RE BRAVE LITTLE FLIES, AT LEAST...
WILLING TO DIE... HEH HEH... JUST TO ANNOY ME...
TWIK
HSS
THIS IS THE END!!!
I'LL DESTROY THIS PLANET ALONG WITH YOU!!!!!

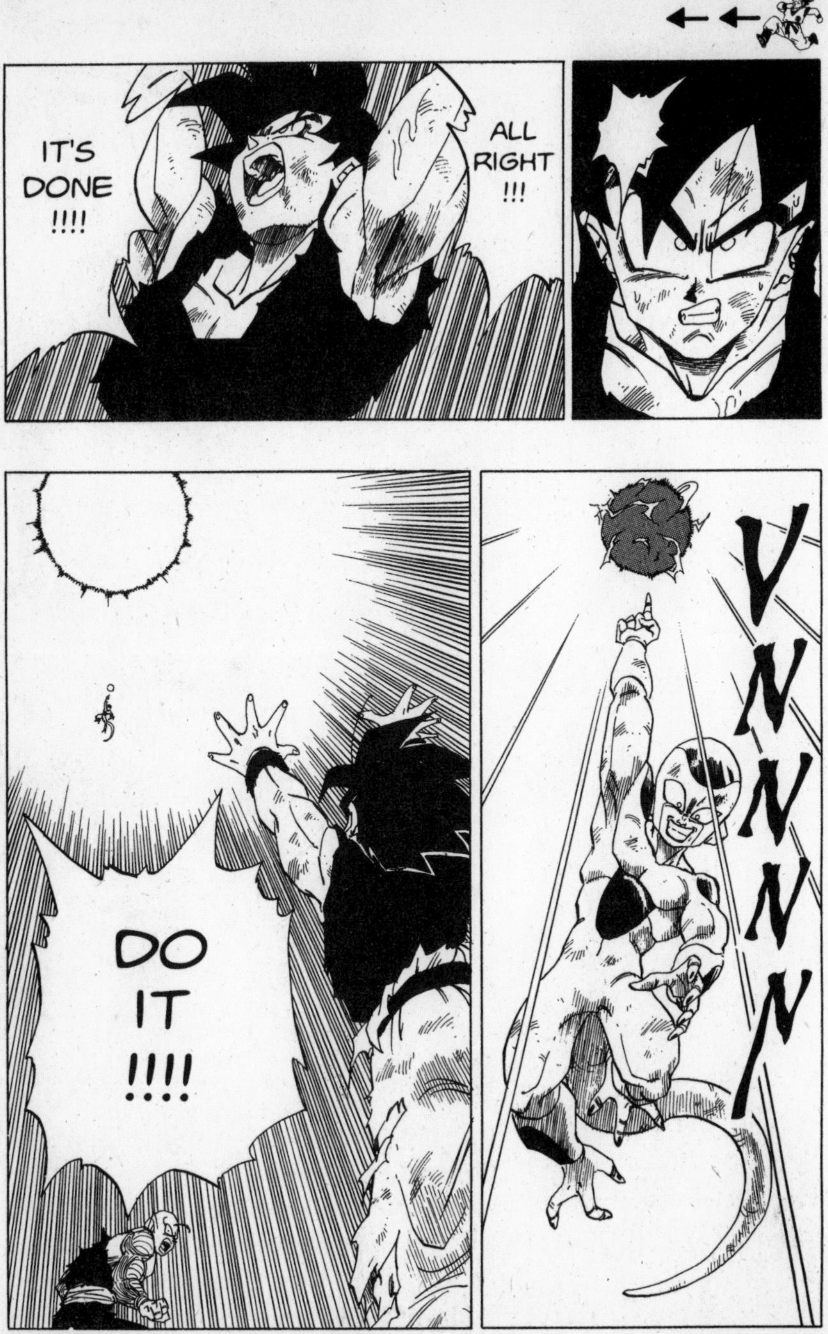
ALL RIGHT !!!
IT'S DONE !!!!
VNNNN
DO IT !!!!

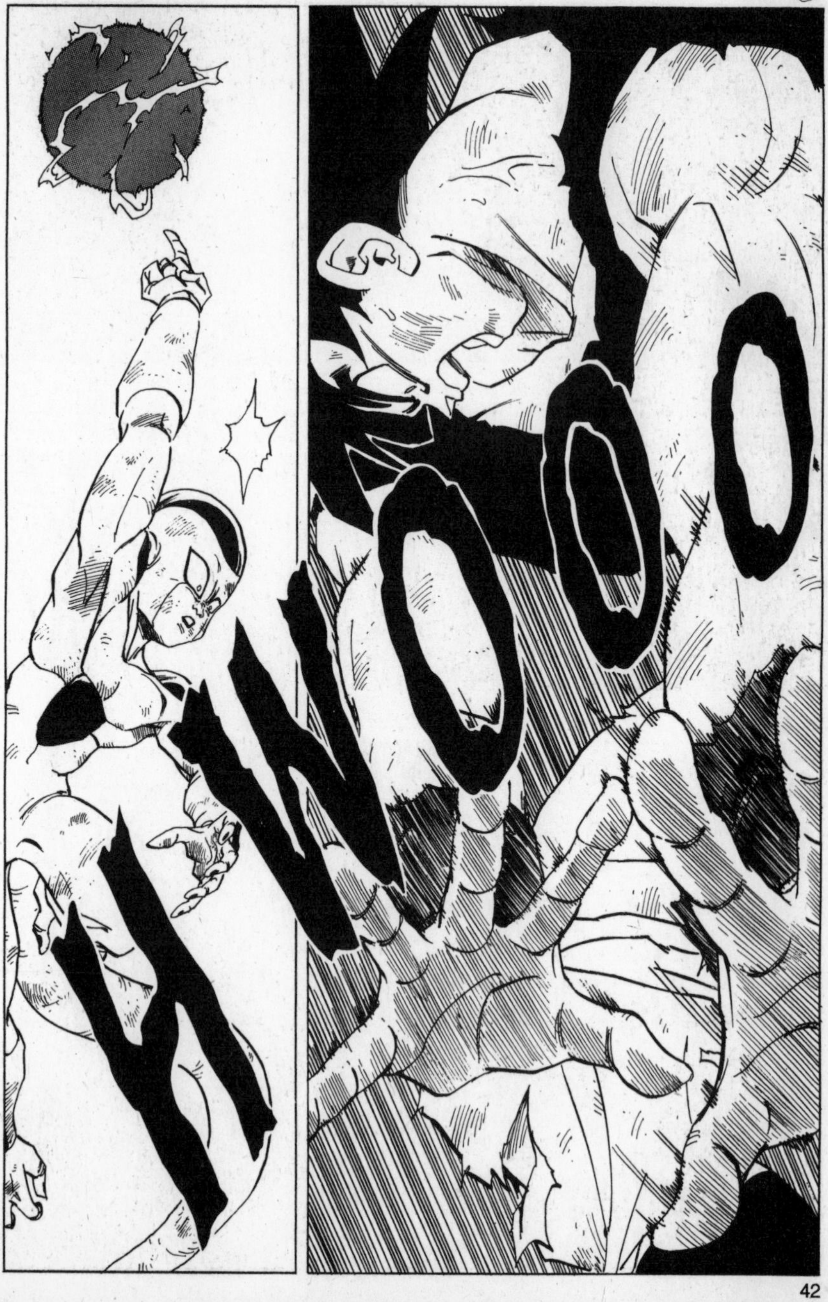
HNOOO

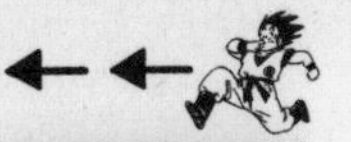

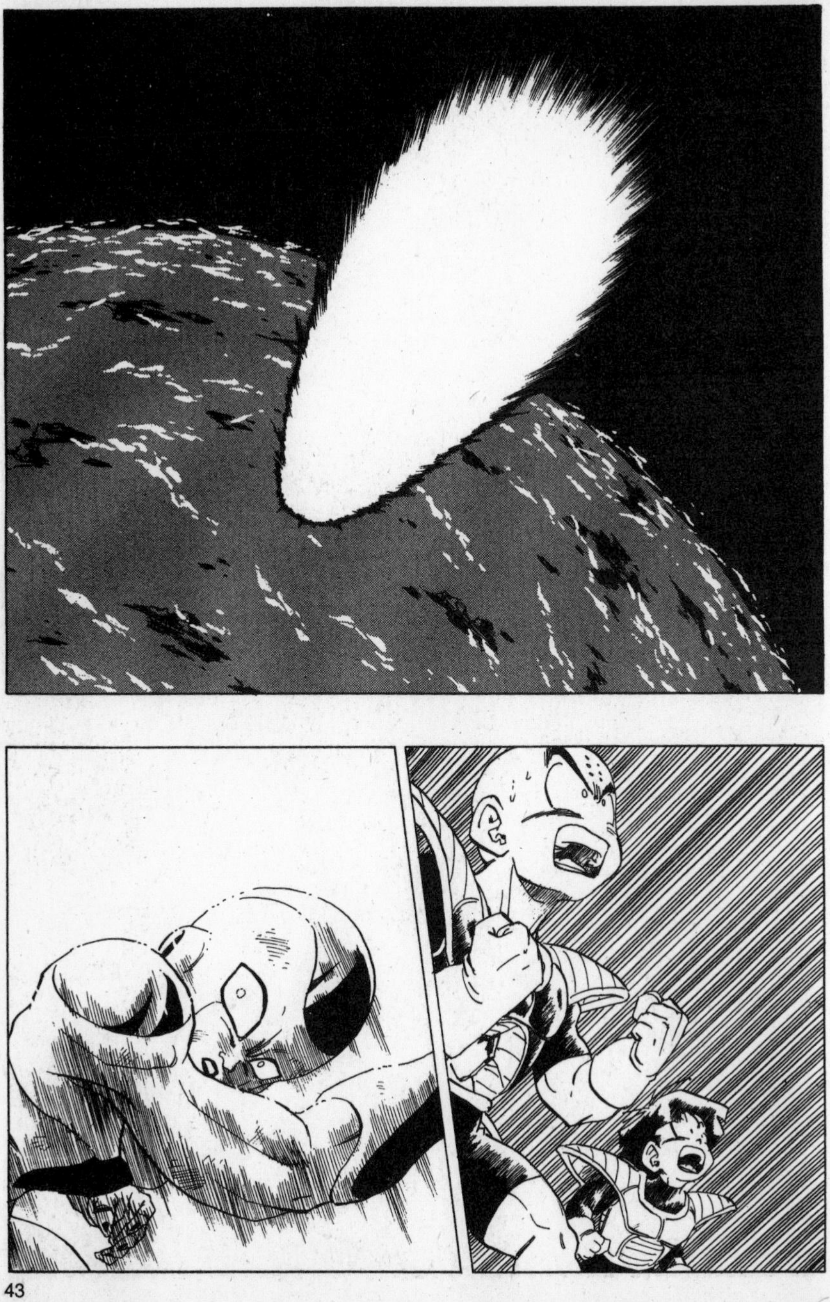

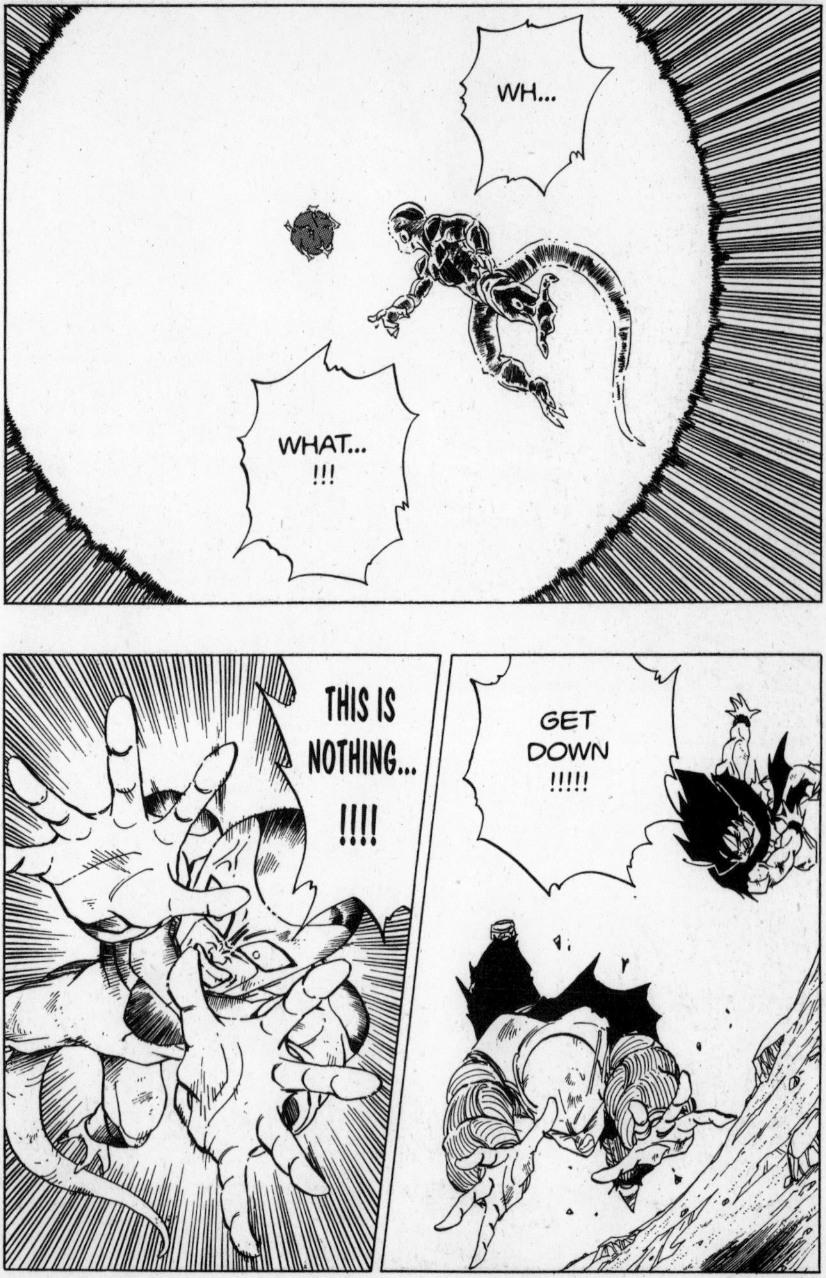
WH...
WHAT... !!!
GET DOWN !!!!!
THIS IS NOTHING... !!!!

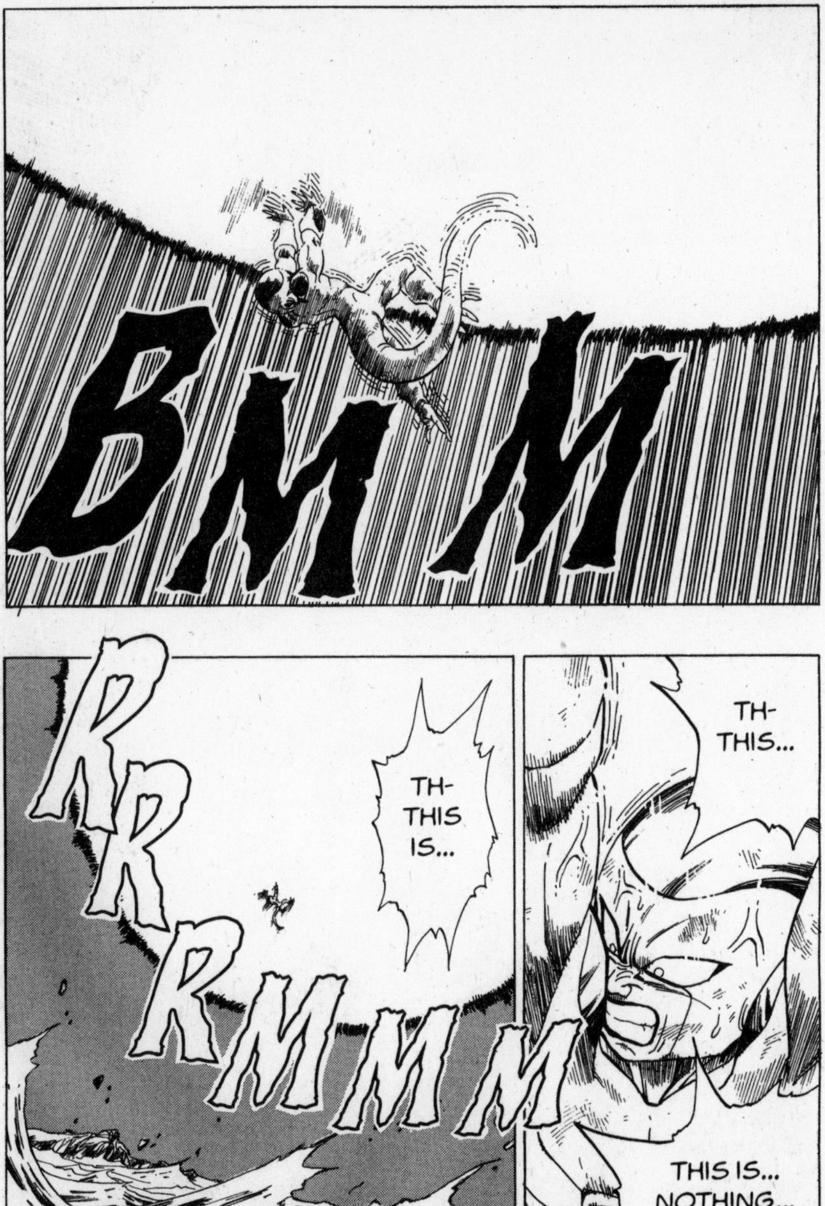
BMM
TH- THIS...
THIS IS... NOTHING... !!!
RRRMMM
TH- THIS IS...

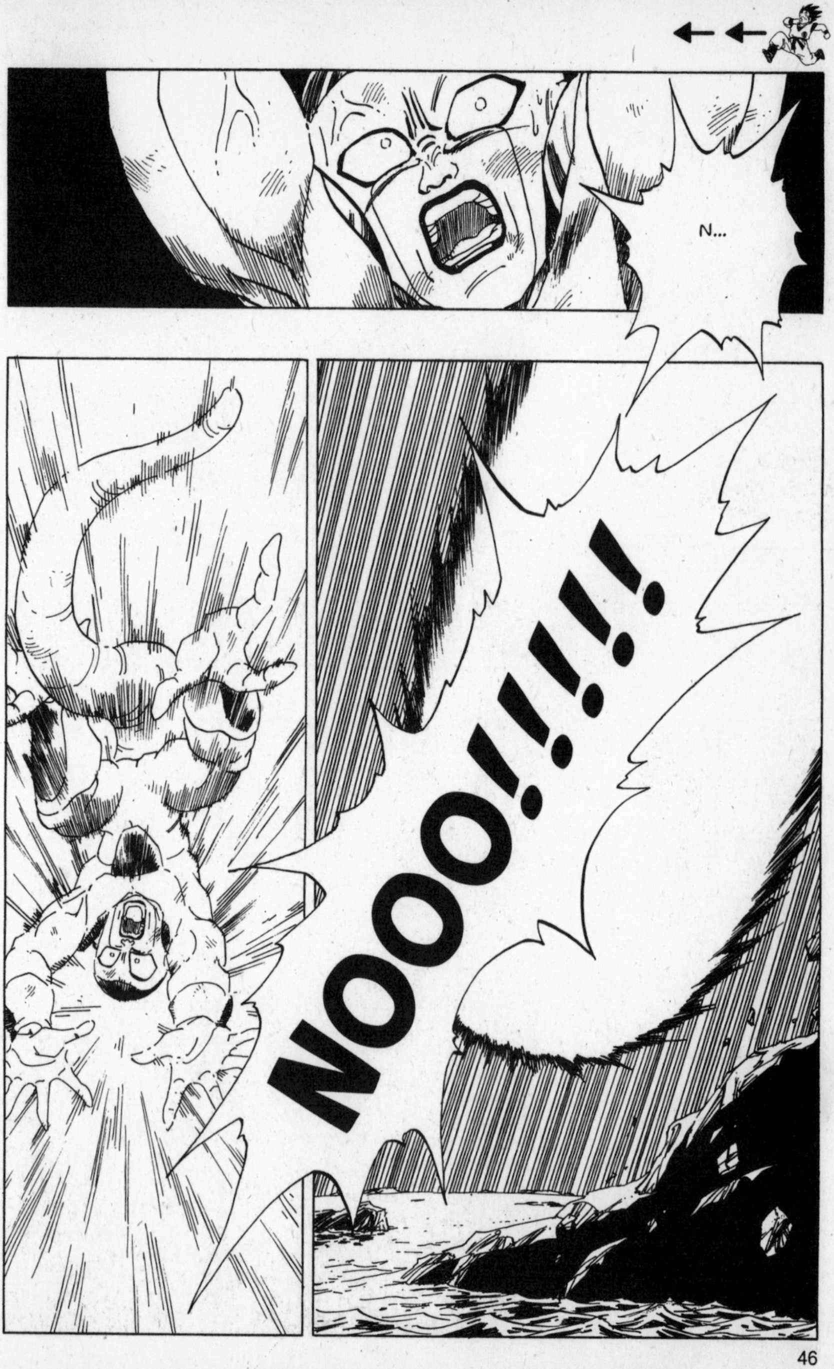
N...
NOOO!!!!!!

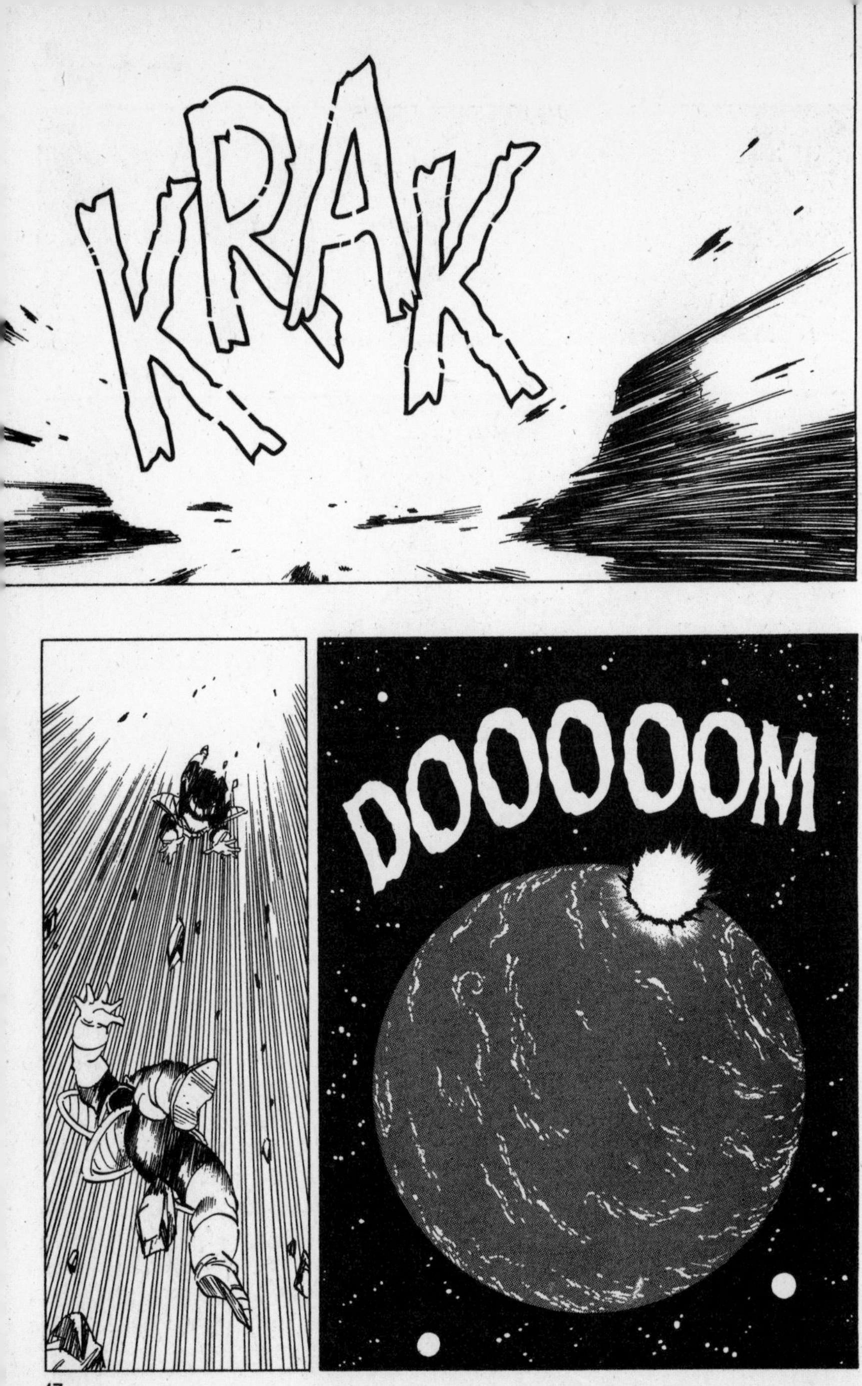
KRAK
DOOOOOM

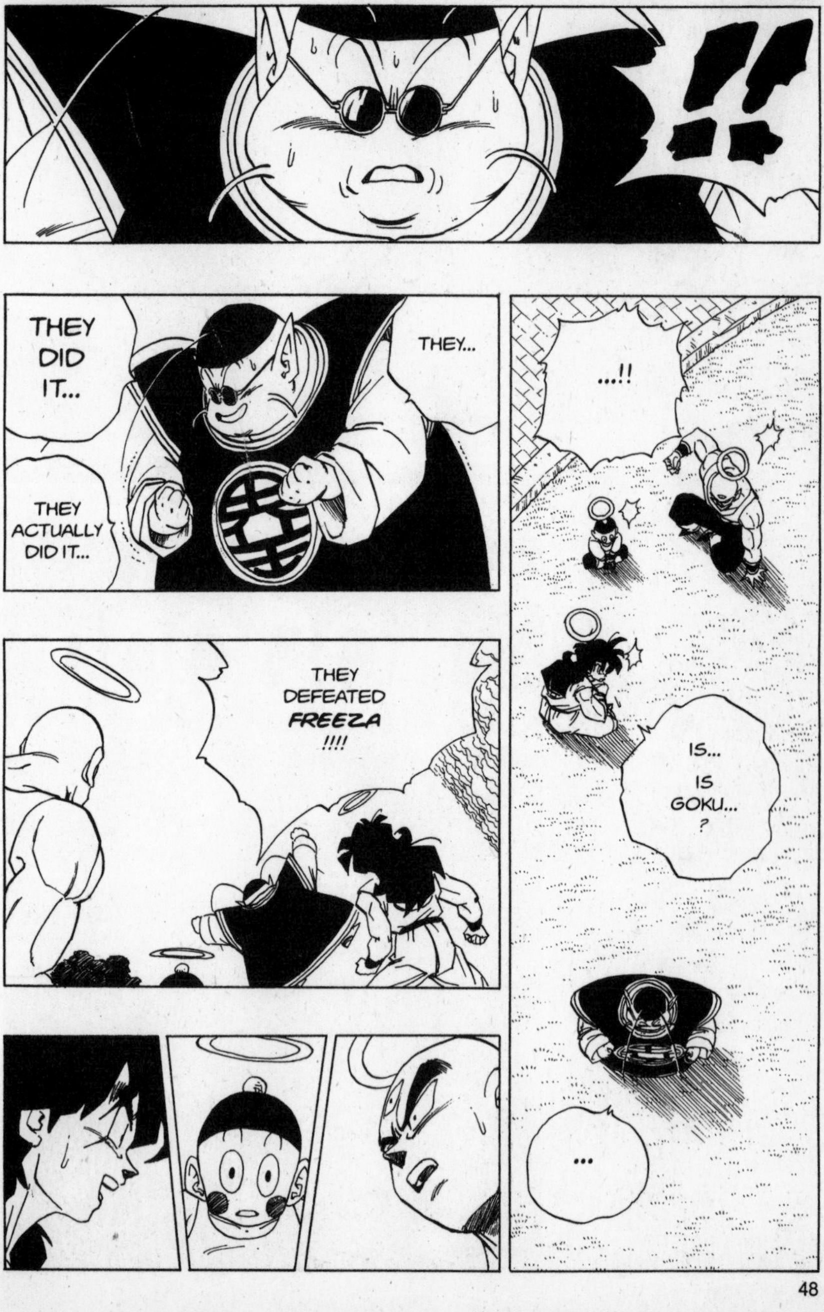
!!
...!!
IS... IS GOKU...?
...
THEY...
THEY DID IT...
THEY ACTUALLY DID IT...
THEY DEFEATED FREEZA!!!!

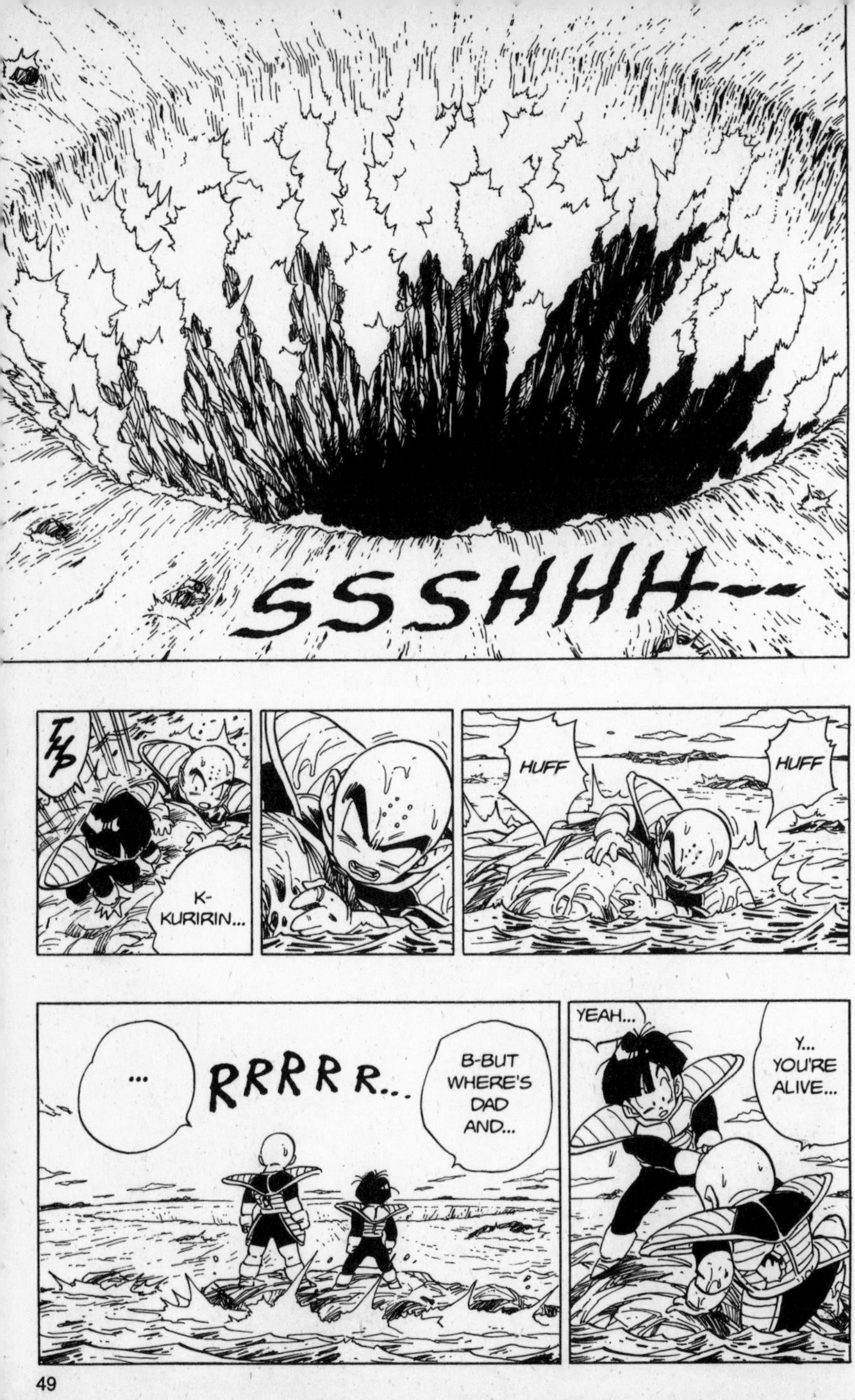
SSSHHH---
HUFF
HUFF
K-KURIRIN...
Y... YOU'RE ALIVE...
YEAH...
B-BUT WHERE'S DAD AND...
RRRRR...
...

DBZ:123 • Life or Death

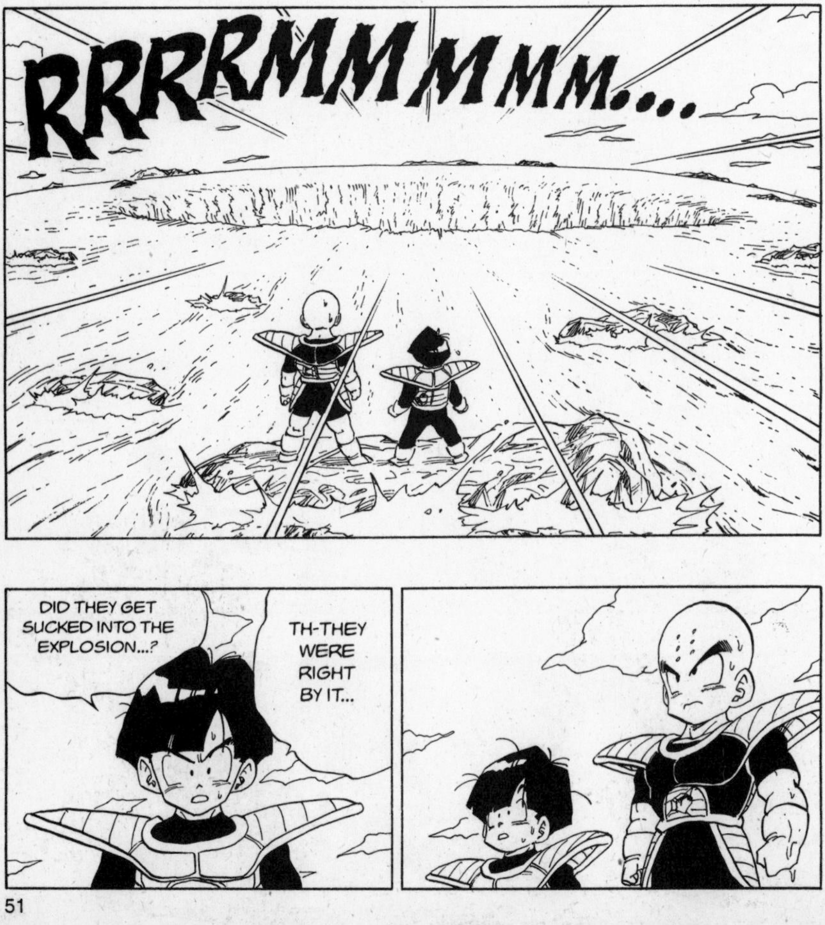
RRRRMMMMM....
TH-THEY WERE RIGHT BY IT...
DID THEY GET SUCKED INTO THE EXPLOSION...?

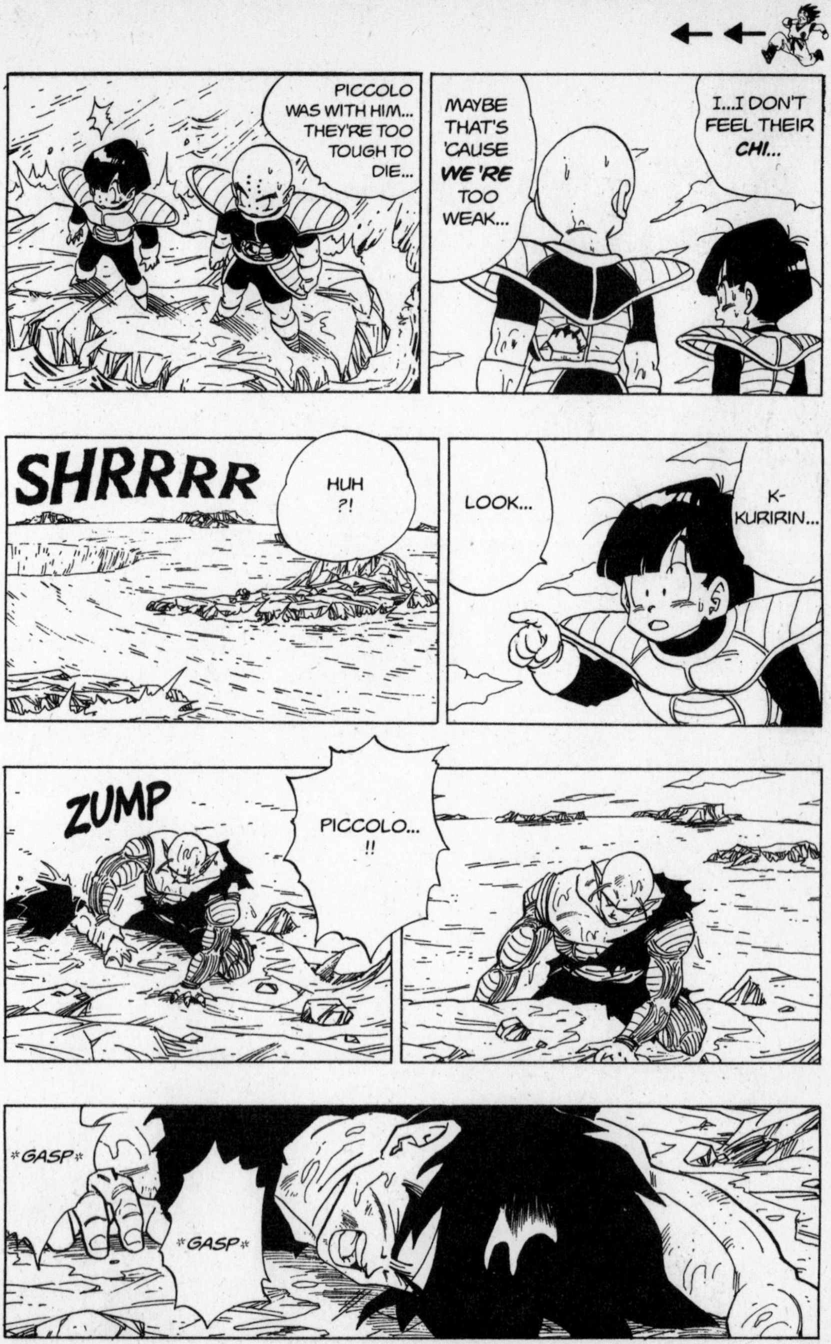
I...I DON'T FEEL THEIR CHI...
MAYBE THAT'S 'CAUSE WE'RE TOO WEAK...
PICCOLO WAS WITH HIM... THEY'RE TOO TOUGH TO DIE...
K-KURIRIN...
LOOK...
HUH ?!
SHRRRR
PICCOLO... !!
ZUMP
GASP
GASP

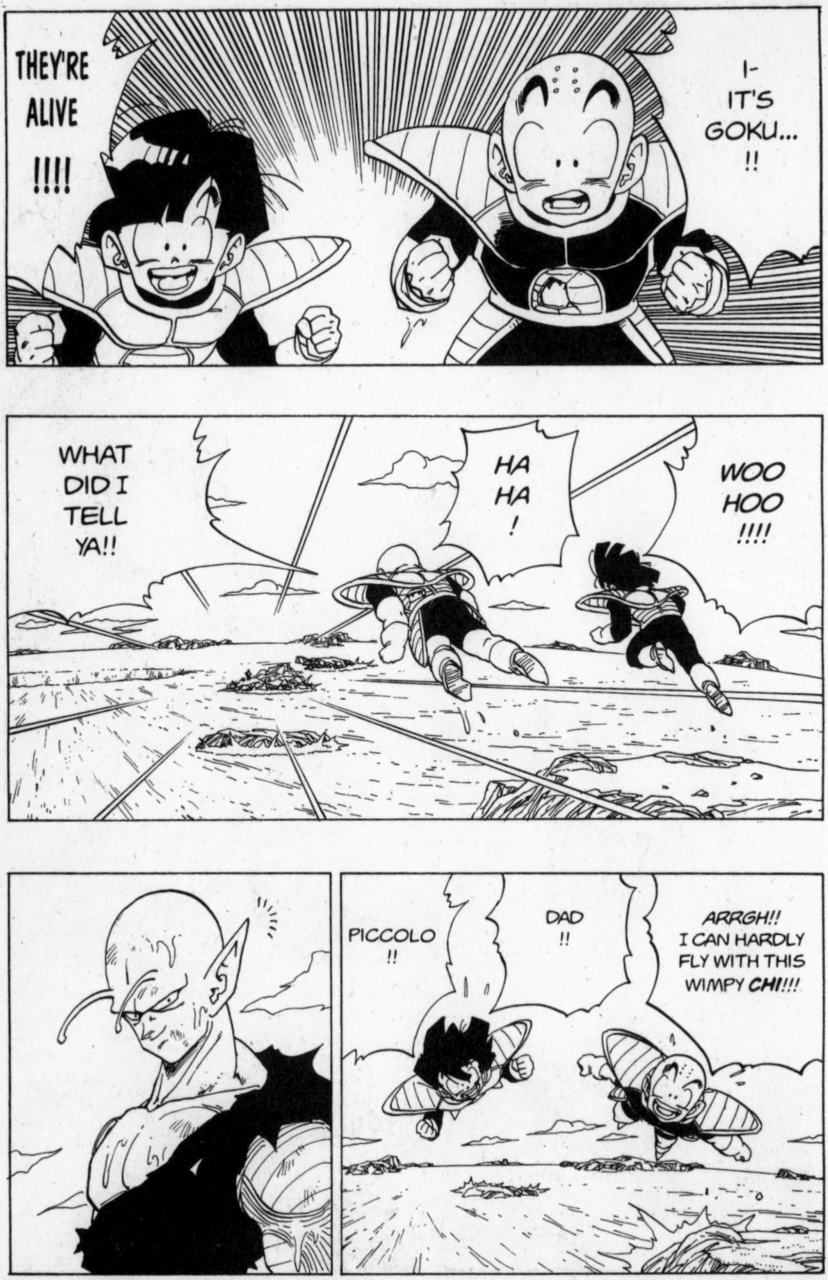
I- IT'S GOKU... !!
THEY'RE ALIVE !!!!
WOO HOO !!!!
HA HA !
WHAT DID I TELL YA!!
ARRGH!! I CAN HARDLY FLY WITH THIS WIMPY CHI!!!
DAD !!
PICCOLO !!

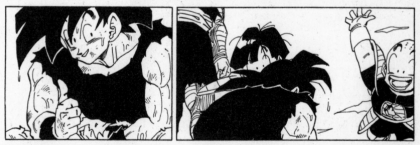

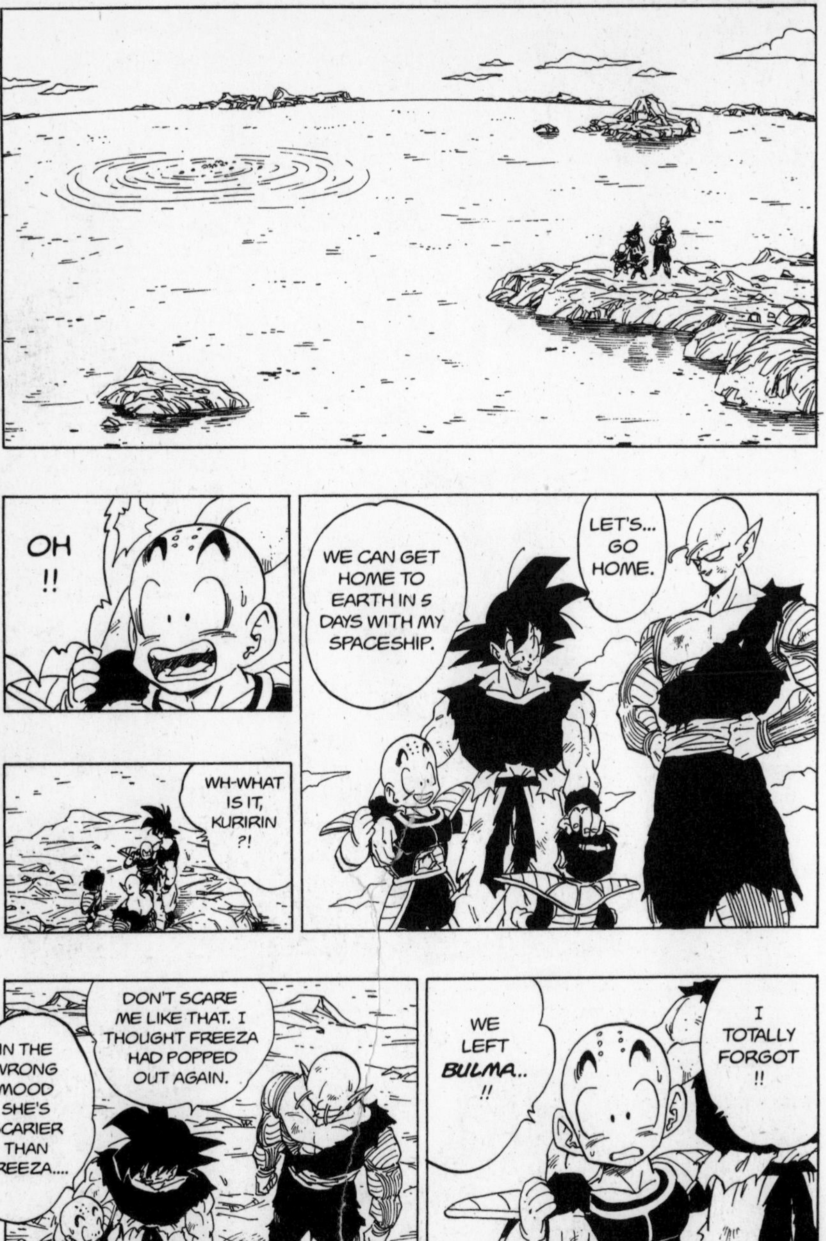
LET'S... GO HOME.
WE CAN GET HOME TO EARTH IN 5 DAYS WITH MY SPACESHIP.
OH !!
WH-WHAT IS IT, KURIRIN ?!
I TOTALLY FORGOT !!
WE LEFT BULMA.. !!
DON'T SCARE ME LIKE THAT. I THOUGHT FREEZA HAD POPPED OUT AGAIN.
IN THE WRONG MOOD SHE'S SCARIER THAN FREEZA....

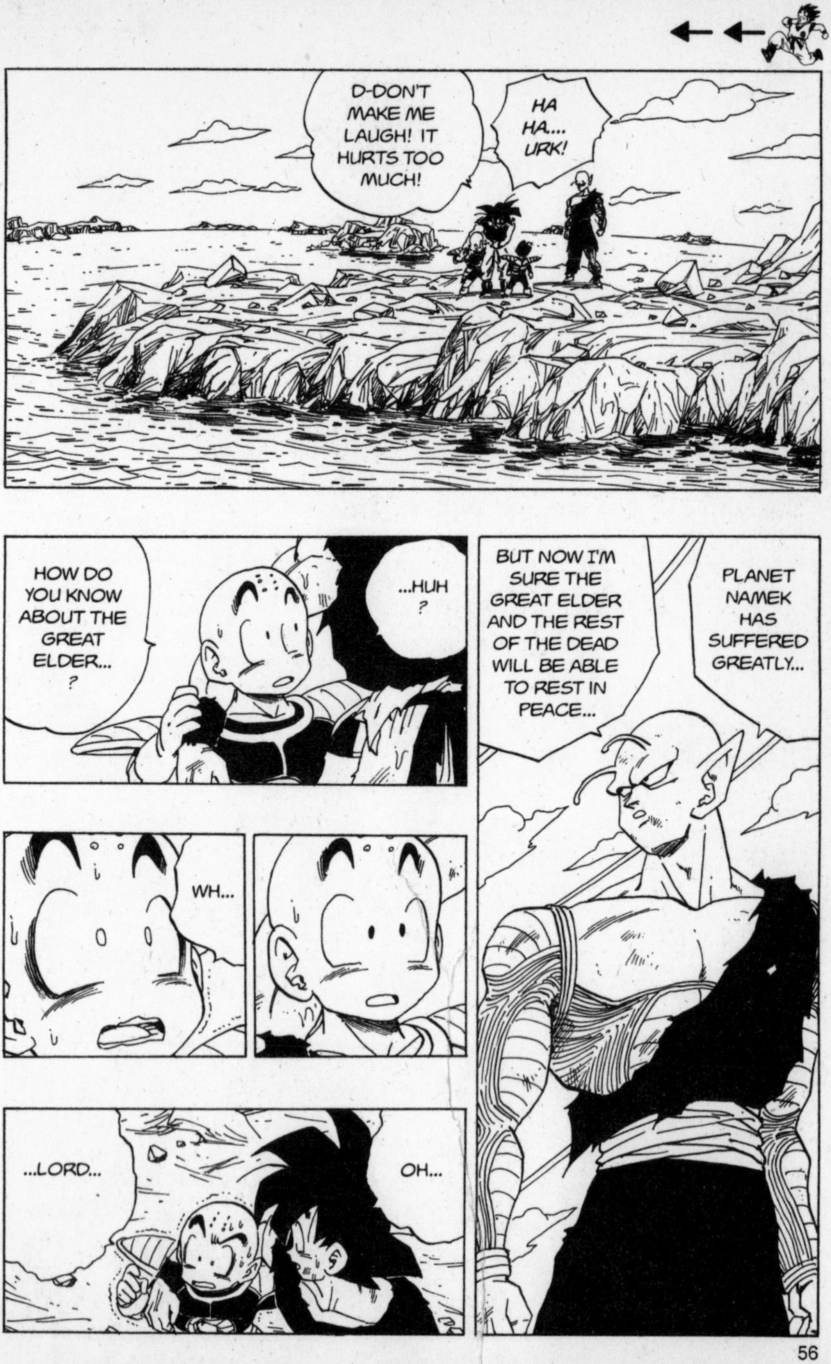

HA HA.... URK!
D-DON'T MAKE ME LAUGH! IT HURTS TOO MUCH!
PLANET NAMEK HAS SUFFERED GREATLY...
BUT NOW I'M SURE THE GREAT ELDER AND THE REST OF THE DEAD WILL BE ABLE TO REST IN PEACE...
...HUH ?
HOW DO YOU KNOW ABOUT THE GREAT ELDER... ?
WH...
OH...
...LORD...

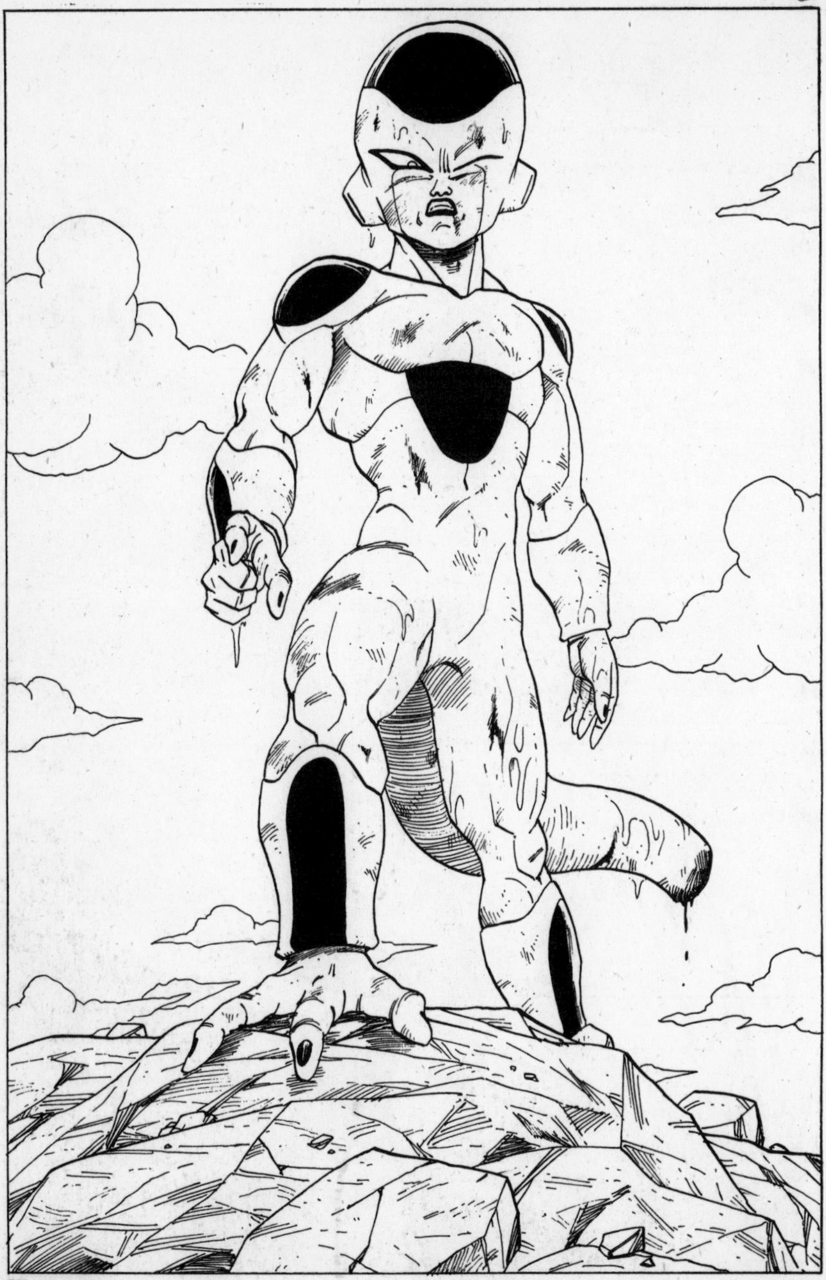

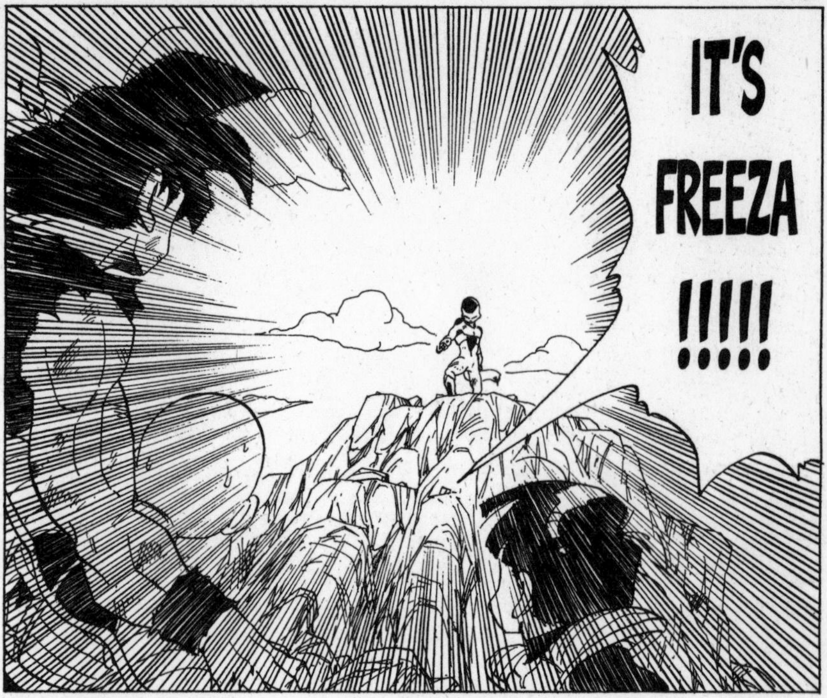
IT'S FREEZA !!!!!
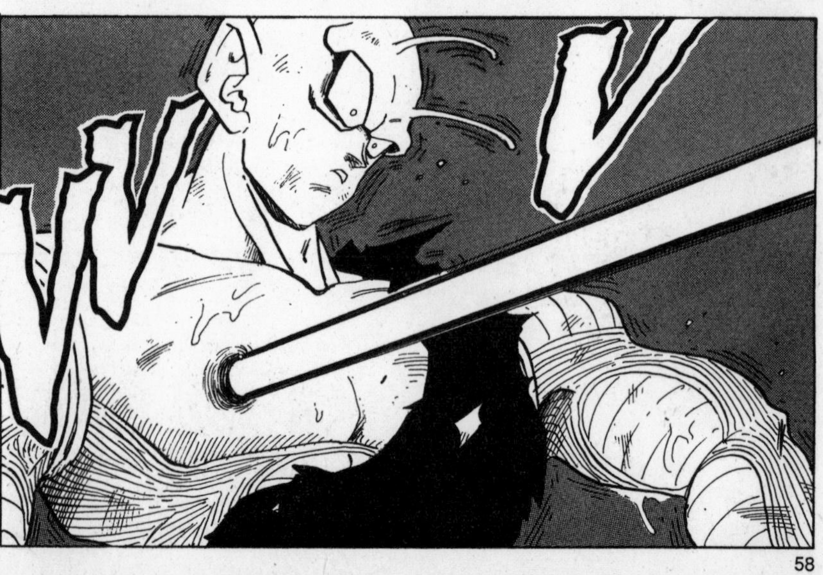
VVV

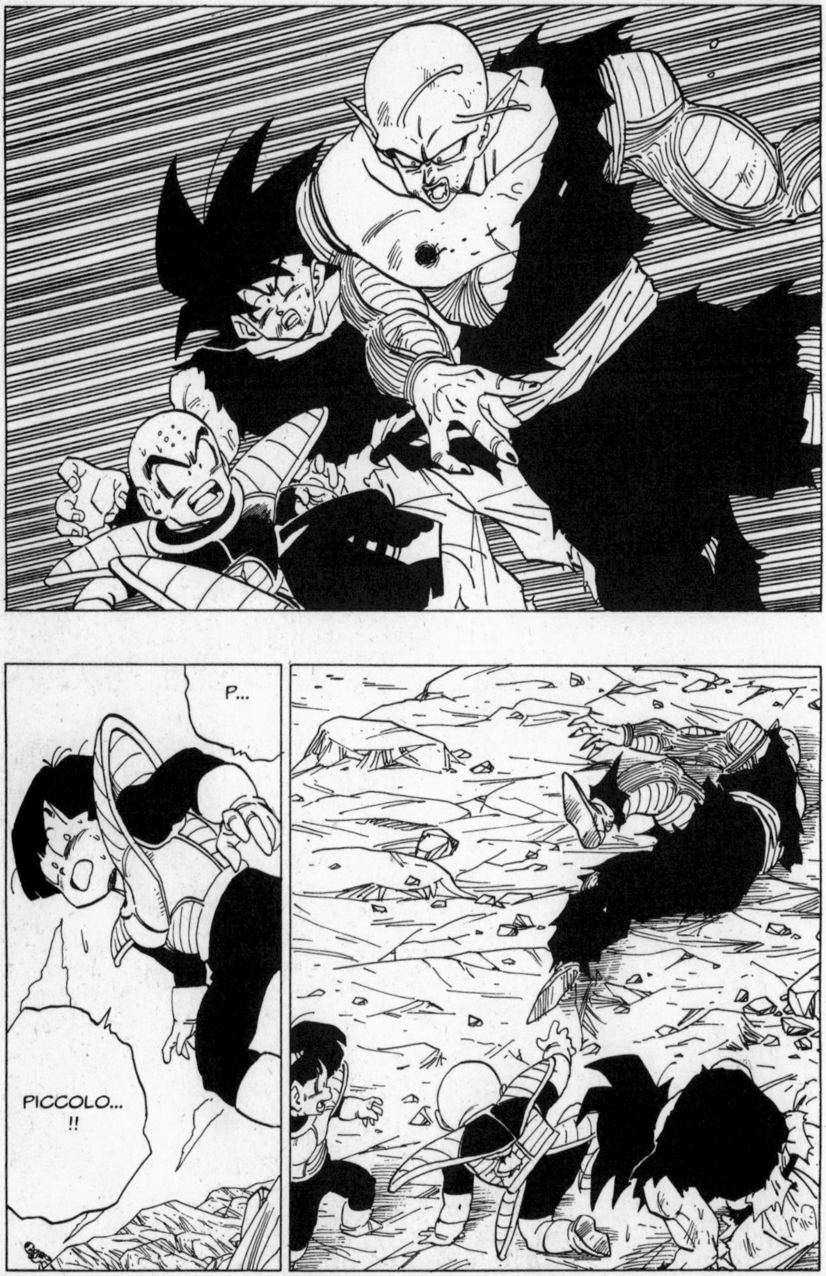
P...
PICCOLO... !!

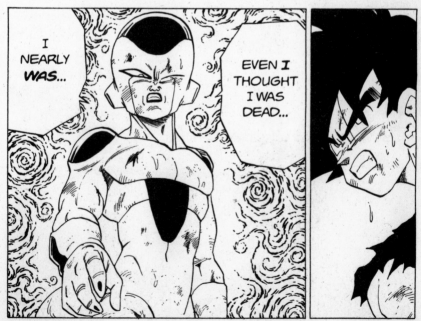

PICCOLO
!!!

I NEARLY
WAS...

EVEN **I**
THOUGHT
I WAS
DEAD...

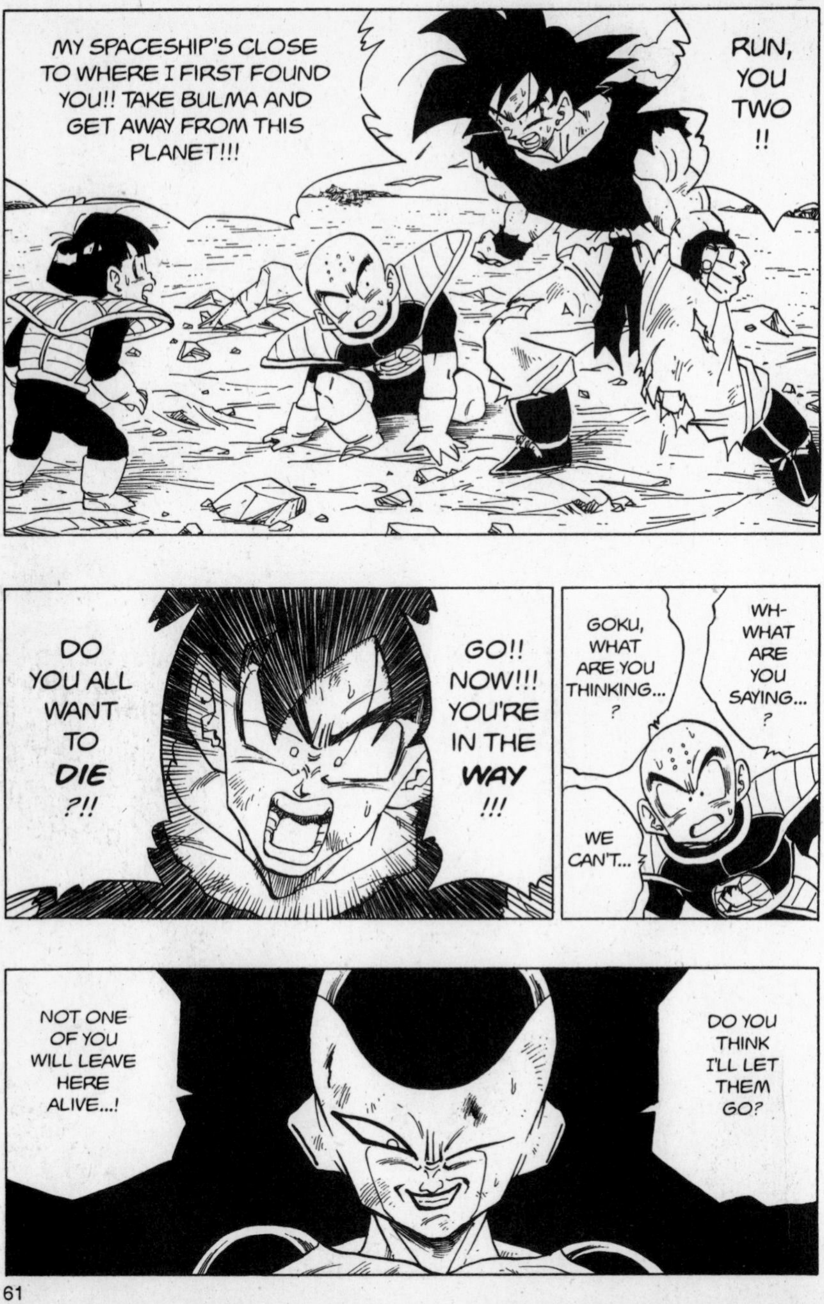
RUN, YOU TWO!!
MY SPACESHIP'S CLOSE TO WHERE I FIRST FOUND YOU!! TAKE BULMA AND GET AWAY FROM THIS PLANET!!!
WH-WHAT ARE YOU SAYING...?
GOKU, WHAT ARE YOU THINKING...?
WE CAN'T...
GO!! NOW!!! YOU'RE IN THE WAY!!!
DO YOU ALL WANT TO DIE?!!
DO YOU THINK I'LL LET THEM GO?
NOT ONE OF YOU WILL LEAVE HERE ALIVE...!

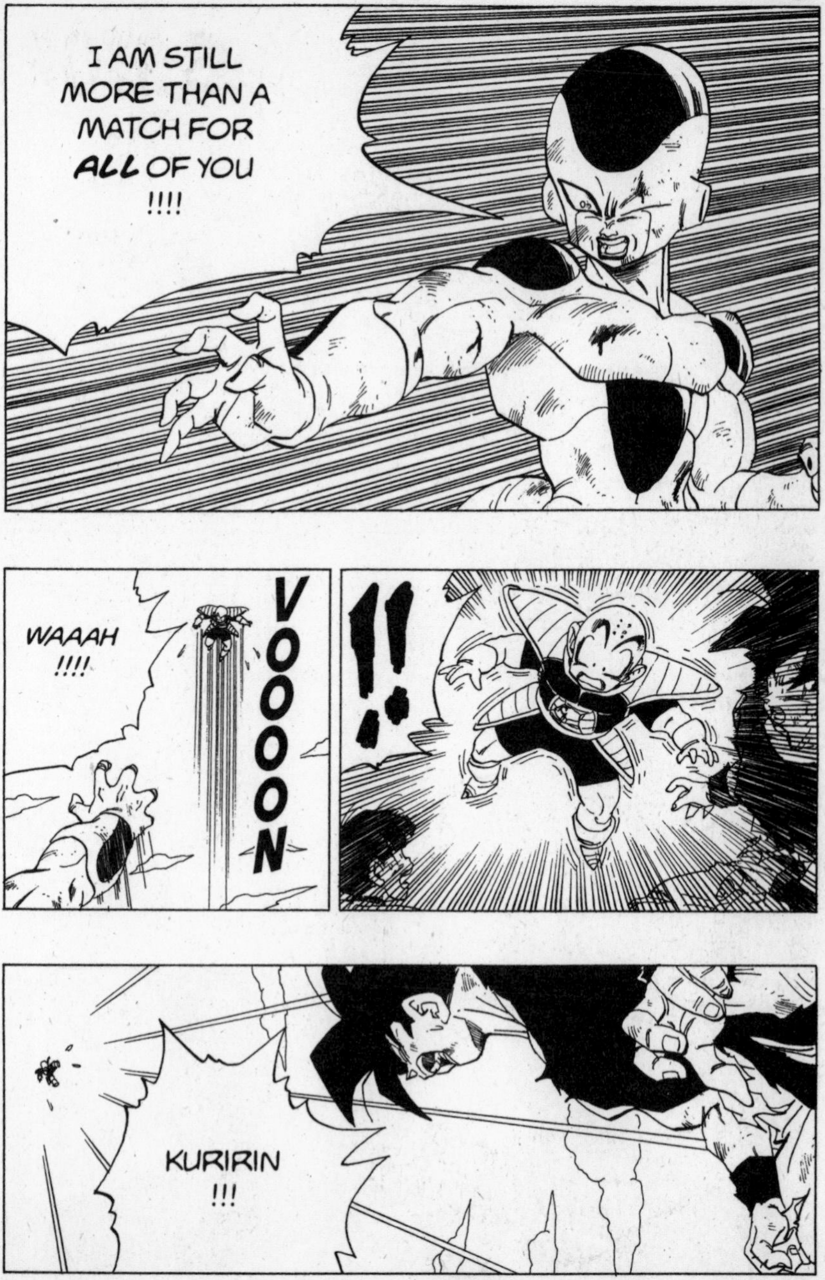
I AM STILL MORE THAN A MATCH FOR ALL OF YOU !!!!
!!
VOOOON
WAAAH !!!!
KURIRIN !!!

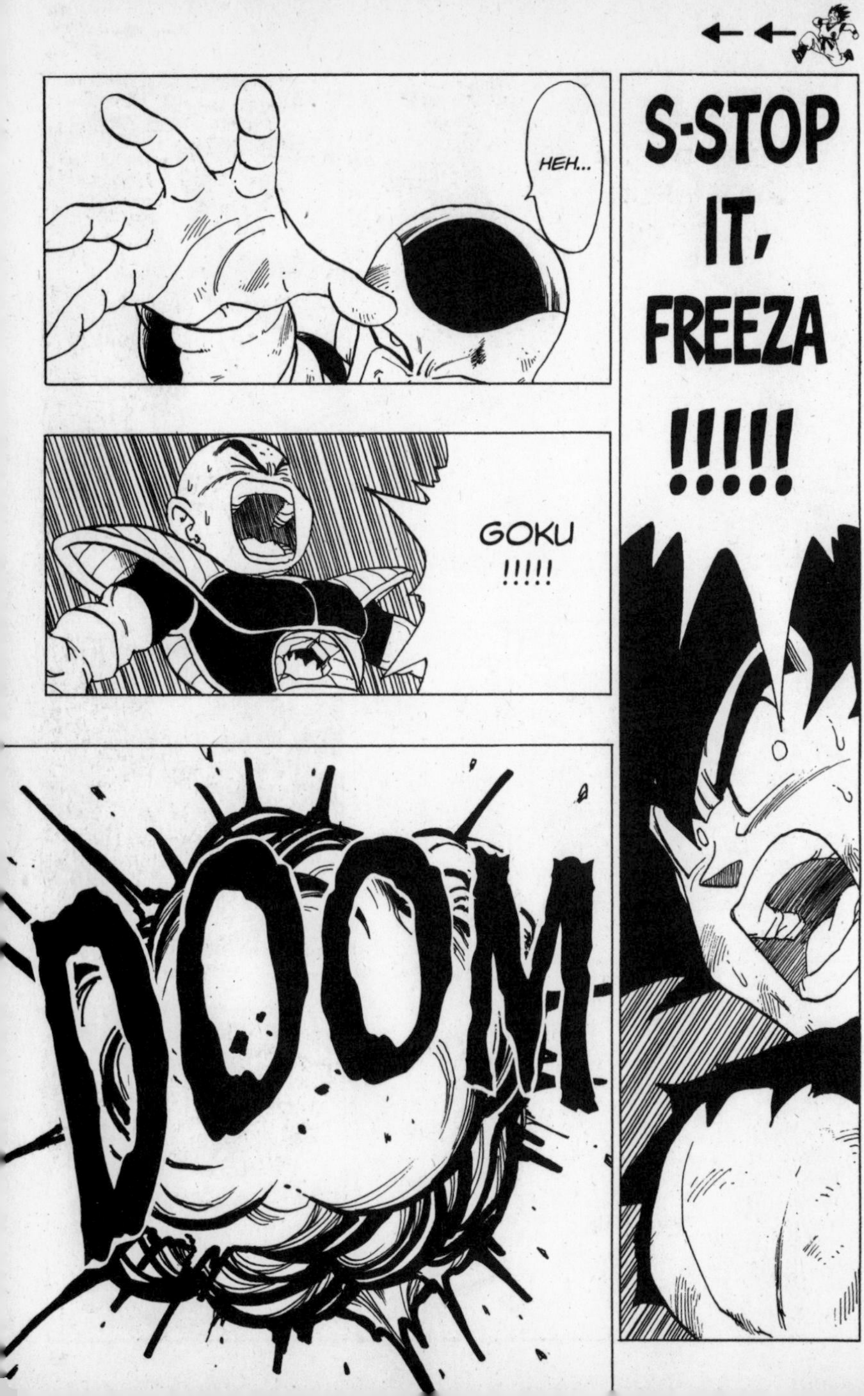
S-STOP IT, FREEZA !!!!!
HEH...
GOKU !!!!!
DOOM

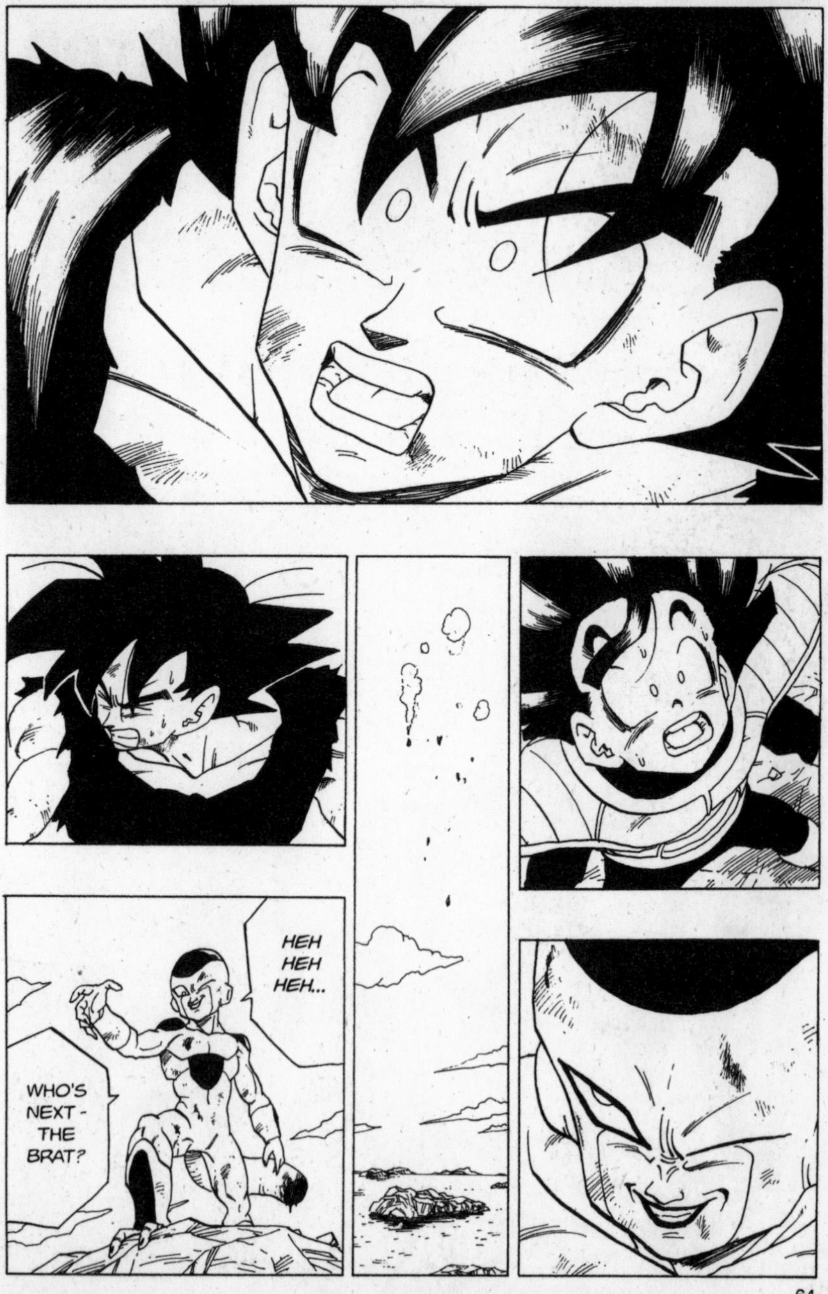
HEH HEH HEH...
WHO'S NEXT - THE BRAT?

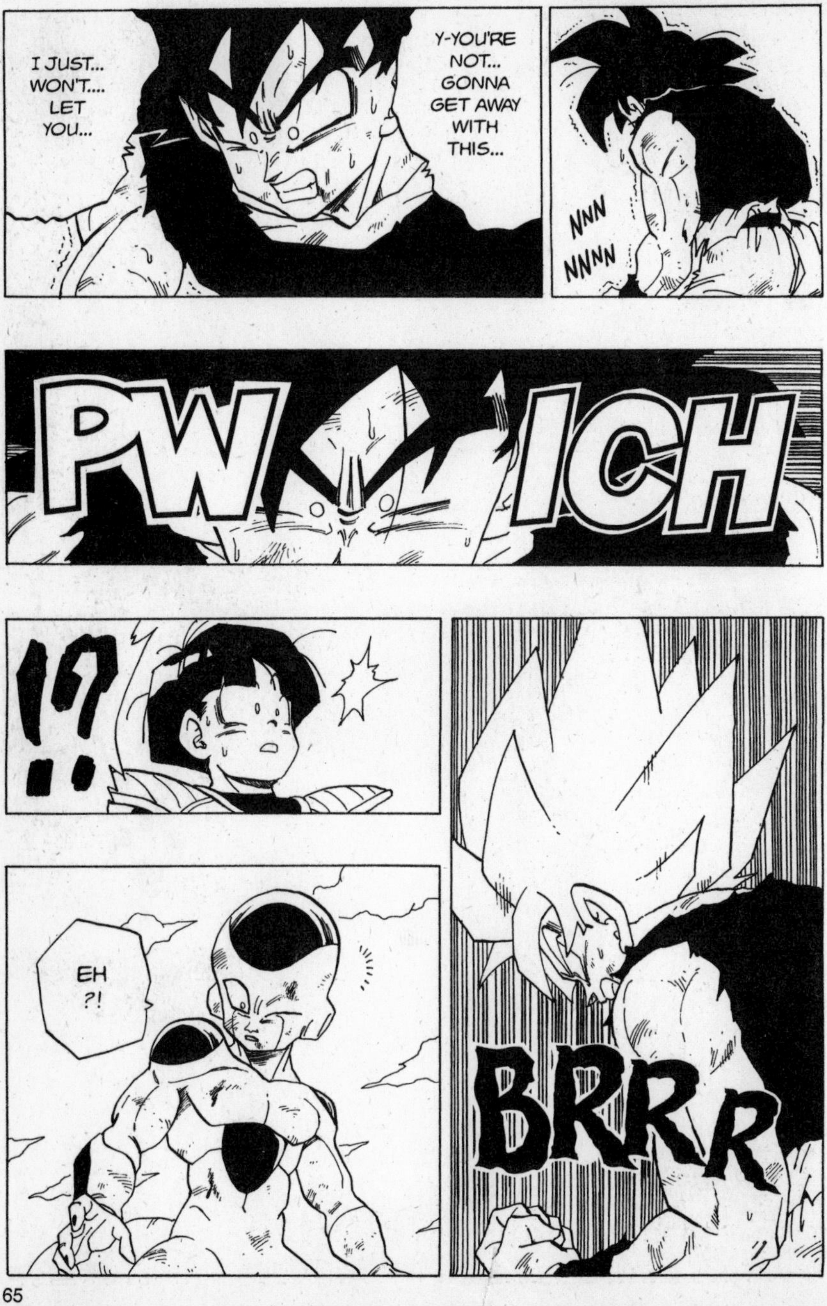
NNN
NNNN
Y-YOU'RE NOT... GONNA GET AWAY WITH THIS...
I JUST... WON'T.... LET YOU...
PW ICH
BRRR
!?
EH ?!

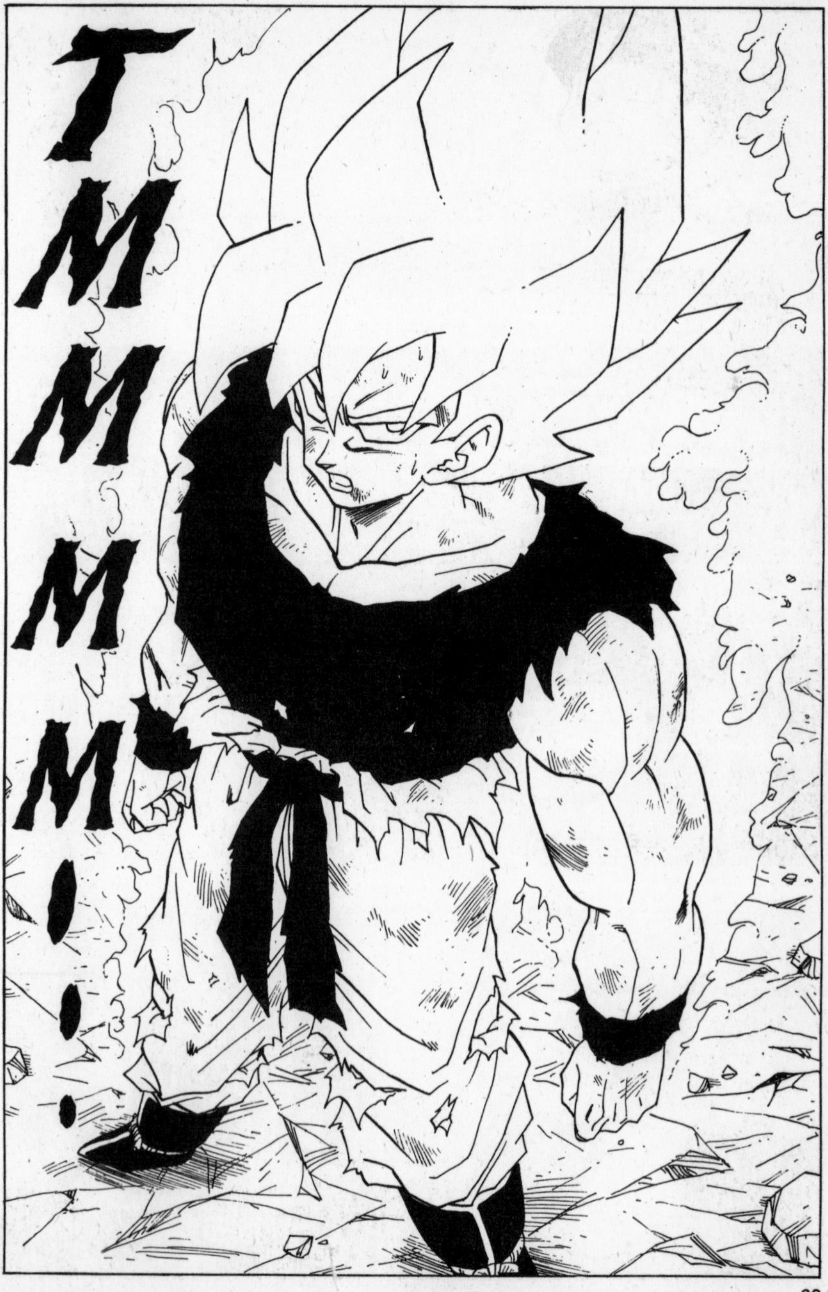
TMMMM...

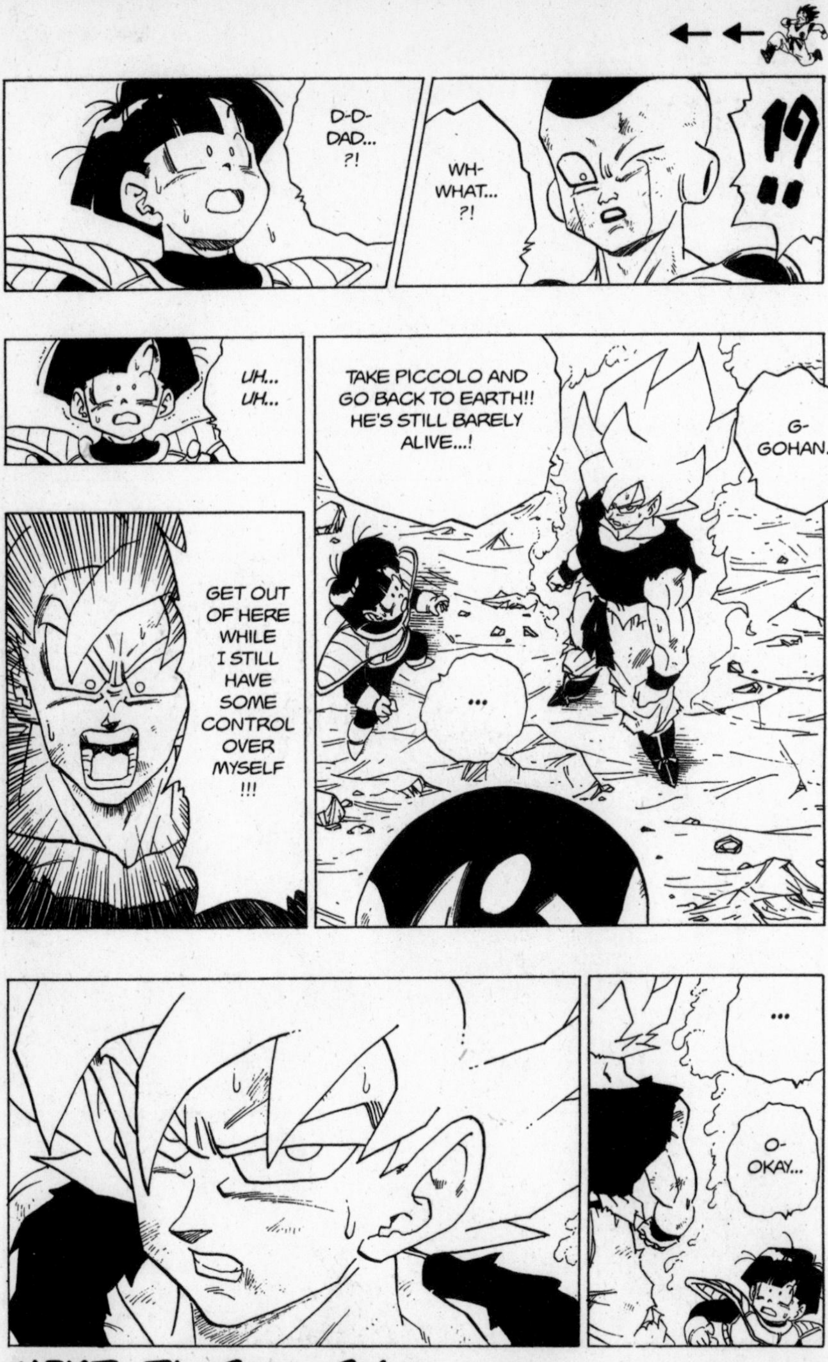
!?!!
WH- WHAT... ?!
D-D- DAD... ?!
G- GOHAN...
TAKE PICCOLO AND GO BACK TO EARTH!! HE'S STILL BARELY ALIVE...!
...
UH... UH...
GET OUT OF HERE WHILE I STILL HAVE SOME CONTROL OVER MYSELF !!!
...
O- OKAY...

NEXT: The Super Saiyan

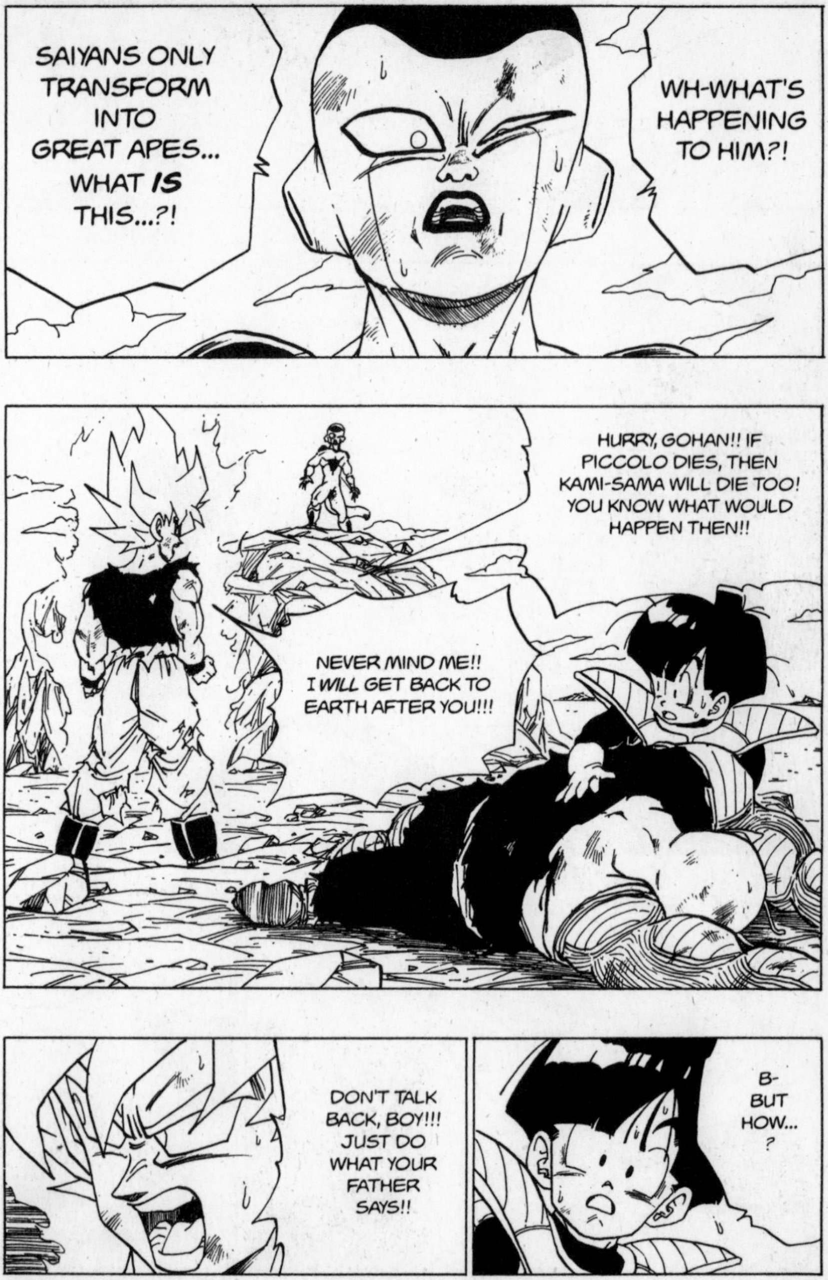
WH-WHAT'S HAPPENING TO HIM?!
SAIYANS ONLY TRANSFORM INTO GREAT APES... WHAT *IS* THIS...?!
HURRY, GOHAN!! IF PICCOLO DIES, THEN KAMI-SAMA WILL DIE TOO! YOU KNOW WHAT WOULD HAPPEN THEN!!
NEVER MIND ME!! I *WILL* GET BACK TO EARTH AFTER YOU!!!
B-BUT HOW...?
DON'T TALK BACK, BOY!!! JUST DO WHAT YOUR FATHER SAYS!!

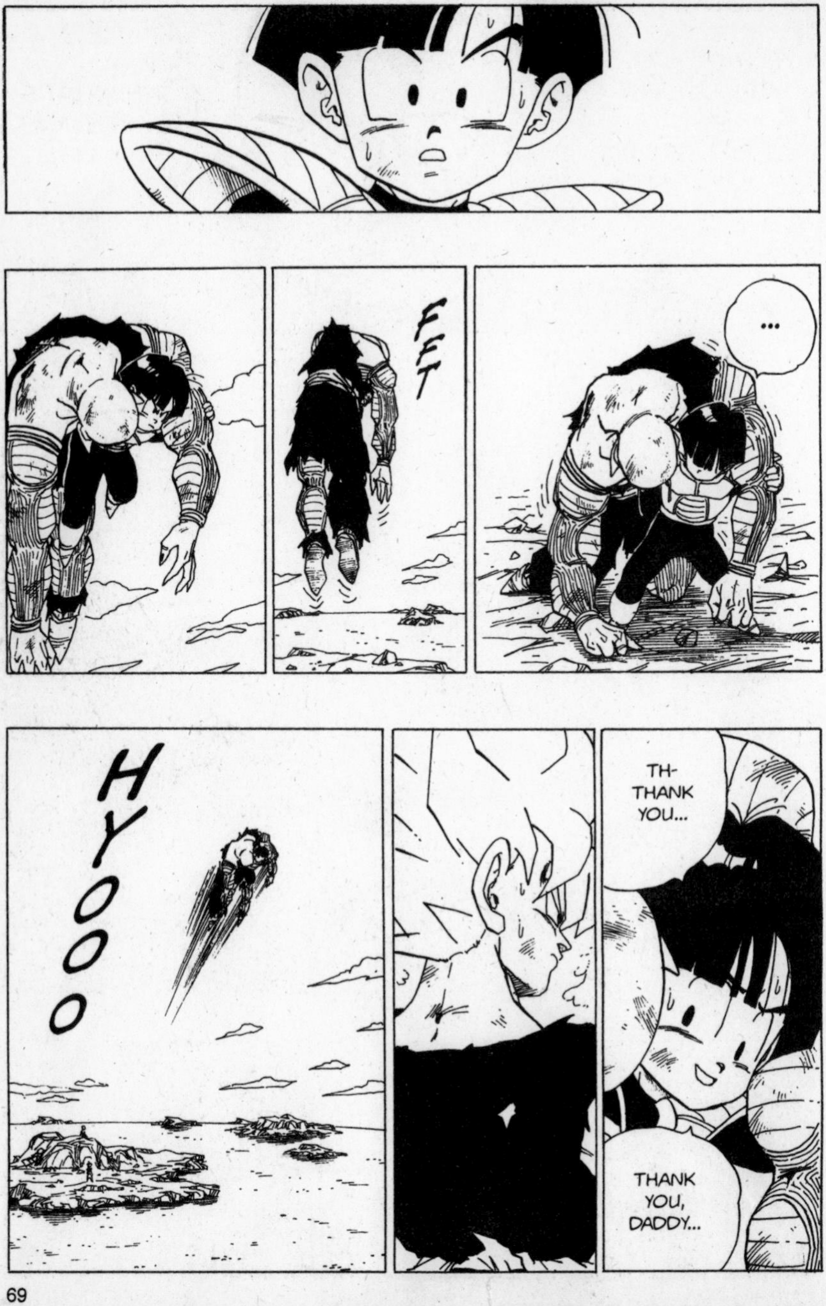
...
FFT
TH-
THANK
YOU...
THANK
YOU,
DADDY...
HYOOO

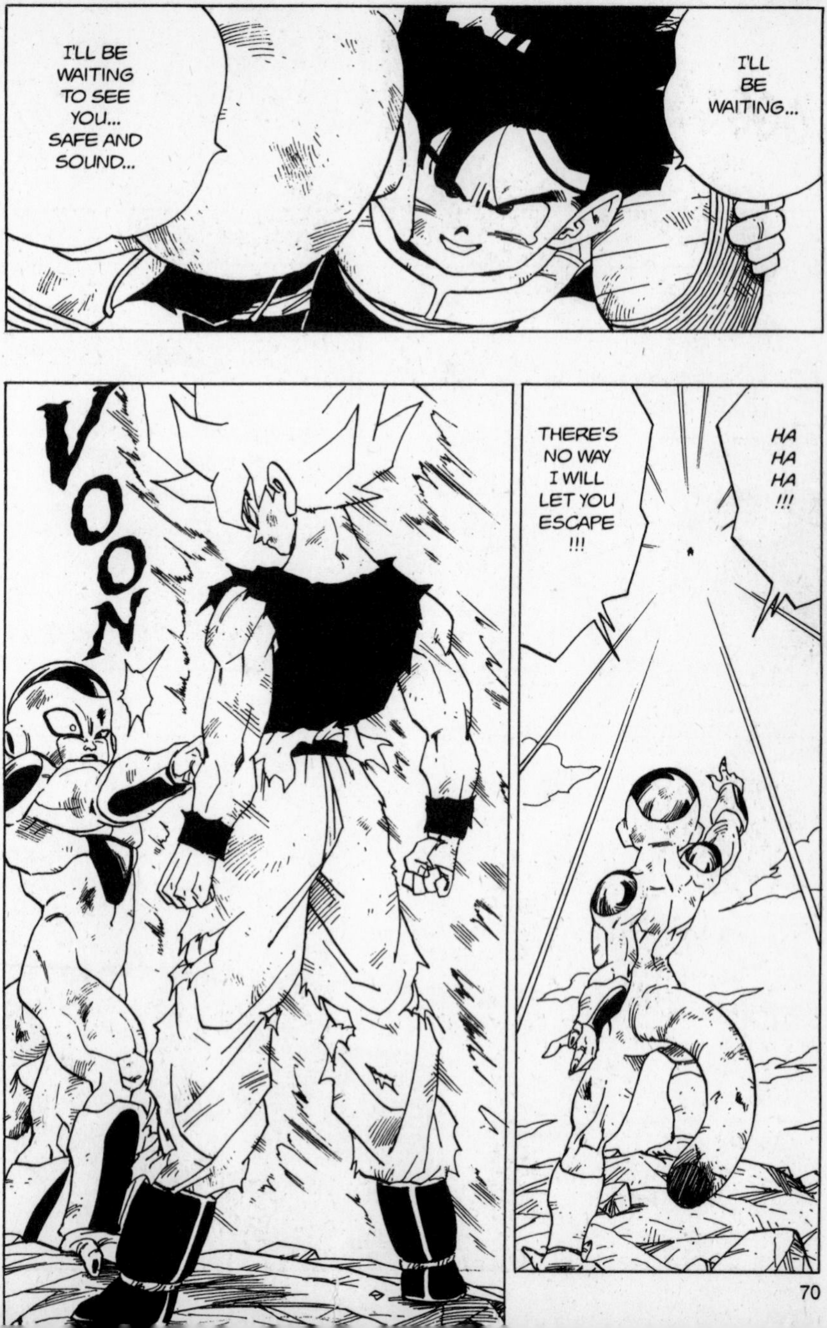
I'LL BE WAITING...
I'LL BE WAITING TO SEE YOU... SAFE AND SOUND...
HA HA HA!!!
THERE'S NO WAY I WILL LET YOU ESCAPE!!!
VOOON

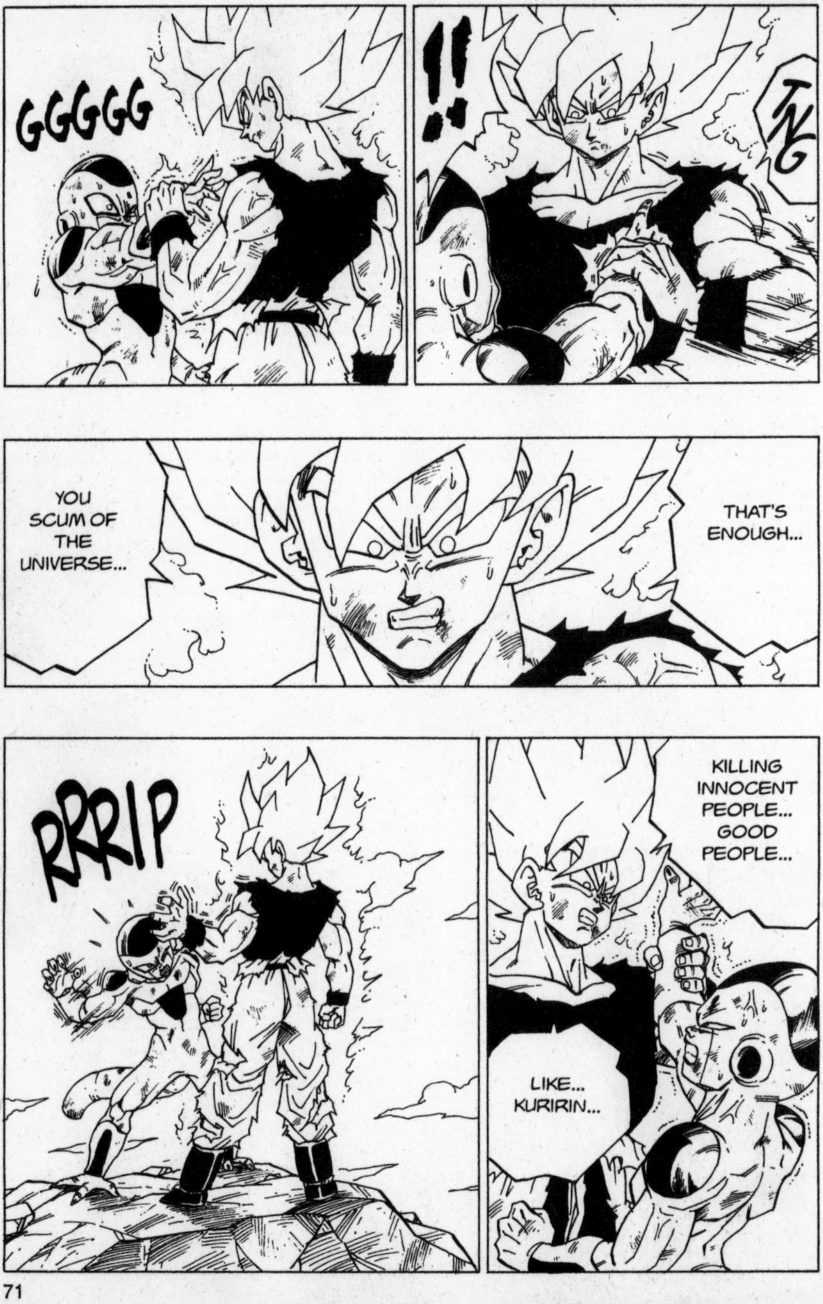
!!
TNG
GGGGG
THAT'S ENOUGH...
YOU SCUM OF THE UNIVERSE...
KILLING INNOCENT PEOPLE... GOOD PEOPLE...
LIKE... KURIRIN...
RRRIP

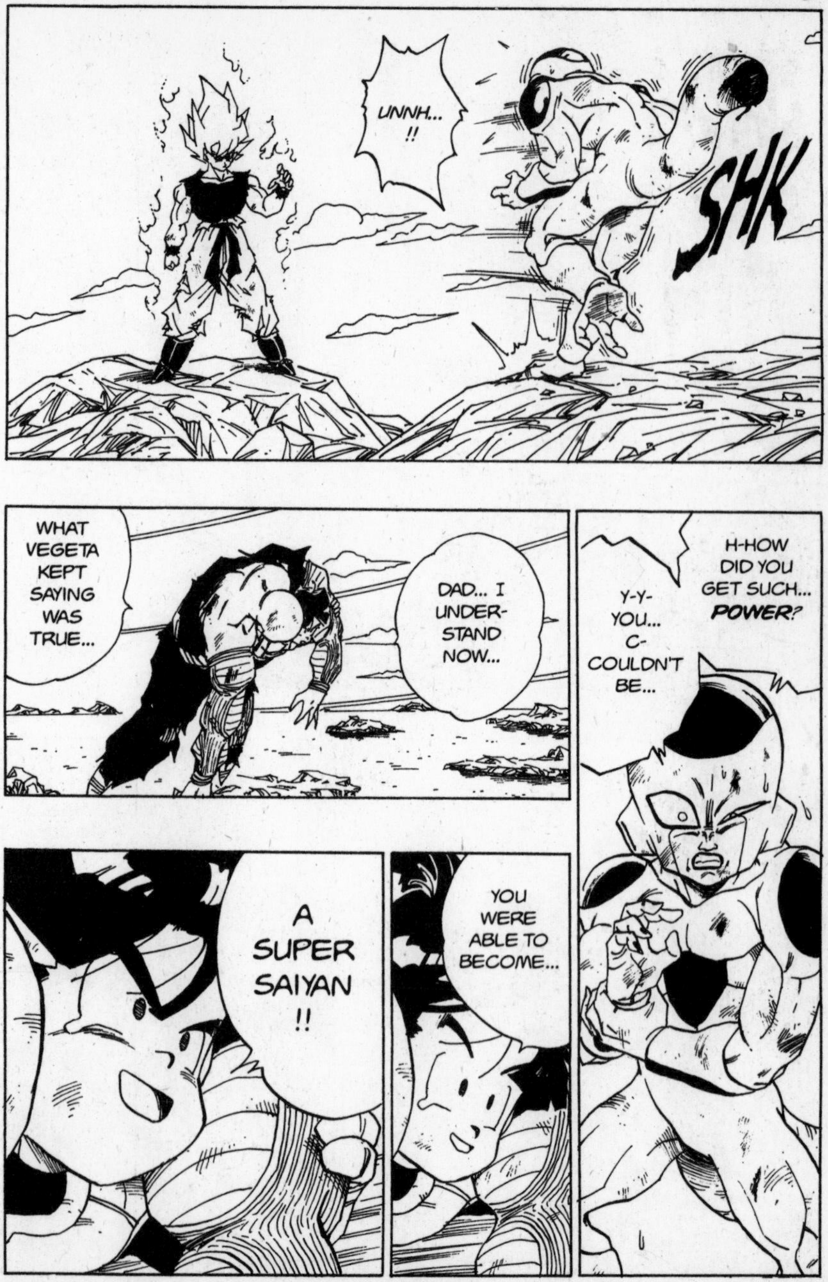
UNNH... !!
SHK
H-HOW DID YOU GET SUCH... POWER?
Y-Y-YOU... C-COULDN'T BE...
DAD... I UNDER-STAND NOW...
WHAT VEGETA KEPT SAYING WAS TRUE...
YOU WERE ABLE TO BECOME...
A SUPER SAIYAN !!

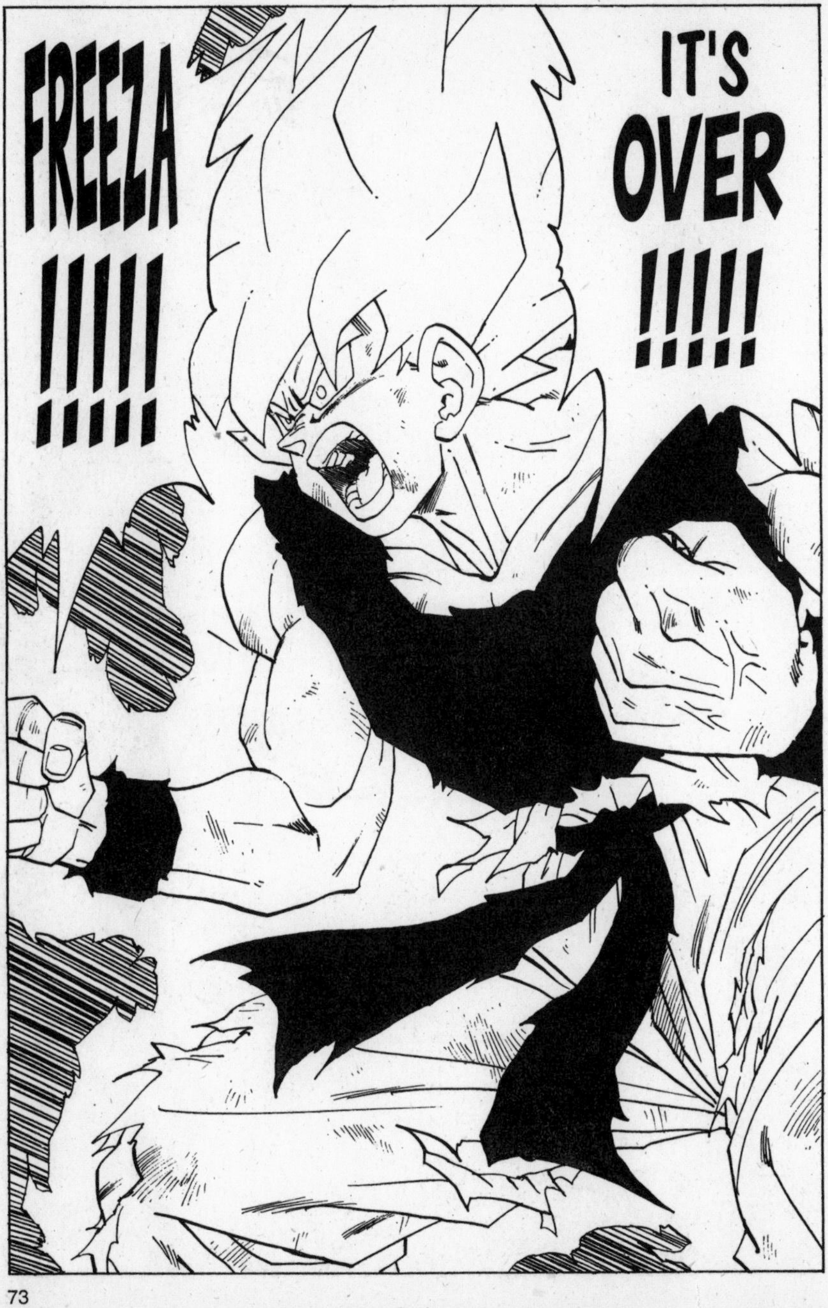
IT'S OVER !!!!!
FREEZA !!!!!

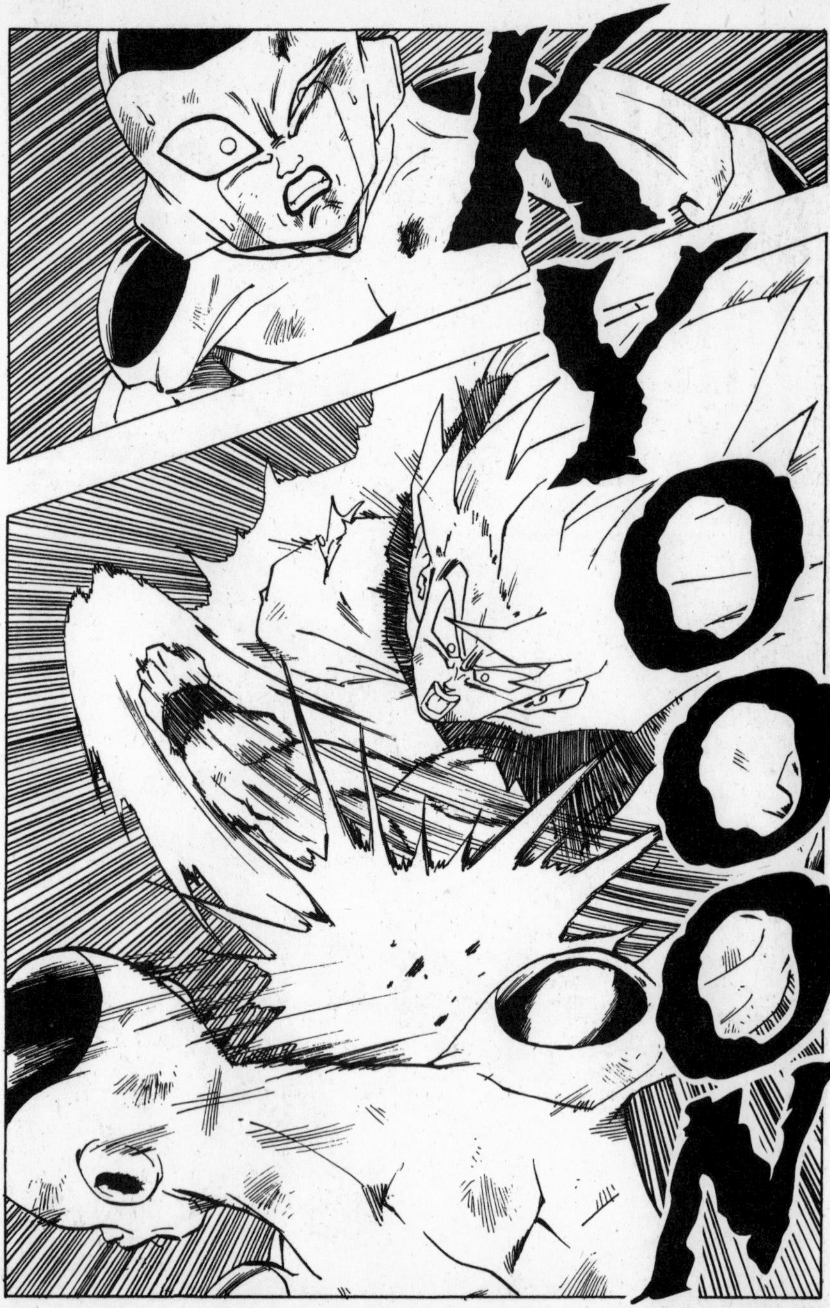
KYOOON

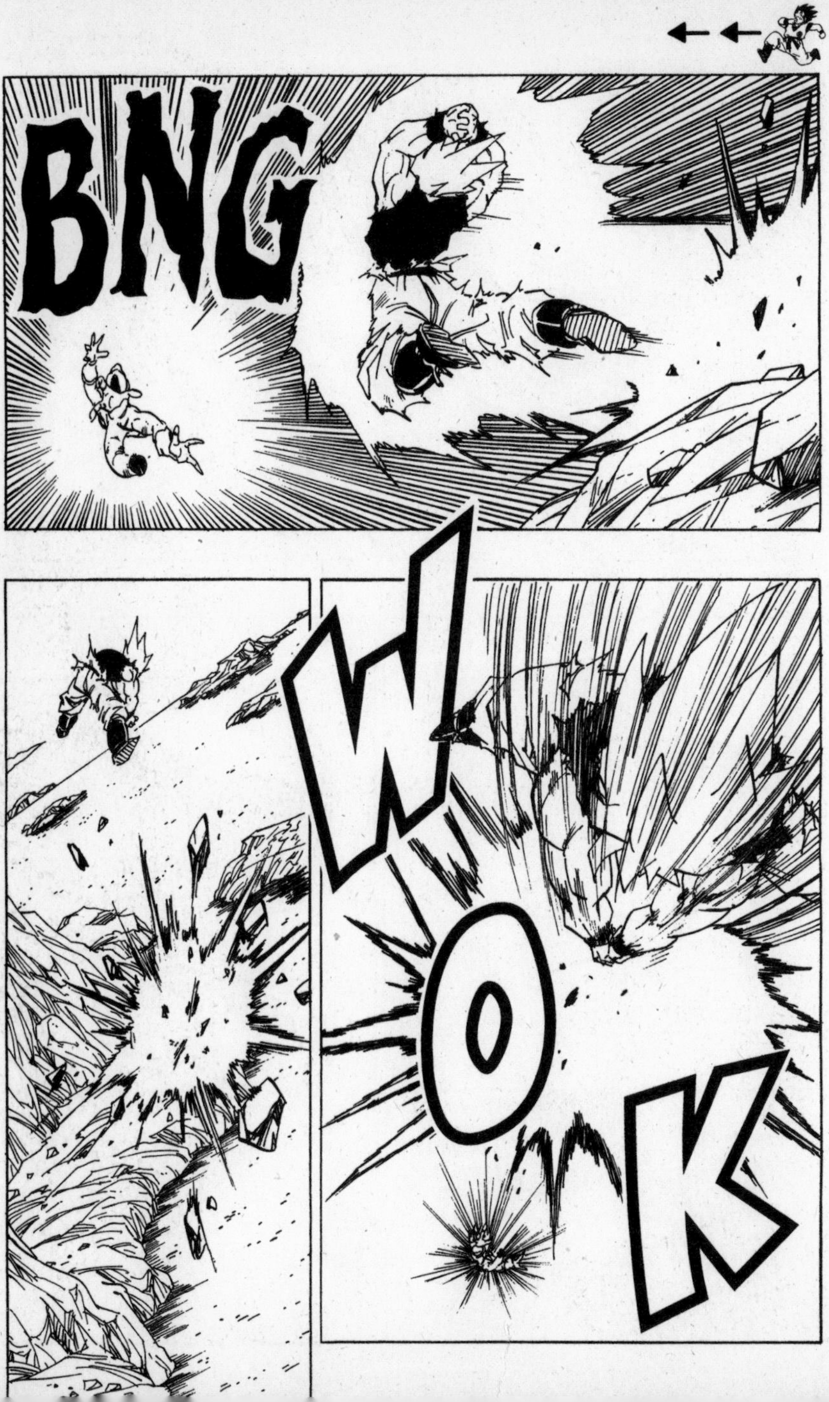
BNG
WOK

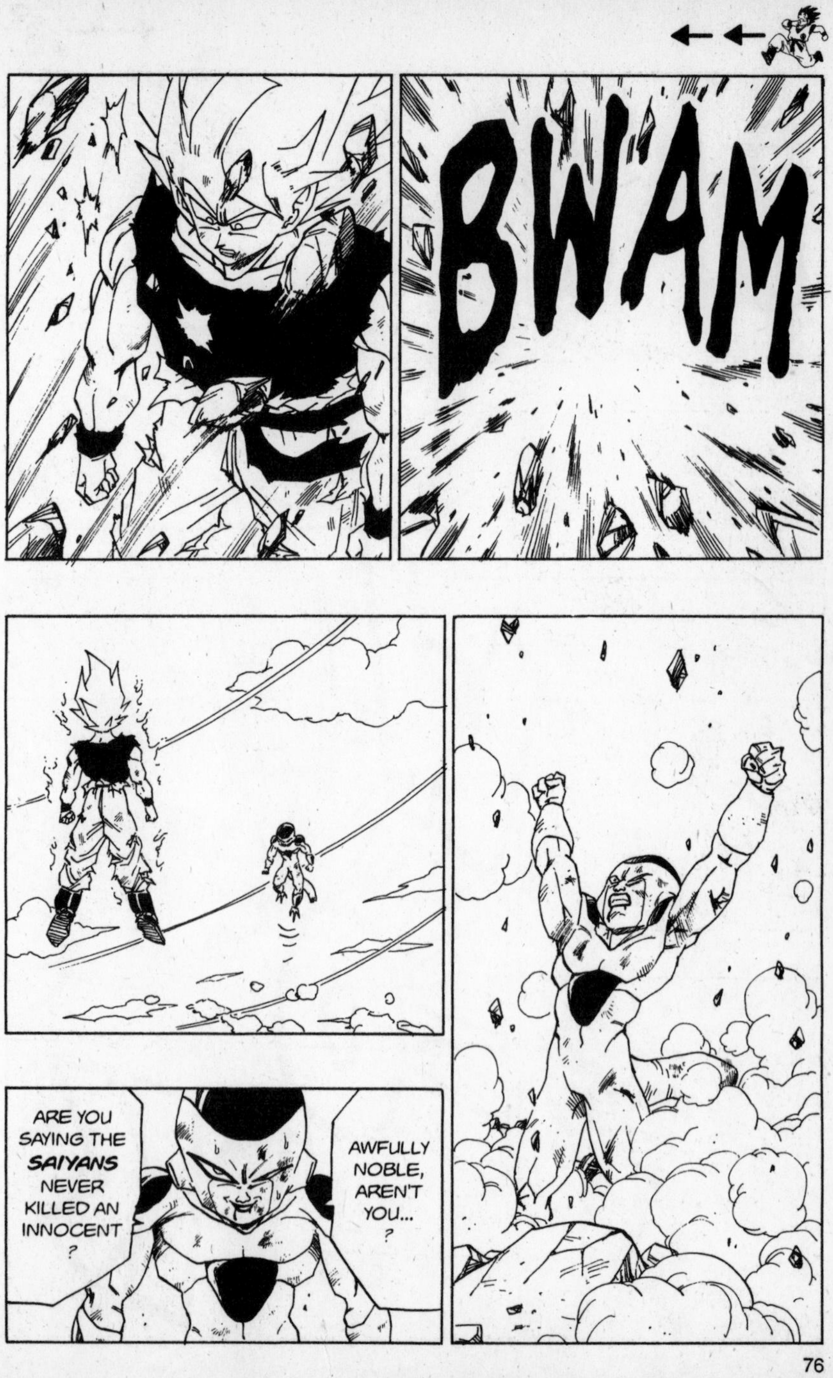
BWAM
AWFULLY NOBLE, AREN'T YOU...?
ARE YOU SAYING THE ***SAIYANS*** NEVER KILLED AN INNOCENT?

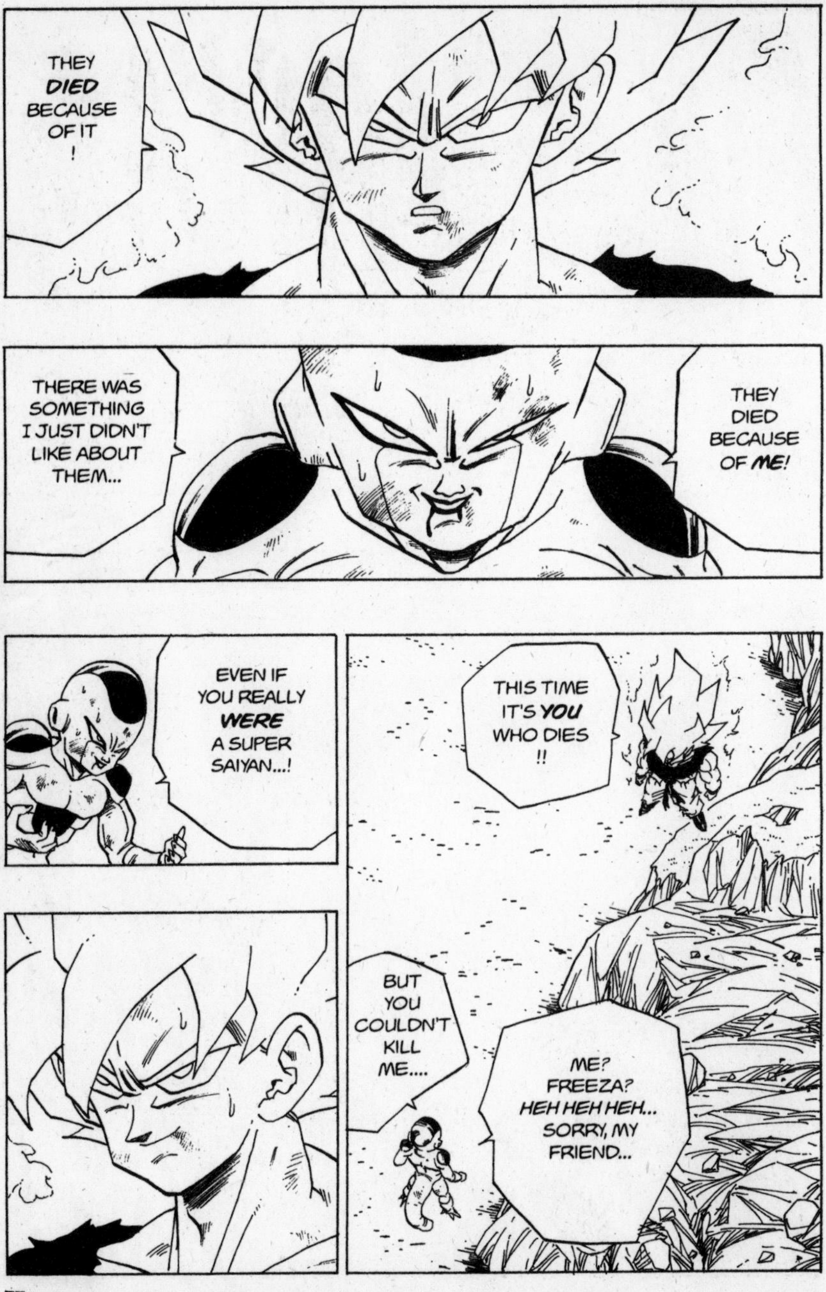
THEY DIED BECAUSE OF IT !
THEY DIED BECAUSE OF ME!
THERE WAS SOMETHING I JUST DIDN'T LIKE ABOUT THEM...
THIS TIME IT'S YOU WHO DIES !!
ME? FREEZA? HEH HEH HEH... SORRY, MY FRIEND...
BUT YOU COULDN'T KILL ME....
EVEN IF YOU REALLY WERE A SUPER SAIYAN...!

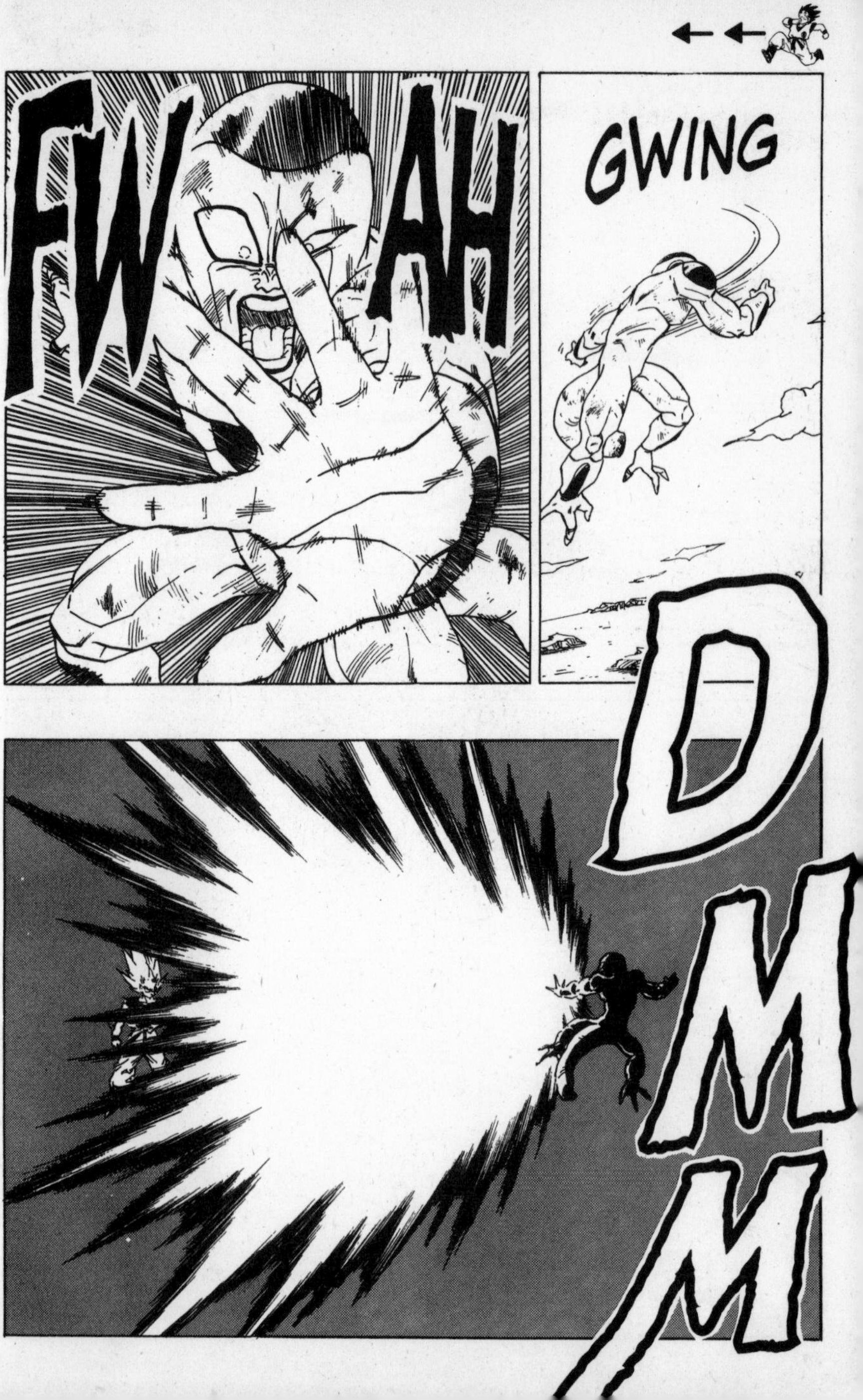
GWING
FW
AH
DMMM

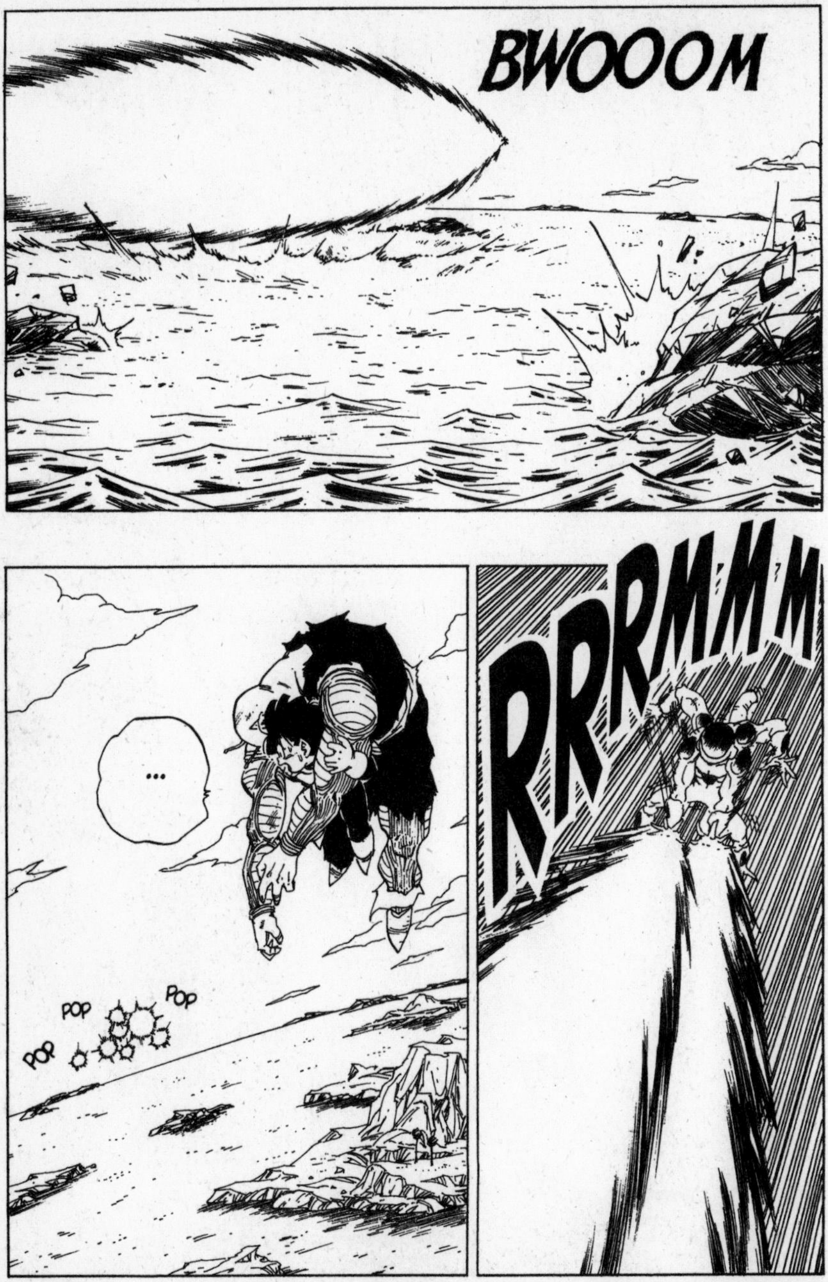
BWOOOM
RRRMMM
...
POP
POP
POP

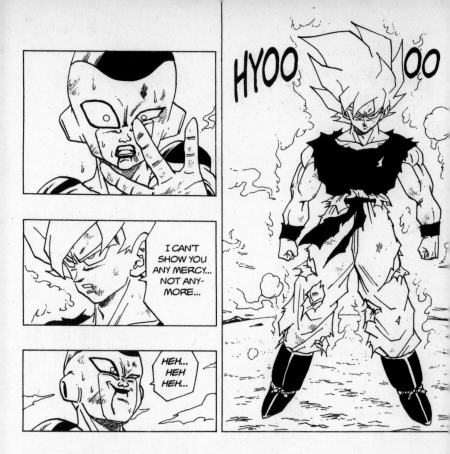

HYOO OO

I CAN'T SHOW YOU ANY MERCY... NOT ANY- MORE...

HEH... HEH... HEH...

SSS...

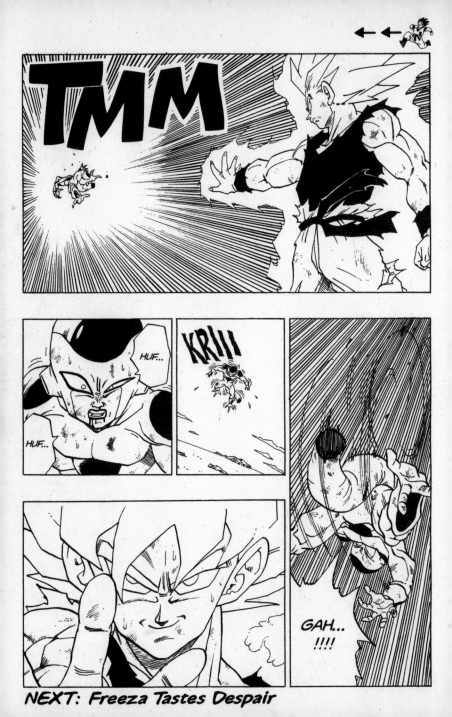

NEXT: *Freeza Tastes Despair*

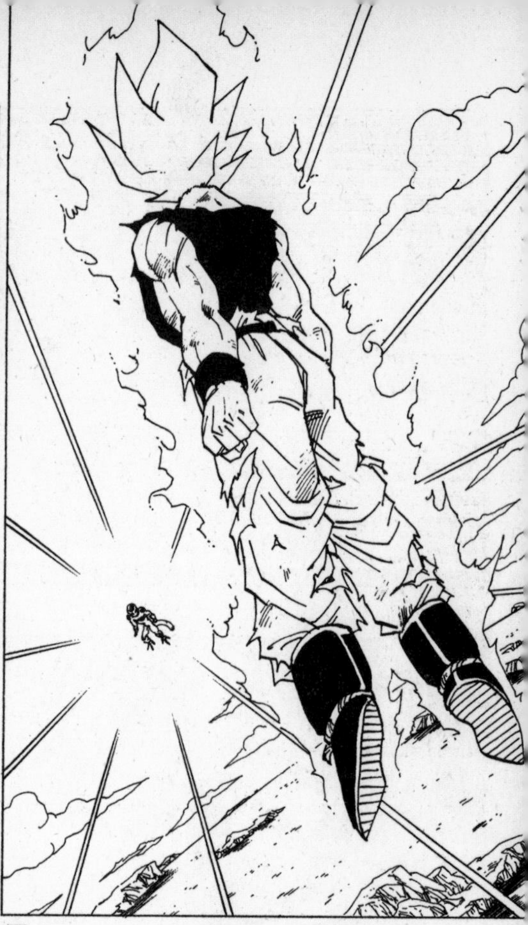

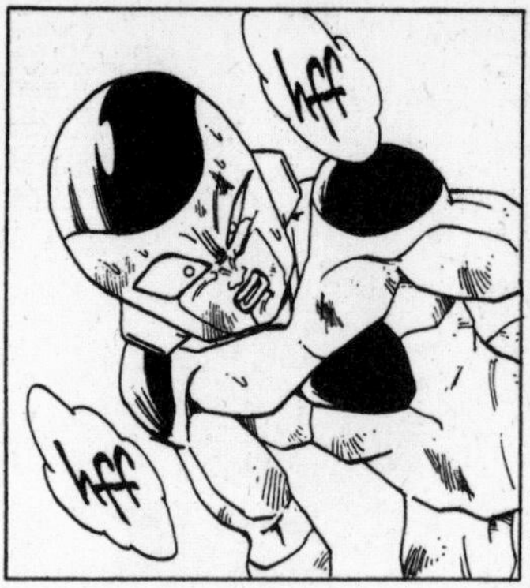
hff
hff

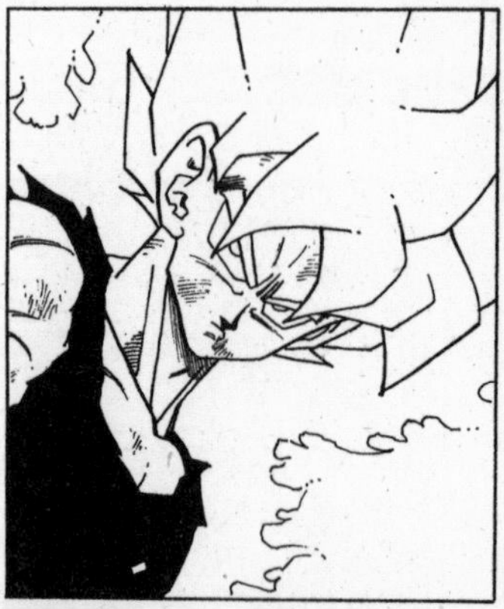

DBZ:125 • The Tables Turn

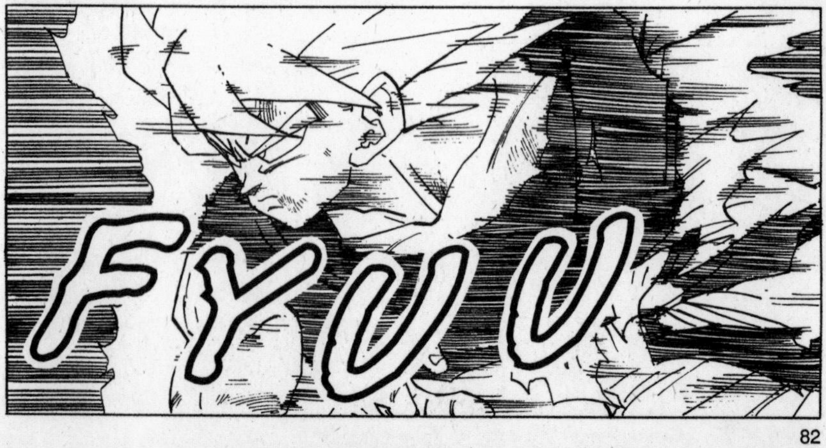
FYUU

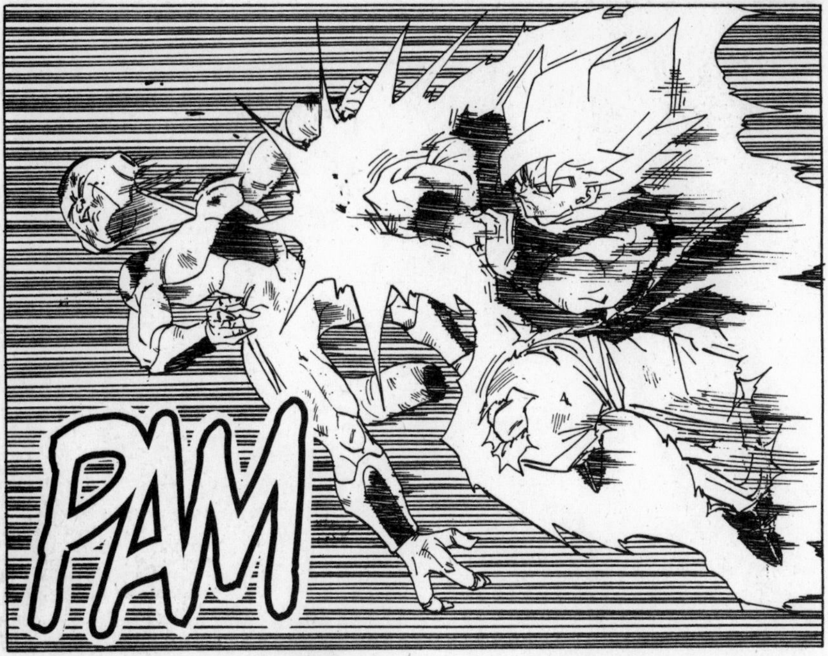
PAM

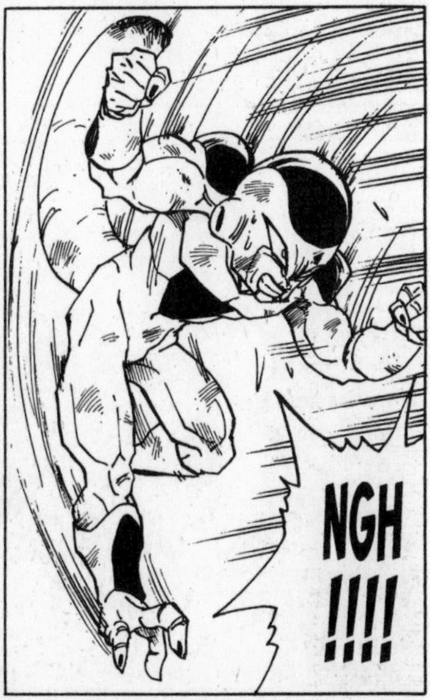
NGH
!!!!

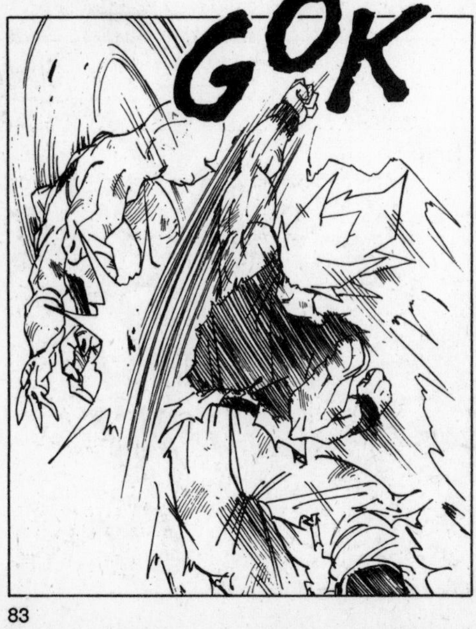
GOK

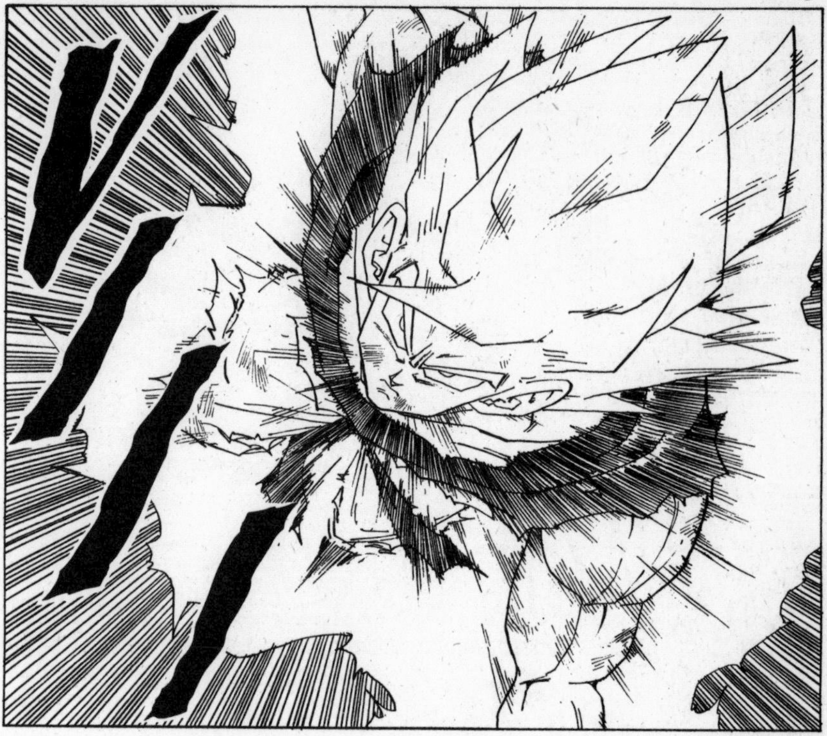

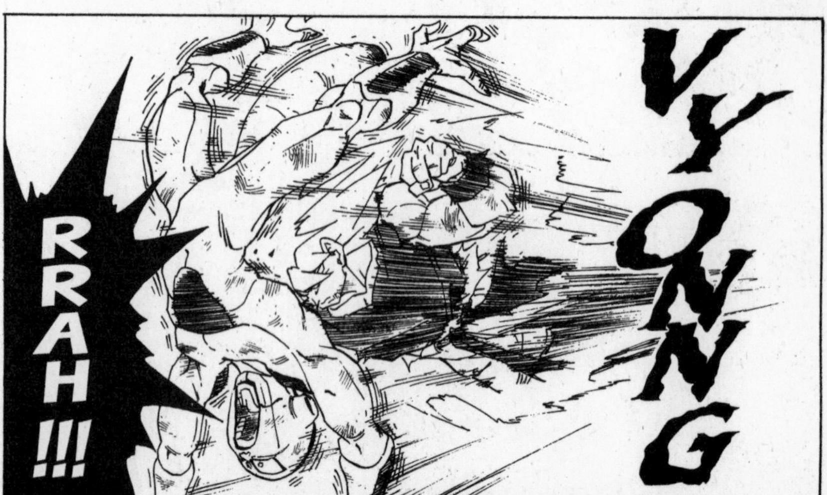
VYONNG
RRAH!!!

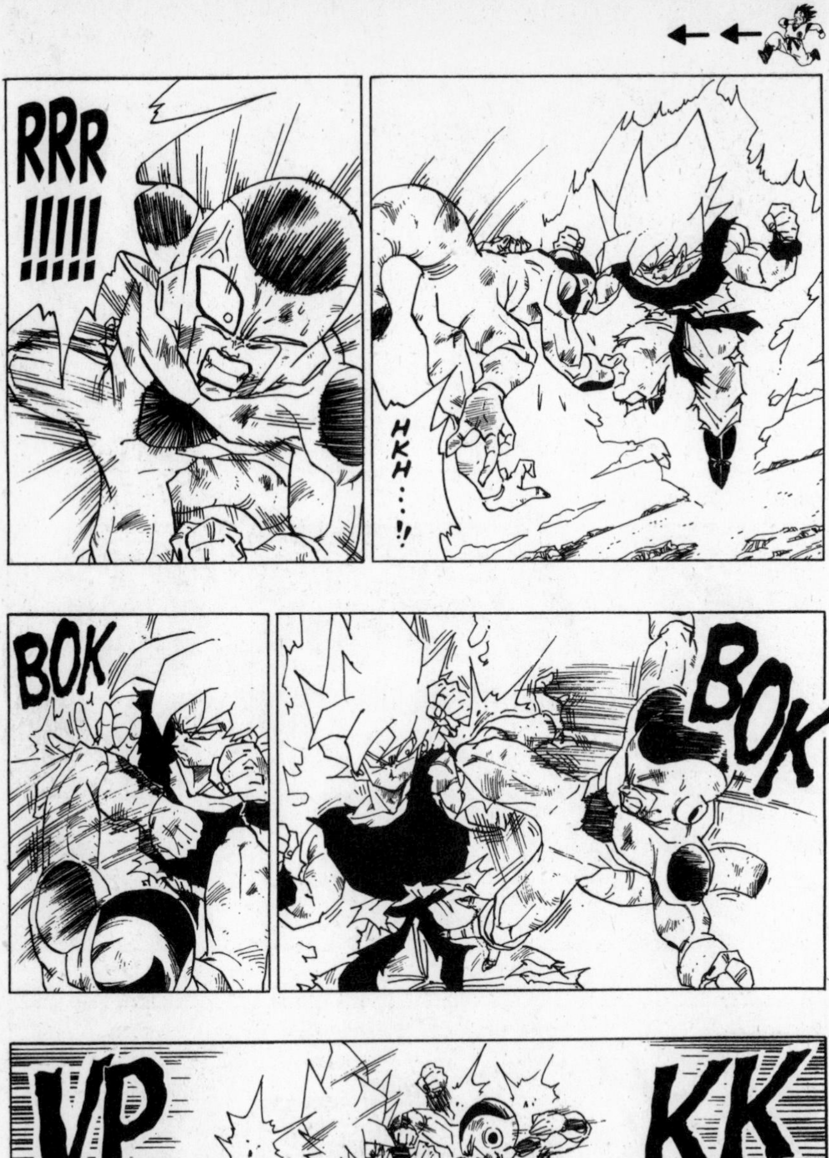
HKH...!!
RRR!!!!!
BOK
BOK
KK KK
VP VVVP

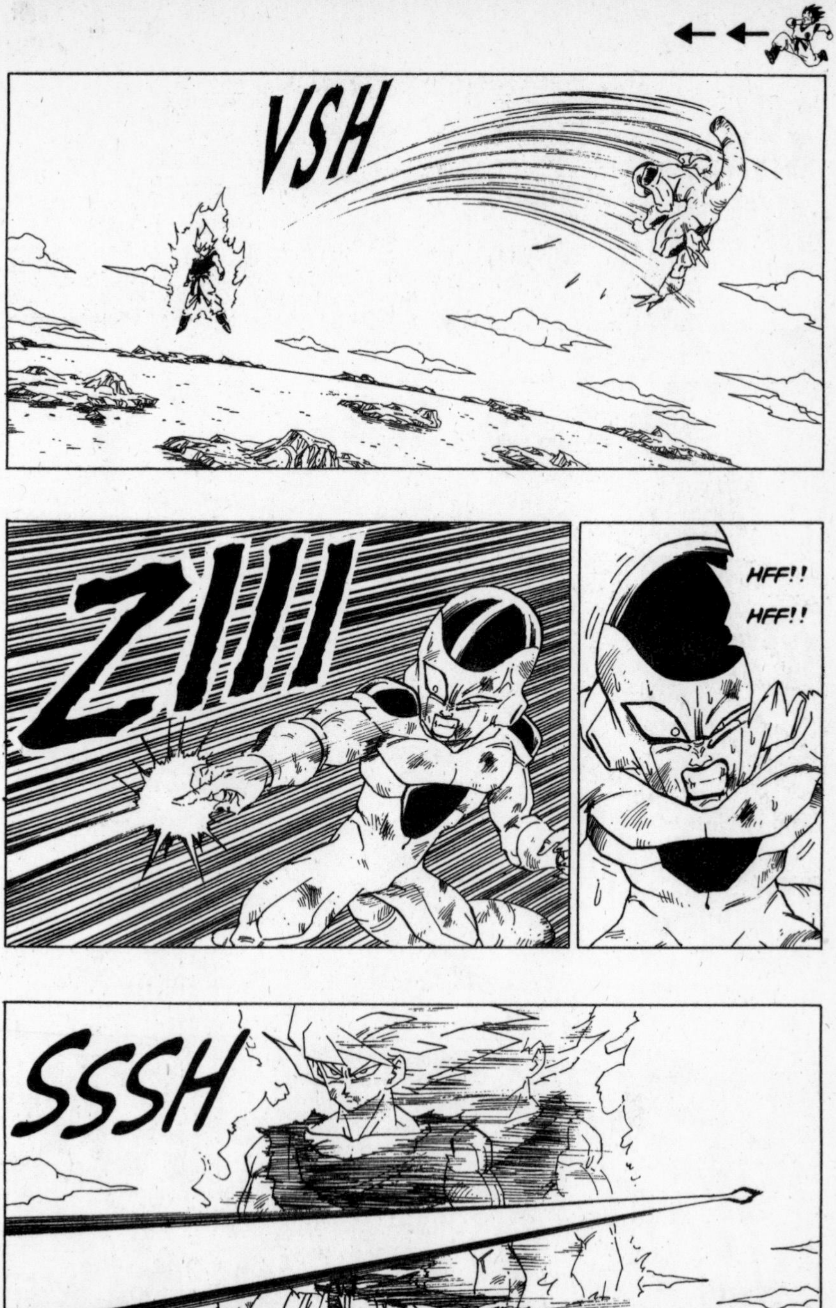
VSH
HFF!!
HFF!!
ZIIII
SSSH

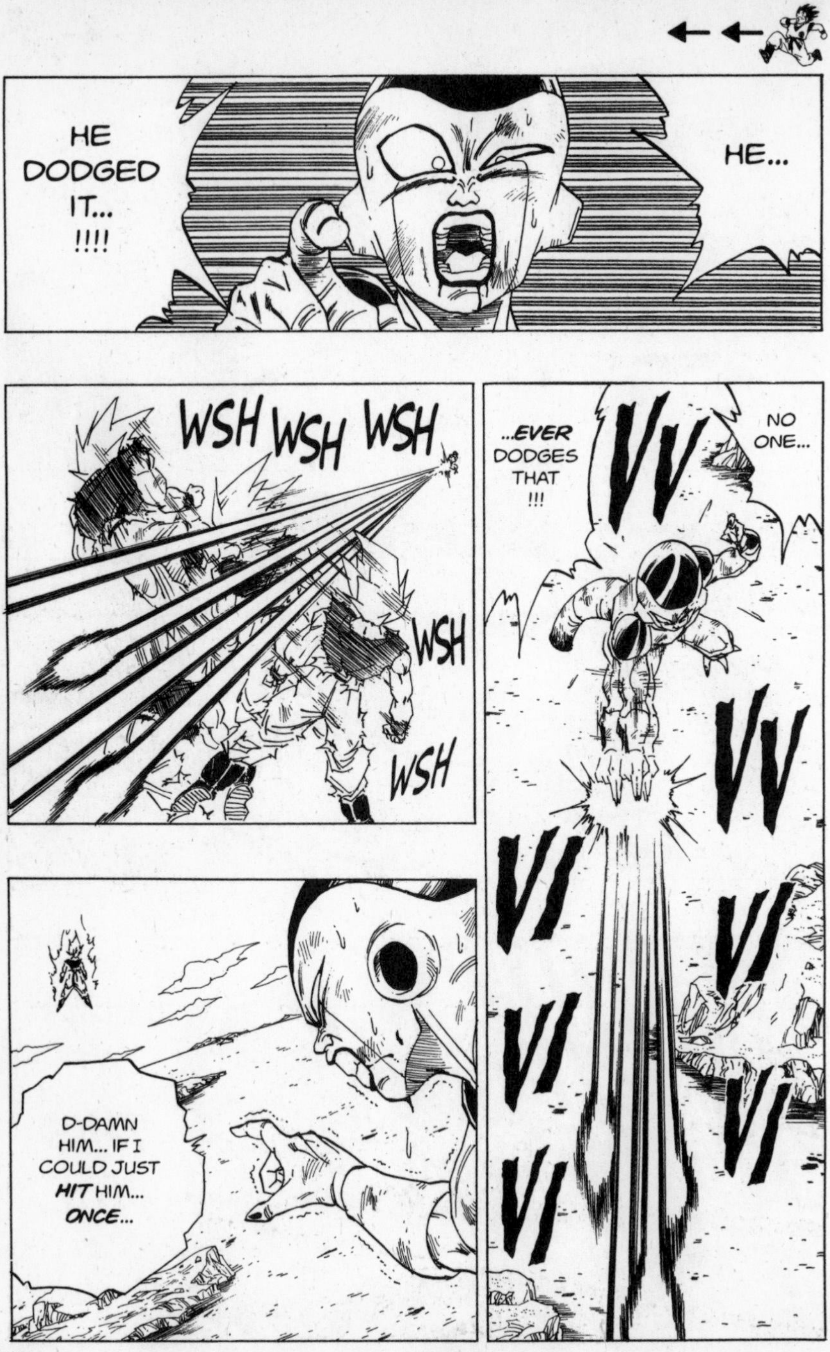
HE...
HE DODGED IT... !!!!
NO ONE...
...EVER DODGES THAT !!!
WSH WSH WSH
WSH
WSH
D-DAMN HIM... IF I COULD JUST HIT HIM... ONCE...

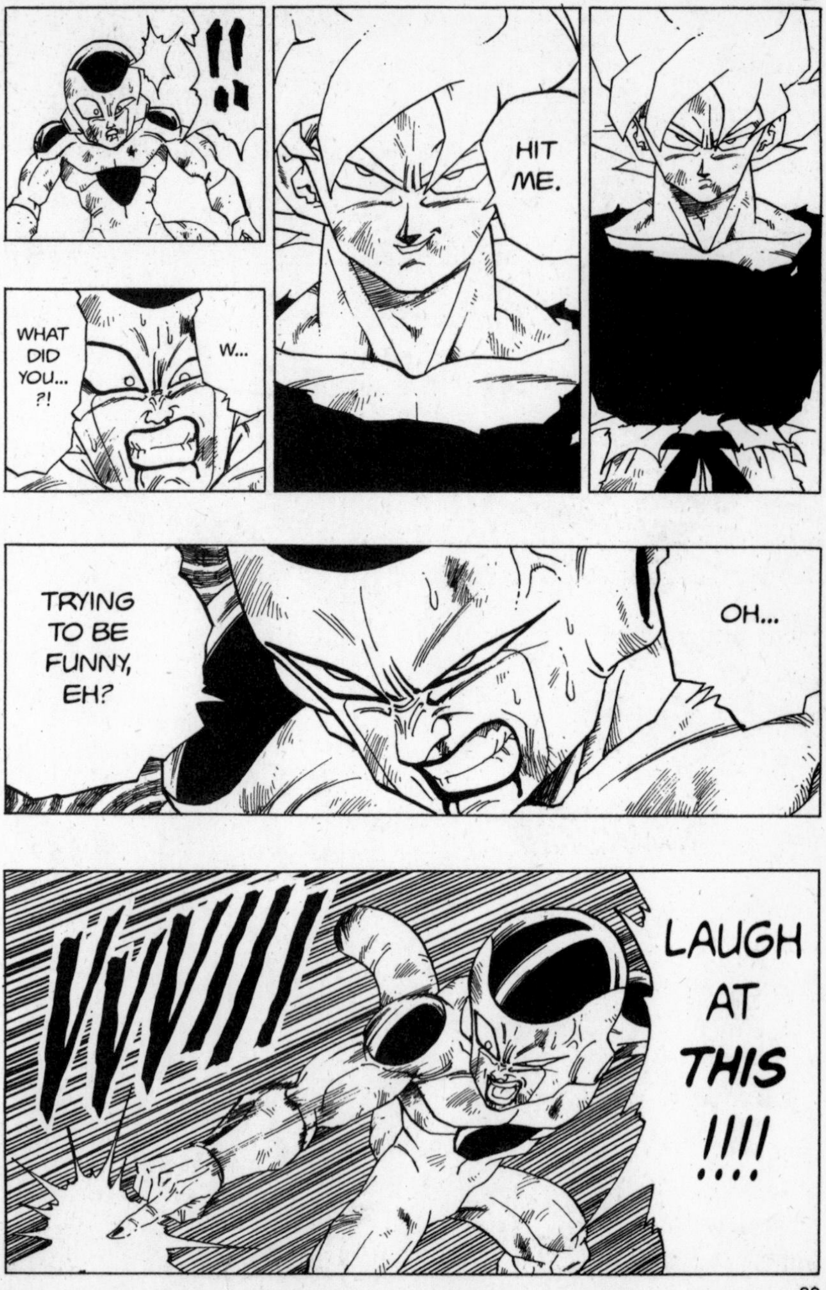
HIT ME.
!!
W...
WHAT DID YOU... ?!
OH...
TRYING TO BE FUNNY, EH?
LAUGH AT THIS !!!!

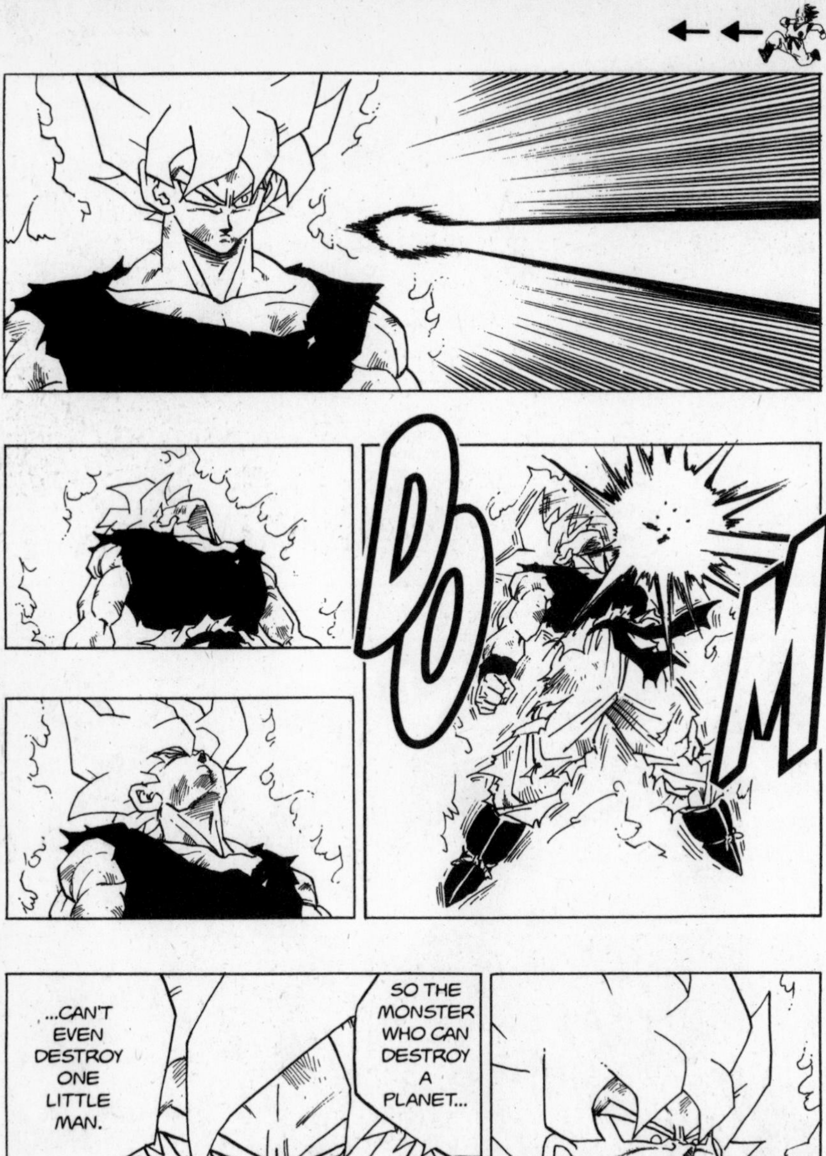
DOOM
SO THE MONSTER WHO CAN DESTROY A PLANET...
...CAN'T EVEN DESTROY ONE LITTLE MAN.

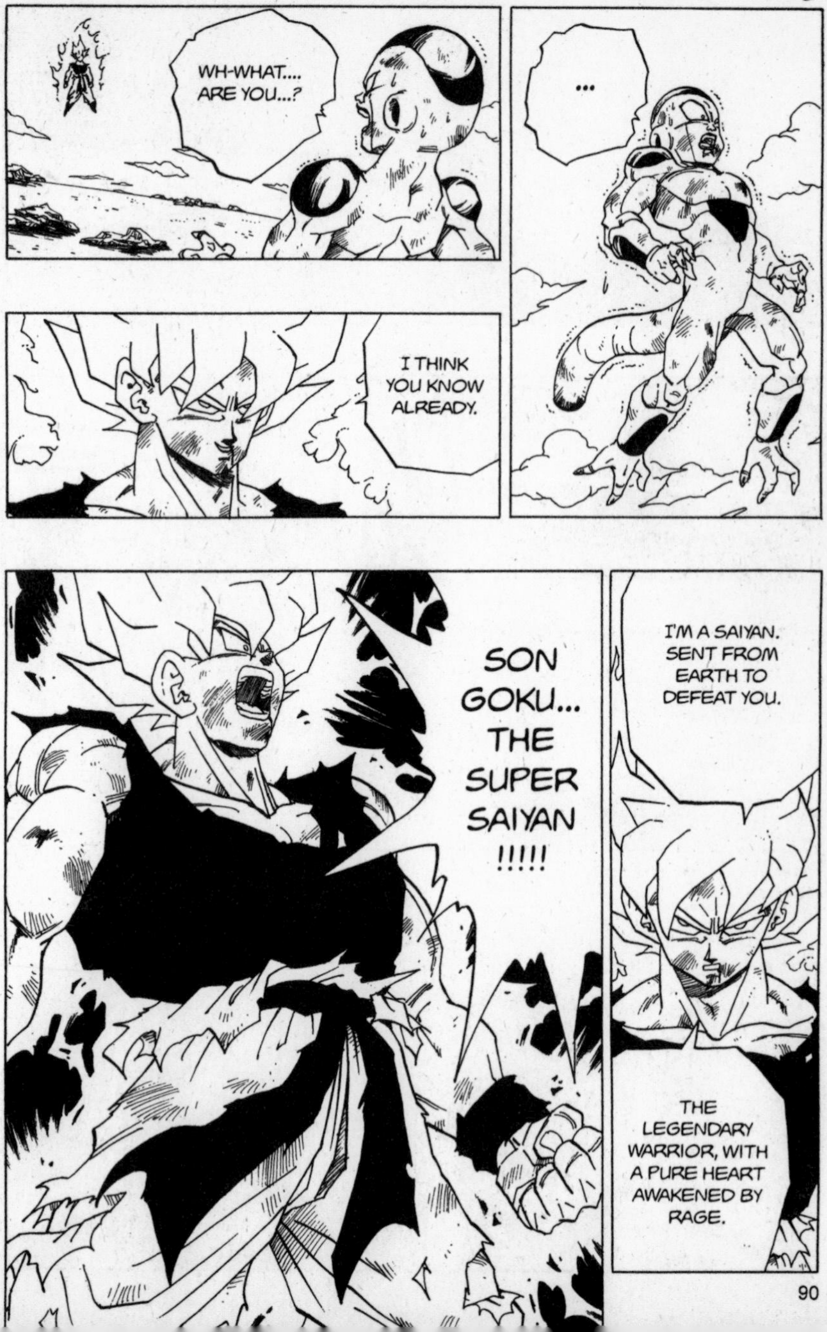
...
WH-WHAT.... ARE YOU...?
I THINK YOU KNOW ALREADY.
I'M A SAIYAN. SENT FROM EARTH TO DEFEAT YOU.
THE LEGENDARY WARRIOR, WITH A PURE HEART AWAKENED BY RAGE.
SON GOKU... THE SUPER SAIYAN !!!!!

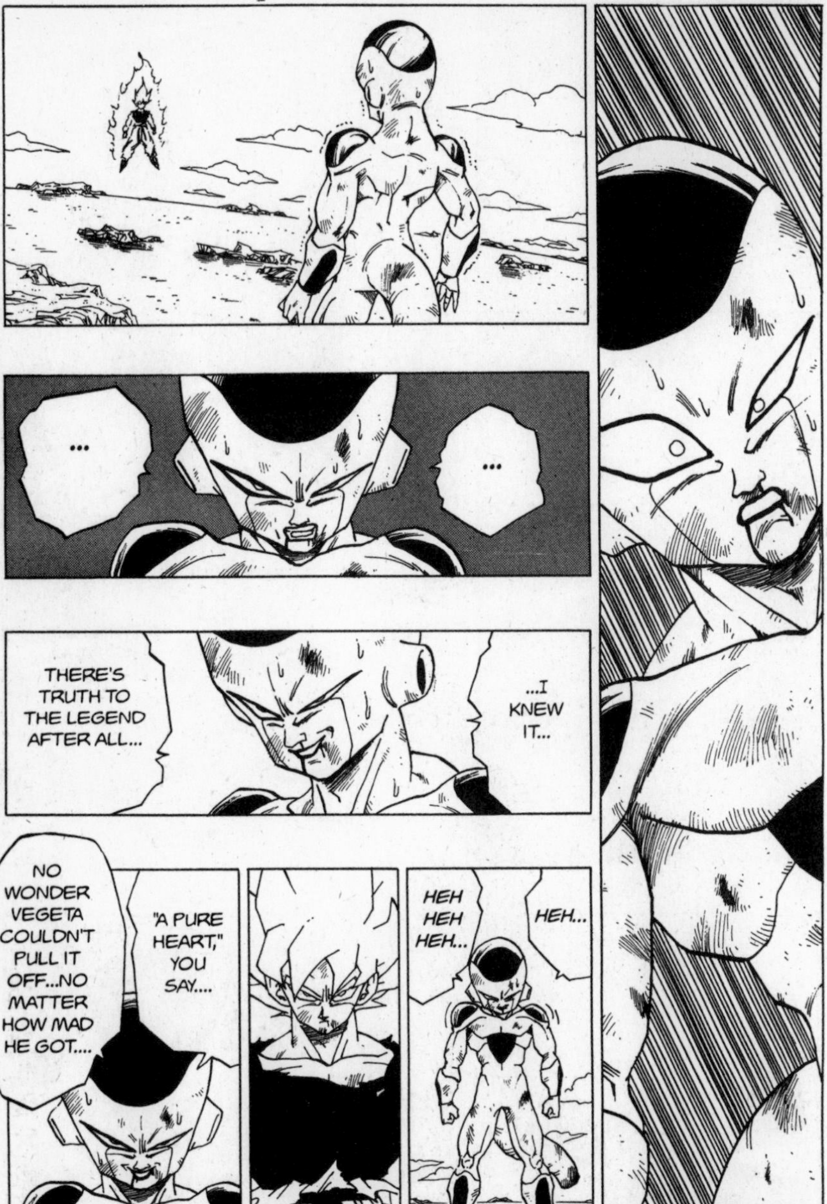
...
...
...I KNEW IT...
THERE'S TRUTH TO THE LEGEND AFTER ALL...
HEH...
HEH HEH HEH...
"A PURE HEART," YOU SAY....
NO WONDER VEGETA COULDN'T PULL IT OFF...NO MATTER HOW MAD HE GOT....

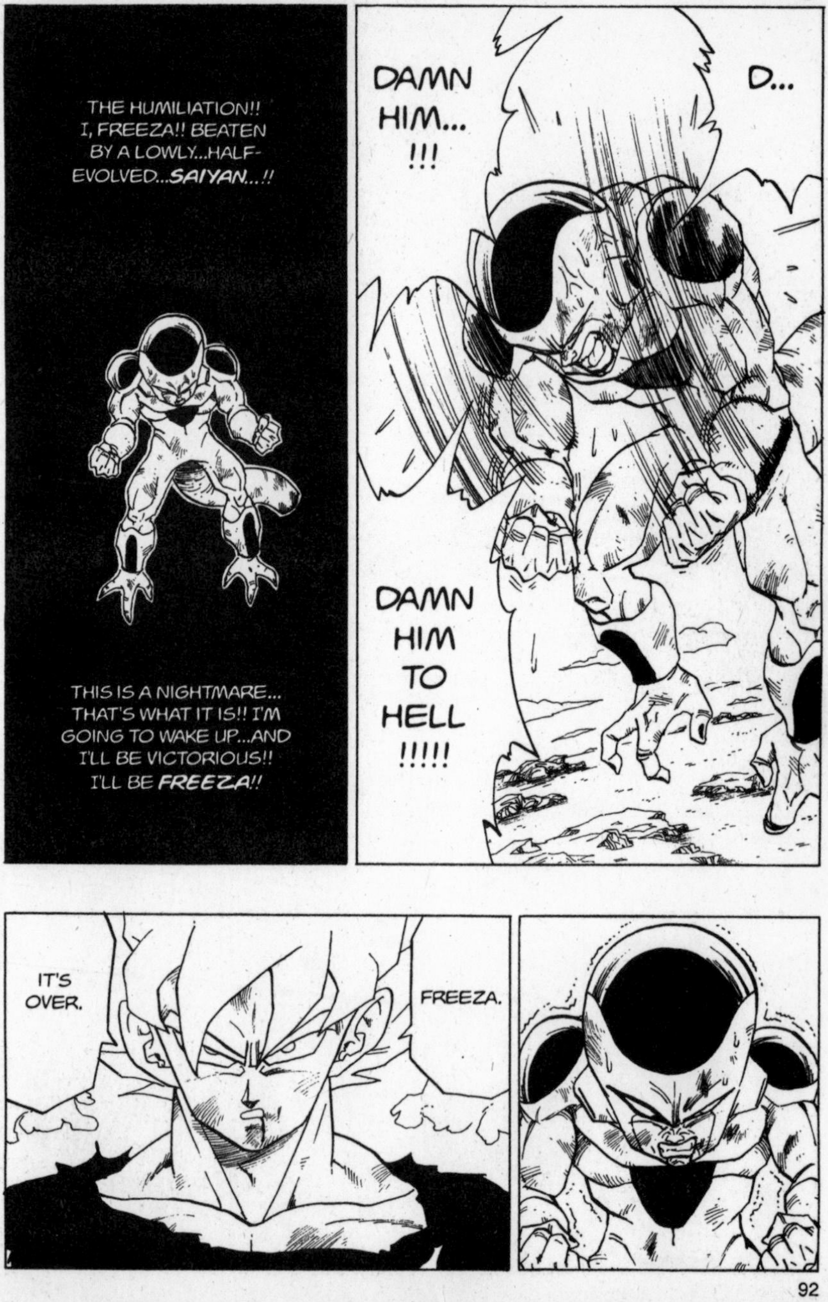
D...
DAMN HIM... !!!
DAMN HIM TO HELL !!!!!
THE HUMILIATION!! I, FREEZA!! BEATEN BY A LOWLY...HALF-EVOLVED...SAIYAN...!!
THIS IS A NIGHTMARE... THAT'S WHAT IT IS!! I'M GOING TO WAKE UP...AND I'LL BE VICTORIOUS!! I'LL BE FREEZA!!
IT'S OVER.
FREEZA.

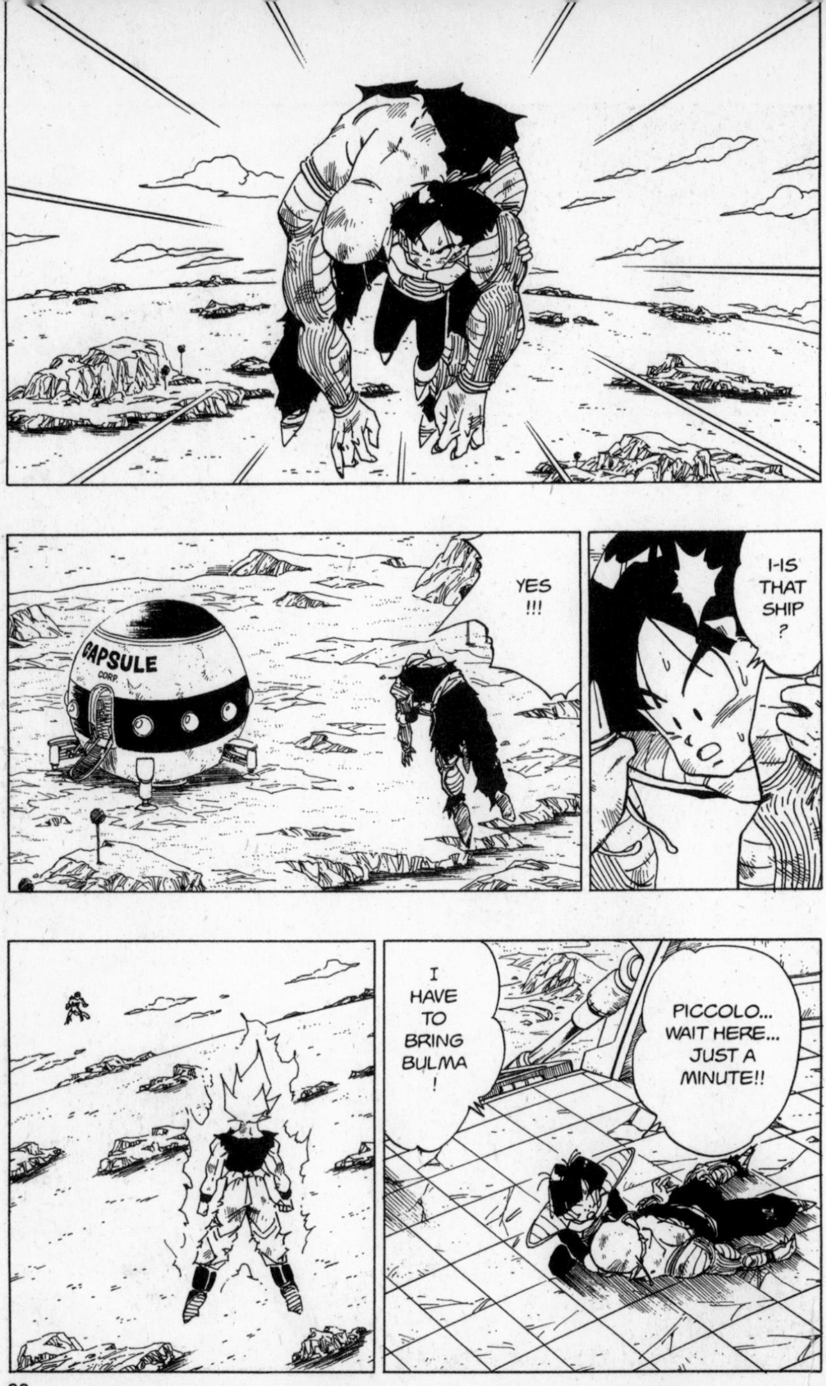
I-IS THAT SHIP ?
YES !!!
CAPSULE
CORP.
PICCOLO... WAIT HERE... JUST A MINUTE!!
I HAVE TO BRING BULMA !

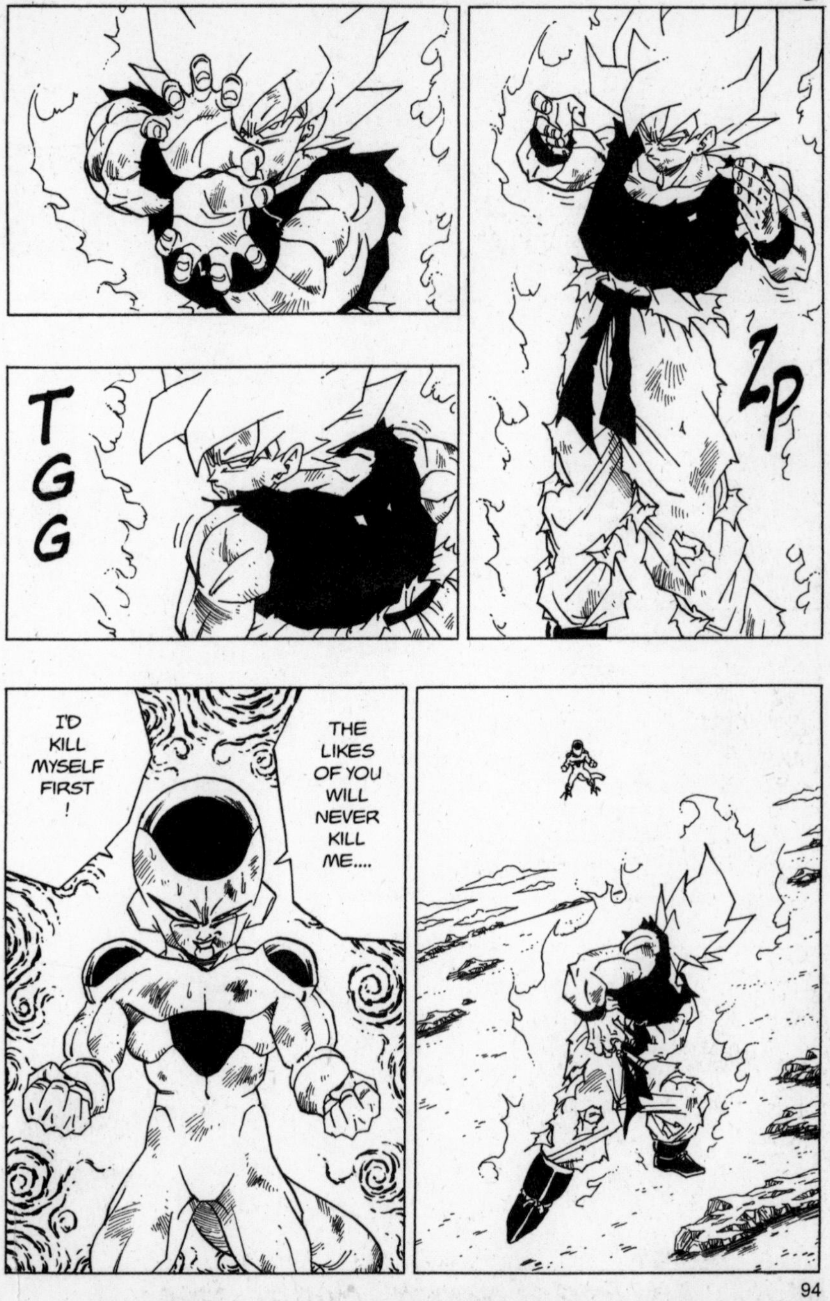
ZP
TGG
THE LIKES OF YOU WILL NEVER KILL ME....
I'D KILL MYSELF FIRST!

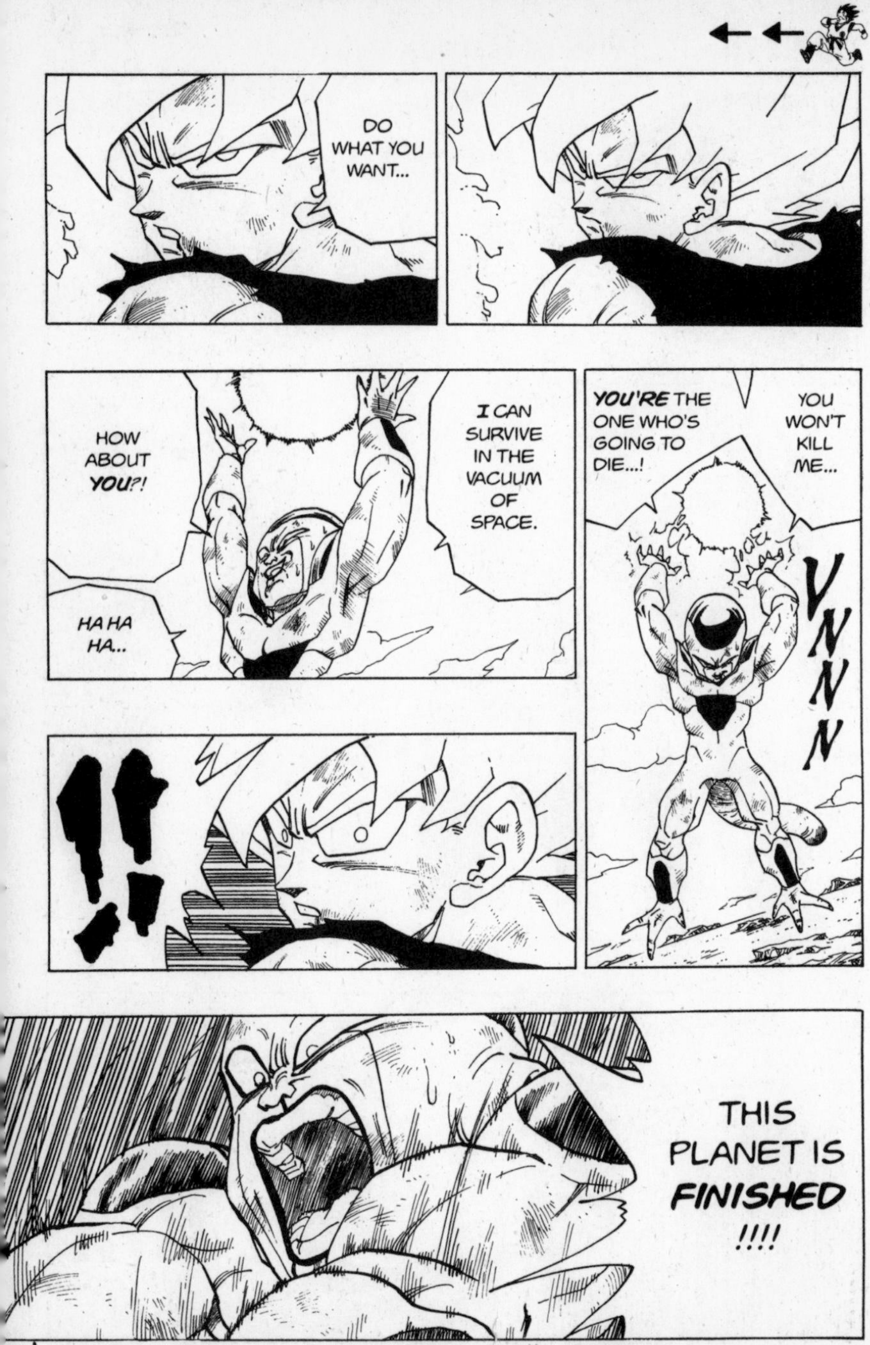
DO WHAT YOU WANT...
YOU WON'T KILL ME...
YOU'RE THE ONE WHO'S GOING TO DIE...!
VNNN
I CAN SURVIVE IN THE VACUUM OF SPACE.
HOW ABOUT YOU?!
HA HA HA...
!!
THIS PLANET IS FINISHED !!!!

NEXT: The End of Namek... And of Hope?

DBZ:126 • The End of Namek?

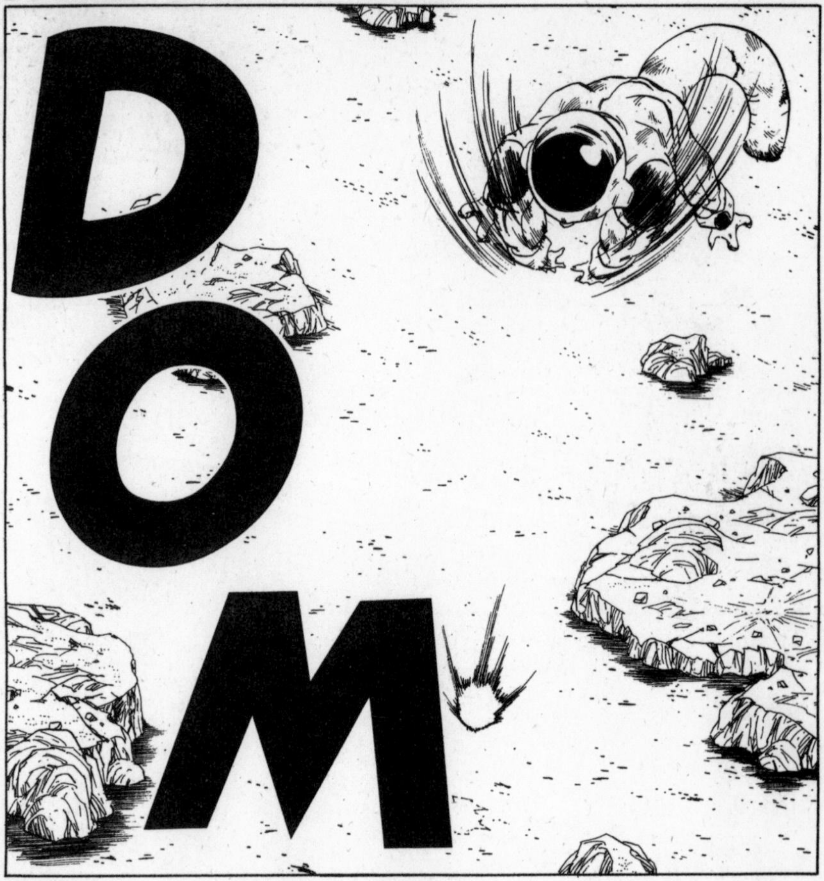
DOM

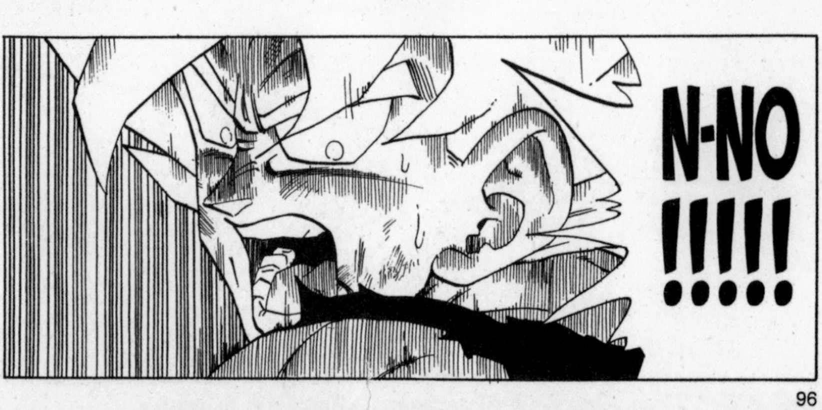
N-NO !!!!!

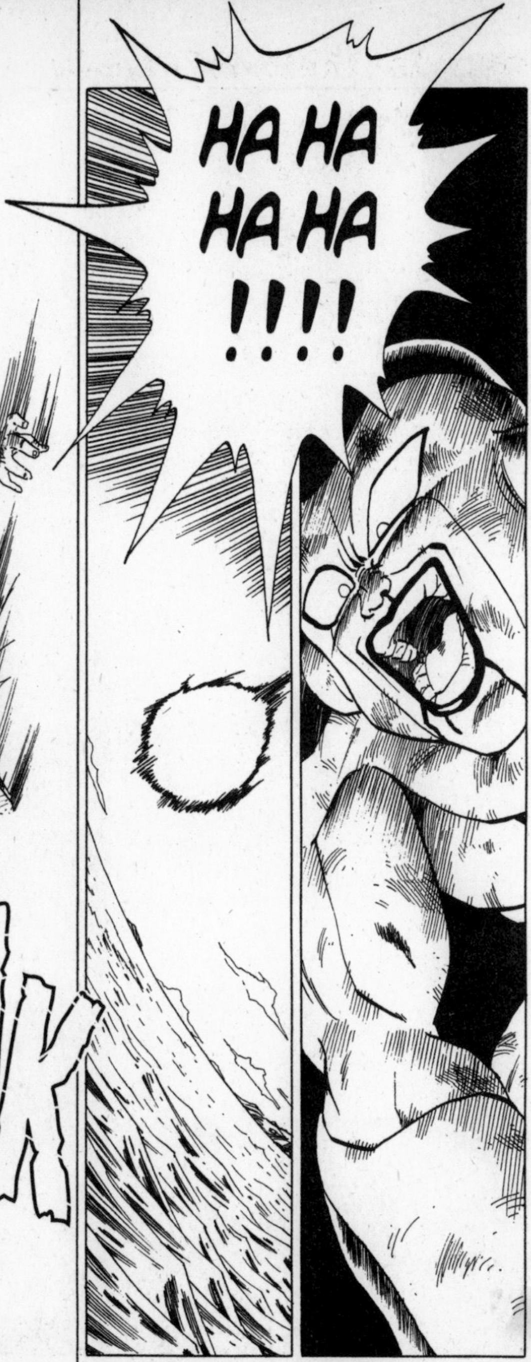
HA HA
HA HA
!!!!
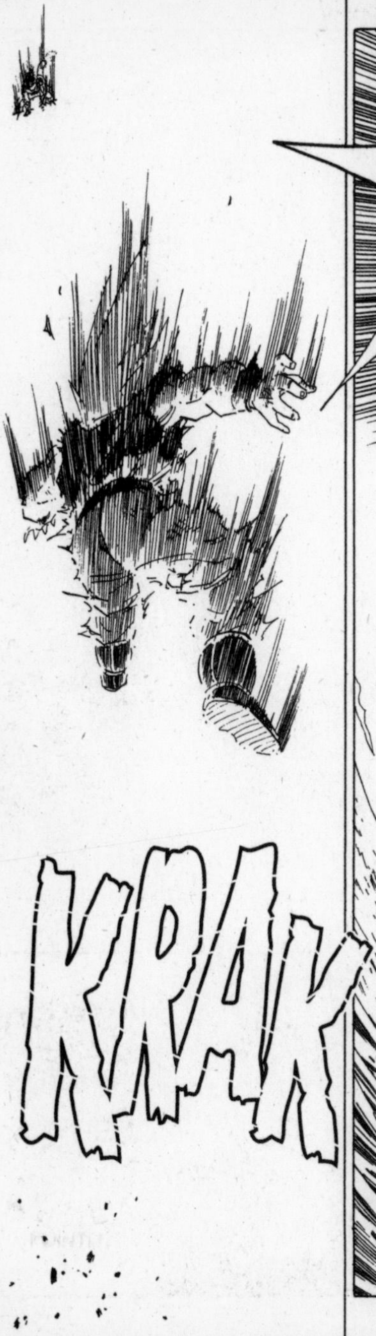
KRAK

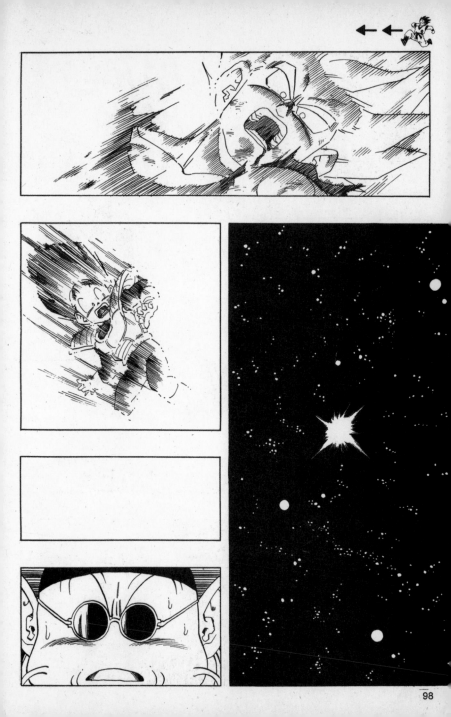

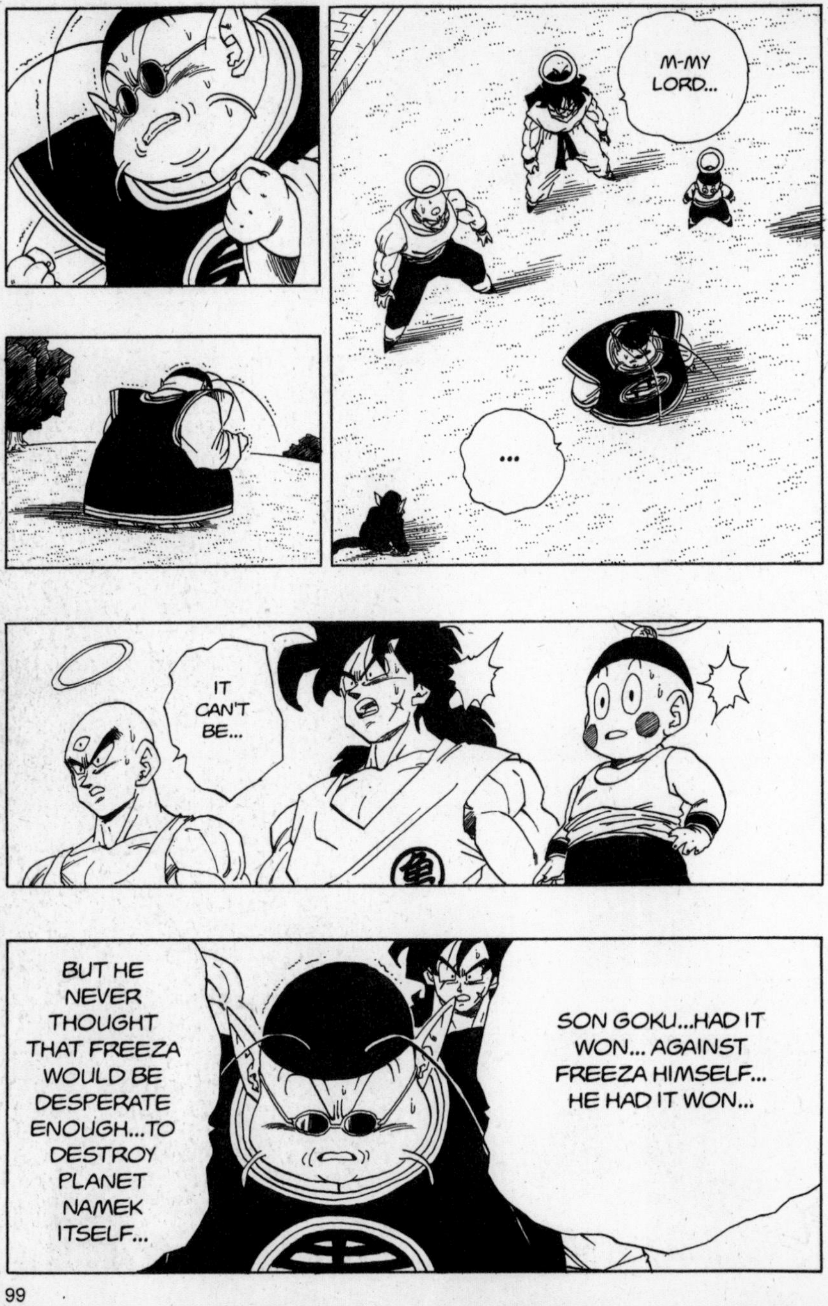
M-MY LORD...
...
IT CAN'T BE...
SON GOKU...HAD IT WON... AGAINST FREEZA HIMSELF... HE HAD IT WON...
BUT HE NEVER THOUGHT THAT FREEZA WOULD BE DESPERATE ENOUGH...TO DESTROY PLANET NAMEK ITSELF...

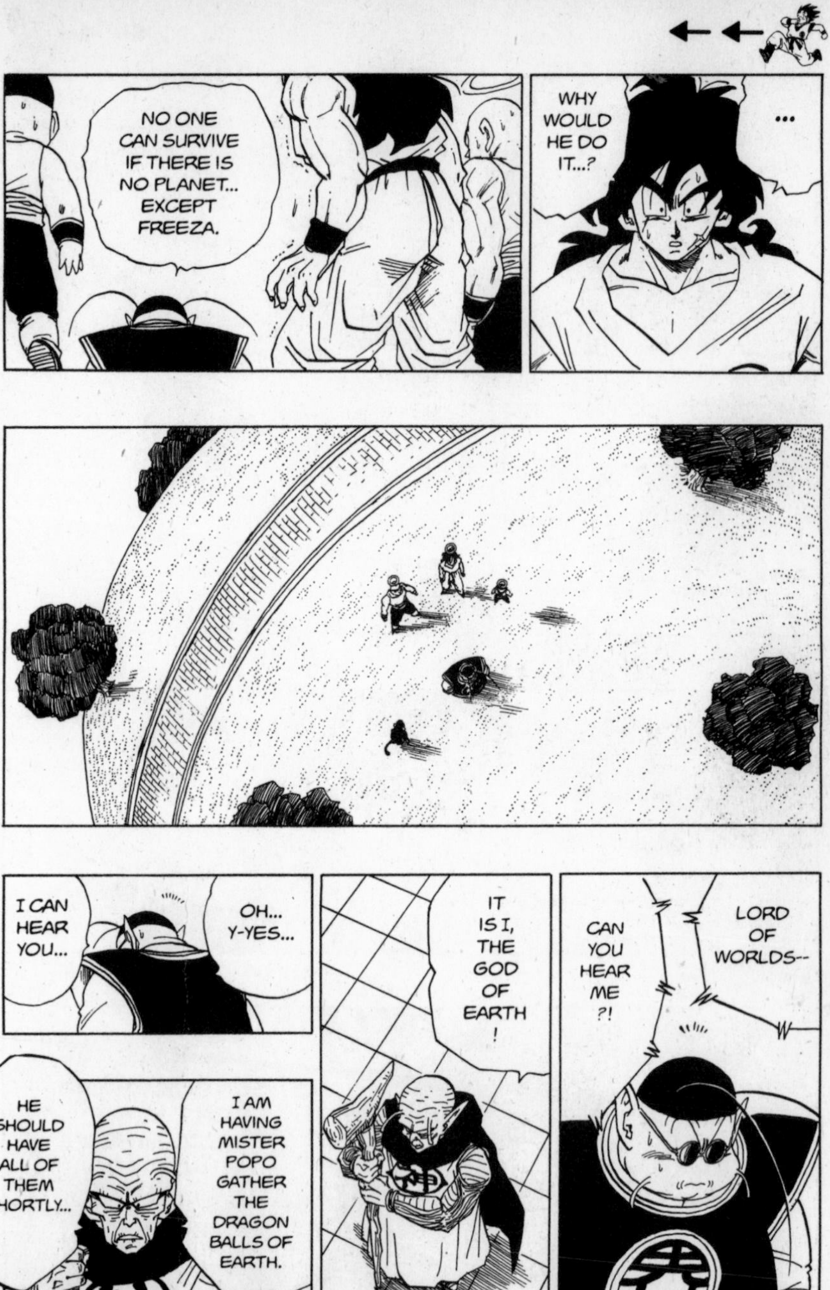
...
WHY WOULD HE DO IT...?
NO ONE CAN SURVIVE IF THERE IS NO PLANET... EXCEPT FREEZA.
LORD OF WORLDS--
CAN YOU HEAR ME ?!
IT IS I, THE GOD OF EARTH!
OH... Y-YES...
I CAN HEAR YOU...
I AM HAVING MISTER POPO GATHER THE DRAGON BALLS OF EARTH.
HE SHOULD HAVE ALL OF THEM SHORTLY...

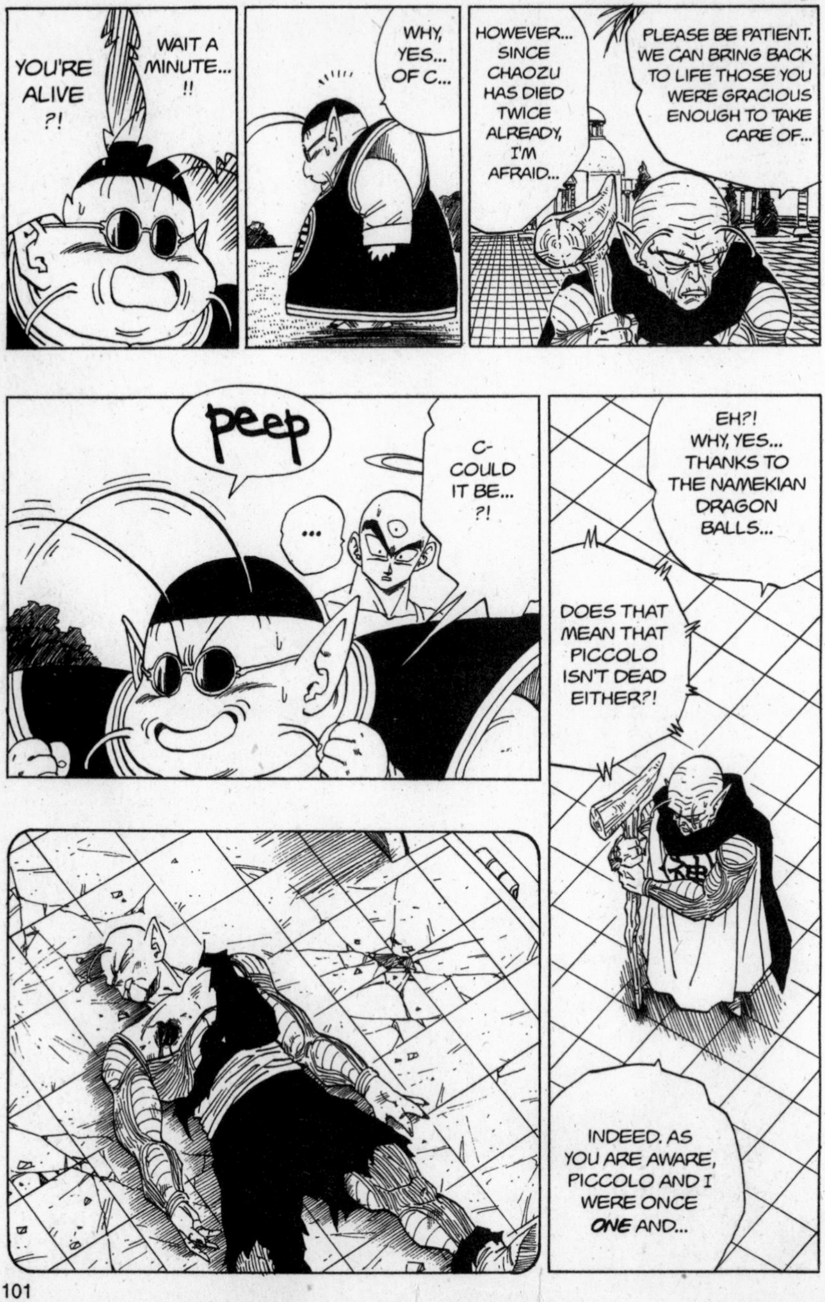
PLEASE BE PATIENT. WE CAN BRING BACK TO LIFE THOSE YOU WERE GRACIOUS ENOUGH TO TAKE CARE OF...
HOWEVER... SINCE CHAOZU HAS DIED TWICE ALREADY, I'M AFRAID...
WHY, YES... OF C...
WAIT A MINUTE... !!
YOU'RE ALIVE ?!
EH?! WHY, YES... THANKS TO THE NAMEKIAN DRAGON BALLS...
DOES THAT MEAN THAT PICCOLO ISN'T DEAD EITHER?!
INDEED. AS YOU ARE AWARE, PICCOLO AND I WERE ONCE *ONE* AND...
C- COULD IT BE... ?!
peep
...

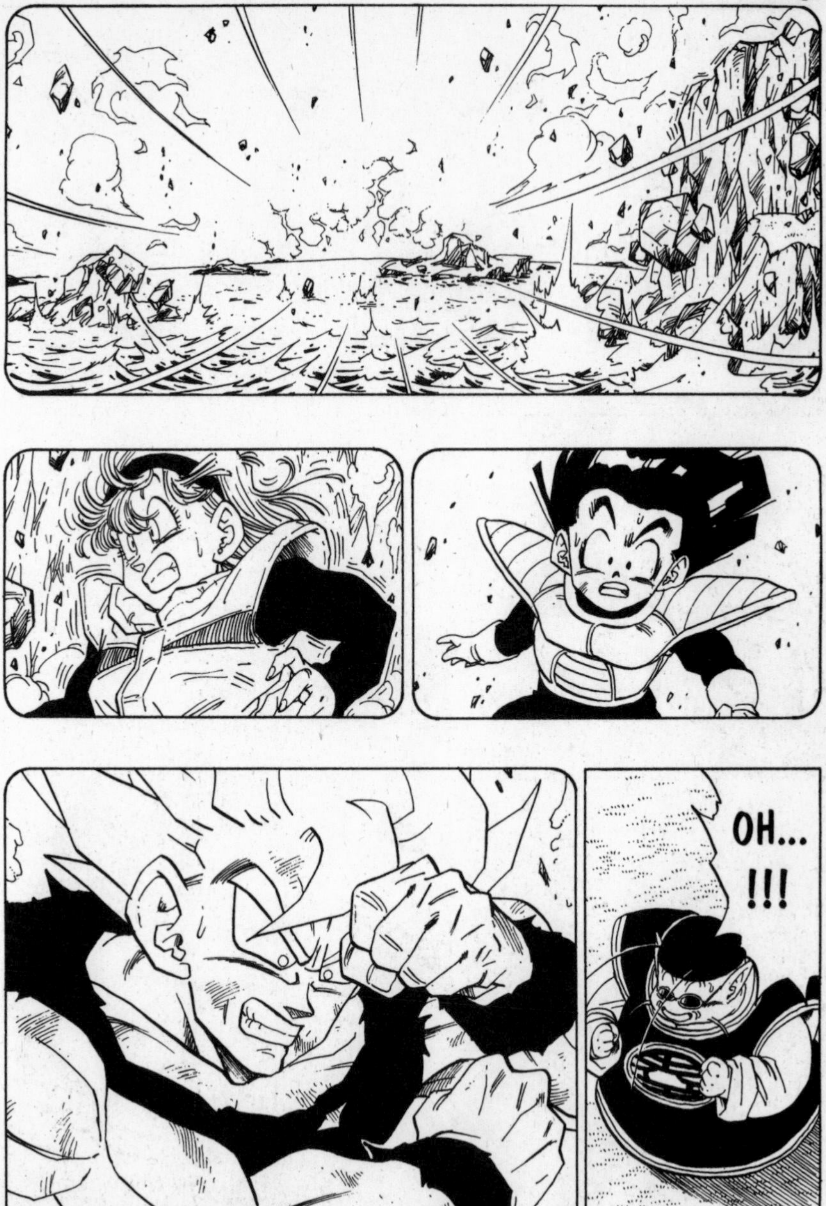
OH...
!!!

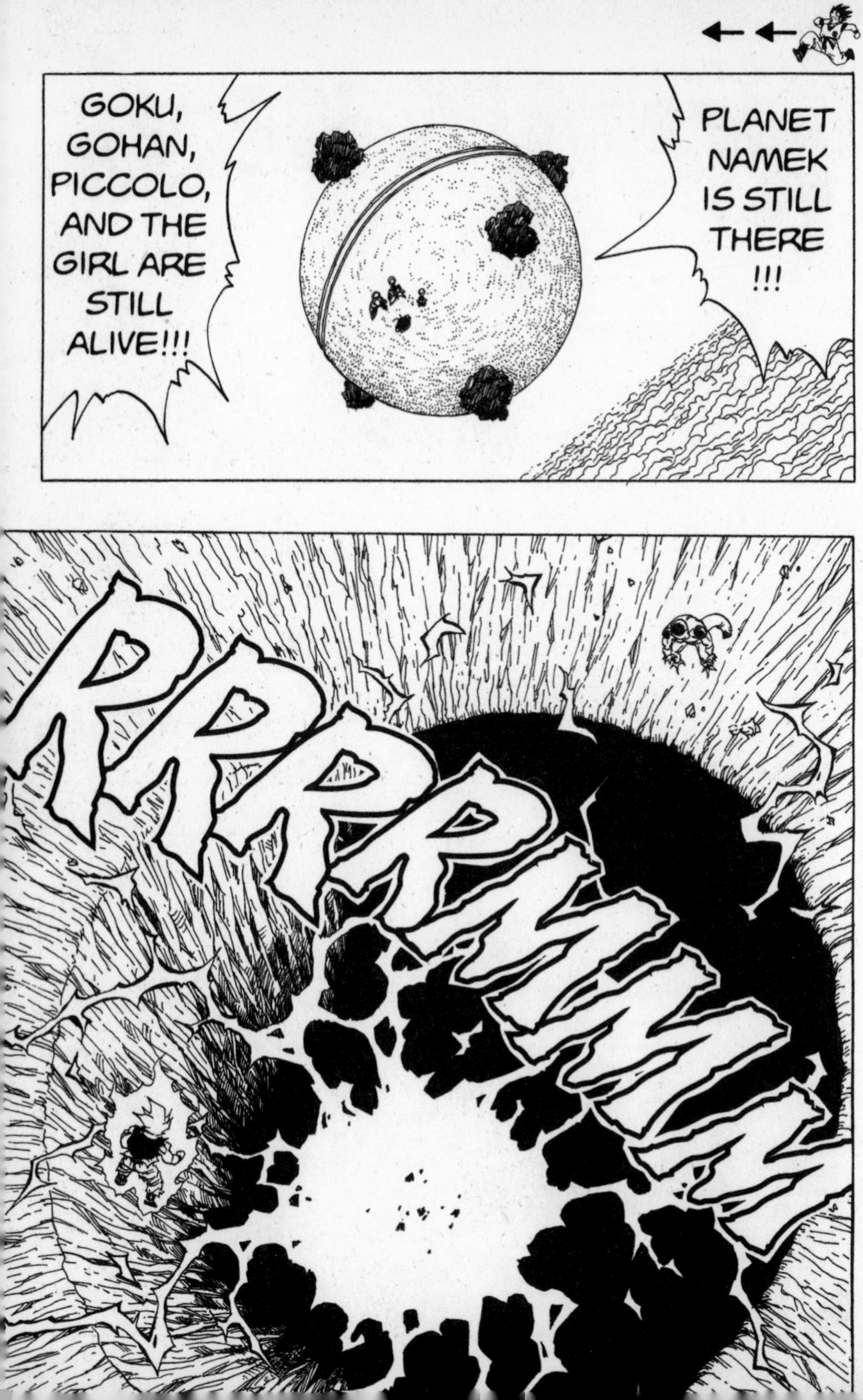
PLANET NAMEK IS STILL THERE!!!
GOKU, GOHAN, PICCOLO, AND THE GIRL ARE STILL ALIVE!!!

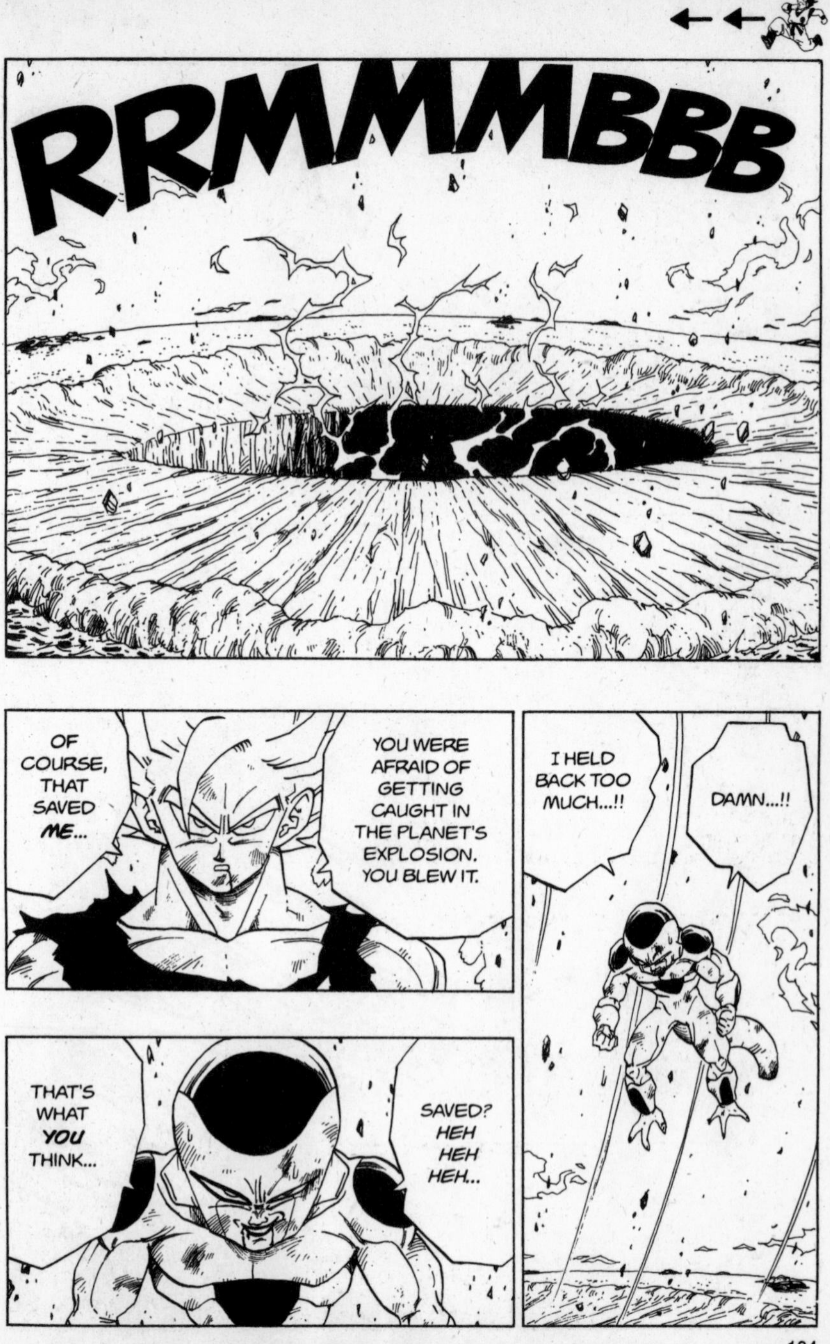
RRMMMBBB
DAMN...!!
I HELD BACK TOO MUCH...!!
YOU WERE AFRAID OF GETTING CAUGHT IN THE PLANET'S EXPLOSION. YOU BLEW IT.
OF COURSE, THAT SAVED ***ME***...
SAVED? ***HEH HEH HEH...***
THAT'S WHAT ***YOU*** THINK...

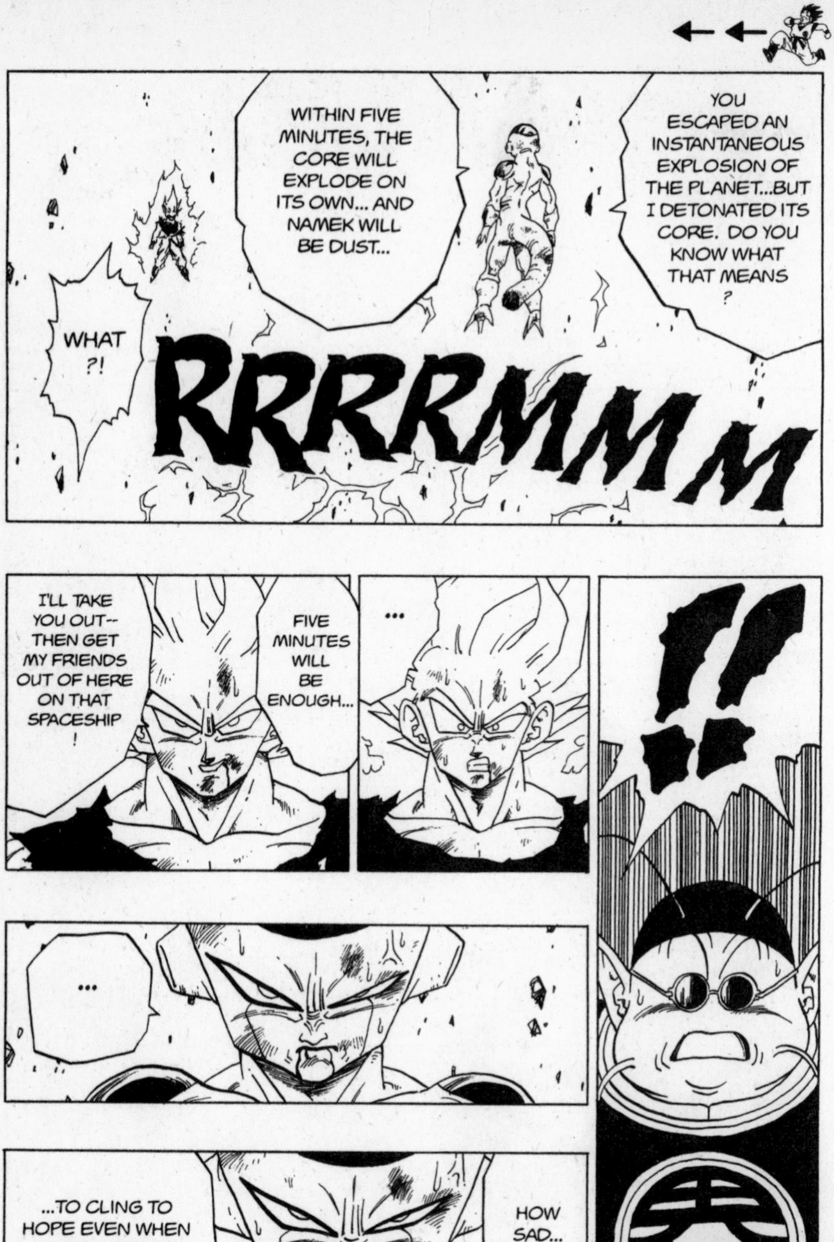
YOU ESCAPED AN INSTANTANEOUS EXPLOSION OF THE PLANET...BUT I DETONATED ITS CORE. DO YOU KNOW WHAT THAT MEANS ?
WITHIN FIVE MINUTES, THE CORE WILL EXPLODE ON ITS OWN... AND NAMEK WILL BE DUST...
WHAT ?!
RRRRMMM M
!!
...
FIVE MINUTES WILL BE ENOUGH...
I'LL TAKE YOU OUT-- THEN GET MY FRIENDS OUT OF HERE ON THAT SPACESHIP !
...
HOW SAD...
...TO CLING TO HOPE EVEN WHEN THINGS ARE SO POINTLESS...

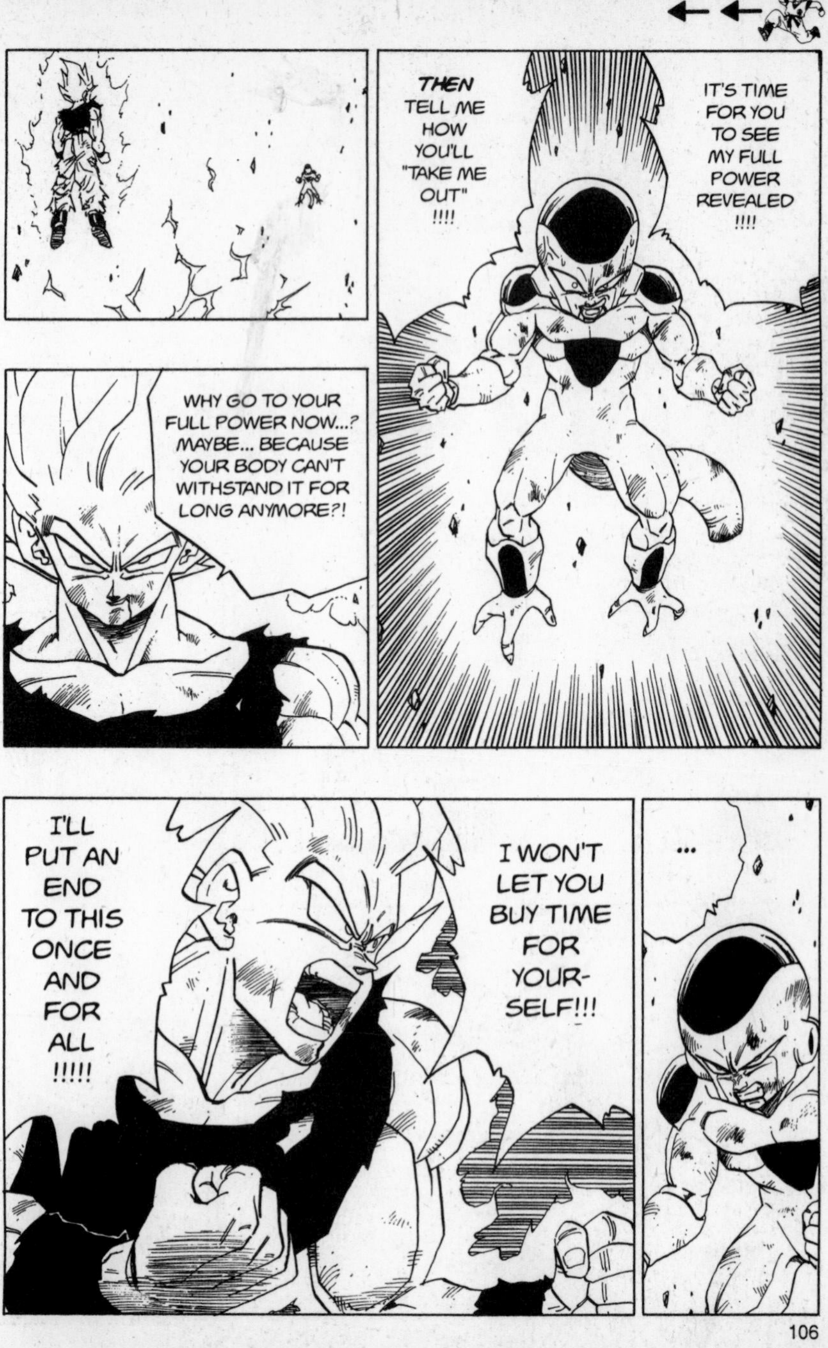

IT'S TIME FOR YOU TO SEE MY FULL POWER REVEALED !!!!
THEN TELL ME HOW YOU'LL "TAKE ME OUT" !!!!
WHY GO TO YOUR FULL POWER NOW...? MAYBE... BECAUSE YOUR BODY CAN'T WITHSTAND IT FOR LONG ANYMORE?!
...
I WON'T LET YOU BUY TIME FOR YOUR-SELF!!!
I'LL PUT AN END TO THIS ONCE AND FOR ALL !!!!!

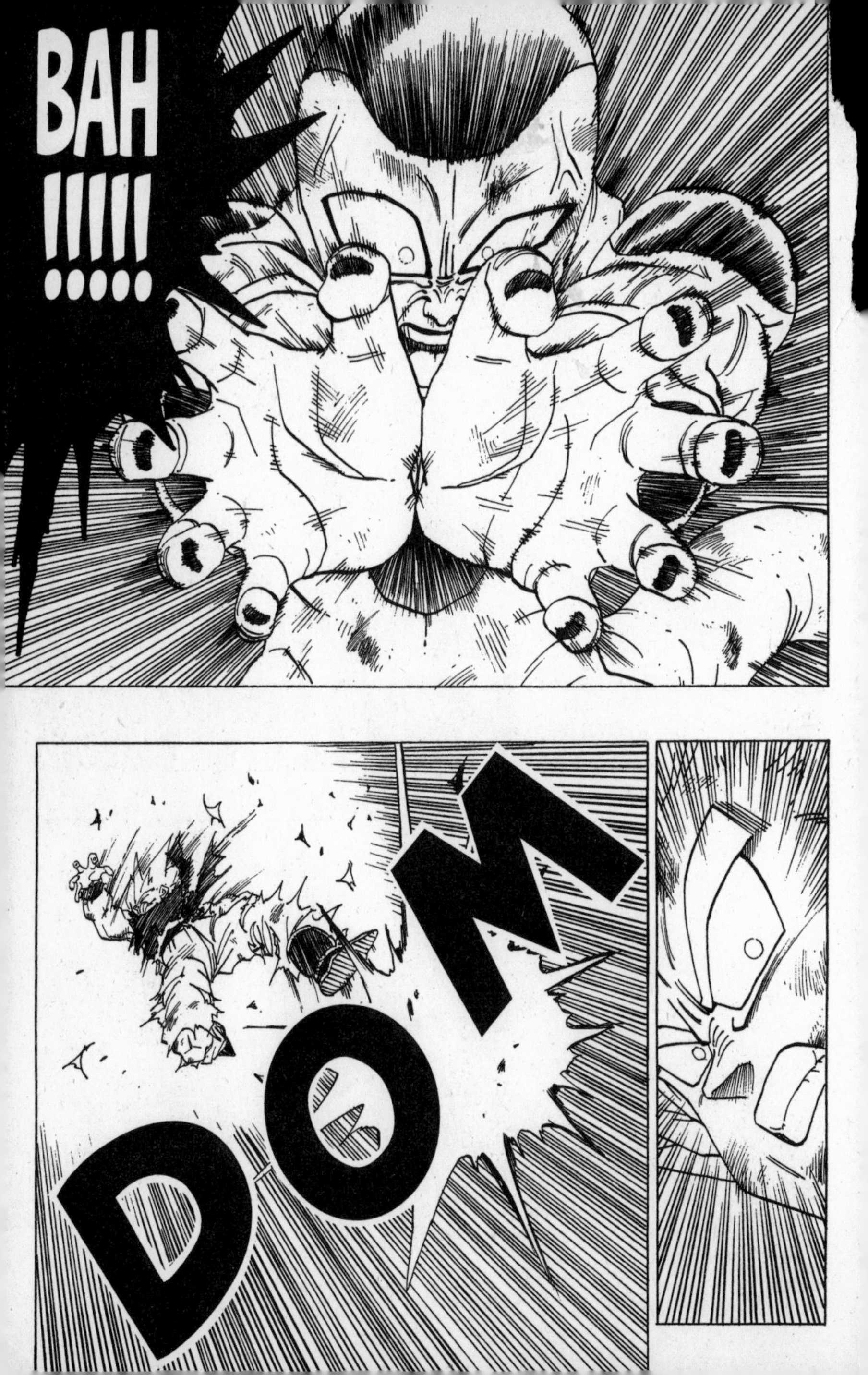
BAH!!!!!
DOM

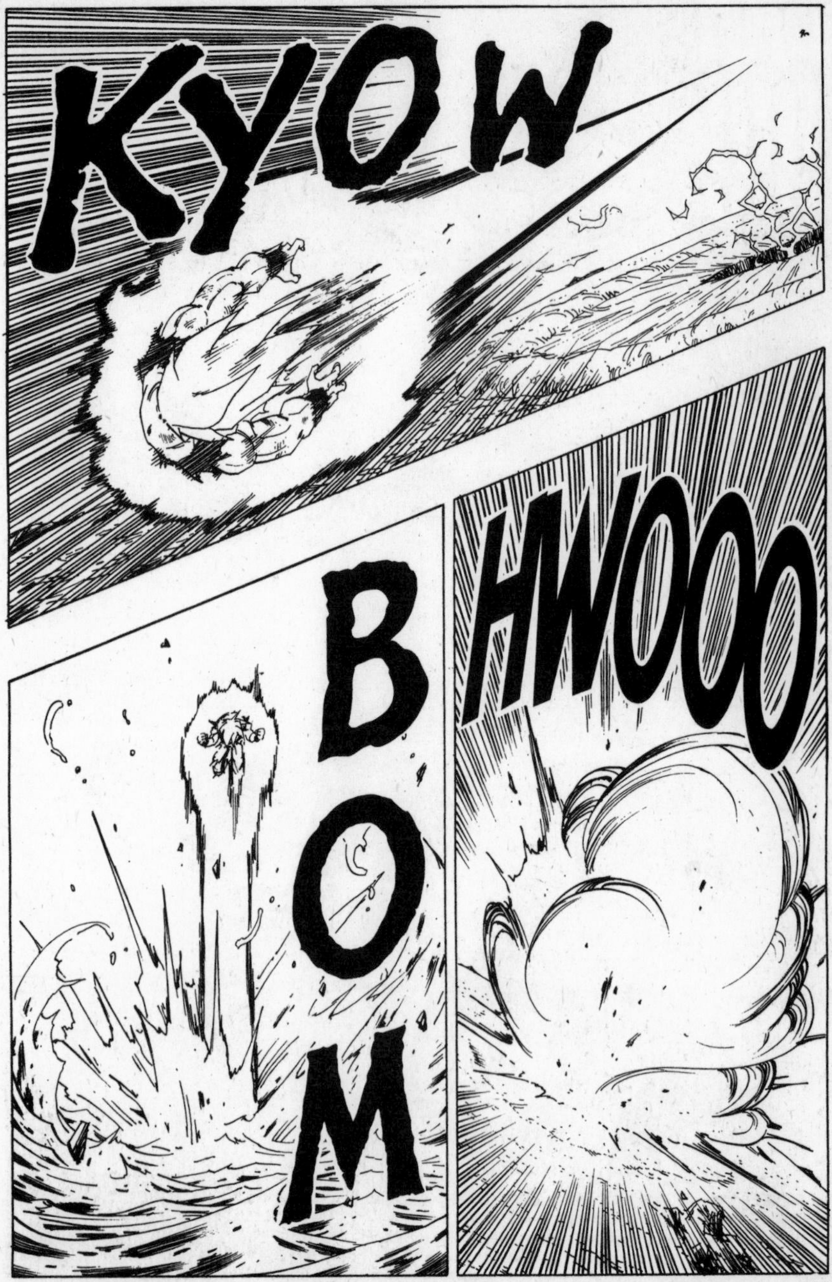
KYOW
HWOOO
BOOM

DBZ:127

Maximum Desperation

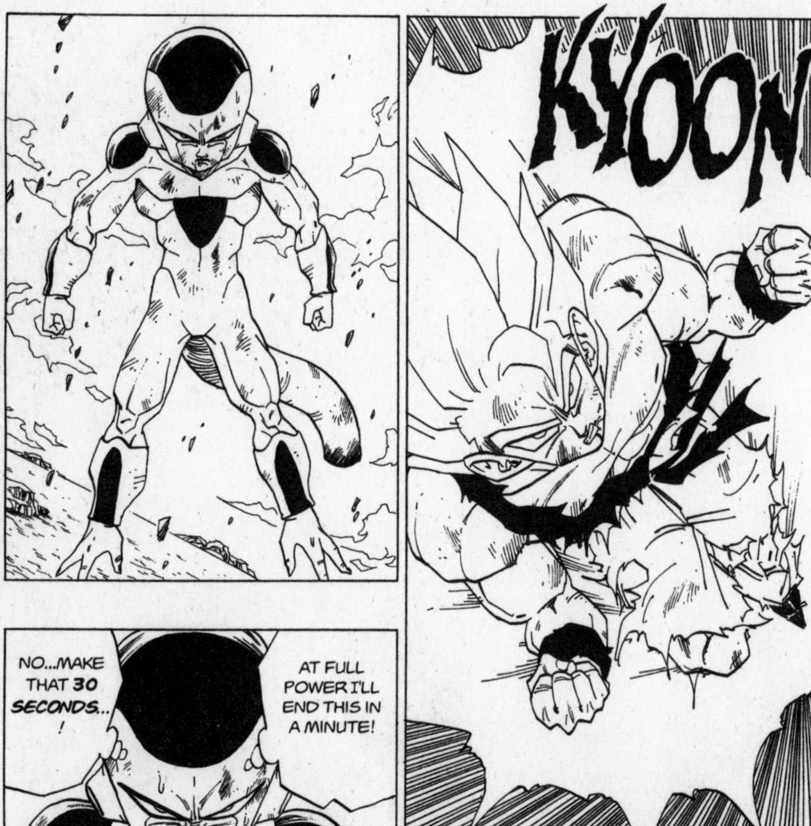
KYOON
AT FULL POWER I'LL END THIS IN A MINUTE!
NO...MAKE THAT 30 SECONDS... !

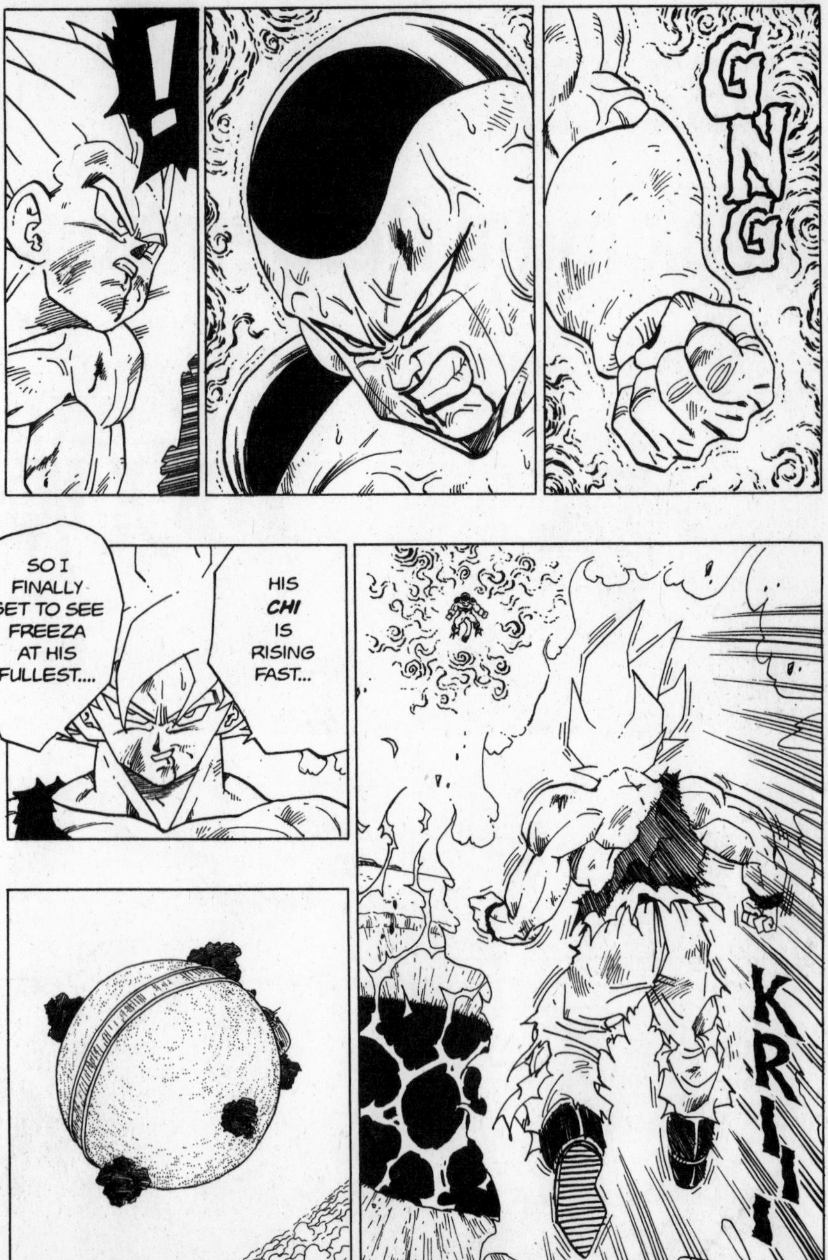
GNG
!
!
KRII
HIS CHI IS RISING FAST...
SO I FINALLY GET TO SEE FREEZA AT HIS FULLEST....

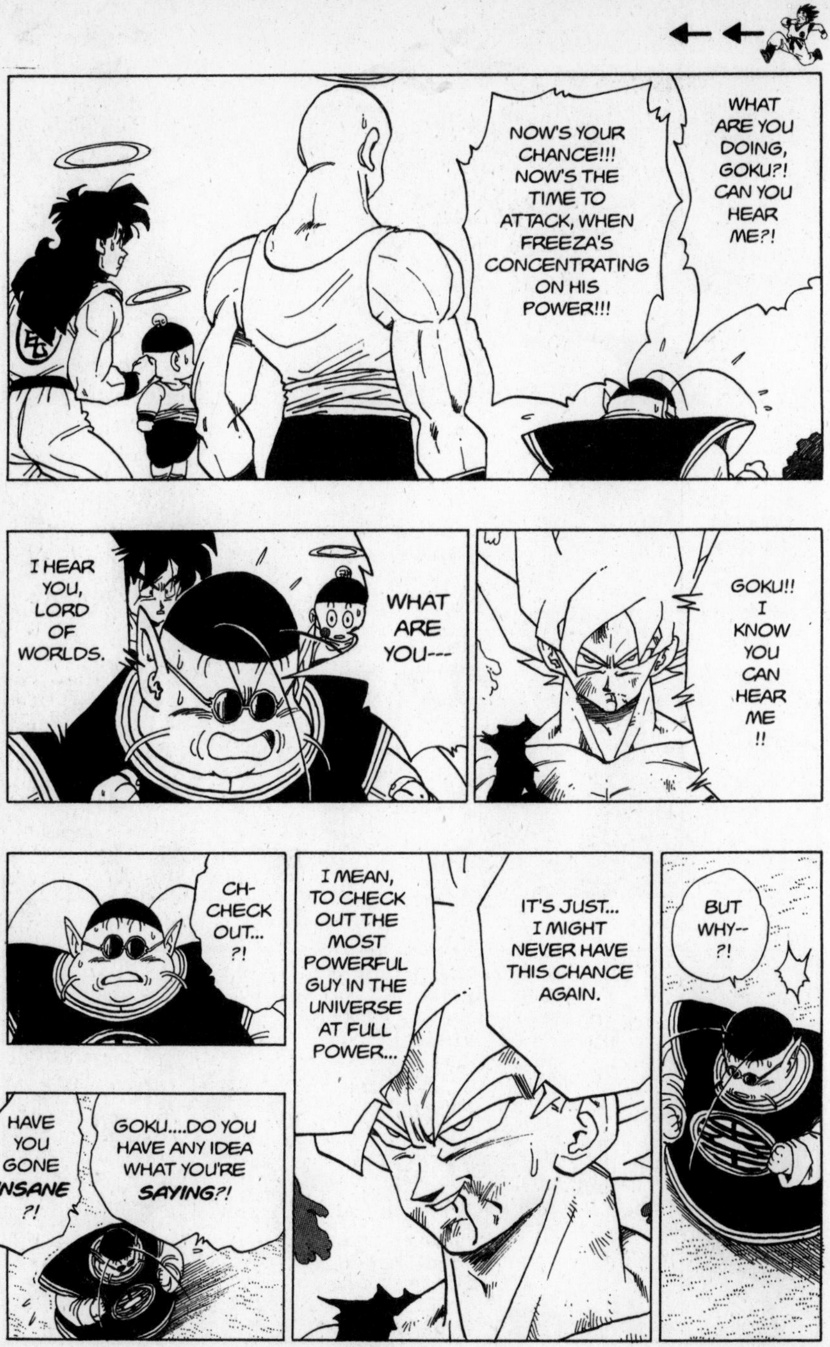
WHAT ARE YOU DOING, GOKU?! CAN YOU HEAR ME?!
NOW'S YOUR CHANCE!!! NOW'S THE TIME TO ATTACK, WHEN FREEZA'S CONCENTRATING ON HIS POWER!!!
GOKU!! I KNOW YOU CAN HEAR ME !!
WHAT ARE YOU---
I HEAR YOU, LORD OF WORLDS.
BUT WHY--?!
IT'S JUST... I MIGHT NEVER HAVE THIS CHANCE AGAIN.
I MEAN, TO CHECK OUT THE MOST POWERFUL GUY IN THE UNIVERSE AT FULL POWER...
CH-CHECK OUT...?!
GOKU....DO YOU HAVE ANY IDEA WHAT YOU'RE *SAYING*?!
HAVE YOU GONE *INSANE*?!

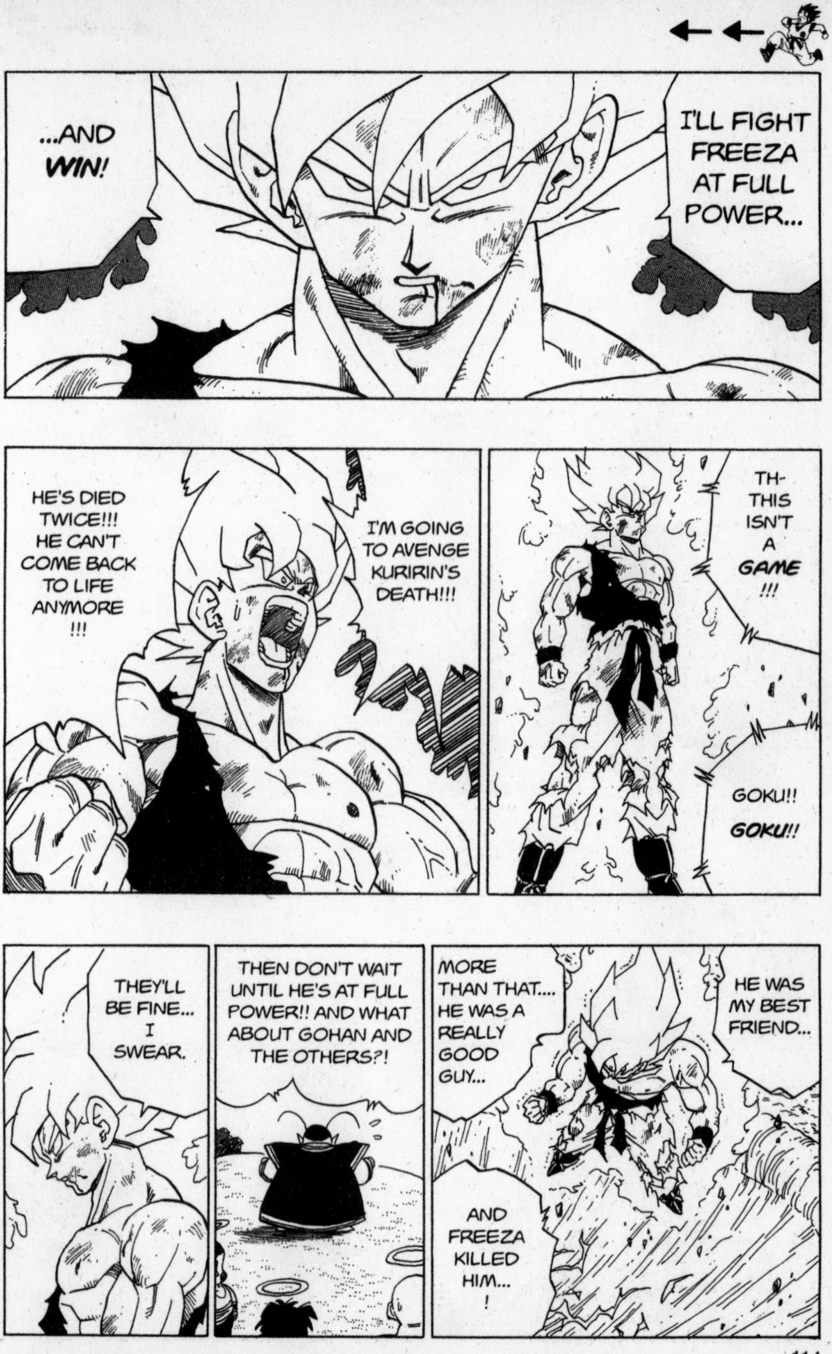
I'LL FIGHT FREEZA AT FULL POWER...
...AND WIN!
TH- THIS ISN'T A GAME !!!
GOKU!! GOKU!!
I'M GOING TO AVENGE KURIRIN'S DEATH!!!
HE'S DIED TWICE!!! HE CAN'T COME BACK TO LIFE ANYMORE !!!
HE WAS MY BEST FRIEND...
MORE THAN THAT.... HE WAS A REALLY GOOD GUY...
AND FREEZA KILLED HIM... !
THEN DON'T WAIT UNTIL HE'S AT FULL POWER!! AND WHAT ABOUT GOHAN AND THE OTHERS?!
THEY'LL BE FINE... I SWEAR.

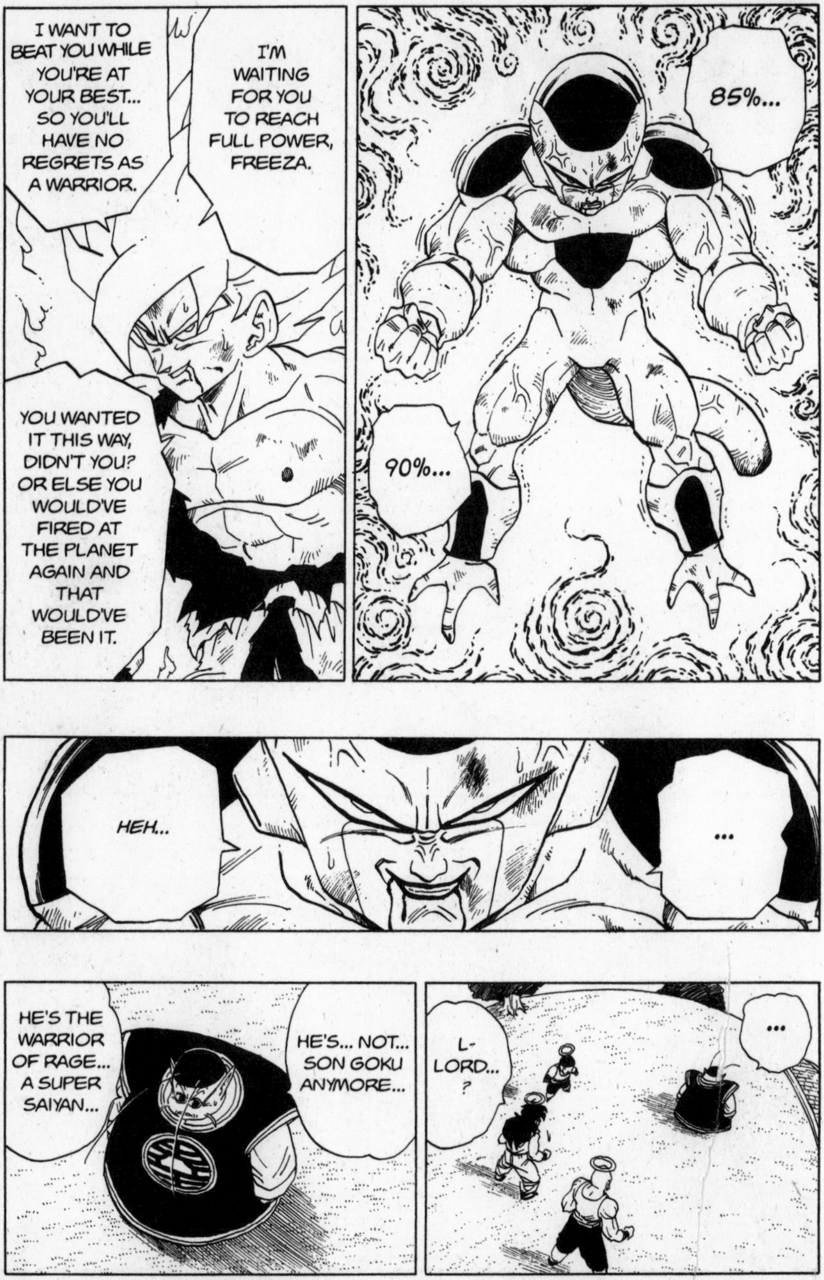
85%...
90%...
I'M WAITING FOR YOU TO REACH FULL POWER, FREEZA.
I WANT TO BEAT YOU WHILE YOU'RE AT YOUR BEST... SO YOU'LL HAVE NO REGRETS AS A WARRIOR.
YOU WANTED IT THIS WAY, DIDN'T YOU? OR ELSE YOU WOULD'VE FIRED AT THE PLANET AGAIN AND THAT WOULD'VE BEEN IT.
...
HEH...
...
L-LORD...?
HE'S... NOT... SON GOKU ANYMORE...
HE'S THE WARRIOR OF RAGE... A SUPER SAIYAN...

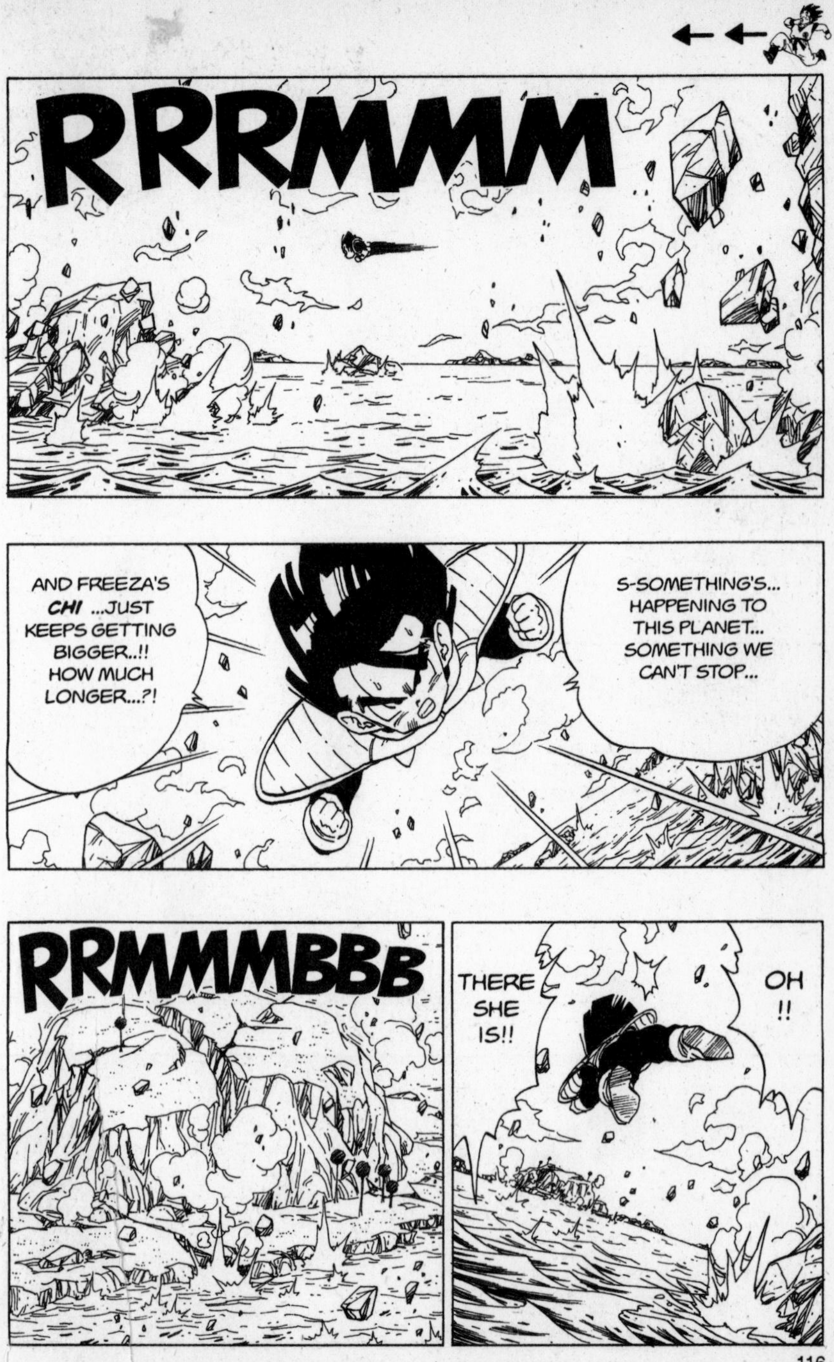
RRRMMM
S-SOMETHING'S... HAPPENING TO THIS PLANET... SOMETHING WE CAN'T STOP...
AND FREEZA'S CHI ...JUST KEEPS GETTING BIGGER..!! HOW MUCH LONGER...?!
OH !!
THERE SHE IS!!
RRMMMBBB

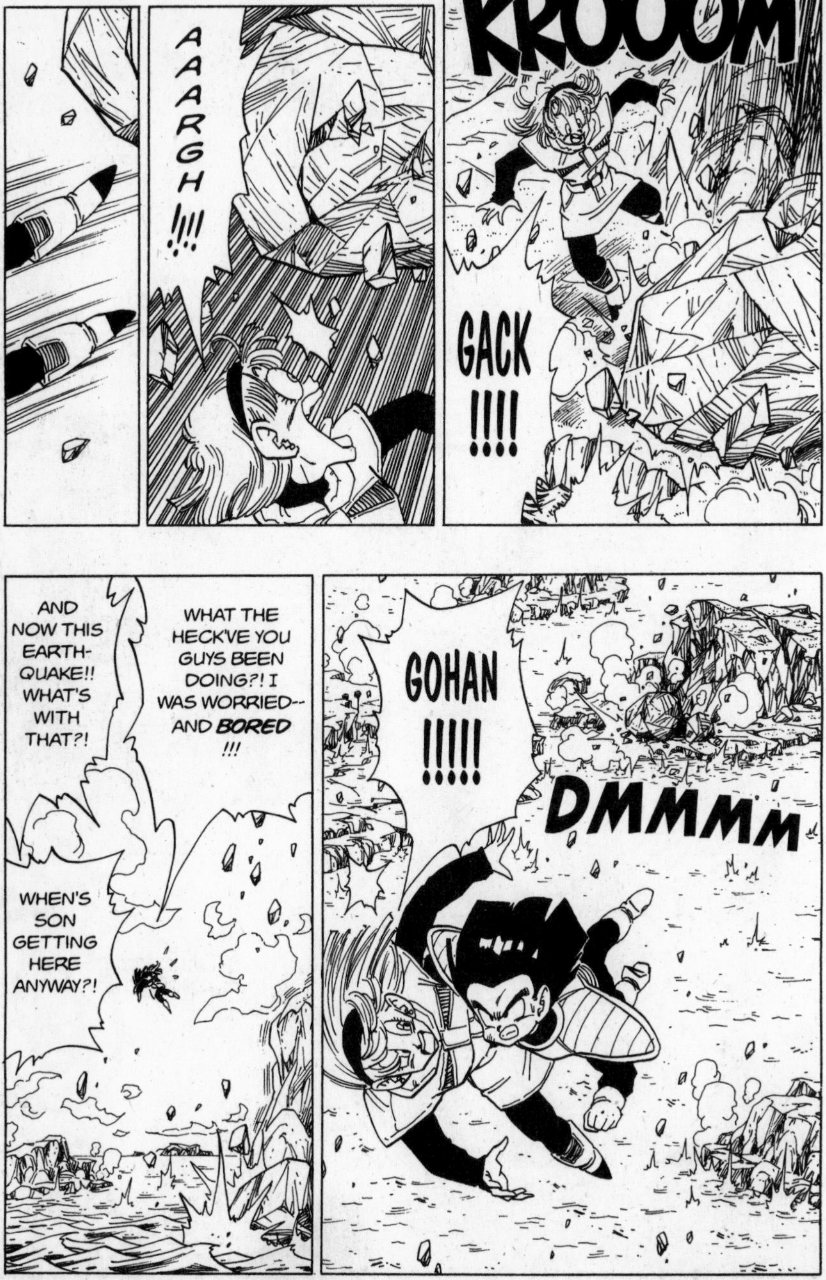
KROOOM
GACK!!!!
AAARGH!!!!
GOHAN!!!!!
DMMMM
WHAT THE HECK'VE YOU GUYS BEEN DOING?! I WAS WORRIED-- AND *BORED*!!!
AND NOW THIS EARTHQUAKE!! WHAT'S WITH THAT?!
WHEN'S SON GETTING HERE ANYWAY?!

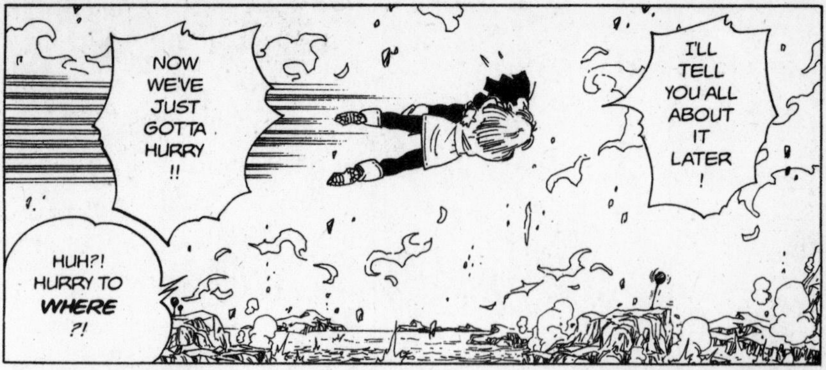
I'LL TELL YOU ALL ABOUT IT LATER!
NOW WE'VE JUST GOTTA HURRY!!
HUH?! HURRY TO *WHERE*?!

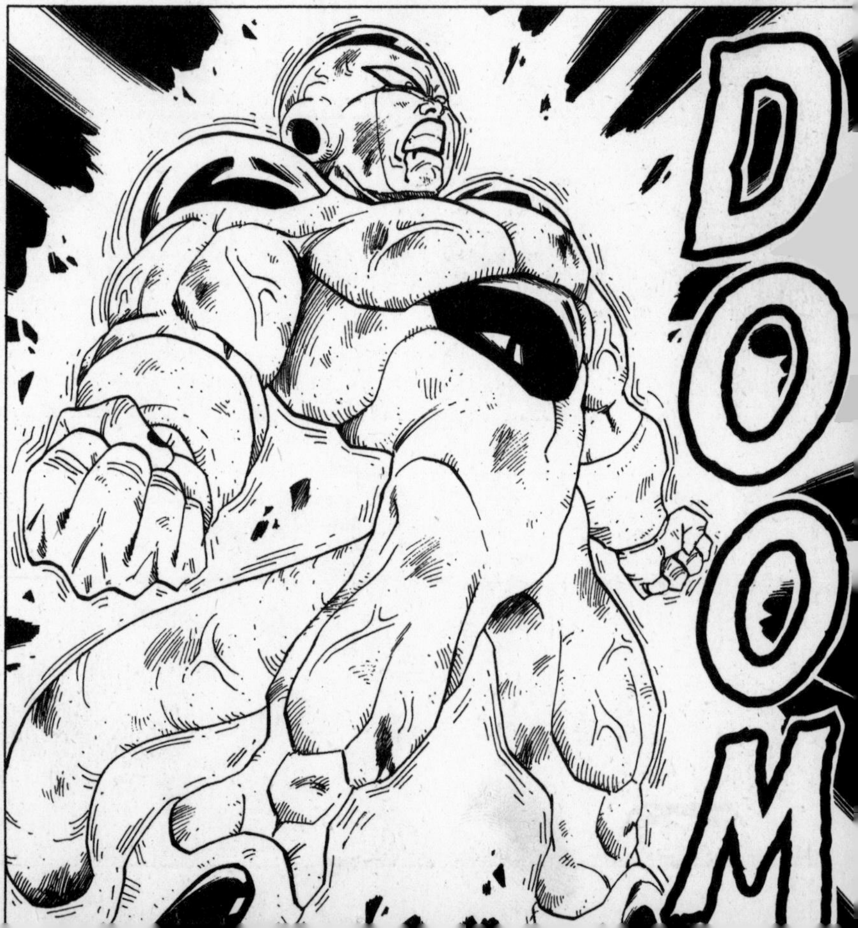
DOOM

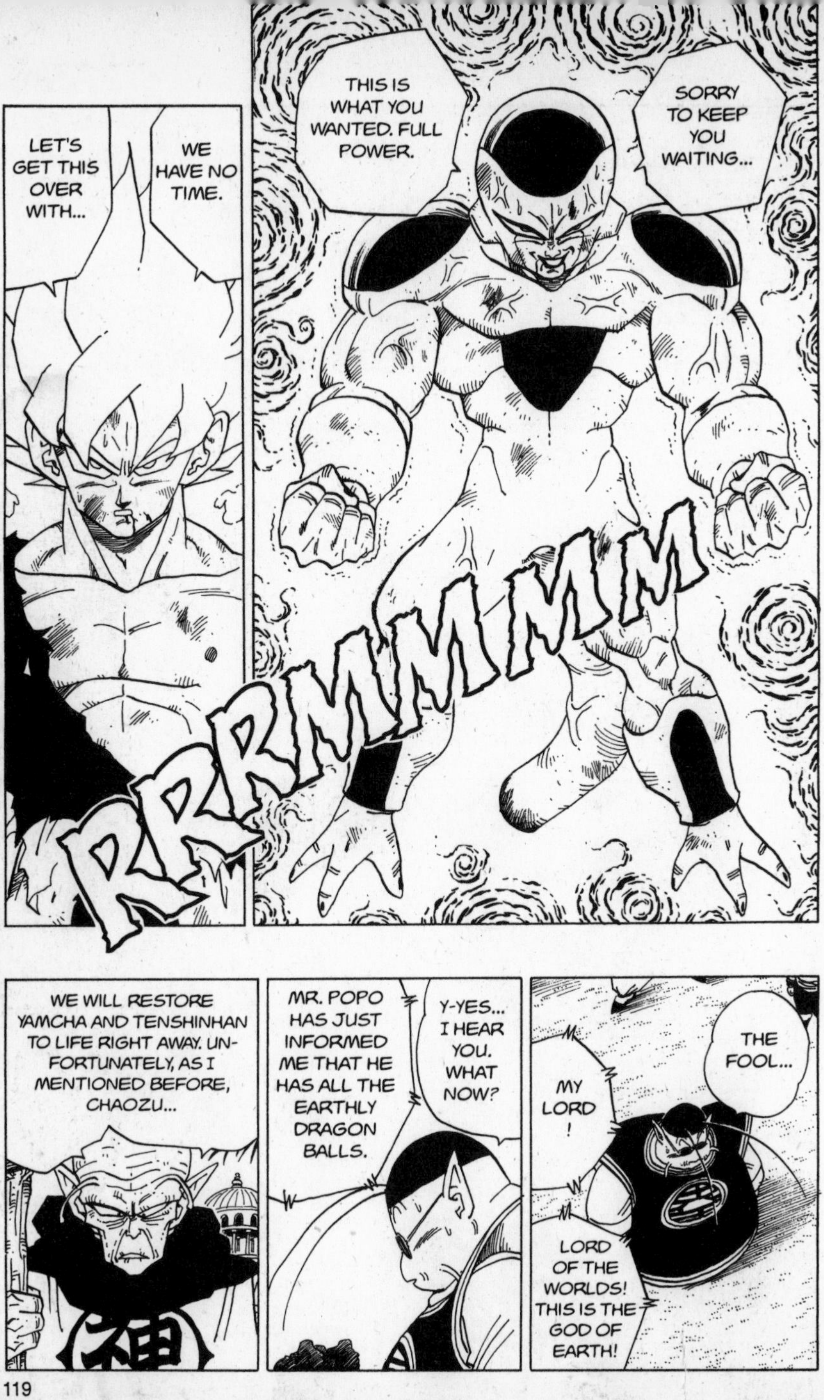
SORRY TO KEEP YOU WAITING...
THIS IS WHAT YOU WANTED. FULL POWER.
RRRMMMMMM
WE HAVE NO TIME.
LET'S GET THIS OVER WITH...
THE FOOL...
MY LORD!
LORD OF THE WORLDS! THIS IS THE GOD OF EARTH!
Y-YES... I HEAR YOU. WHAT NOW?
MR. POPO HAS JUST INFORMED ME THAT HE HAS ALL THE EARTHLY DRAGON BALLS.
WE WILL RESTORE YAMCHA AND TENSHINHAN TO LIFE RIGHT AWAY. UN-FORTUNATELY, AS I MENTIONED BEFORE, CHAOZU...

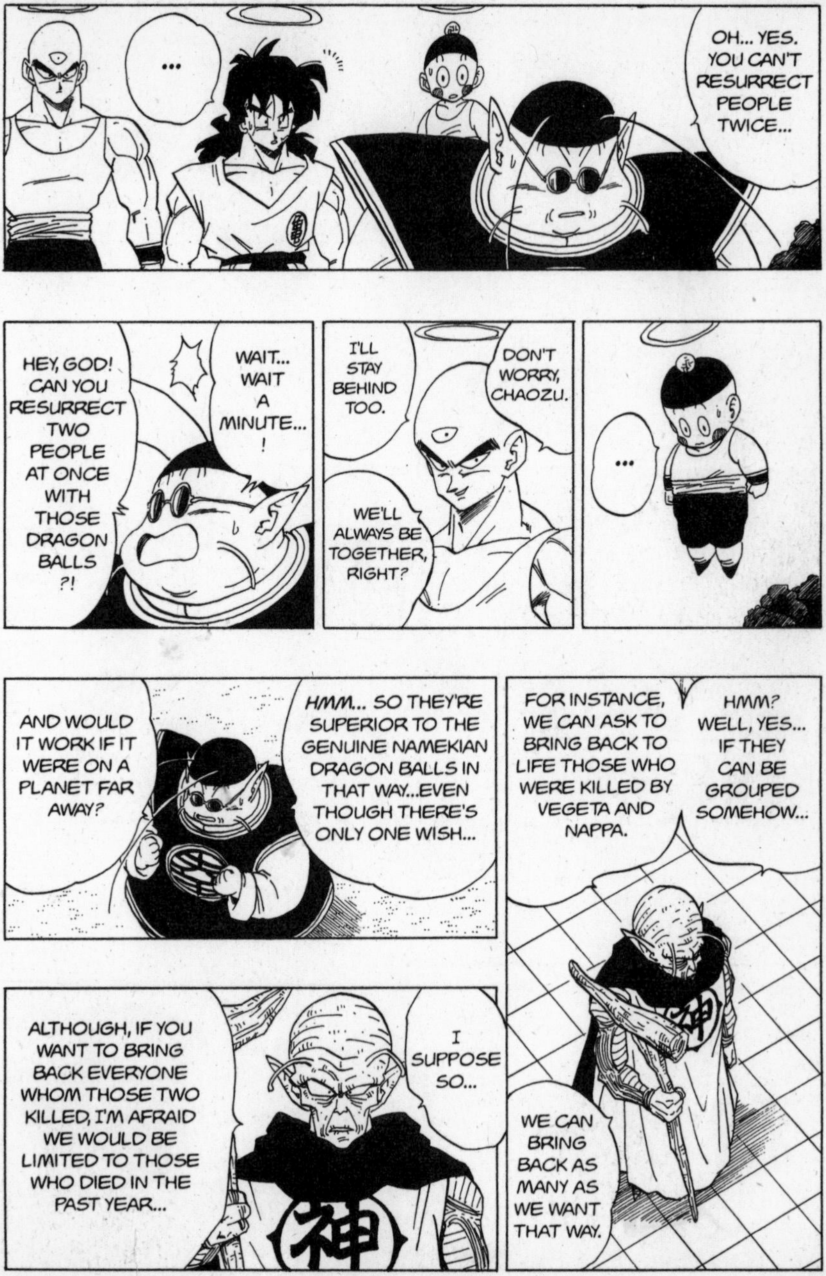
OH... YES. YOU CAN'T RESURRECT PEOPLE TWICE...
...
...
DON'T WORRY, CHAOZU.
I'LL STAY BEHIND TOO.
WE'LL ALWAYS BE TOGETHER, RIGHT?
WAIT... WAIT A MINUTE... !
HEY, GOD! CAN YOU RESURRECT TWO PEOPLE AT ONCE WITH THOSE DRAGON BALLS ?!
HMM? WELL, YES... IF THEY CAN BE GROUPED SOMEHOW...
FOR INSTANCE, WE CAN ASK TO BRING BACK TO LIFE THOSE WHO WERE KILLED BY VEGETA AND NAPPA.
WE CAN BRING BACK AS MANY AS WE WANT THAT WAY.
HMM... SO THEY'RE SUPERIOR TO THE GENUINE NAMEKIAN DRAGON BALLS IN THAT WAY...EVEN THOUGH THERE'S ONLY ONE WISH...
AND WOULD IT WORK IF IT WERE ON A PLANET FAR AWAY?
I SUPPOSE SO...
ALTHOUGH, IF YOU WANT TO BRING BACK EVERYONE WHOM THOSE TWO KILLED, I'M AFRAID WE WOULD BE LIMITED TO THOSE WHO DIED IN THE PAST YEAR...

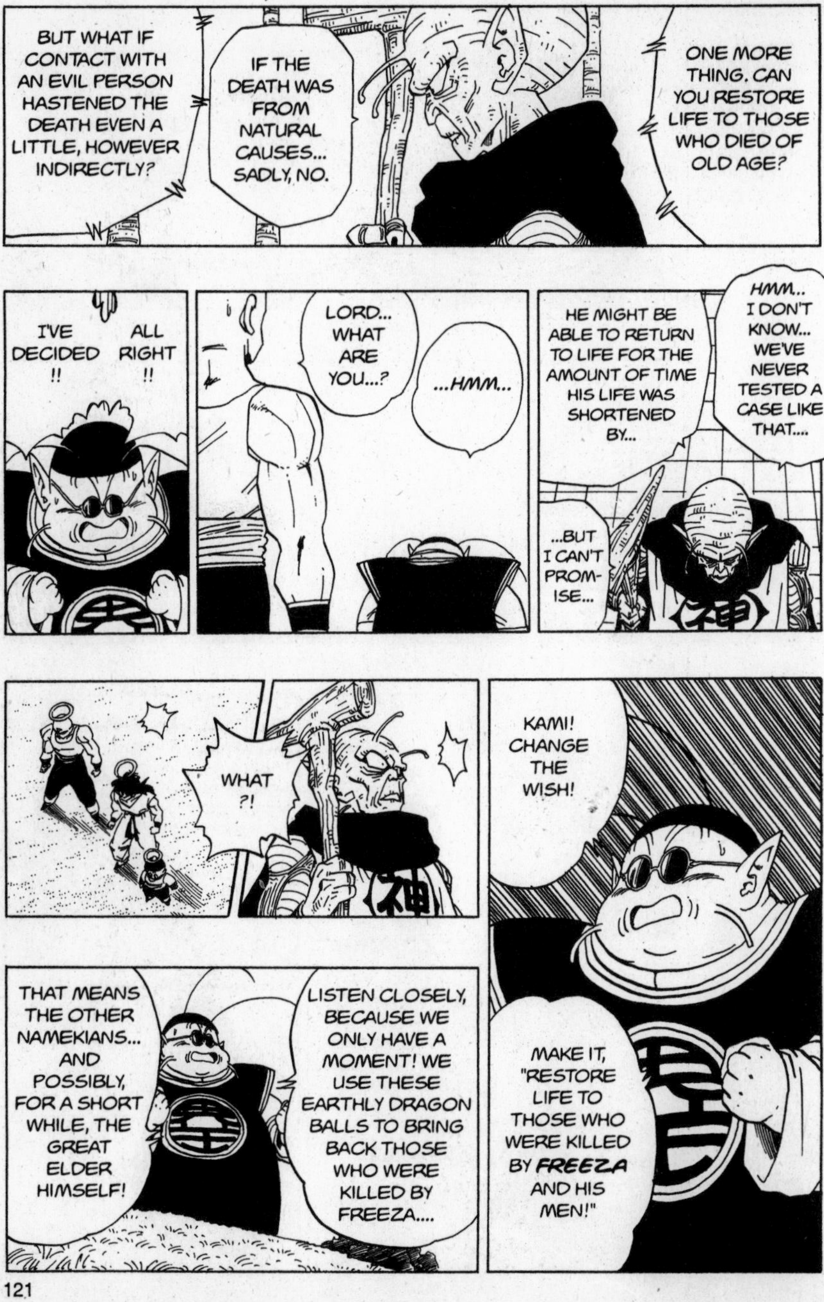
ONE MORE THING. CAN YOU RESTORE LIFE TO THOSE WHO DIED OF OLD AGE?
IF THE DEATH WAS FROM NATURAL CAUSES... SADLY, NO.
BUT WHAT IF CONTACT WITH AN EVIL PERSON HASTENED THE DEATH EVEN A LITTLE, HOWEVER INDIRECTLY?
HMM... I DON'T KNOW... WE'VE NEVER TESTED A CASE LIKE THAT....
HE MIGHT BE ABLE TO RETURN TO LIFE FOR THE AMOUNT OF TIME HIS LIFE WAS SHORTENED BY...
...BUT I CAN'T PROM-ISE...
LORD... WHAT ARE YOU...?
...HMM...
ALL RIGHT !!
I'VE DECIDED !!
KAMI! CHANGE THE WISH!
MAKE IT, "RESTORE LIFE TO THOSE WHO WERE KILLED BY *FREEZA* AND HIS MEN!"
WHAT ?!
LISTEN CLOSELY, BECAUSE WE ONLY HAVE A MOMENT! WE USE THESE EARTHLY DRAGON BALLS TO BRING BACK THOSE WHO WERE KILLED BY FREEZA....
THAT MEANS THE OTHER NAMEKIANS... AND POSSIBLY, FOR A SHORT WHILE, THE GREAT ELDER HIMSELF!

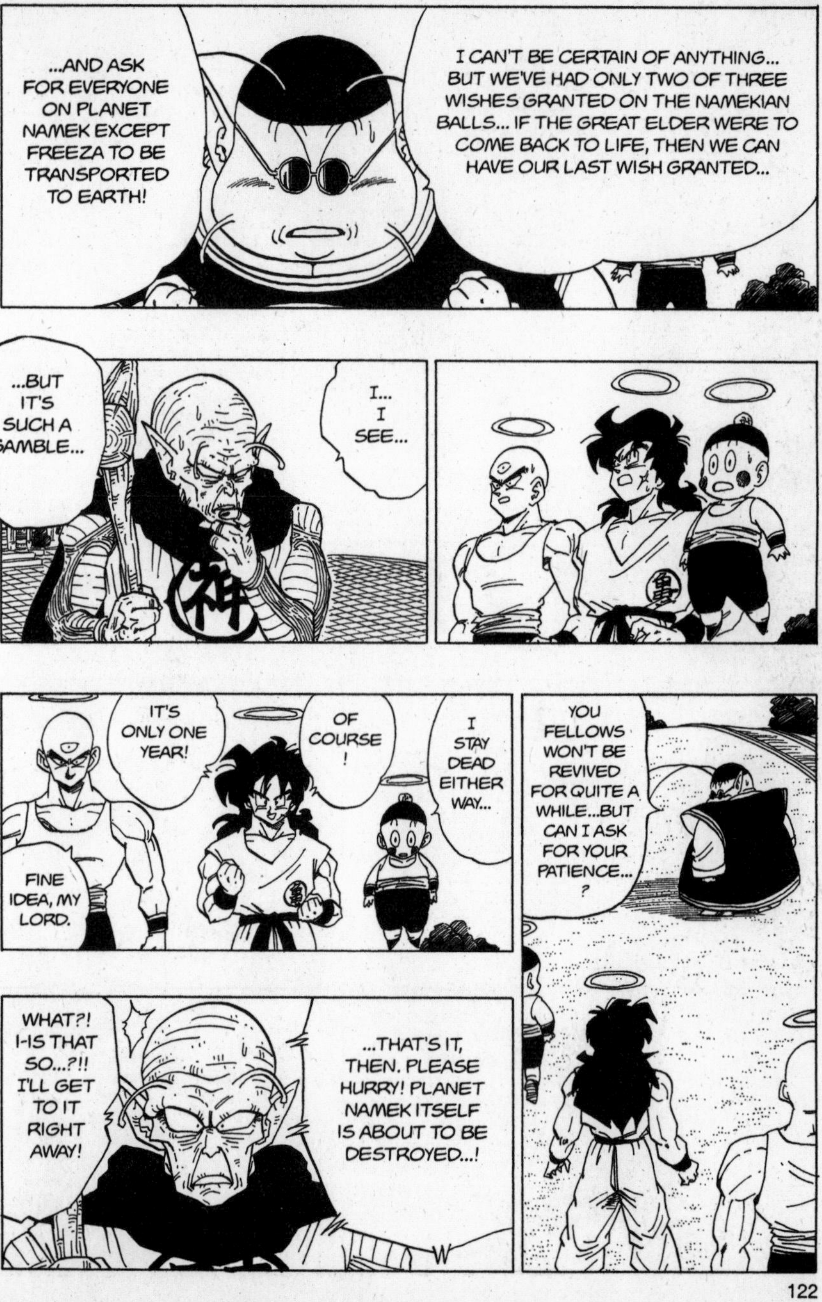

I CAN'T BE CERTAIN OF ANYTHING... BUT WE'VE HAD ONLY TWO OF THREE WISHES GRANTED ON THE NAMEKIAN BALLS... IF THE GREAT ELDER WERE TO COME BACK TO LIFE, THEN WE CAN HAVE OUR LAST WISH GRANTED...
...AND ASK FOR EVERYONE ON PLANET NAMEK EXCEPT FREEZA TO BE TRANSPORTED TO EARTH!
I... I SEE...
...BUT IT'S SUCH A GAMBLE...
YOU FELLOWS WON'T BE REVIVED FOR QUITE A WHILE...BUT CAN I ASK FOR YOUR PATIENCE...?
I STAY DEAD EITHER WAY...
OF COURSE!
IT'S ONLY ONE YEAR!
FINE IDEA, MY LORD.
...THAT'S IT, THEN. PLEASE HURRY! PLANET NAMEK ITSELF IS ABOUT TO BE DESTROYED...!
WHAT?! I-IS THAT SO...?!! I'LL GET TO IT RIGHT AWAY!

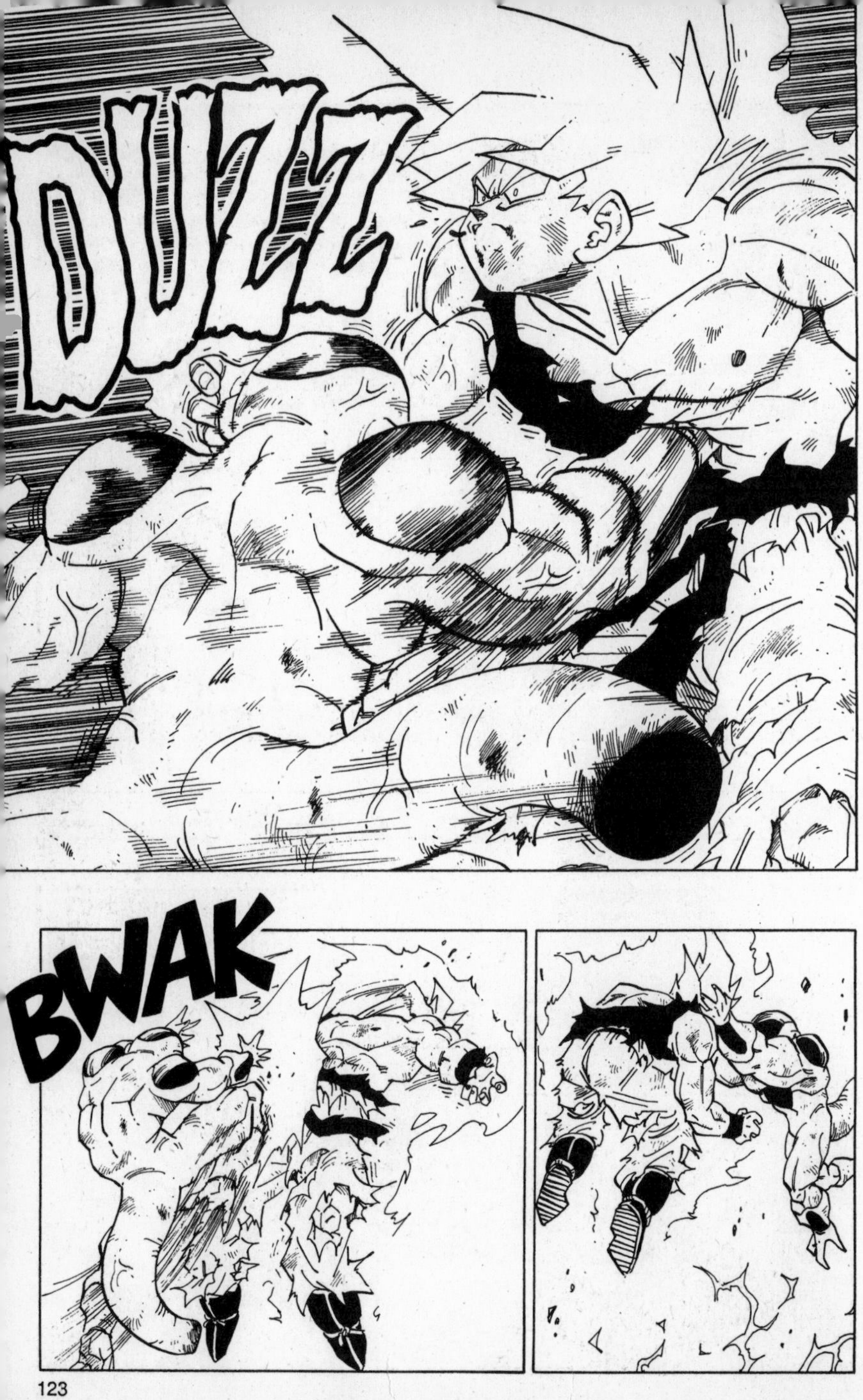
DUZZ
BWAK

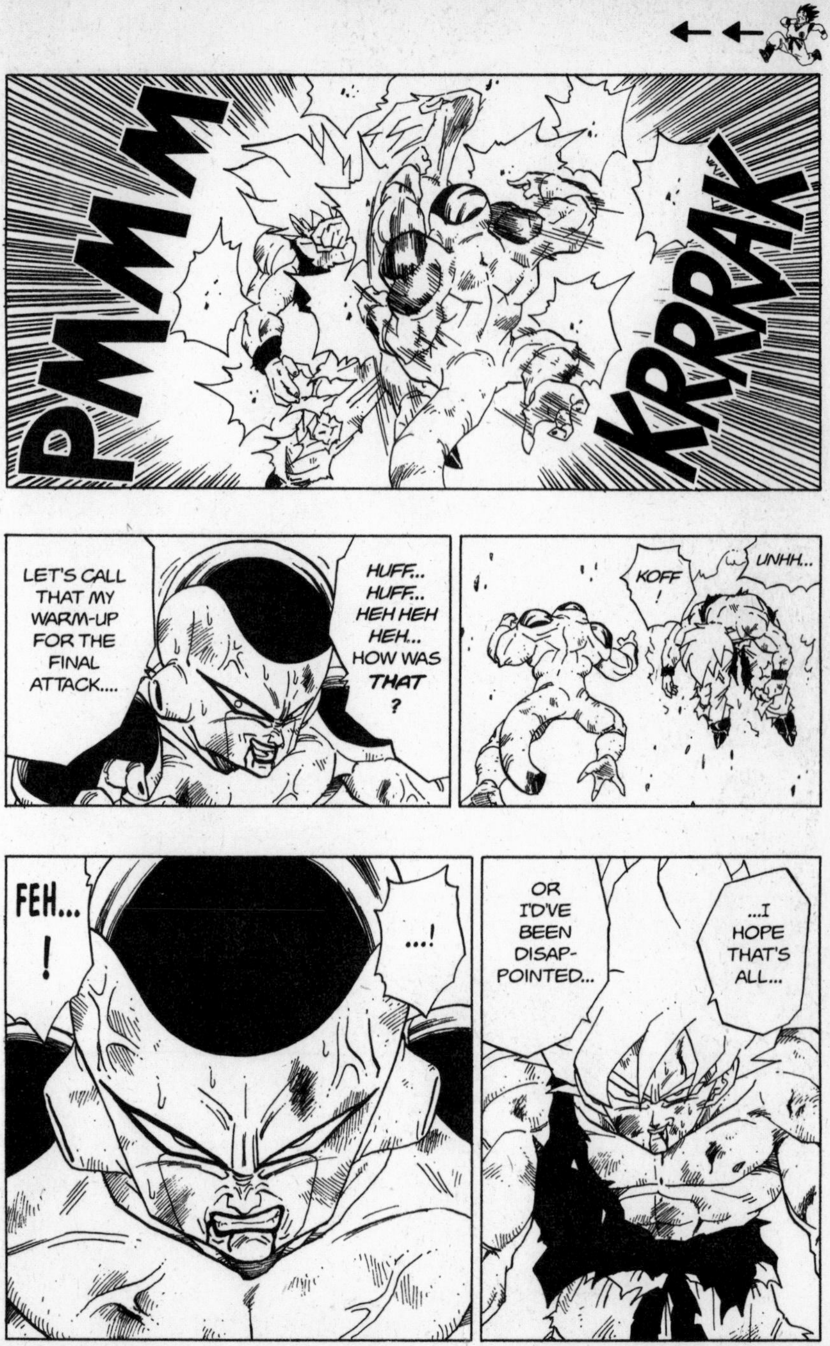
KRRAK
PMMM
...UNHH...
KOFF!
HUFF... HUFF... HEH HEH HEH... HOW WAS *THAT*?
LET'S CALL THAT MY WARM-UP FOR THE FINAL ATTACK....
...I HOPE THAT'S ALL...
OR I'D'VE BEEN DISAP-POINTED...
...!
FEH...!

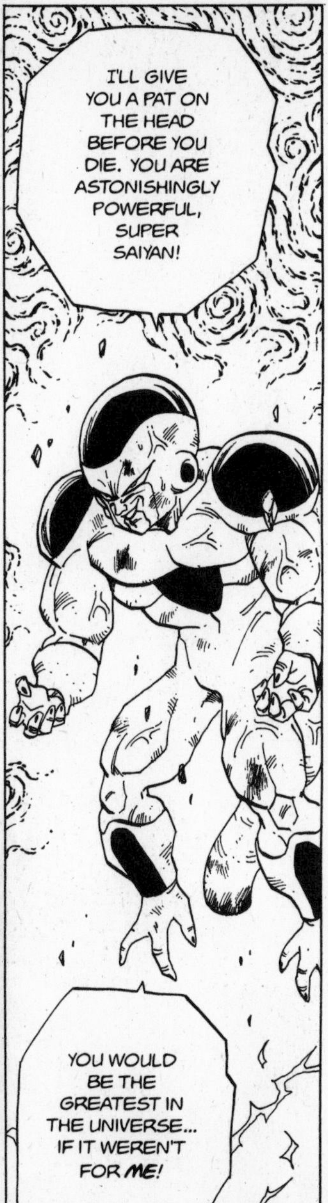
I'LL GIVE YOU A PAT ON THE HEAD BEFORE YOU DIE. YOU ARE ASTONISHINGLY POWERFUL, SUPER SAIYAN!
YOU WOULD BE THE GREATEST IN THE UNIVERSE... IF IT WEREN'T FOR *ME!*
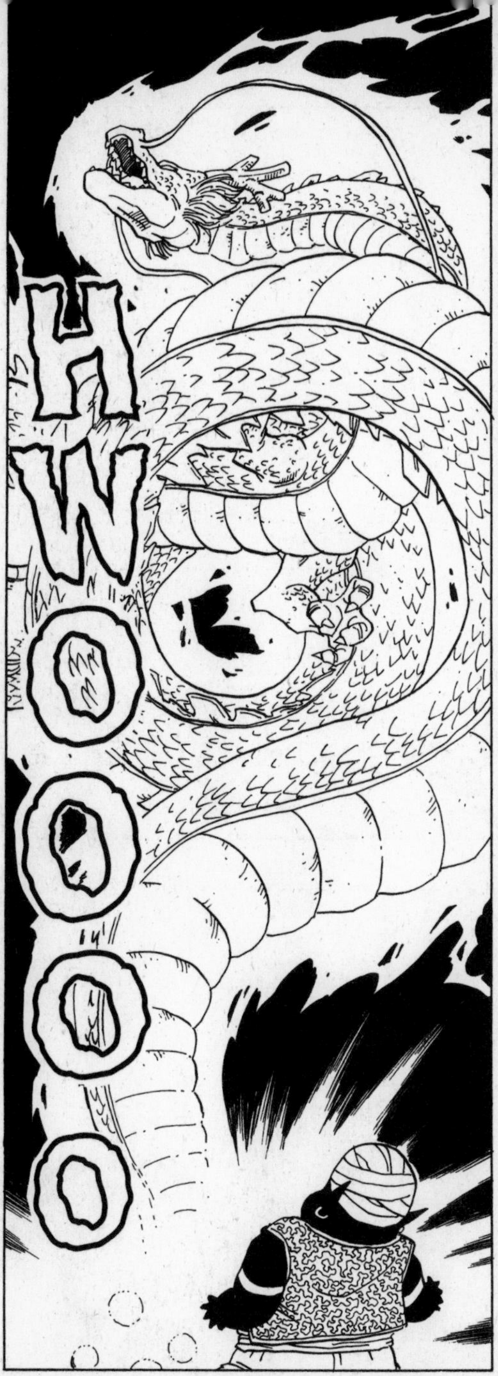
HWOOOO

DBZ:128

Two Warriors, One Finish

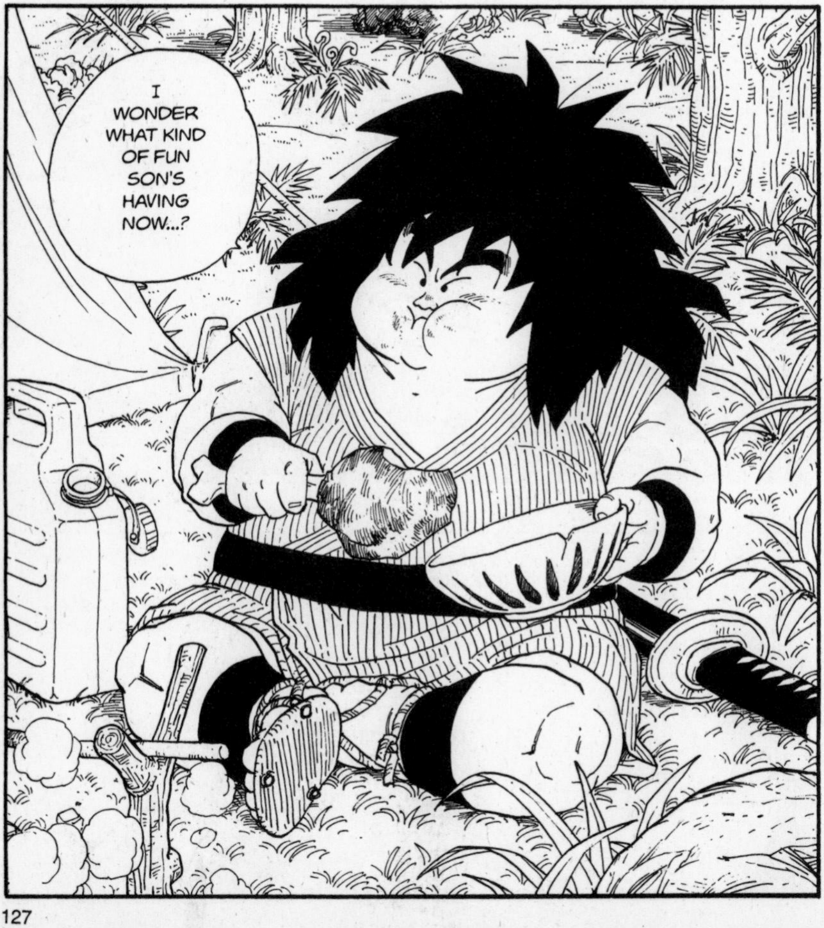
I WONDER WHAT KIND OF FUN SON'S HAVING NOW...?

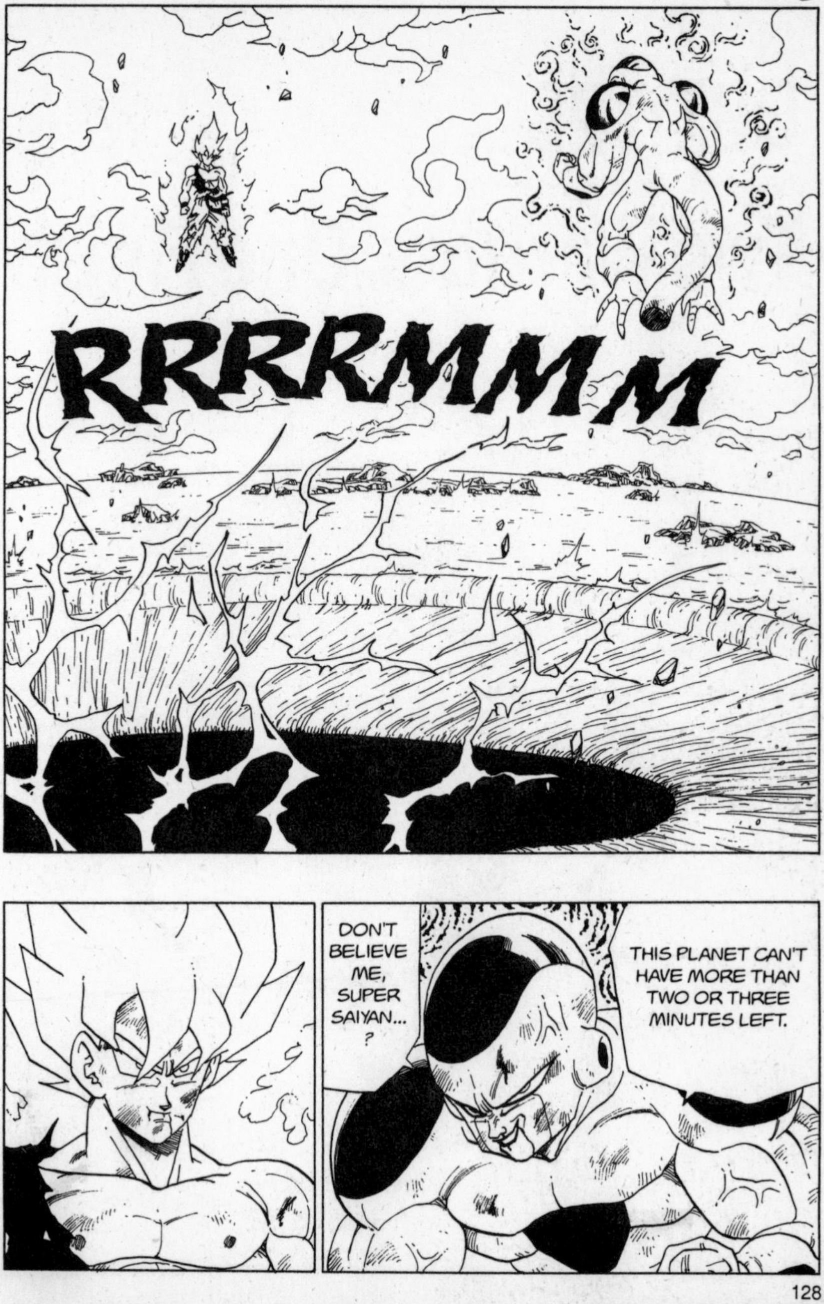
RRRRMMM
THIS PLANET CAN'T HAVE MORE THAN TWO OR THREE MINUTES LEFT.
DON'T BELIEVE ME, SUPER SAIYAN... ?

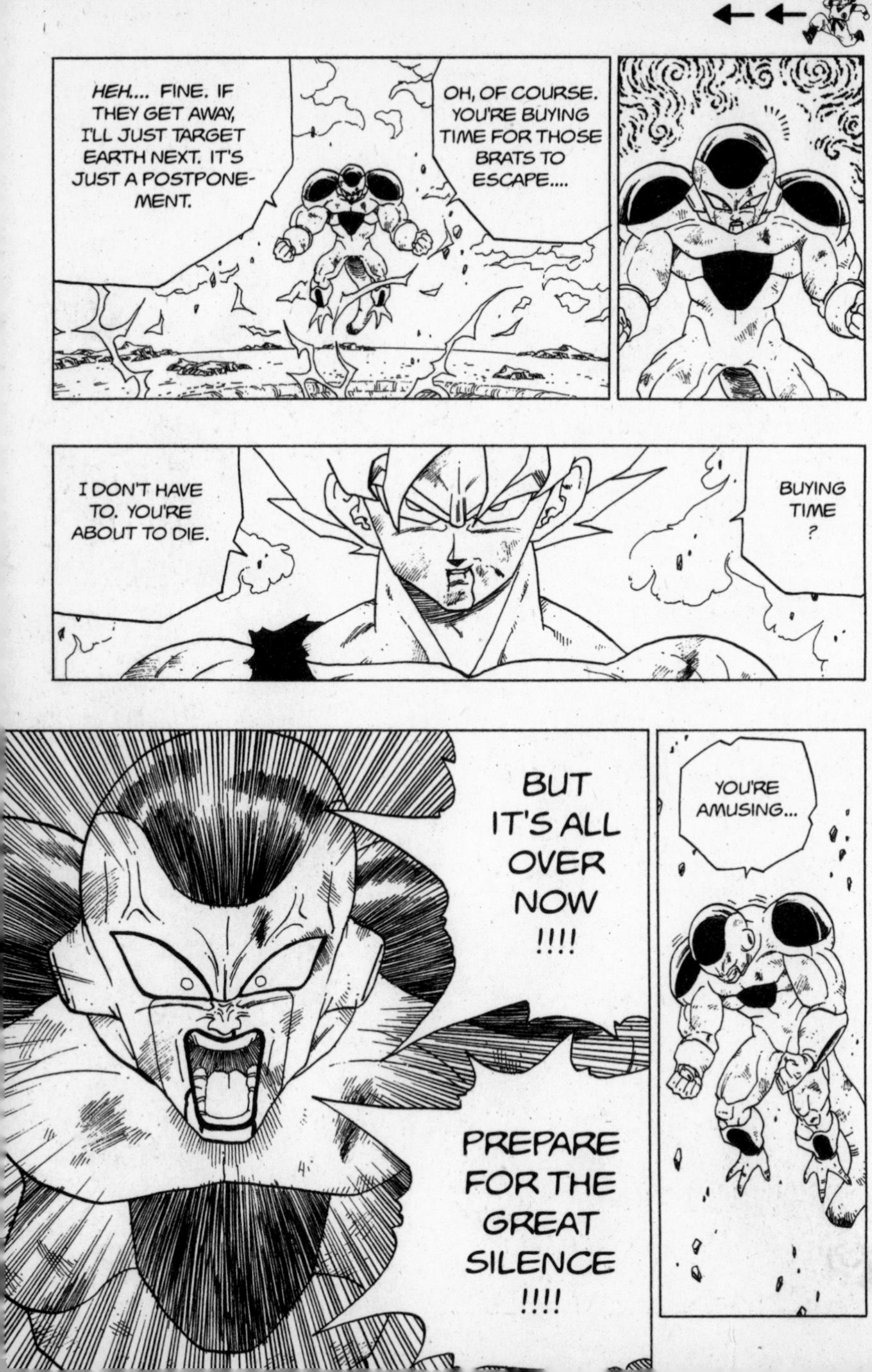
OH, OF COURSE. YOU'RE BUYING TIME FOR THOSE BRATS TO ESCAPE....
HEH.... FINE. IF THEY GET AWAY, I'LL JUST TARGET EARTH NEXT. IT'S JUST A POSTPONE-MENT.
BUYING TIME ?
I DON'T HAVE TO. YOU'RE ABOUT TO DIE.
YOU'RE AMUSING...
BUT IT'S ALL OVER NOW !!!!
PREPARE FOR THE GREAT SILENCE !!!!

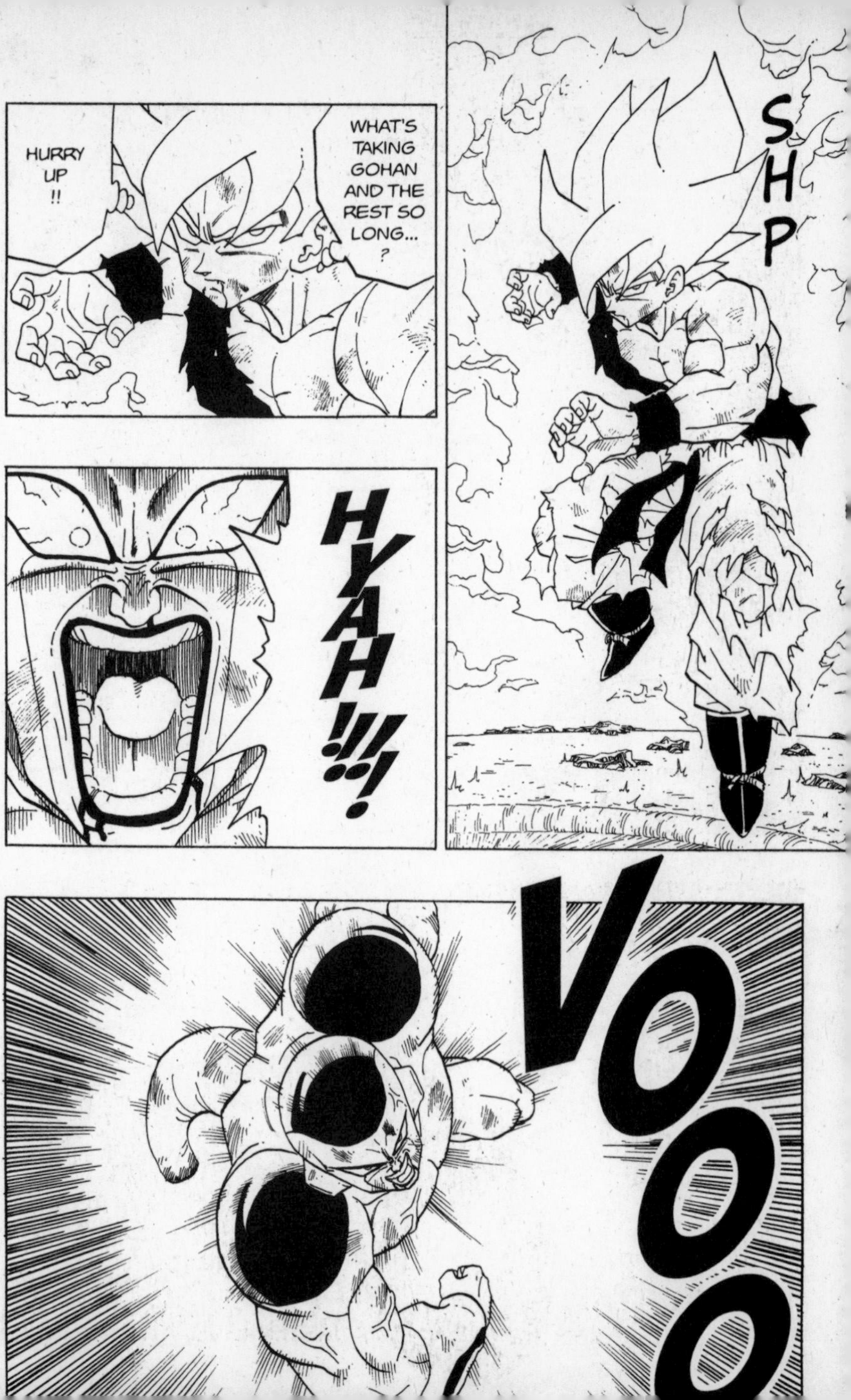
SHP
WHAT'S TAKING GOHAN AND THE REST SO LONG...?
HURRY UP!!
HYAH!!!!
VOOO

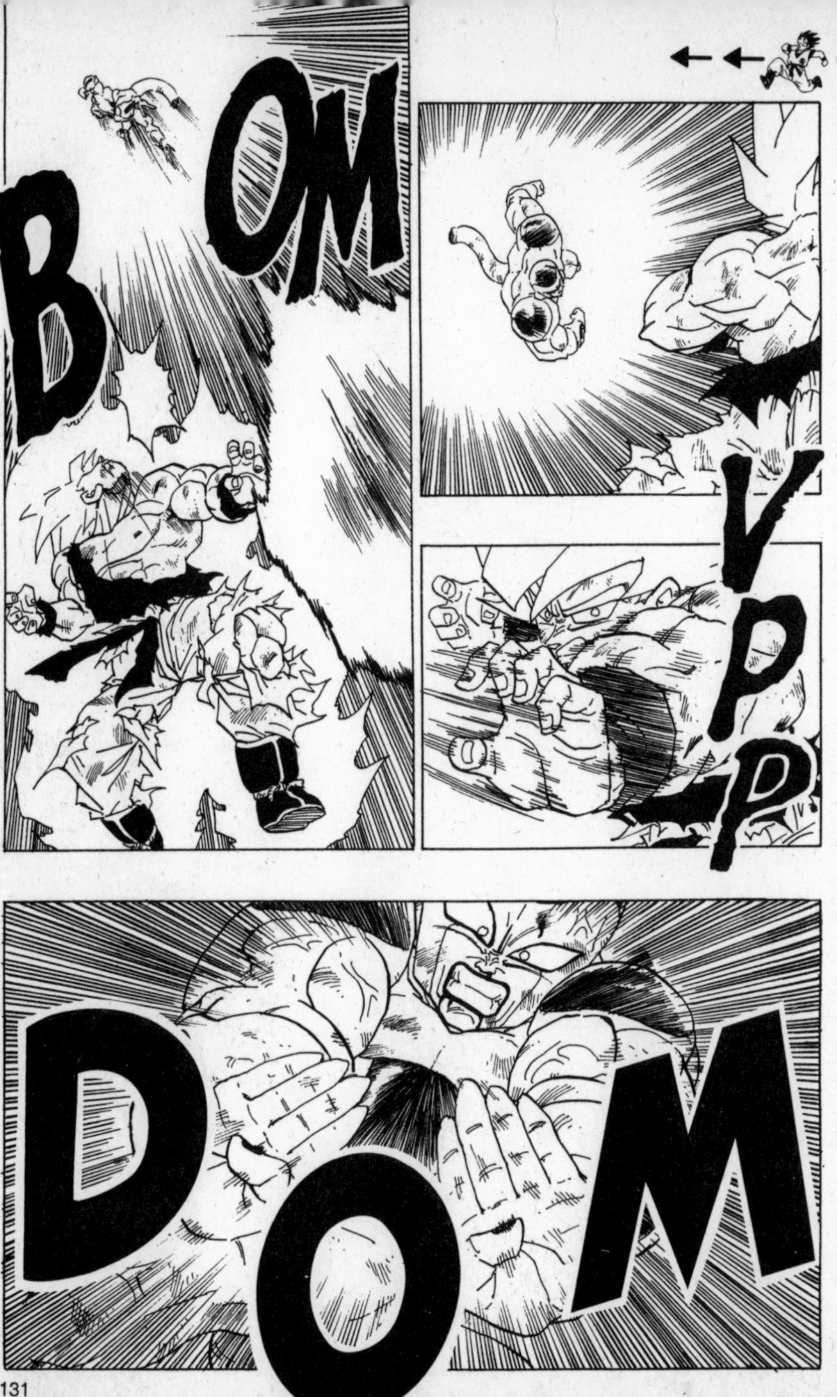
VPP
BOOM
DOM

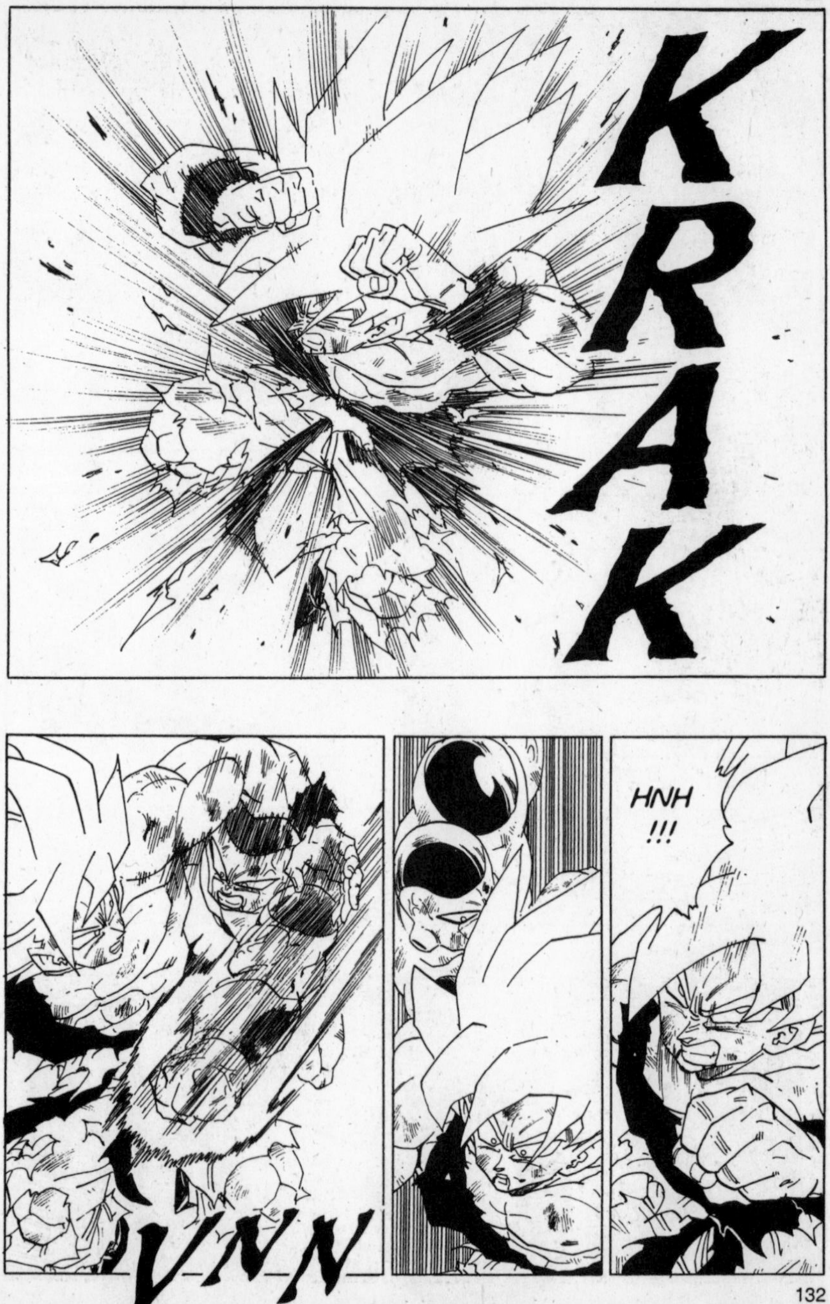
KRAK
HNH !!!
VNN

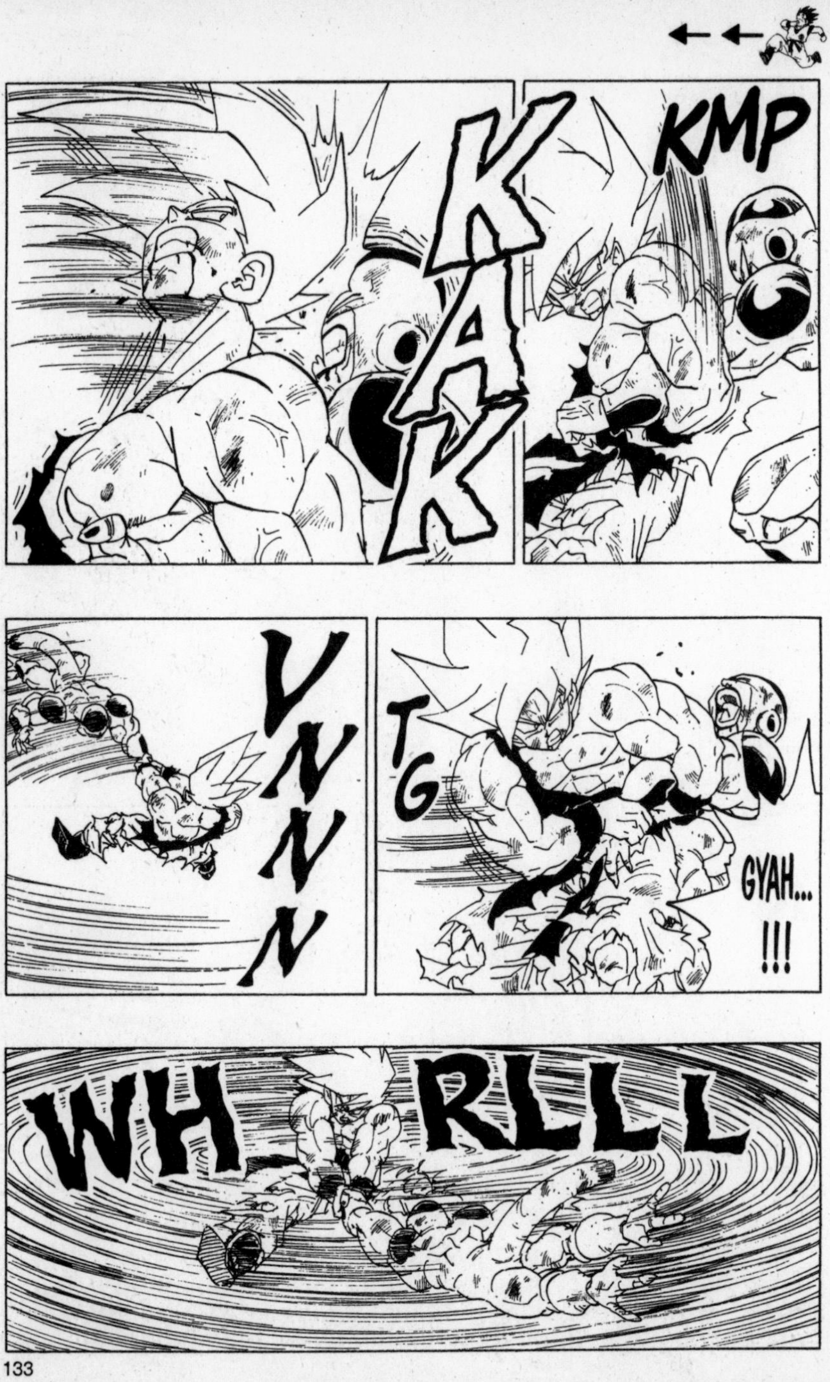
KMP
KAK
TG
GYAH... !!!
VNNN
WH RLLL

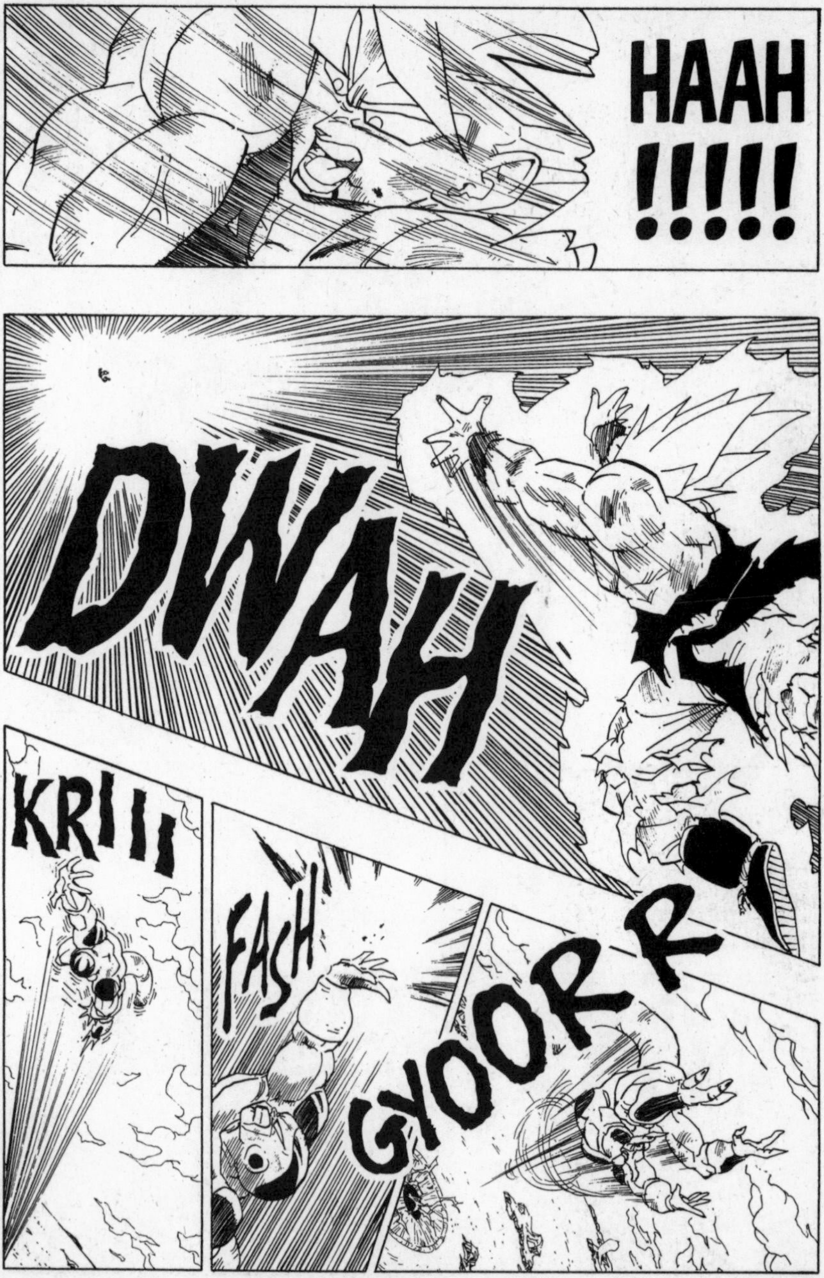
HAAH !!!!!
DWAH
GYOORR
FASH
KRIII

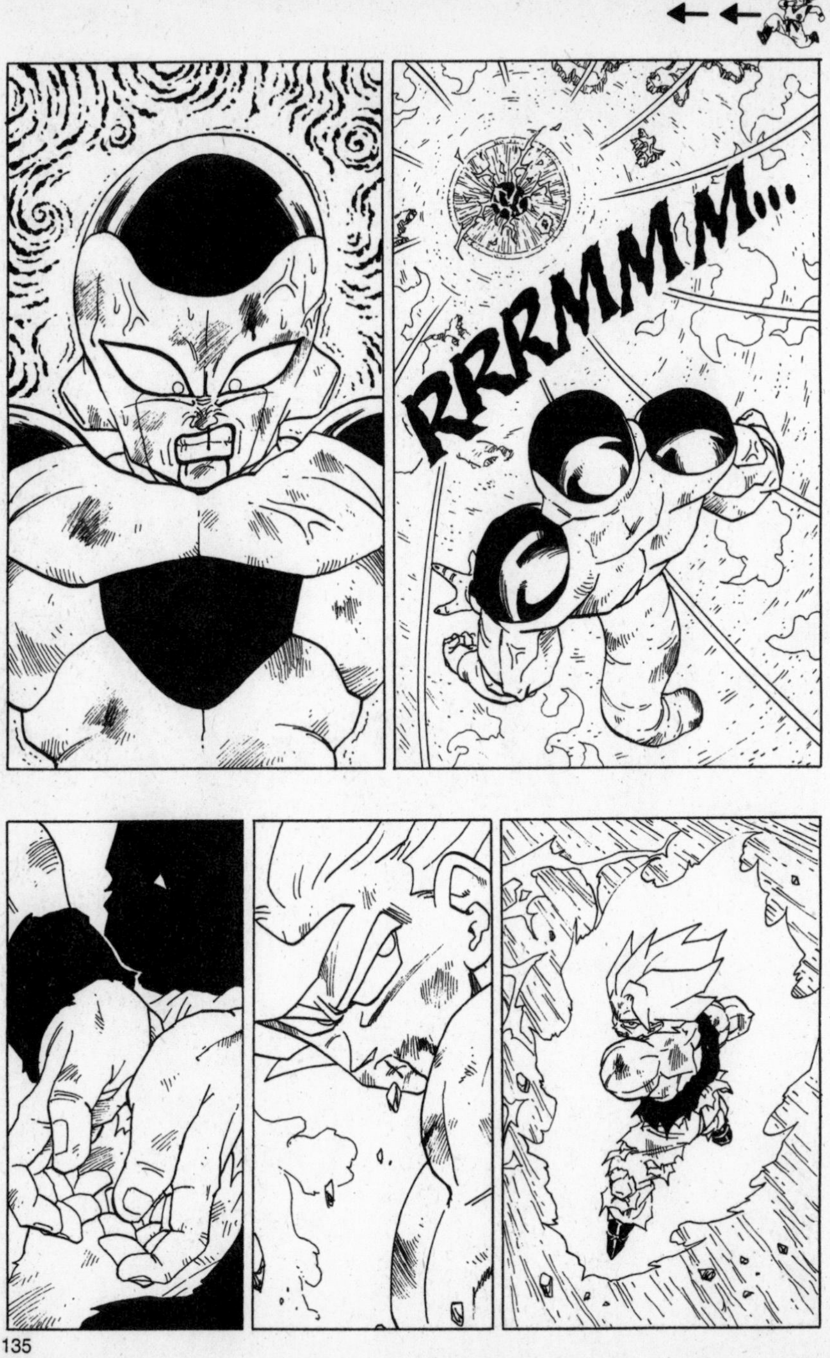
RRRMMM...

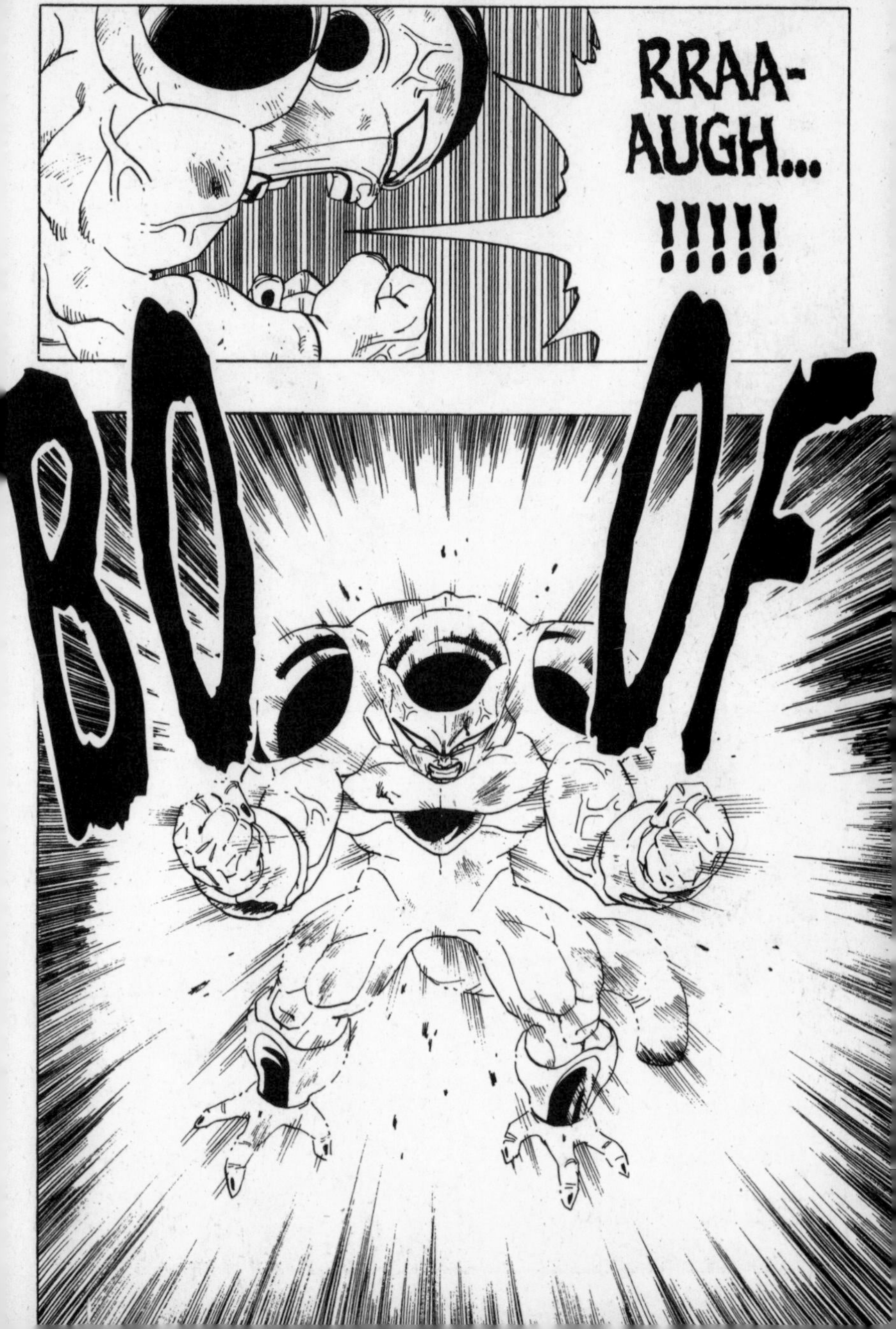
RRAA-
AUGH...
!!!!!
BOOF

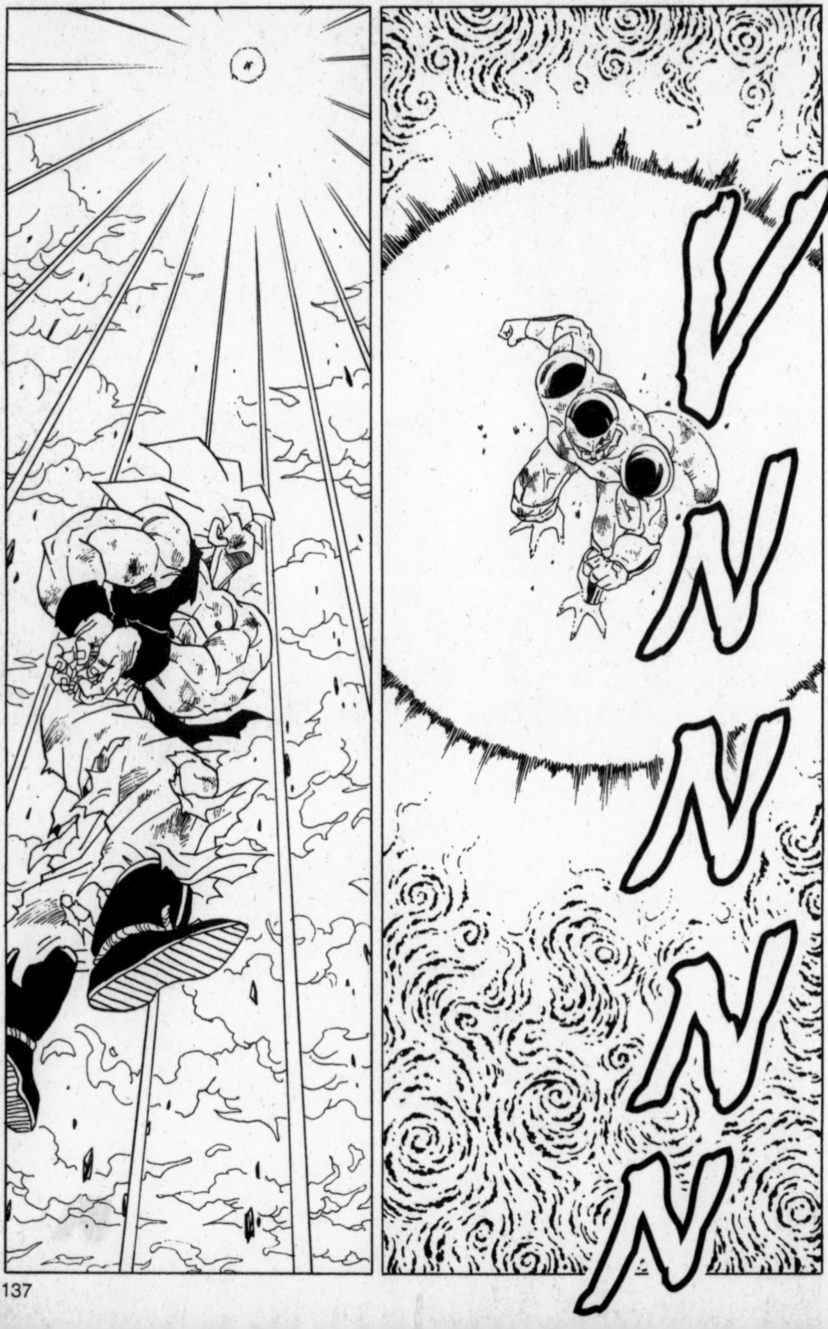
VNNNNN

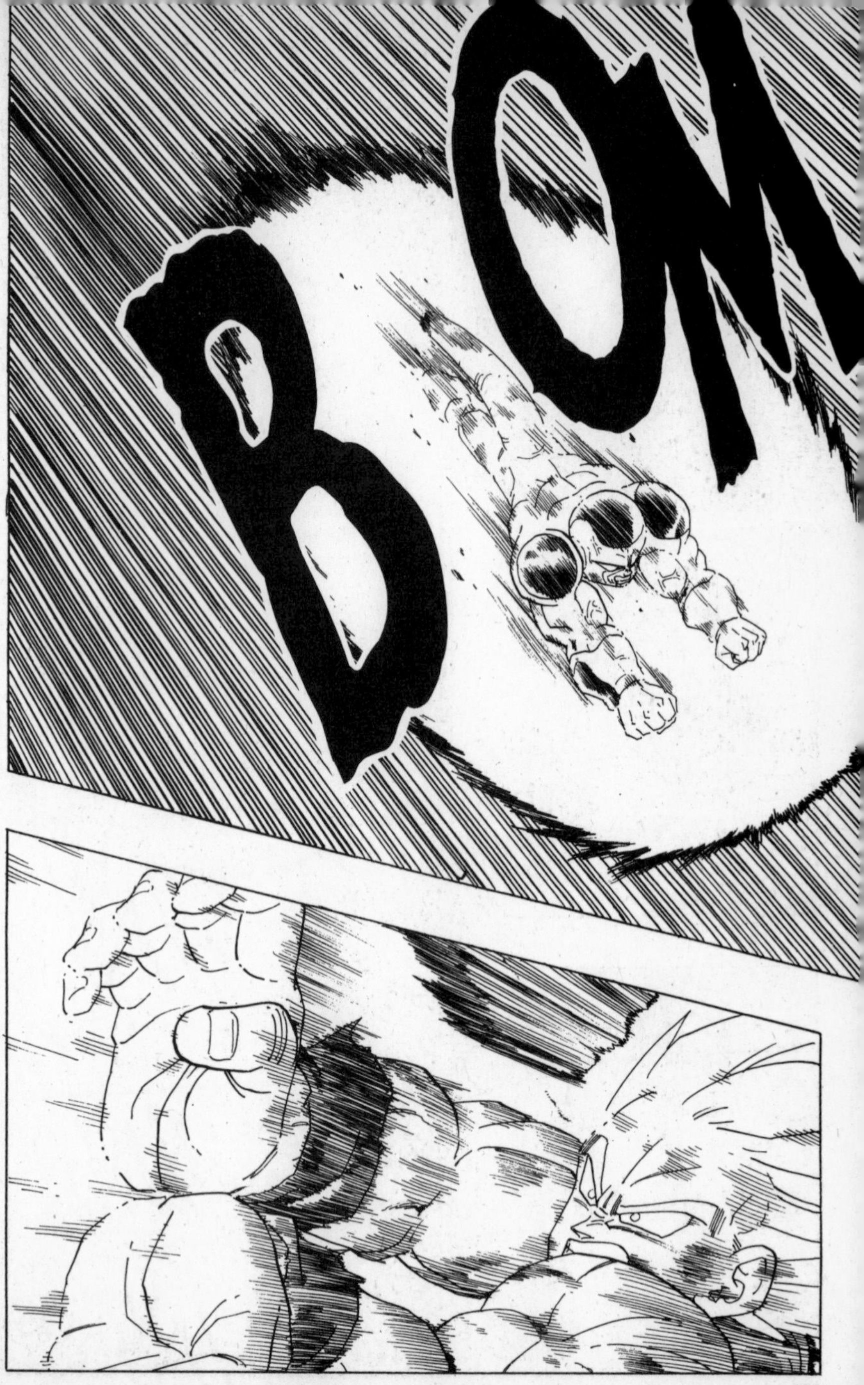
BOOM

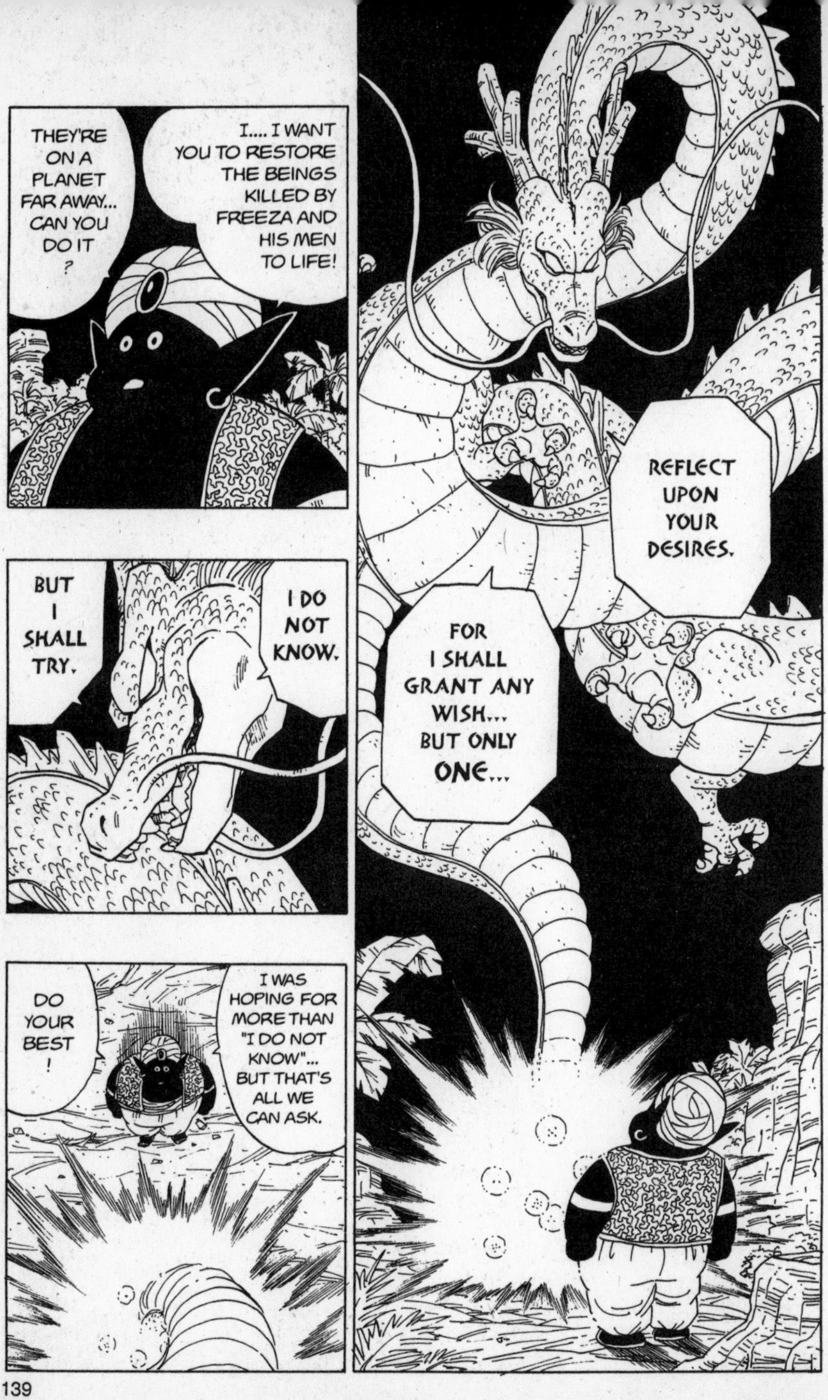
REFLECT UPON YOUR DESIRES.
FOR I SHALL GRANT ANY WISH... BUT ONLY ONE...
I.... I WANT YOU TO RESTORE THE BEINGS KILLED BY FREEZA AND HIS MEN TO LIFE!
THEY'RE ON A PLANET FAR AWAY... CAN YOU DO IT ?
I DO NOT KNOW.
BUT I SHALL TRY.
I WAS HOPING FOR MORE THAN "I DO NOT KNOW"... BUT THAT'S ALL WE CAN ASK.
DO YOUR BEST !

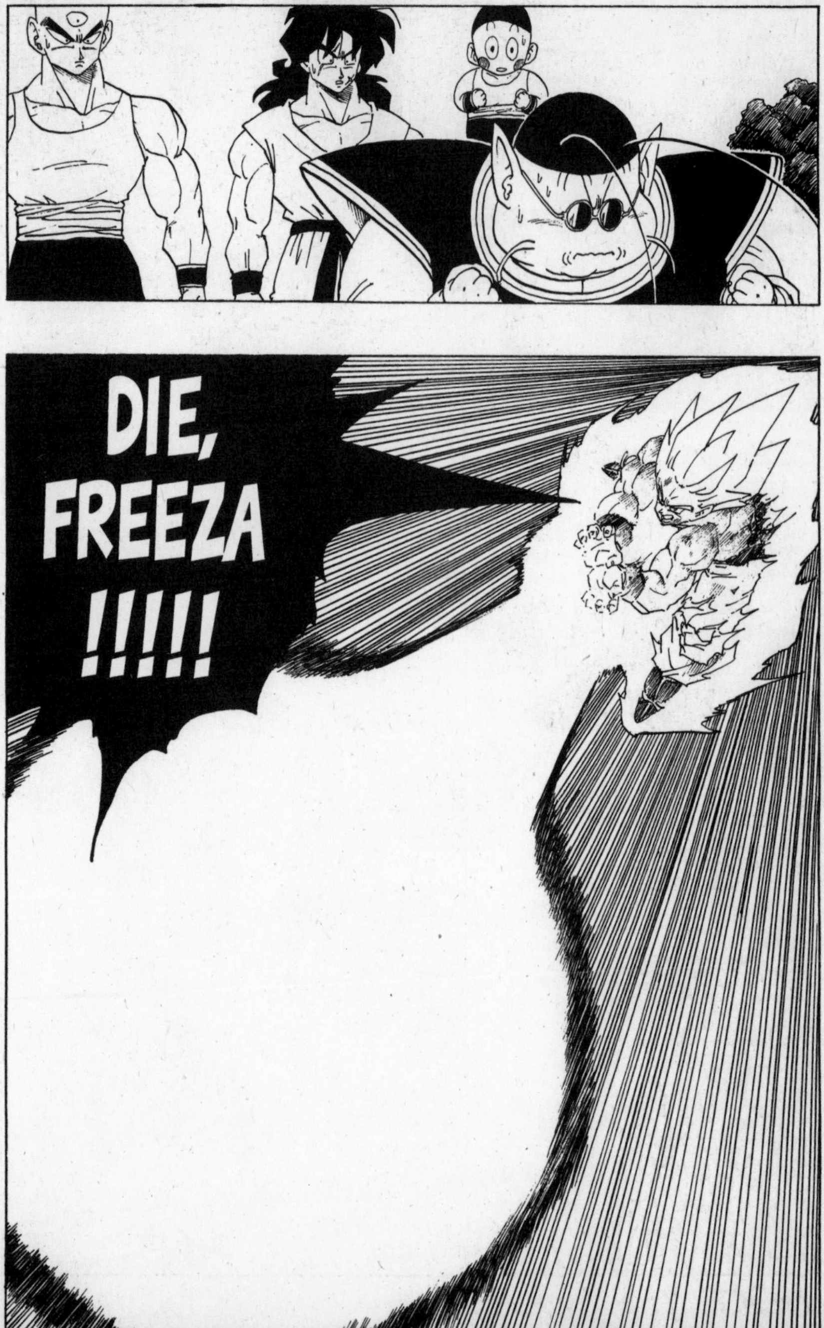
DIE, FREEZA !!!!!

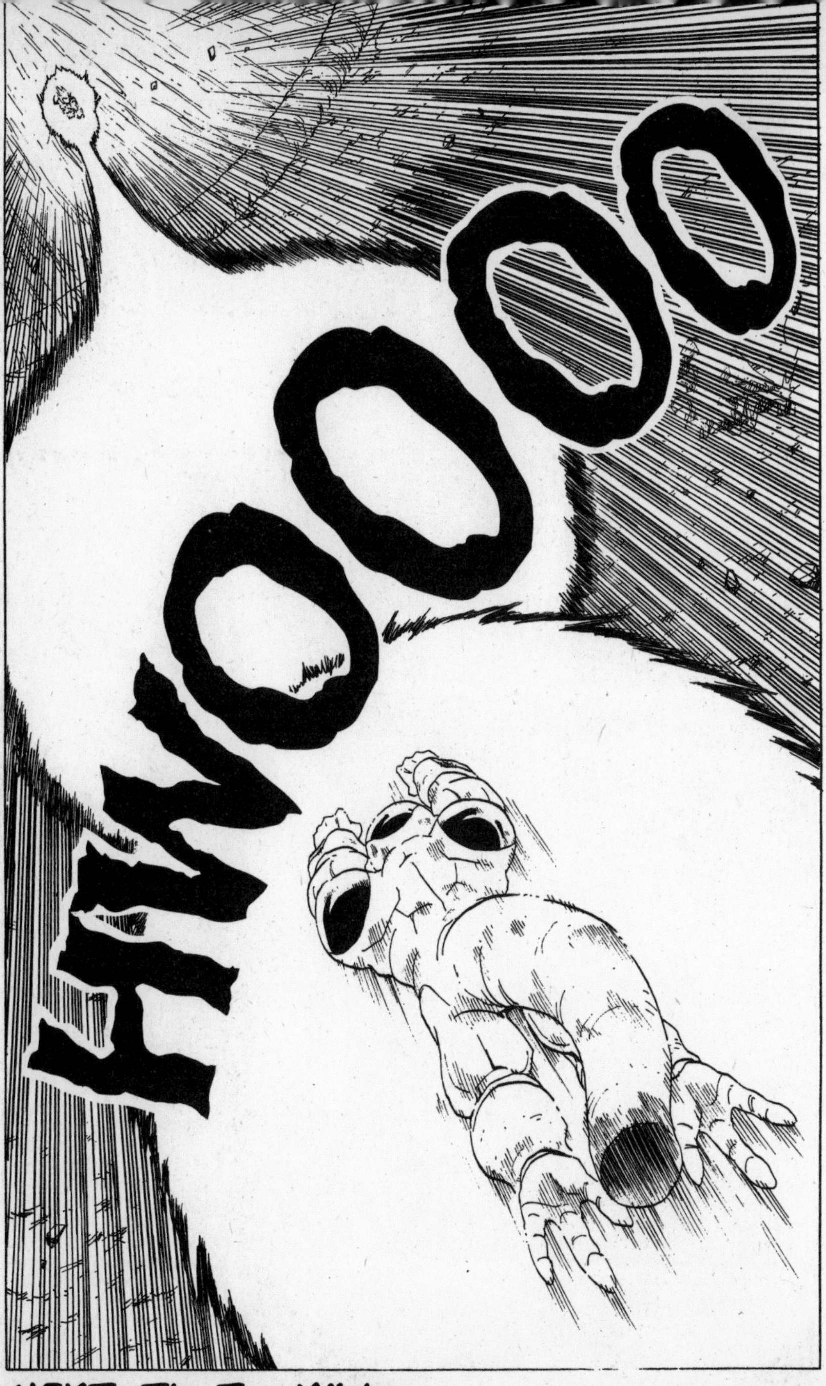
HWOOOOO

NEXT: The Two Wishes

DBZ:129 • The Two Wishes

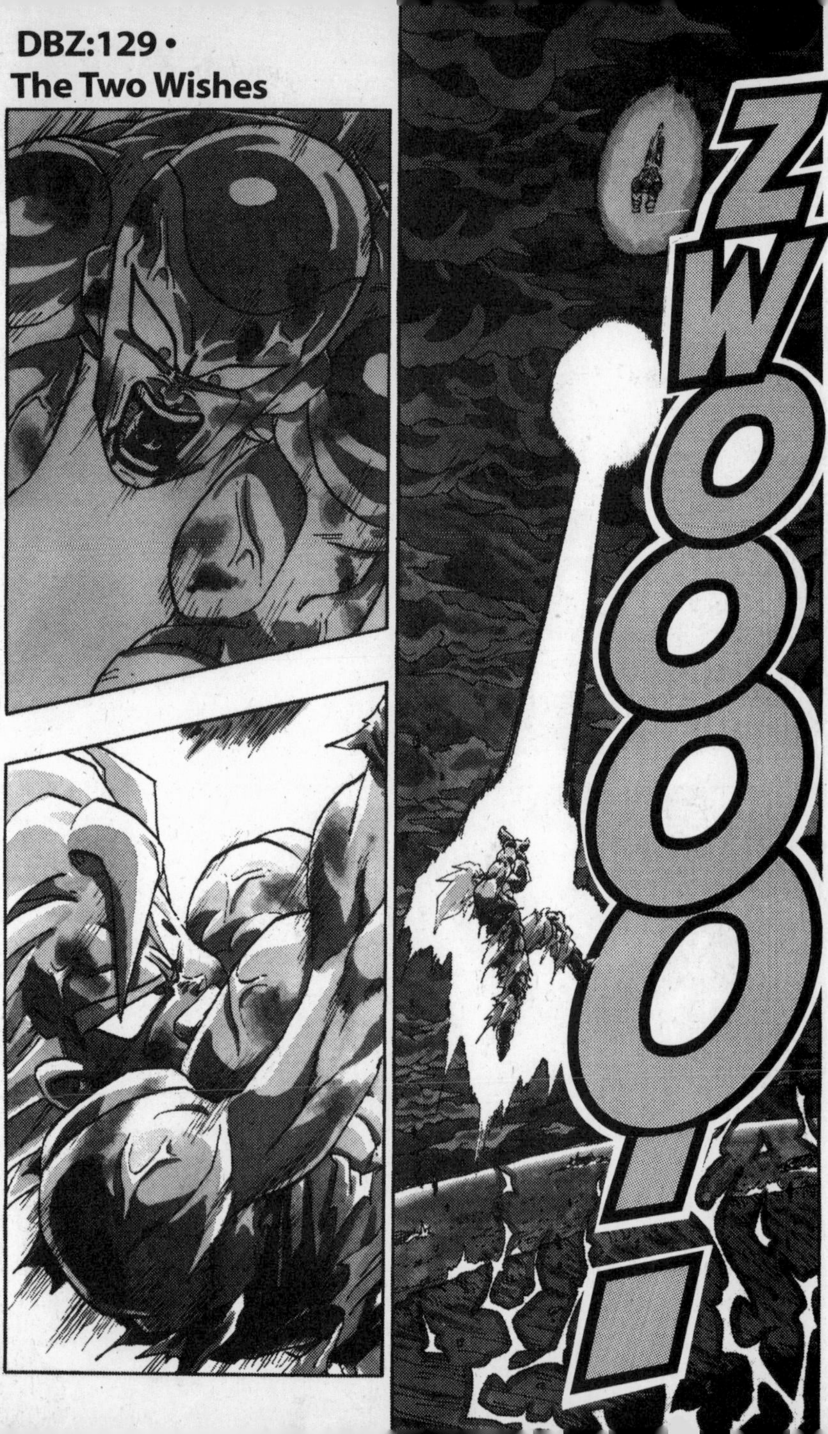
ZWOOOOO!!

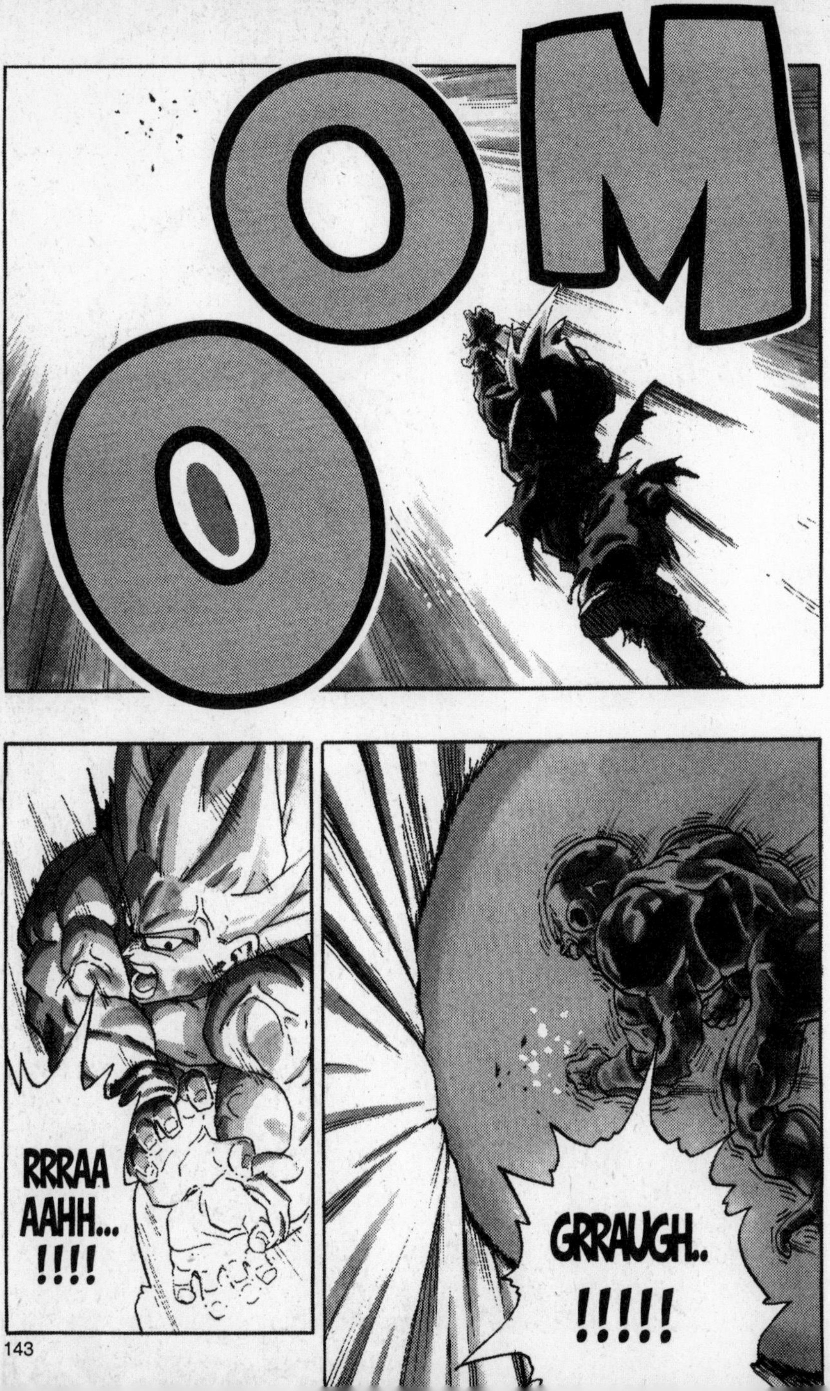
OOM
GRRAUGH..
!!!!!
RRRAA
AAHH...
!!!!

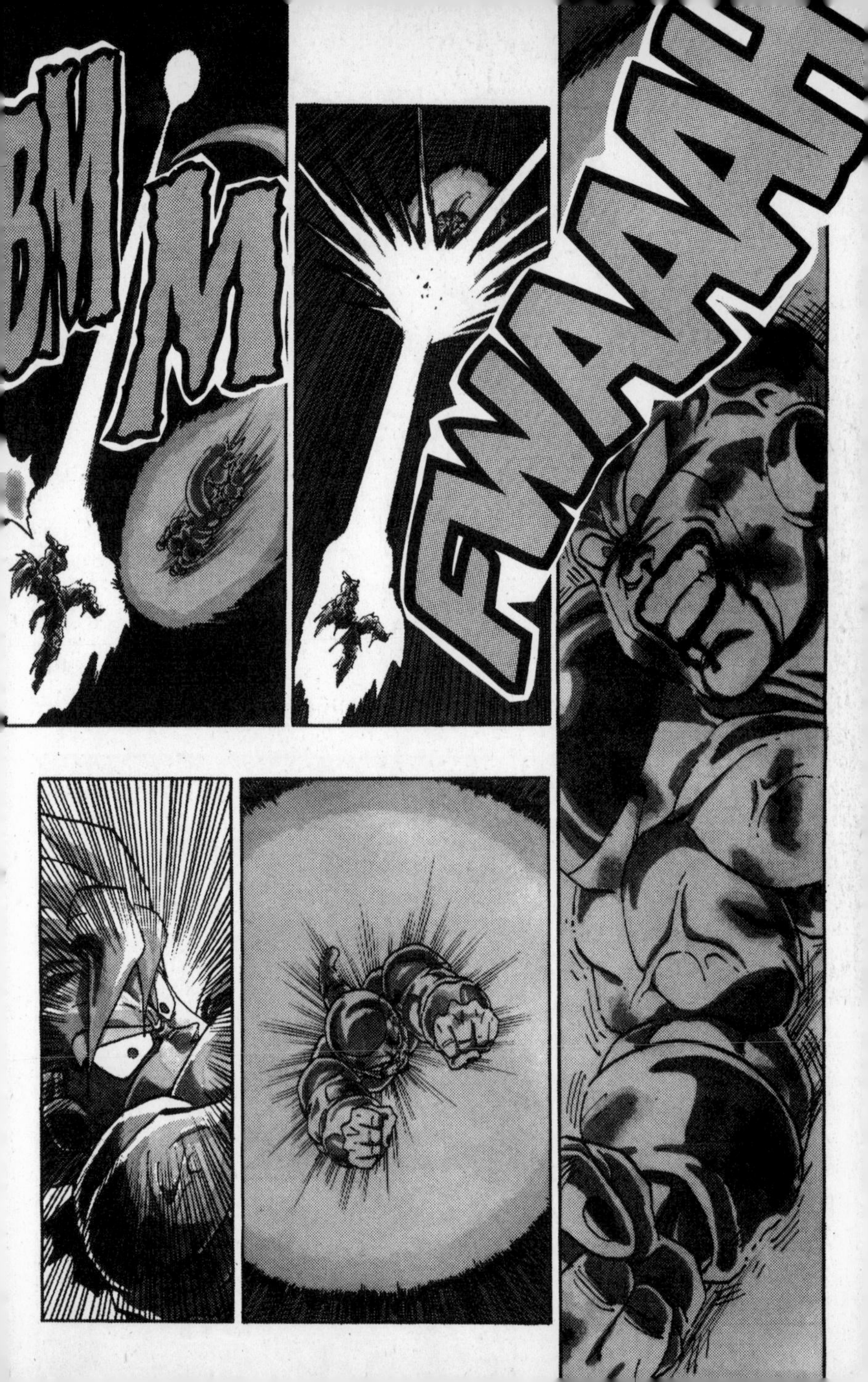
FWAAAH
BMM

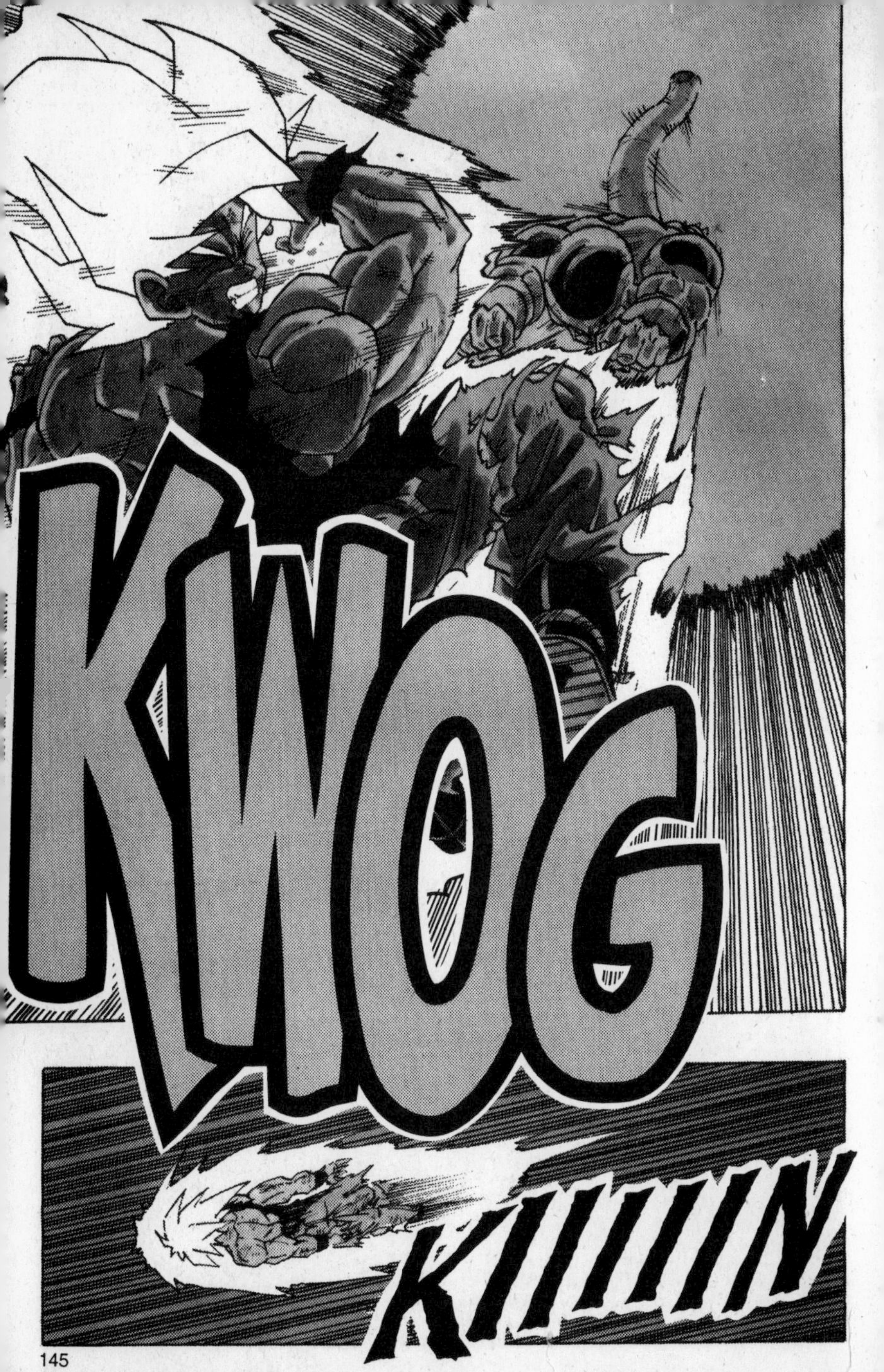
KWOG
KIIIIIN

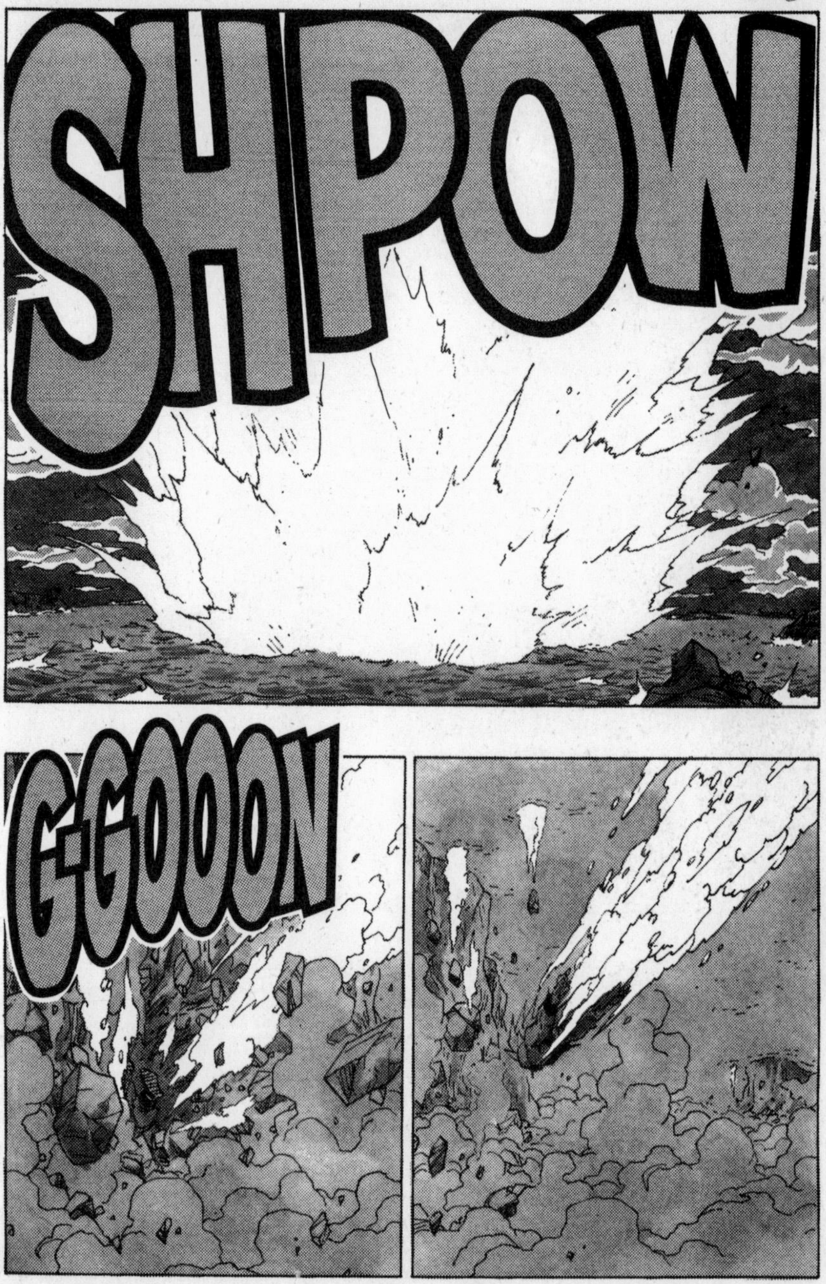
SHPOW
G-GOOON

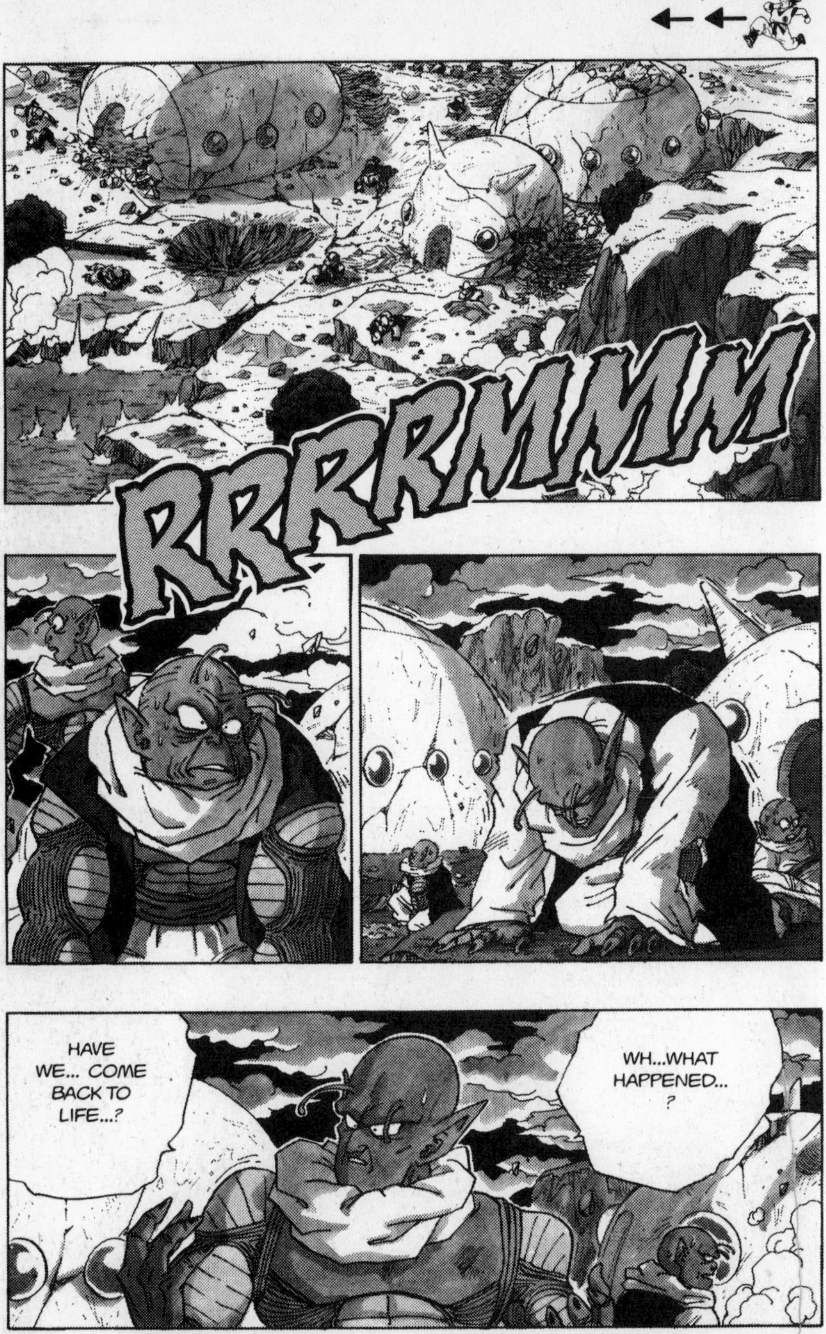
RRRRMMMM
WH...WHAT HAPPENED... ?
HAVE WE... COME BACK TO LIFE...?

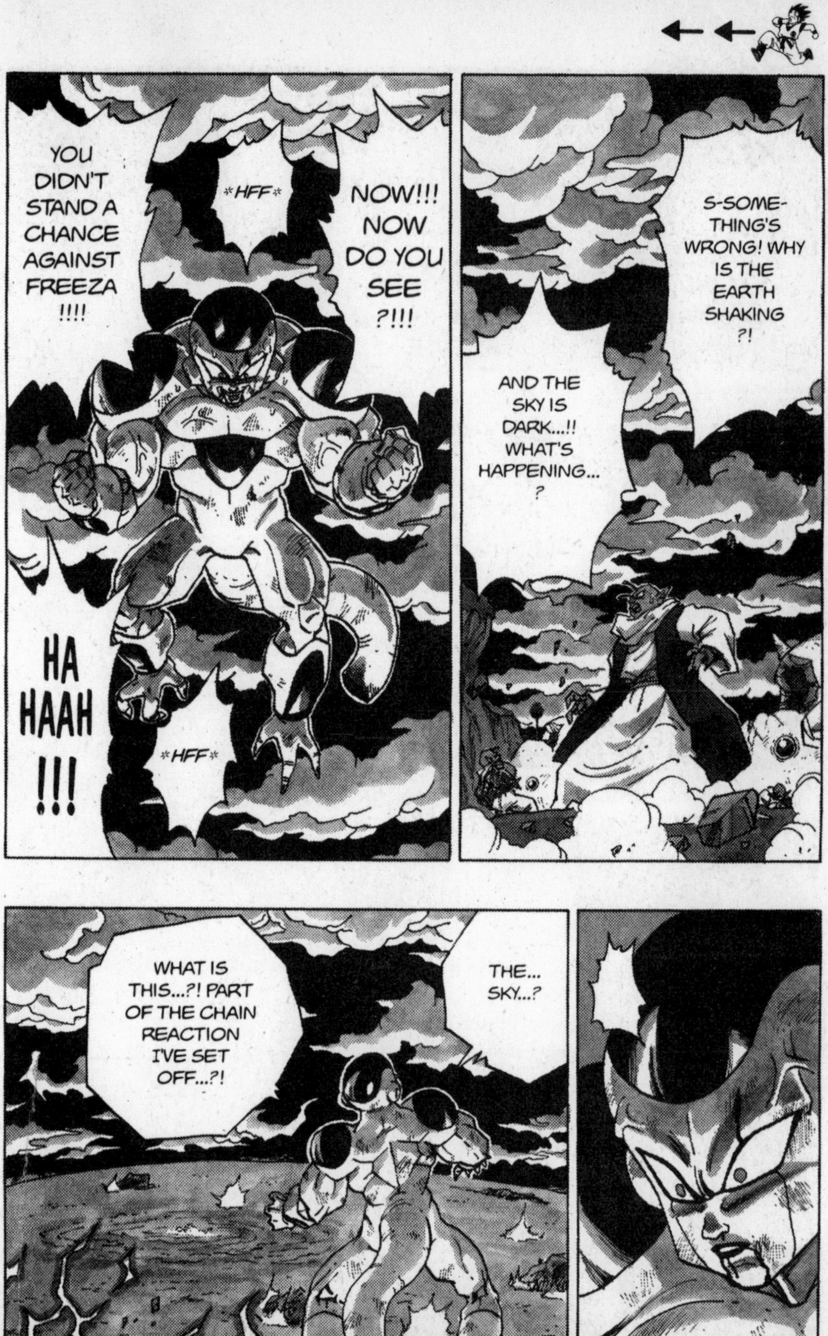
S-SOME-THING'S WRONG! WHY IS THE EARTH SHAKING ?!
AND THE SKY IS DARK...!! WHAT'S HAPPENING... ?
NOW!!! NOW DO YOU SEE ?!!!
HFF
YOU DIDN'T STAND A CHANCE AGAINST FREEZA !!!!
HA HAAH !!!
HFF
THE... SKY...?
WHAT IS THIS...?! PART OF THE CHAIN REACTION I'VE SET OFF...?!

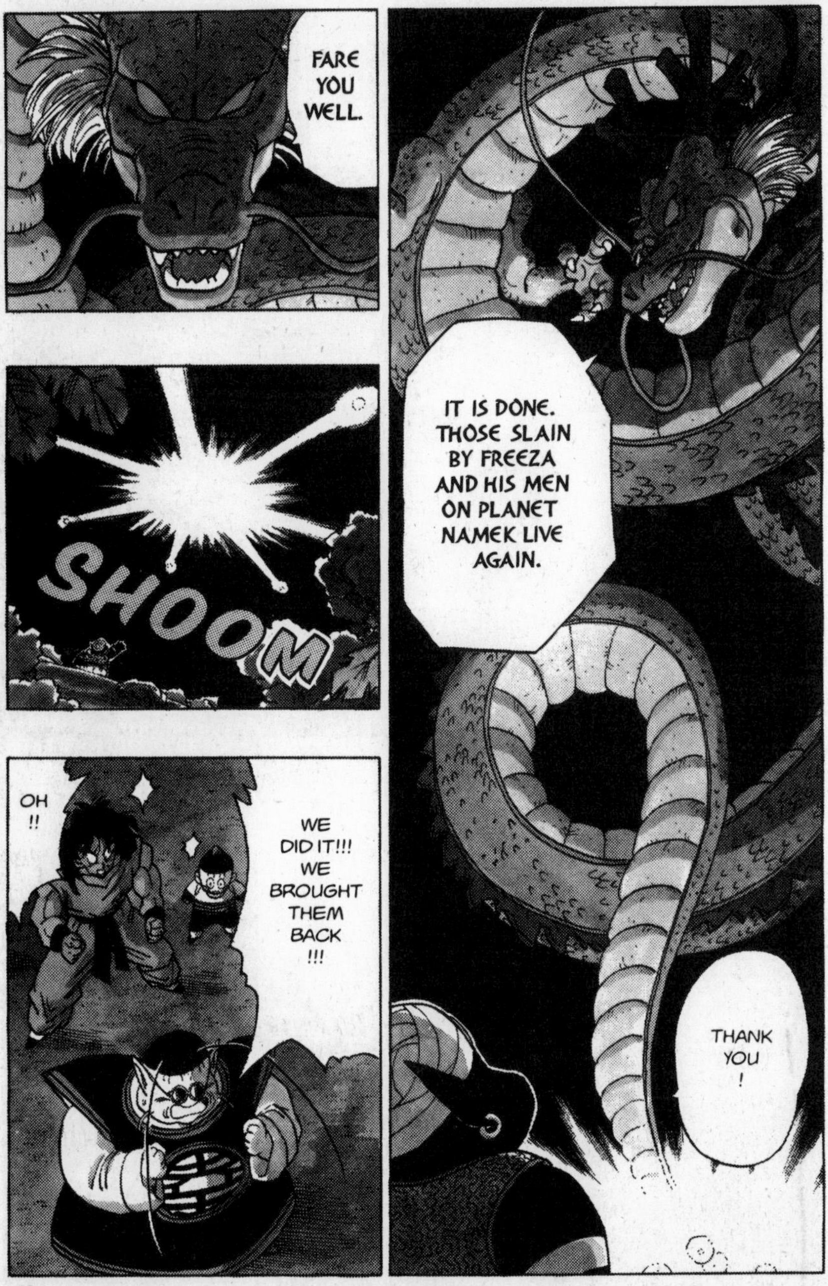
IT IS DONE. THOSE SLAIN BY FREEZA AND HIS MEN ON PLANET NAMEK LIVE AGAIN.
THANK YOU !
FARE YOU WELL.
SHOOM
WE DID IT!!! WE BROUGHT THEM BACK !!!
OH !!

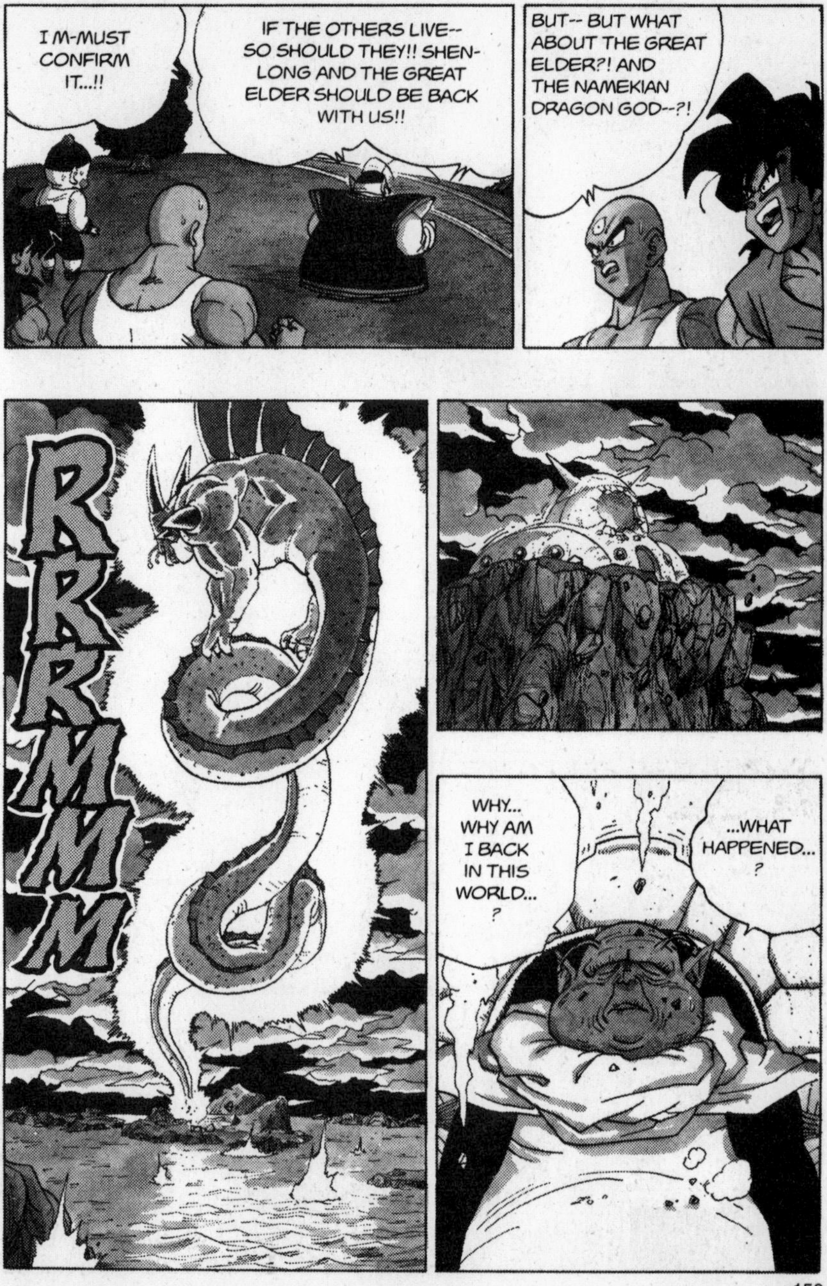
BUT-- BUT WHAT ABOUT THE GREAT ELDER?! AND THE NAMEKIAN DRAGON GOD--?!
IF THE OTHERS LIVE-- SO SHOULD THEY!! SHEN-LONG AND THE GREAT ELDER SHOULD BE BACK WITH US!!
I M-MUST CONFIRM IT...!!
...WHAT HAPPENED...?
WHY... WHY AM I BACK IN THIS WORLD...?
RRRMMM

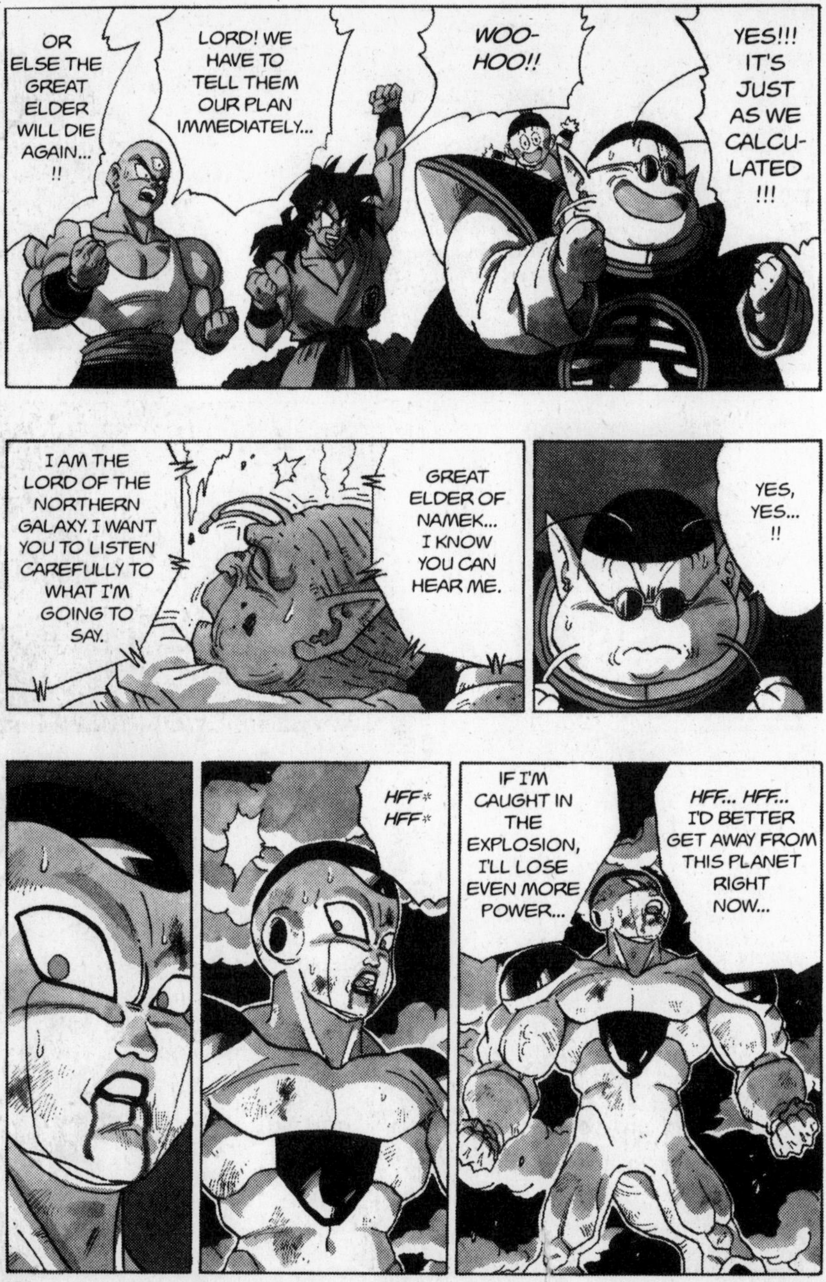

YES!!! IT'S JUST AS WE CALCULATED !!!
WOO-HOO!!
LORD! WE HAVE TO TELL THEM OUR PLAN IMMEDIATELY...
OR ELSE THE GREAT ELDER WILL DIE AGAIN... !!
YES, YES... !!
GREAT ELDER OF NAMEK... I KNOW YOU CAN HEAR ME.
I AM THE LORD OF THE NORTHERN GALAXY. I WANT YOU TO LISTEN CAREFULLY TO WHAT I'M GOING TO SAY.
HFF... HFF... I'D BETTER GET AWAY FROM THIS PLANET RIGHT NOW...
IF I'M CAUGHT IN THE EXPLOSION, I'LL LOSE EVEN MORE POWER...
HFF* HFF*

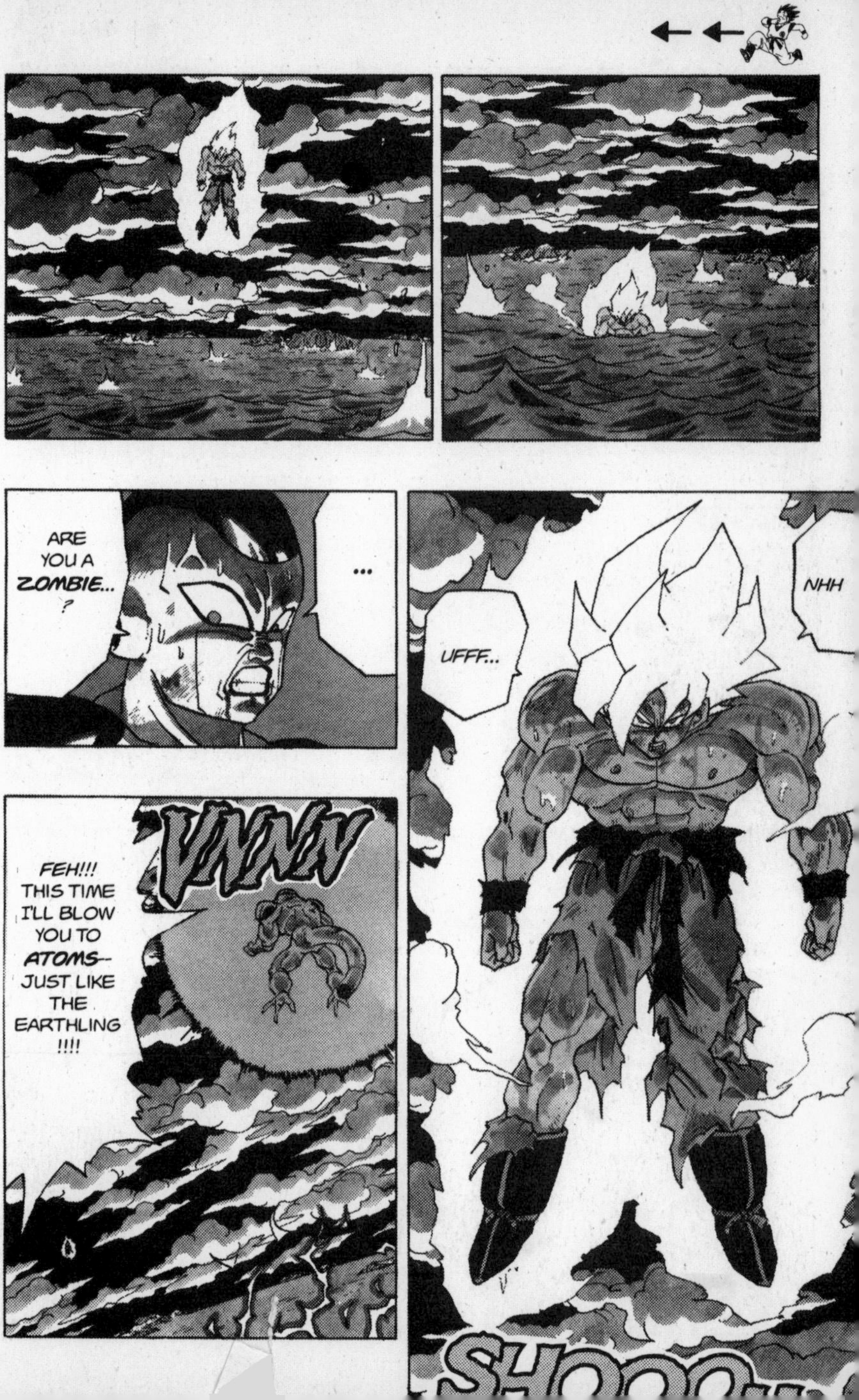
NHH
UFFF...
SHOOO...
...
ARE YOU A ZOMBIE...?
VNNN
FEH!!! THIS TIME I'LL BLOW YOU TO ATOMS-- JUST LIKE THE EARTHLING !!!!

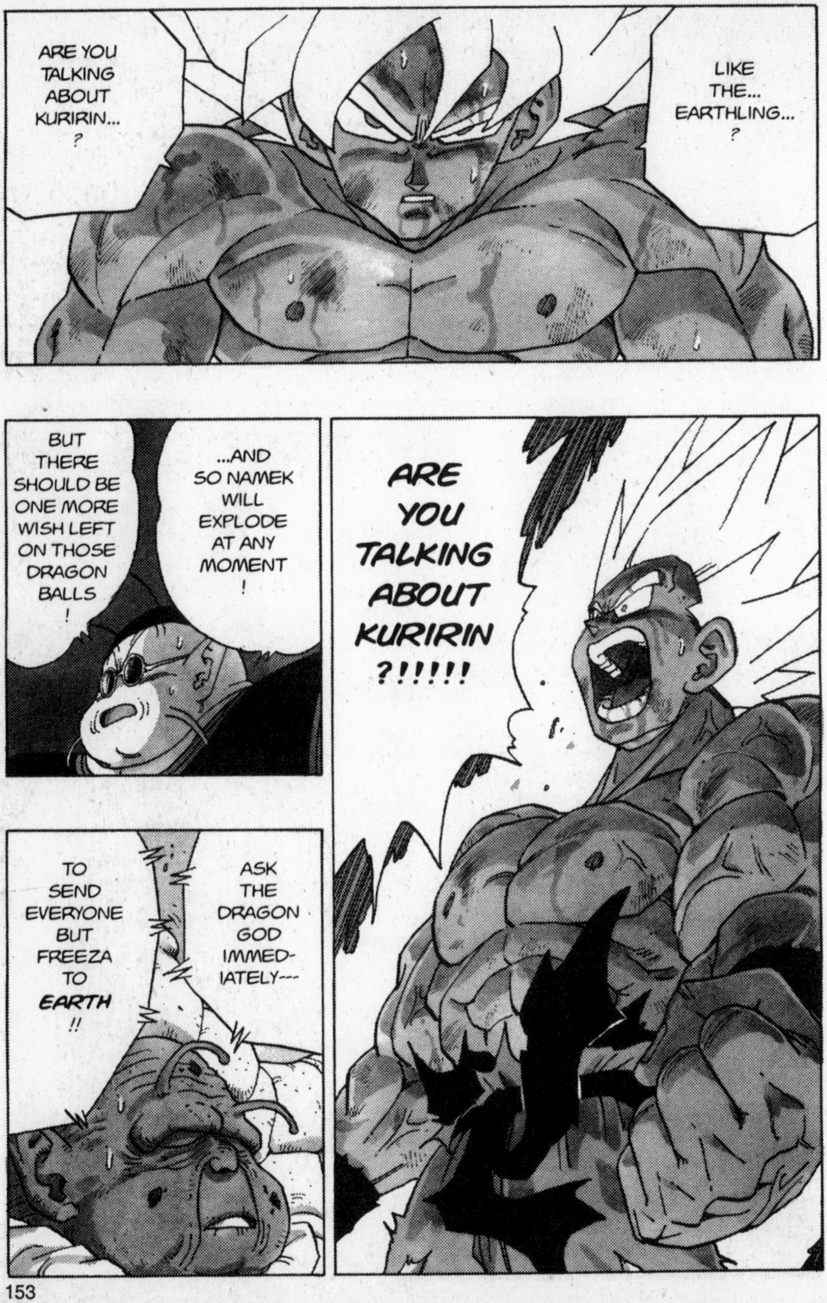
LIKE THE... EARTHLING... ?
ARE YOU TALKING ABOUT KURIRIN... ?
ARE YOU TALKING ABOUT KURIRIN ?!!!!!
...AND SO NAMEK WILL EXPLODE AT ANY MOMENT !
BUT THERE SHOULD BE ONE MORE WISH LEFT ON THOSE DRAGON BALLS !
ASK THE DRAGON GOD IMMED-IATELY---
TO SEND EVERYONE BUT FREEZA TO EARTH !!

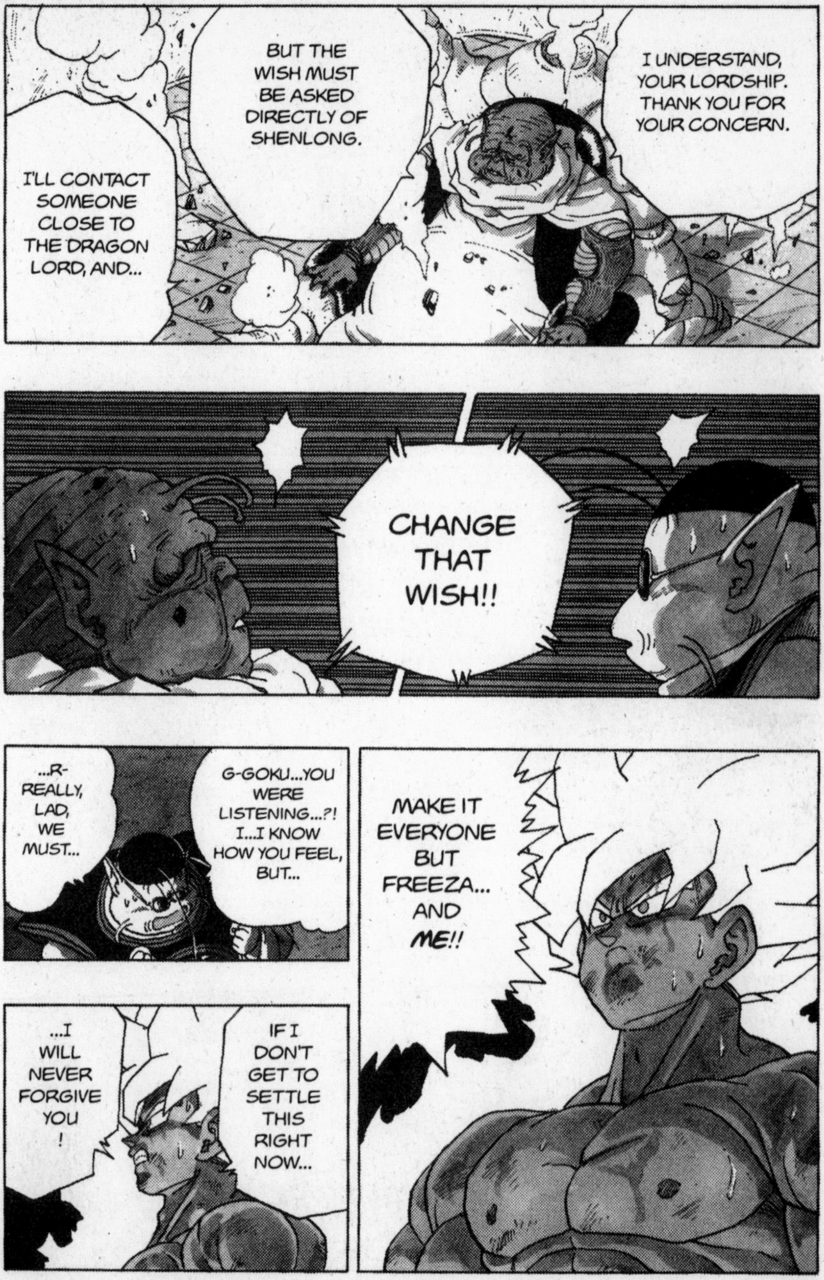
I UNDERSTAND, YOUR LORDSHIP. THANK YOU FOR YOUR CONCERN.
BUT THE WISH MUST BE ASKED DIRECTLY OF SHENLONG.
I'LL CONTACT SOMEONE CLOSE TO THE DRAGON LORD, AND...
CHANGE THAT WISH!!
MAKE IT EVERYONE BUT FREEZA... AND *ME*!!
G-GOKU...YOU WERE LISTENING...?! I...I KNOW HOW YOU FEEL, BUT...
...R-REALLY, LAD, WE MUST...
IF I DON'T GET TO SETTLE THIS RIGHT NOW...
...I WILL NEVER FORGIVE YOU!

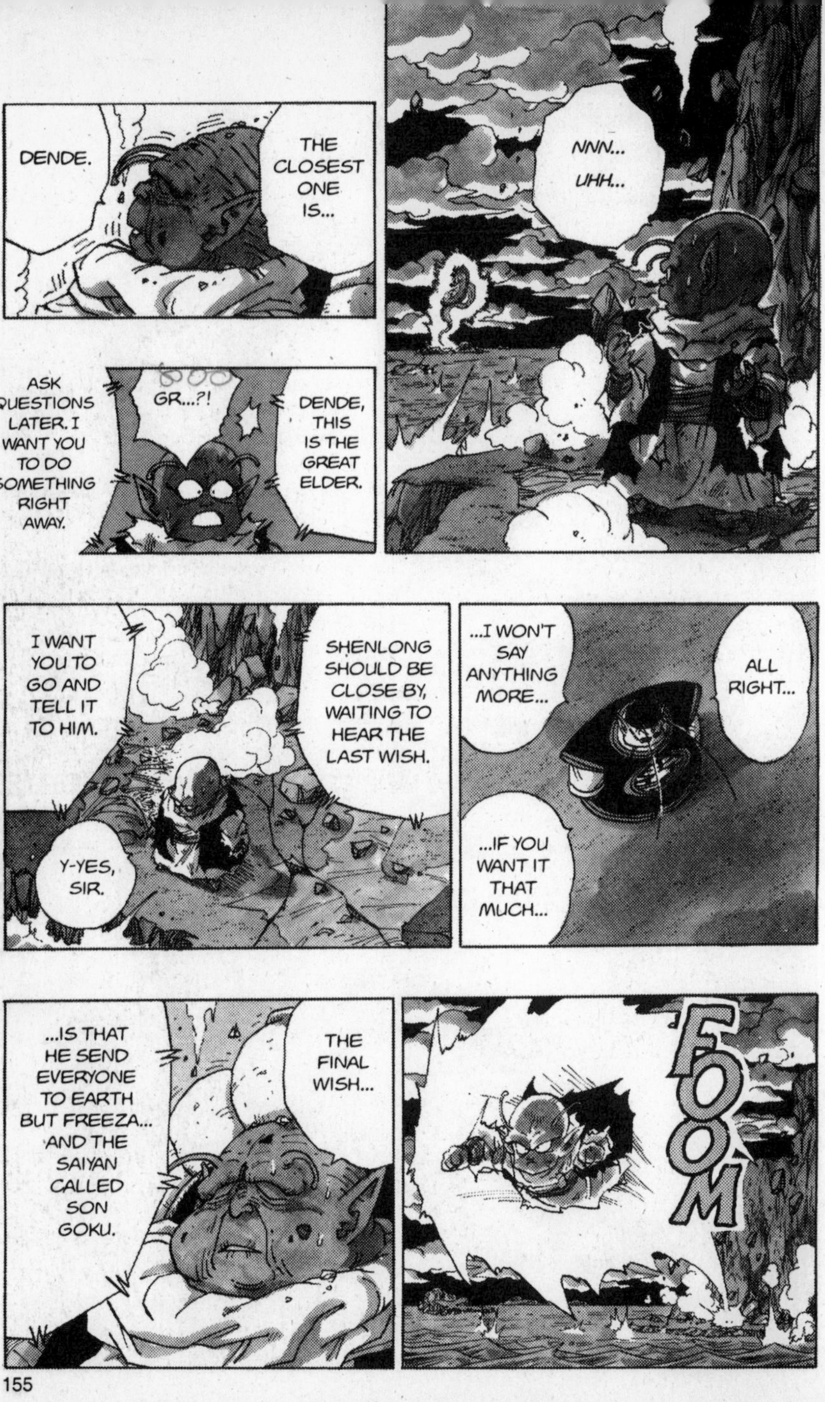
NNN...
UHH...
THE CLOSEST ONE IS...
DENDE.
DENDE, THIS IS THE GREAT ELDER.
GR...?!
ASK QUESTIONS LATER. I WANT YOU TO DO SOMETHING RIGHT AWAY.
ALL RIGHT...
...I WON'T SAY ANYTHING MORE...
...IF YOU WANT IT THAT MUCH...
SHENLONG SHOULD BE CLOSE BY, WAITING TO HEAR THE LAST WISH.
I WANT YOU TO GO AND TELL IT TO HIM.
Y-YES, SIR.
FOOM
THE FINAL WISH...
...IS THAT HE SEND EVERYONE TO EARTH BUT FREEZA... AND THE SAIYAN CALLED SON GOKU.

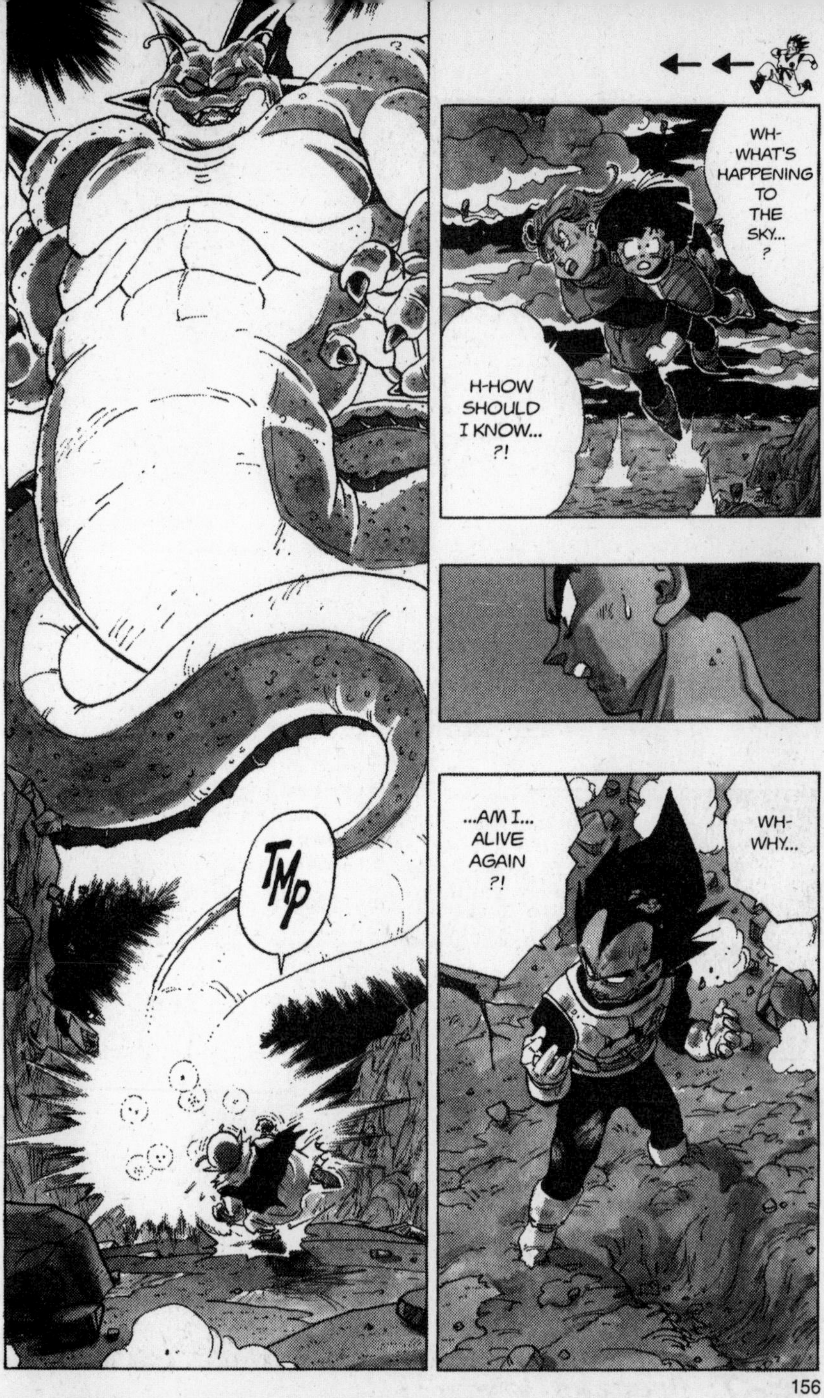
WH- WHAT'S HAPPENING TO THE SKY... ?
H-HOW SHOULD I KNOW... ?!
WH- WHY...
...AM I... ALIVE AGAIN ?!
TMP

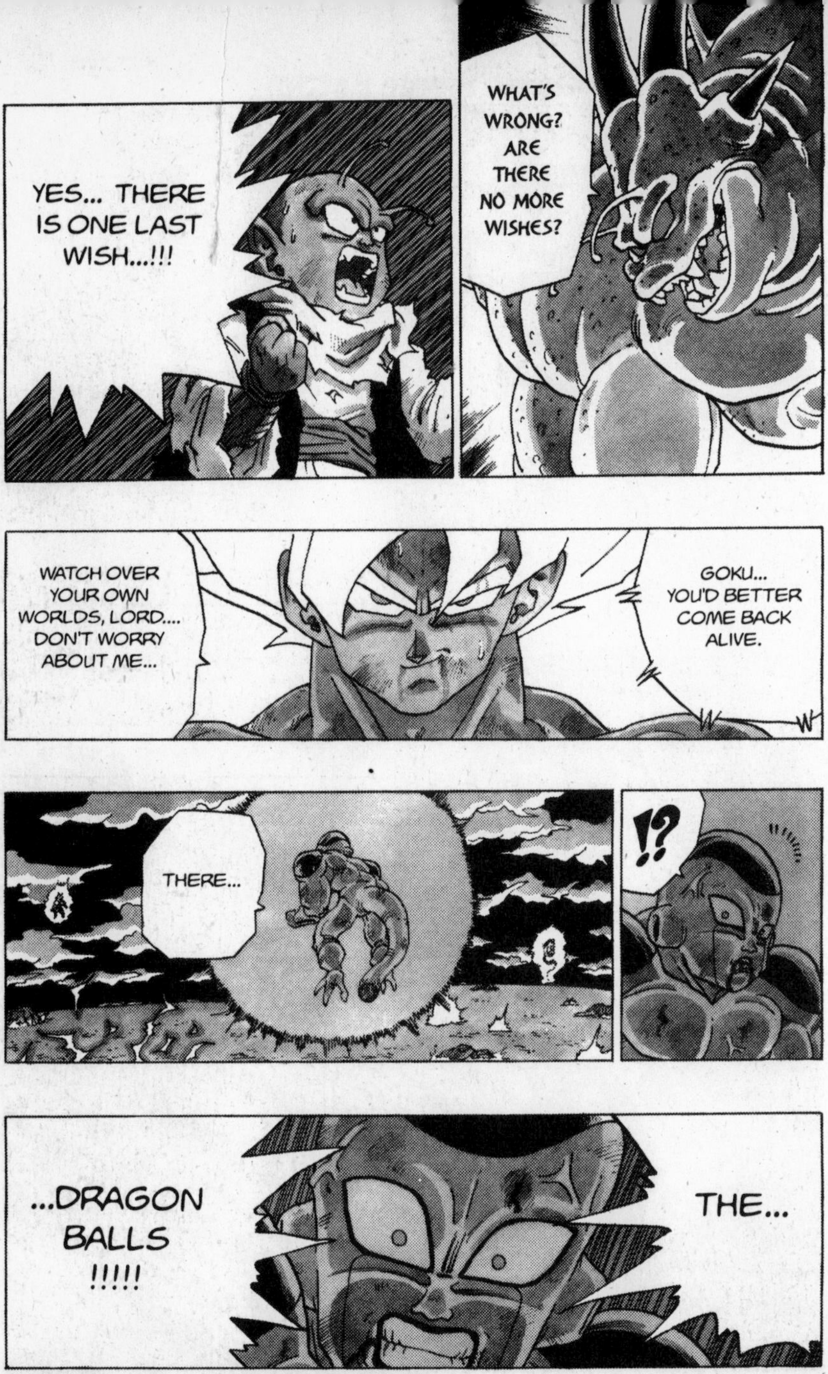
WHAT'S WRONG? ARE THERE NO MORE WISHES?
YES... THERE IS ONE LAST WISH...!!!
GOKU... YOU'D BETTER COME BACK ALIVE.
WATCH OVER YOUR OWN WORLDS, LORD.... DON'T WORRY ABOUT ME...
!?
THERE...
THE...
...DRAGON BALLS !!!!!

NEXT: Freeza's Wish???

DBZ:130 • The Quiet, Fierce Battle

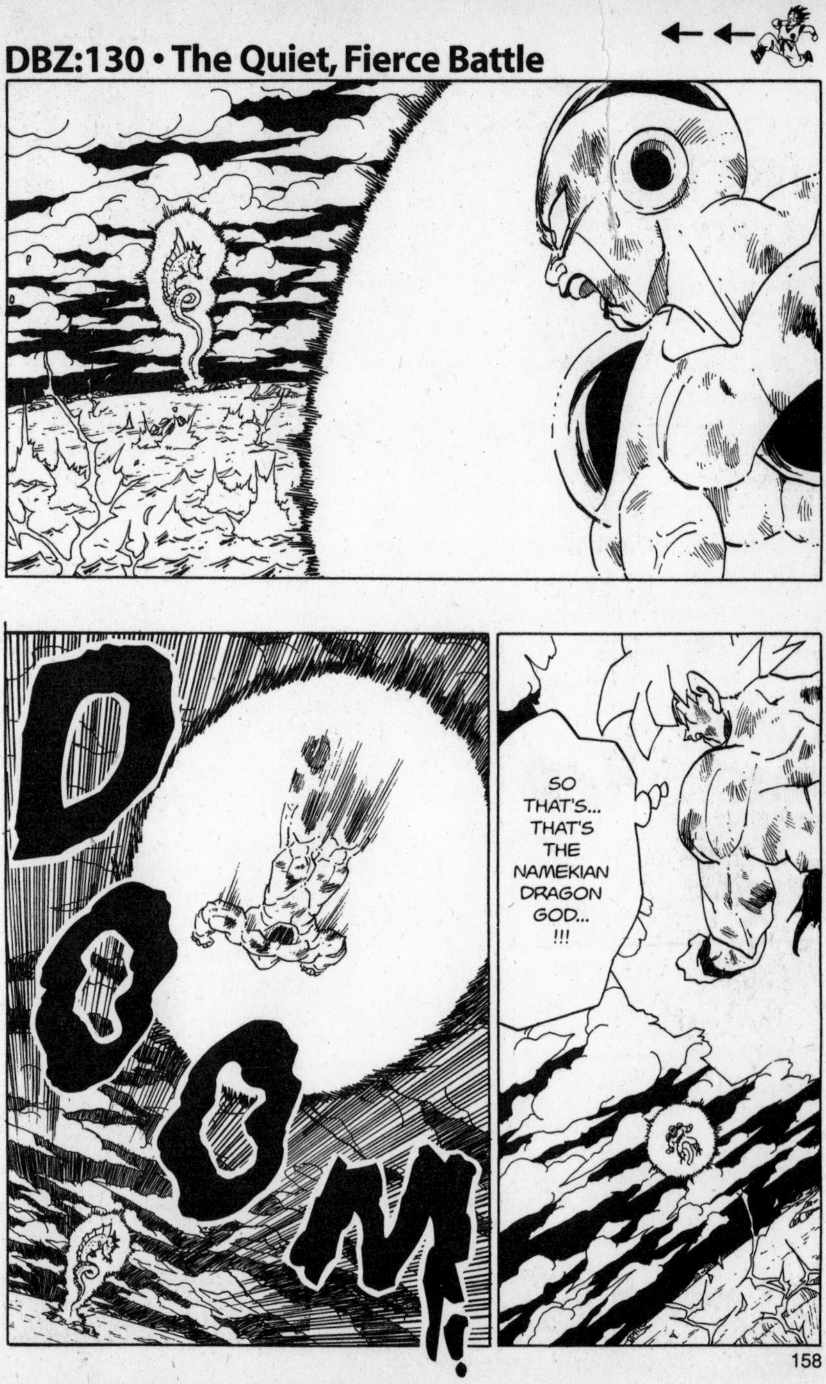
SO THAT'S... THAT'S THE NAMEKIAN DRAGON GOD... !!!
DOOOM!

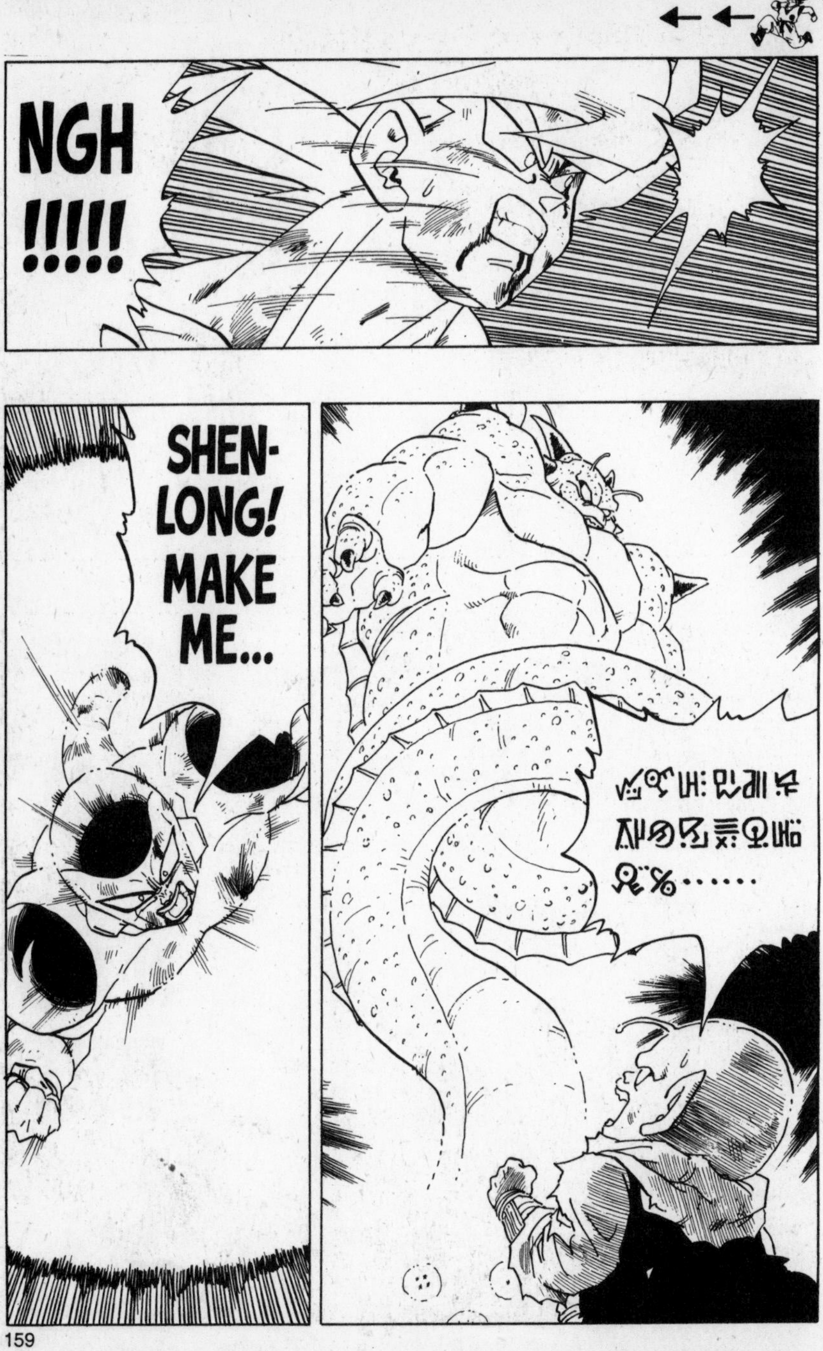
NGH!!!!!
SHEN-LONG! MAKE ME...

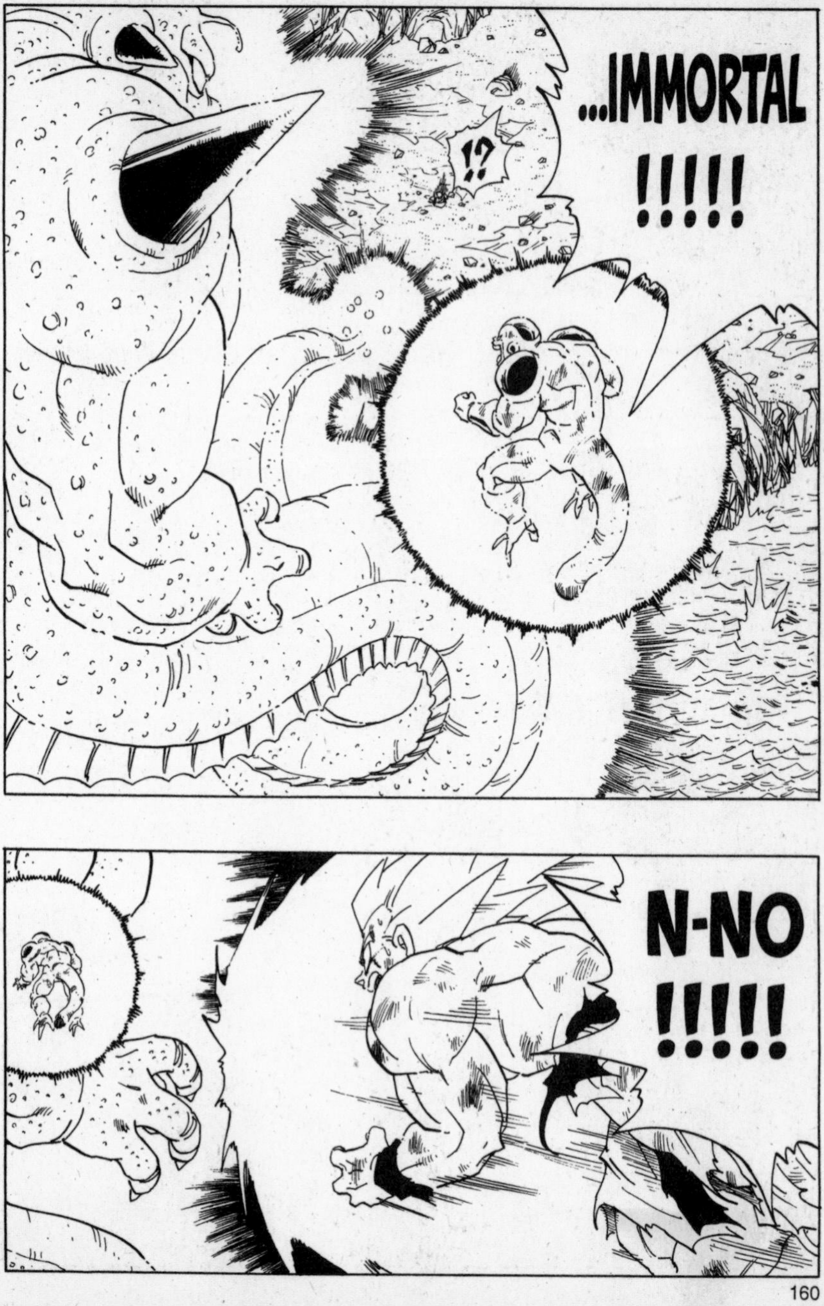
...IMMORTAL !!!!!
!?
N-NO !!!!!

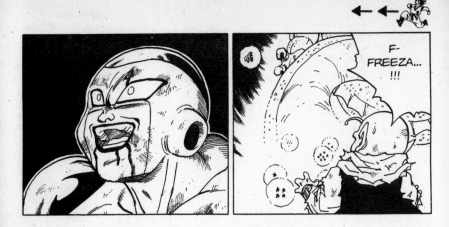

F-
FREEZA...
!!!

V/̈O⌃¡⼌:⺌⼌⼅⼌
⼌O⼌⺌⼌O⼌⼌O
Ö:⼌⼌⼌F⸚⼌V
S⼌D⼌⼌⼌.!!!!!

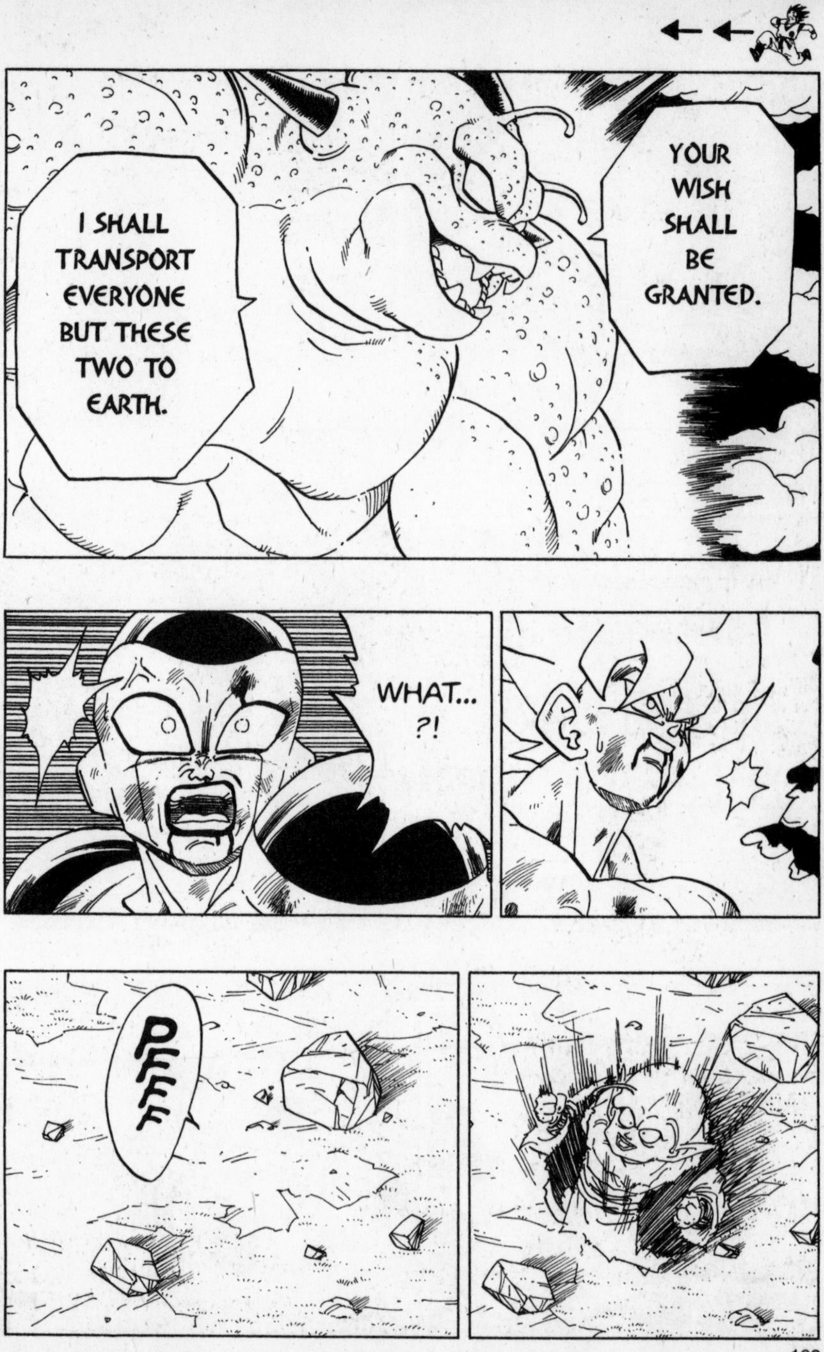
YOUR WISH SHALL BE GRANTED.
I SHALL TRANSPORT EVERYONE BUT THESE TWO TO EARTH.
WHAT... ?!
PFFF

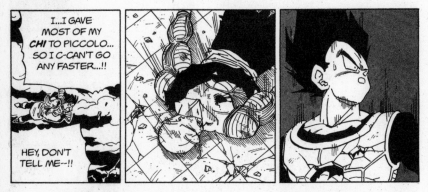

I...I GAVE MOST OF MY *CHI* TO PICCOLO... SO I C-CAN'T GO ANY FASTER...!!

HEY, DON'T TELL ME--!!

PFF

HUH ?!

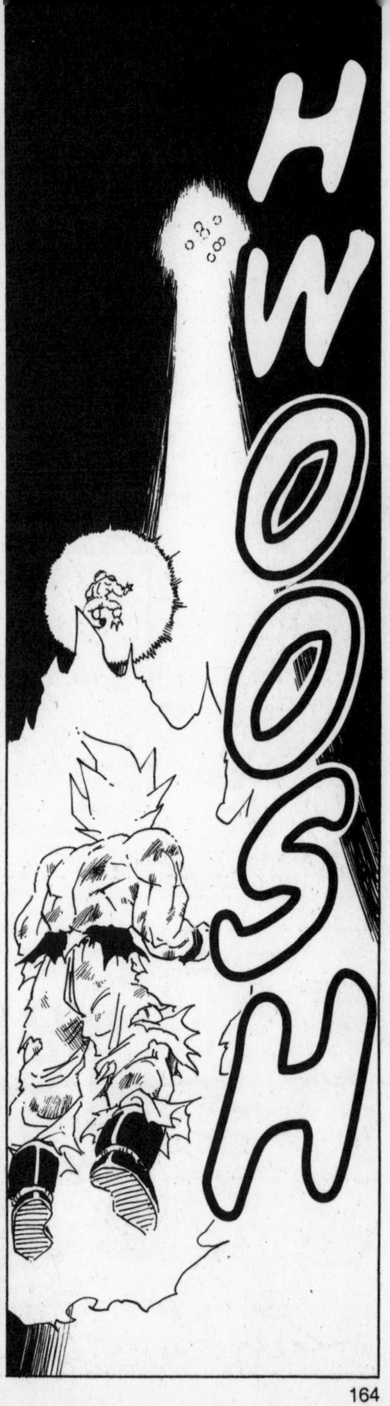
WHOOSH

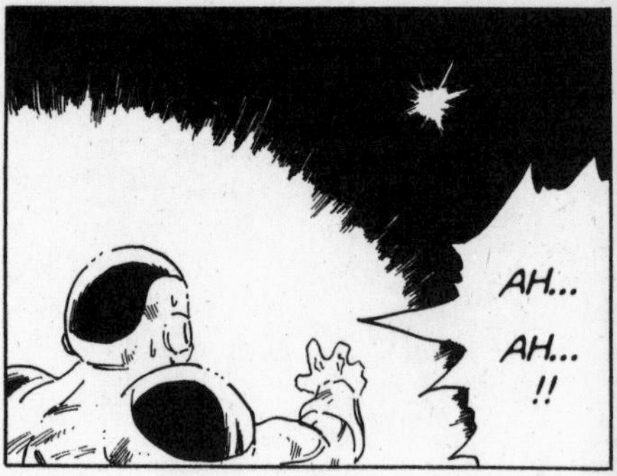
AH...
AH... !!

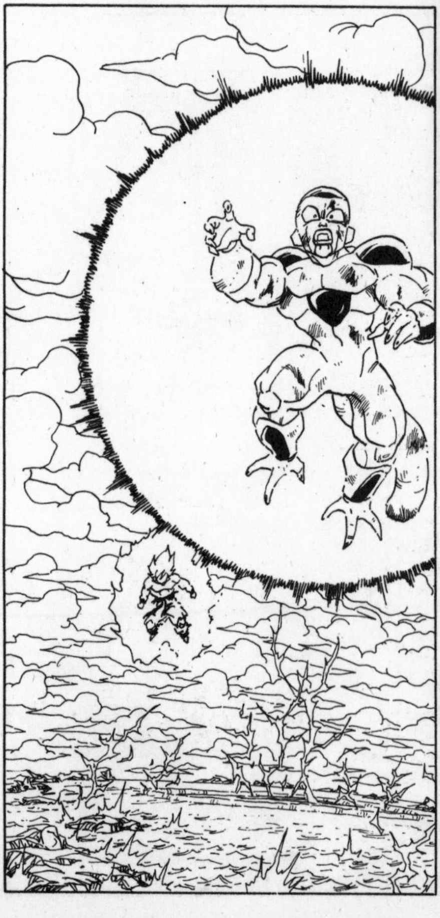

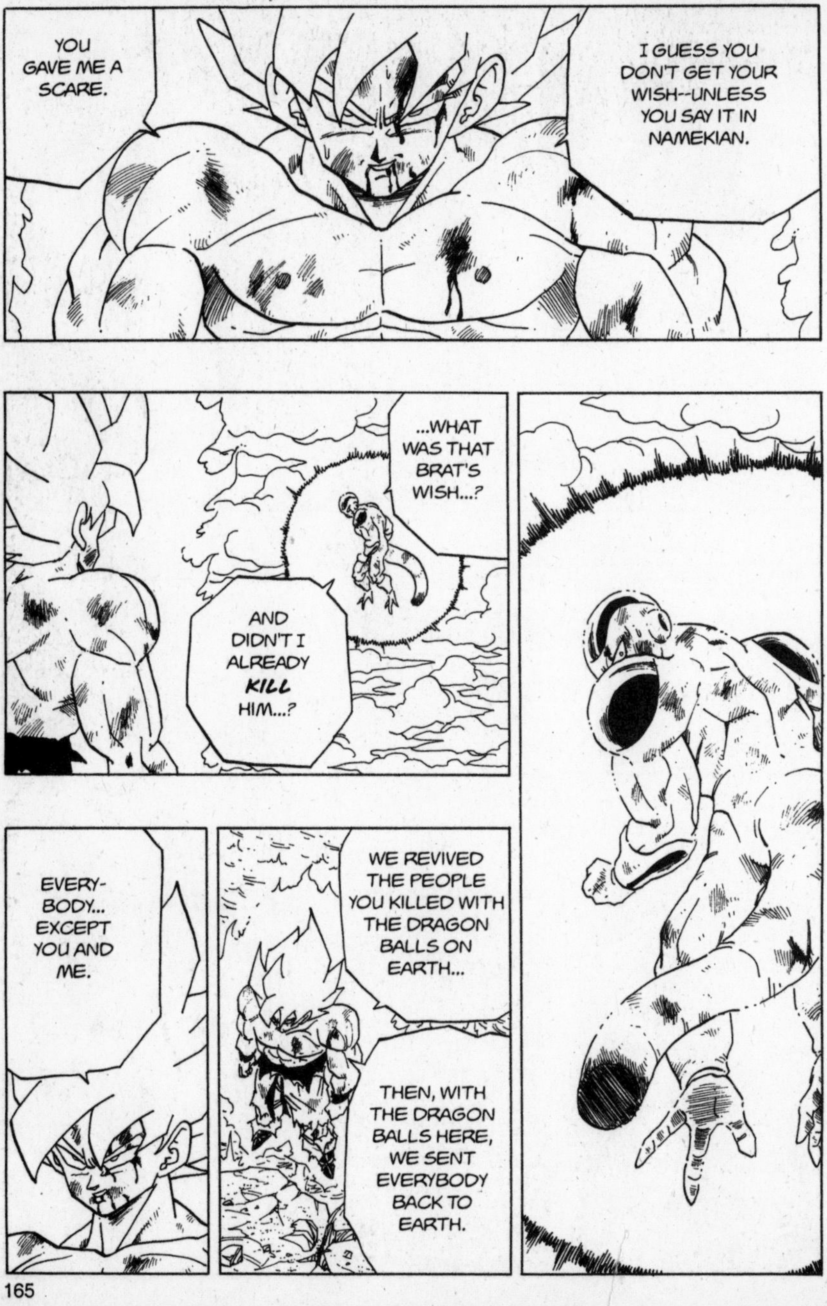
I GUESS YOU DON'T GET YOUR WISH--UNLESS YOU SAY IT IN NAMEKIAN.
YOU GAVE ME A SCARE.
...WHAT WAS THAT BRAT'S WISH...?
AND DIDN'T I ALREADY **KILL** HIM...?
WE REVIVED THE PEOPLE YOU KILLED WITH THE DRAGON BALLS ON EARTH...
THEN, WITH THE DRAGON BALLS HERE, WE SENT EVERYBODY BACK TO EARTH.
EVERY-BODY... EXCEPT YOU AND ME.

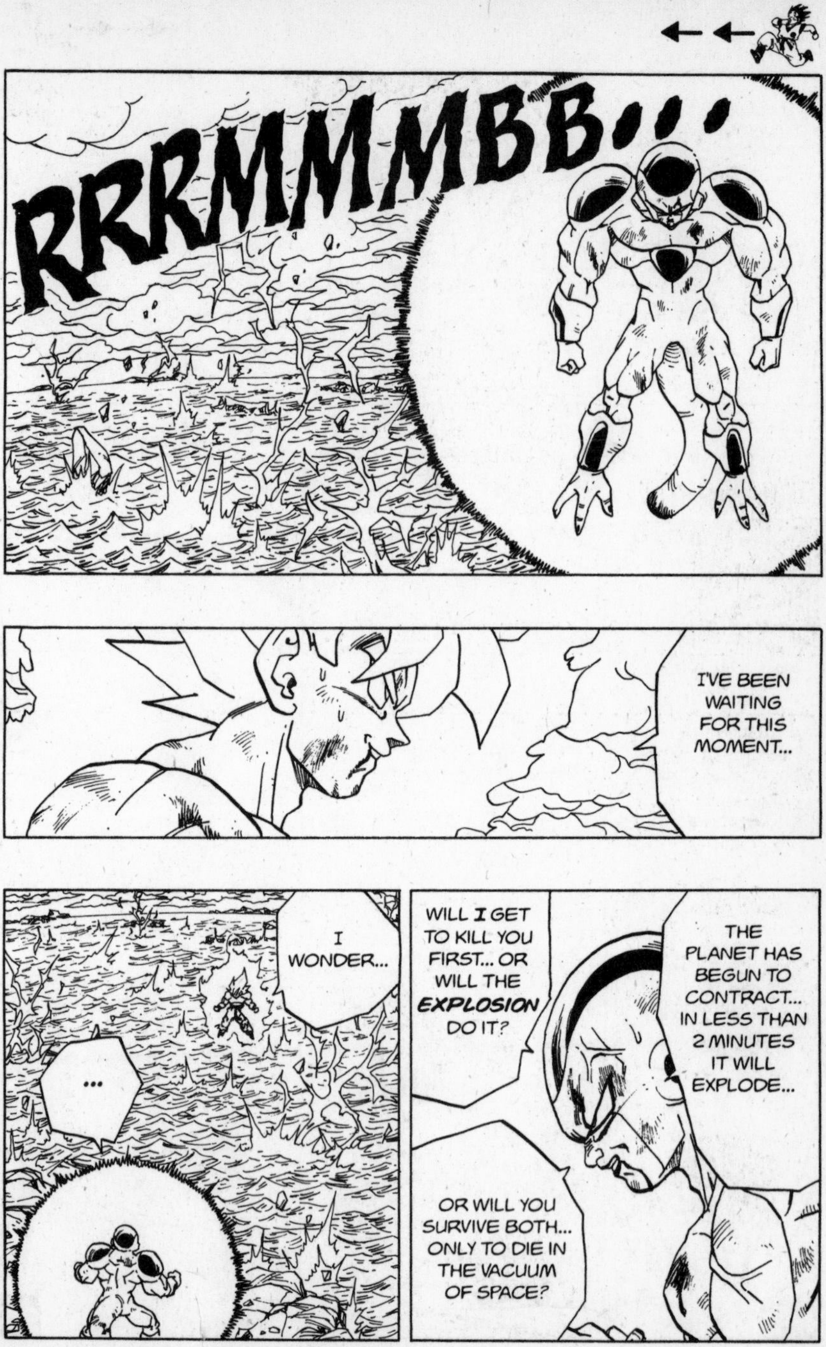
RRRMMMBB...
I'VE BEEN WAITING FOR THIS MOMENT...
THE PLANET HAS BEGUN TO CONTRACT... IN LESS THAN 2 MINUTES IT WILL EXPLODE...
WILL I GET TO KILL YOU FIRST... OR WILL THE EXPLOSION DO IT?
OR WILL YOU SURVIVE BOTH... ONLY TO DIE IN THE VACUUM OF SPACE?
I WONDER...
...

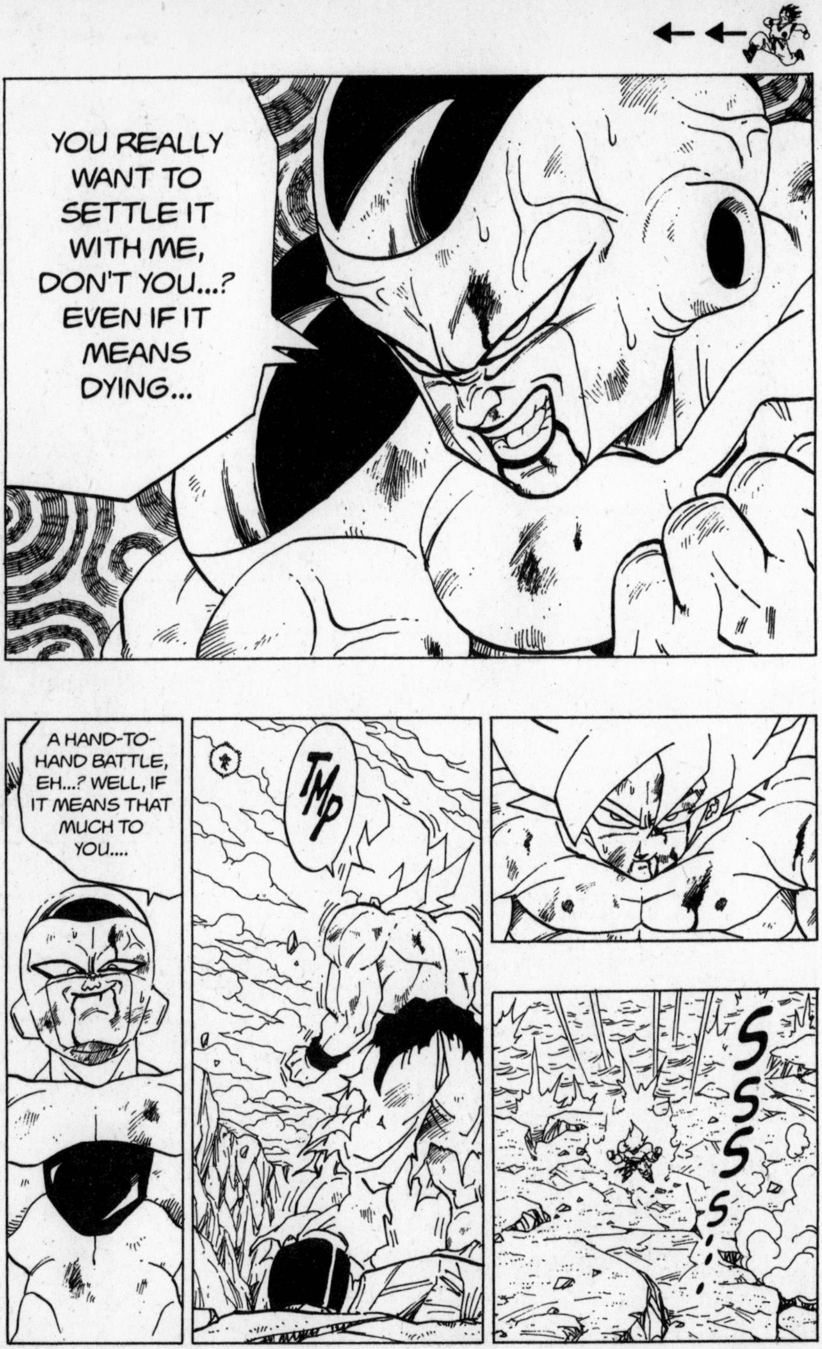
YOU REALLY WANT TO SETTLE IT WITH ME, DON'T YOU...? EVEN IF IT MEANS DYING...
SSSS...
TMP
A HAND-TO-HAND BATTLE, EH...? WELL, IF IT MEANS THAT MUCH TO YOU....

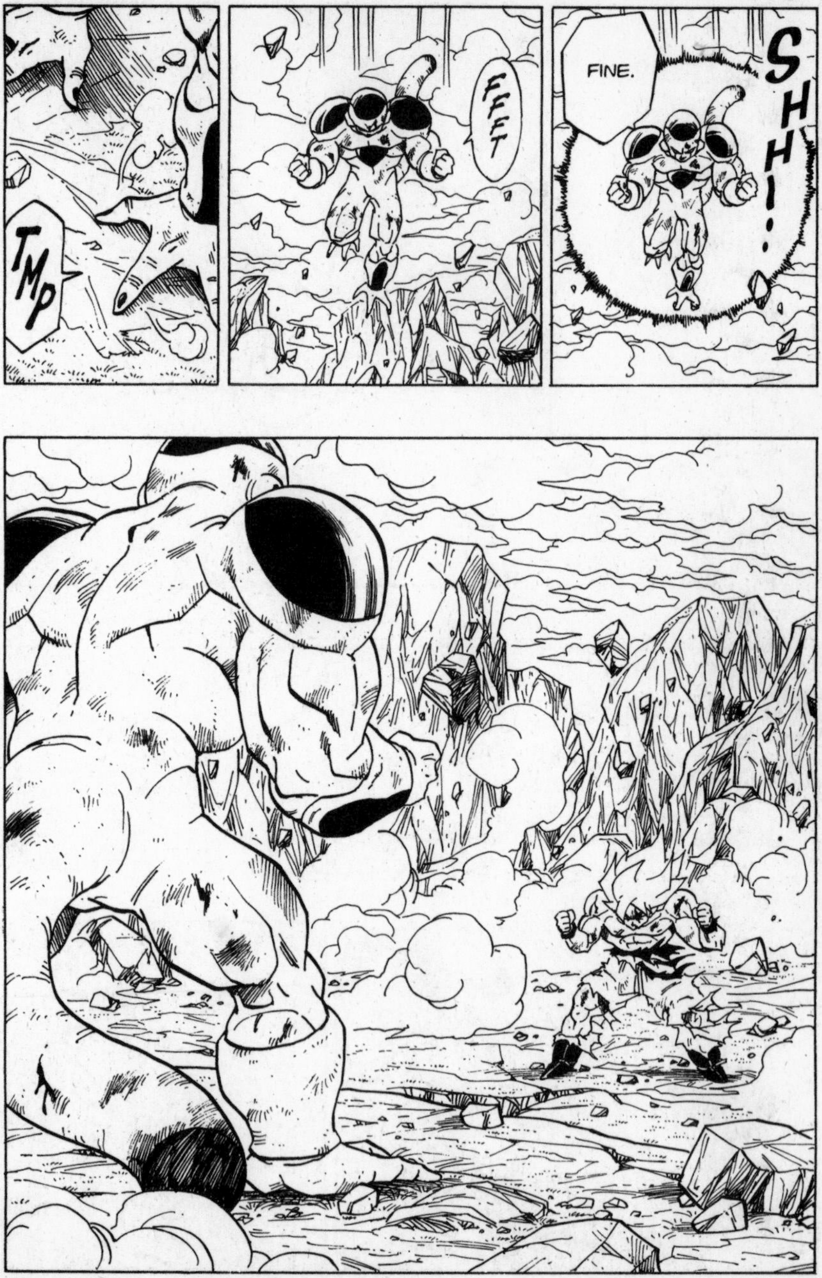
FINE.
SHHI!!
FFFT
TMP

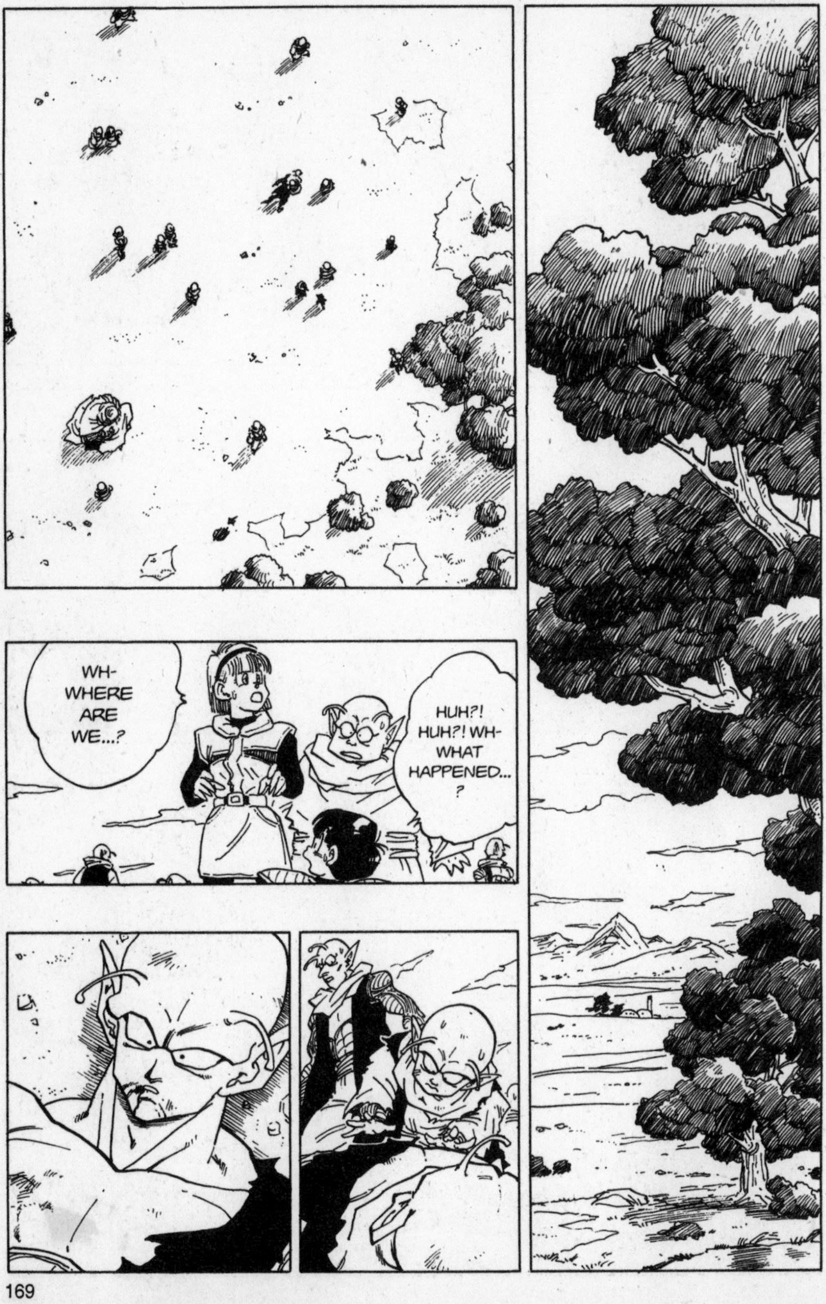
HUH?! HUH?! WH- WHAT HAPPENED... ?
WH- WHERE ARE WE...?

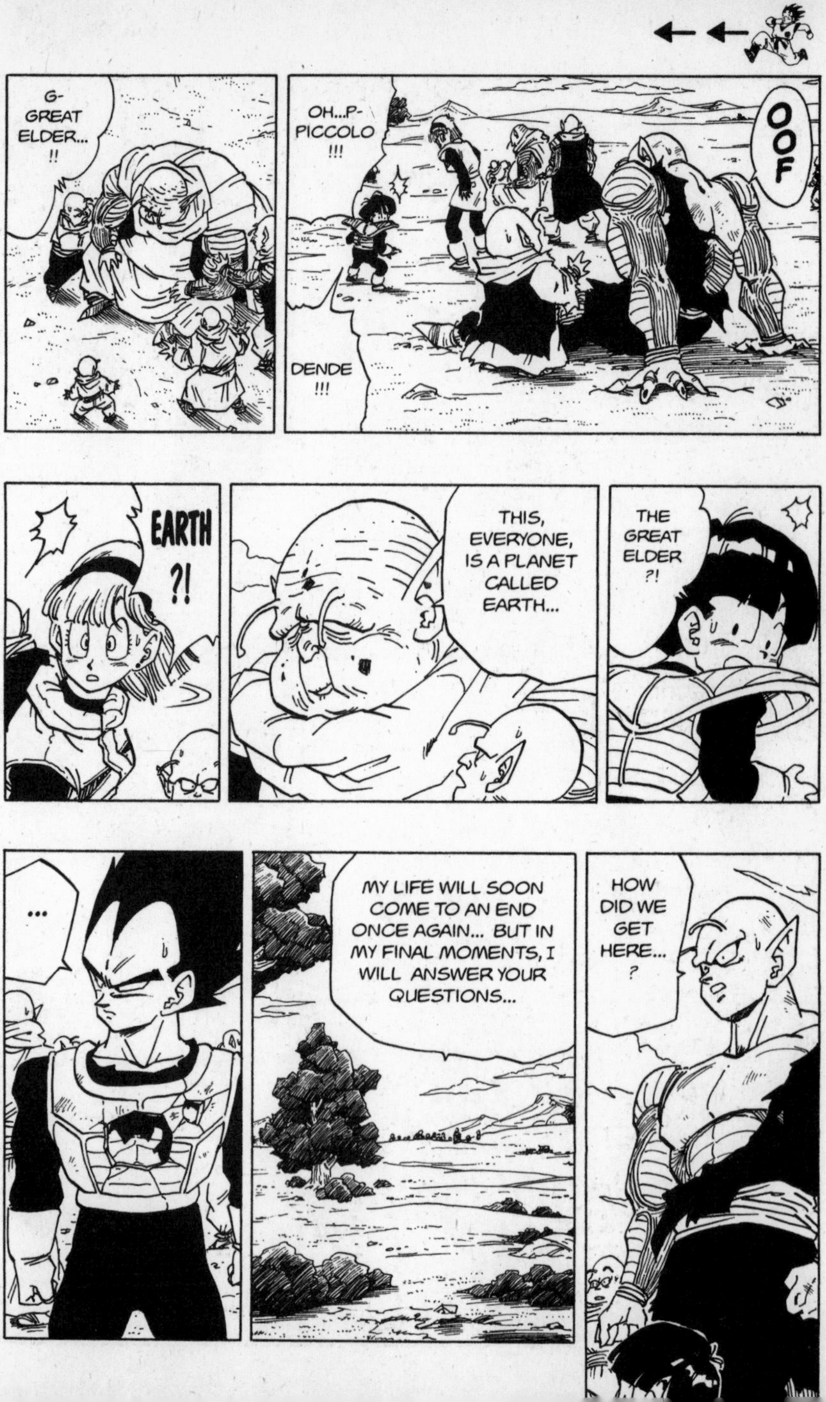
OOF
OH...P-PICCOLO !!!
DENDE !!!
G-GREAT ELDER... !!
THE GREAT ELDER ?!
THIS, EVERYONE, IS A PLANET CALLED EARTH...
EARTH ?!
HOW DID WE GET HERE... ?
MY LIFE WILL SOON COME TO AN END ONCE AGAIN... BUT IN MY FINAL MOMENTS, I WILL ANSWER YOUR QUESTIONS...
...

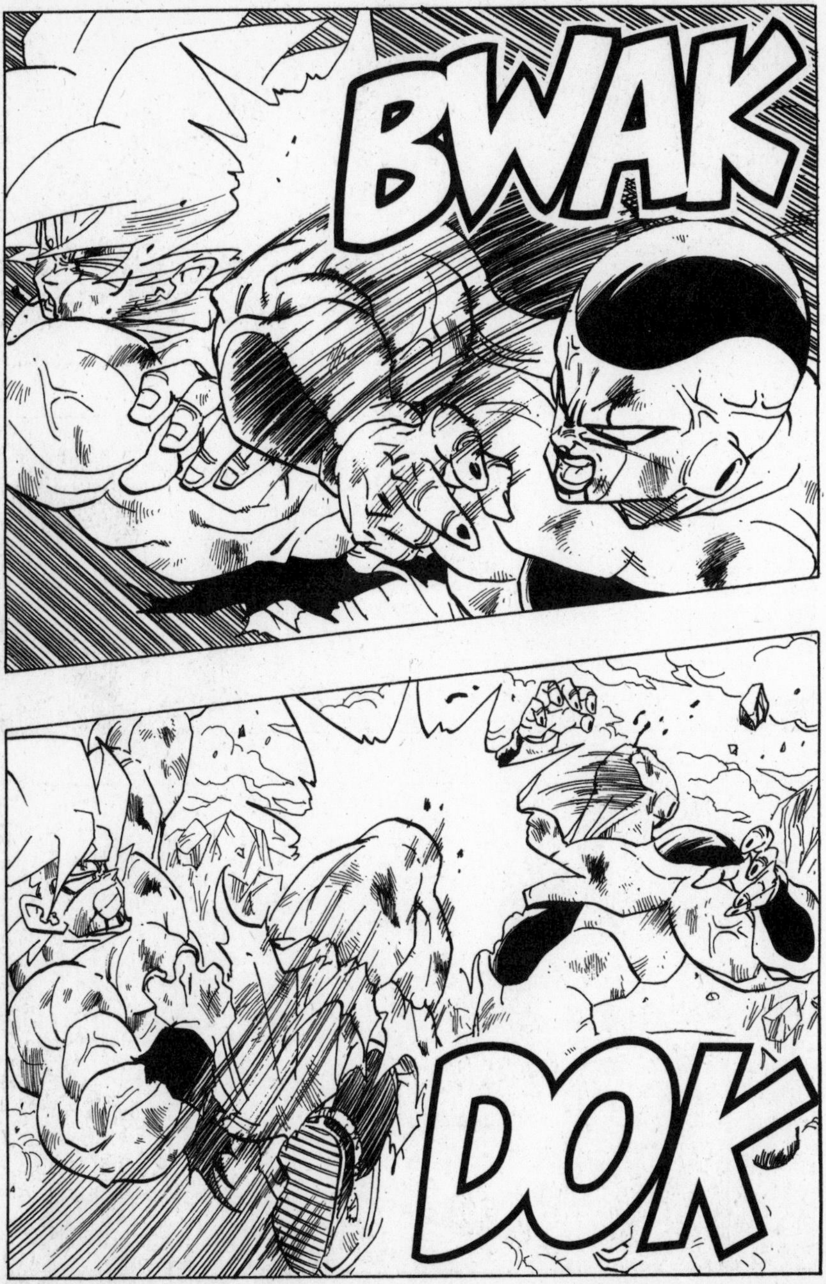
BWAK
DOK

DBZ:131 • Son Goku Quits

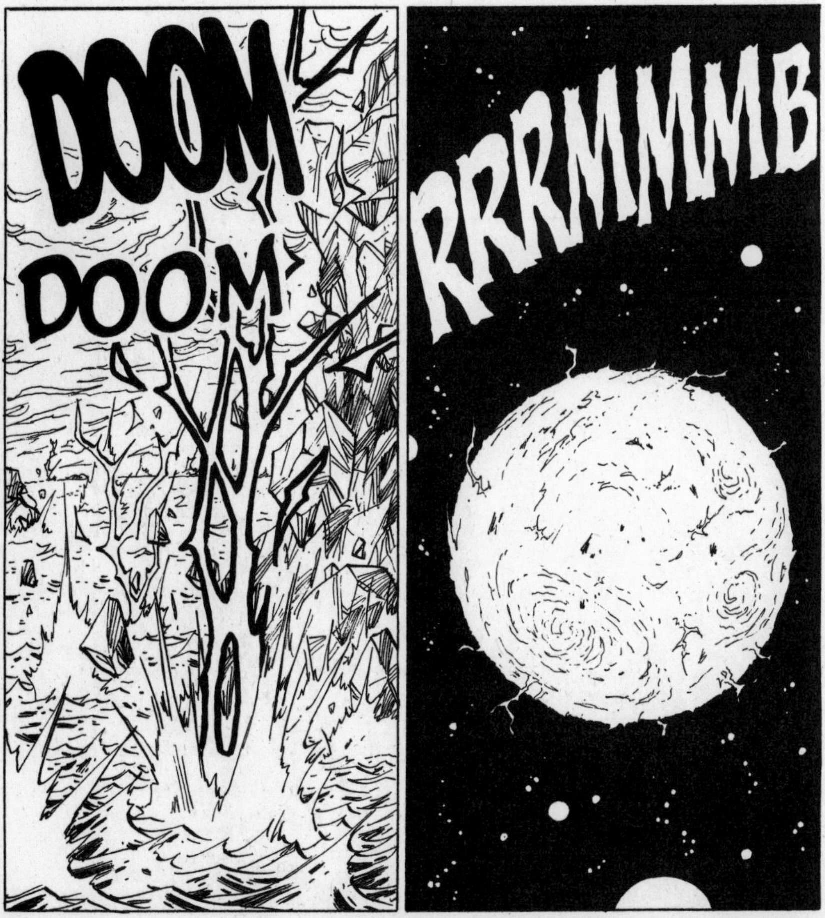
RRRMMMB
DOOM
DOOM

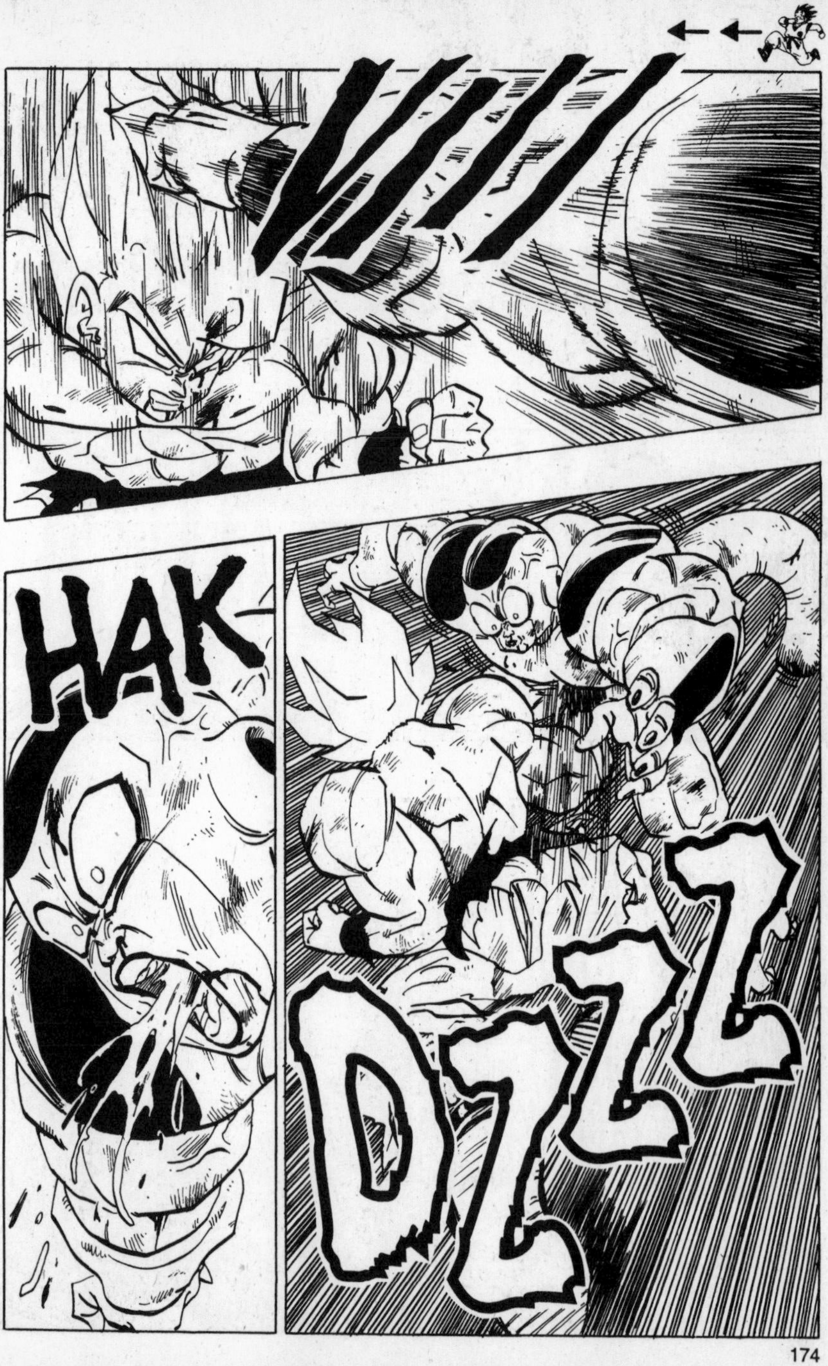
DZZ
HAK

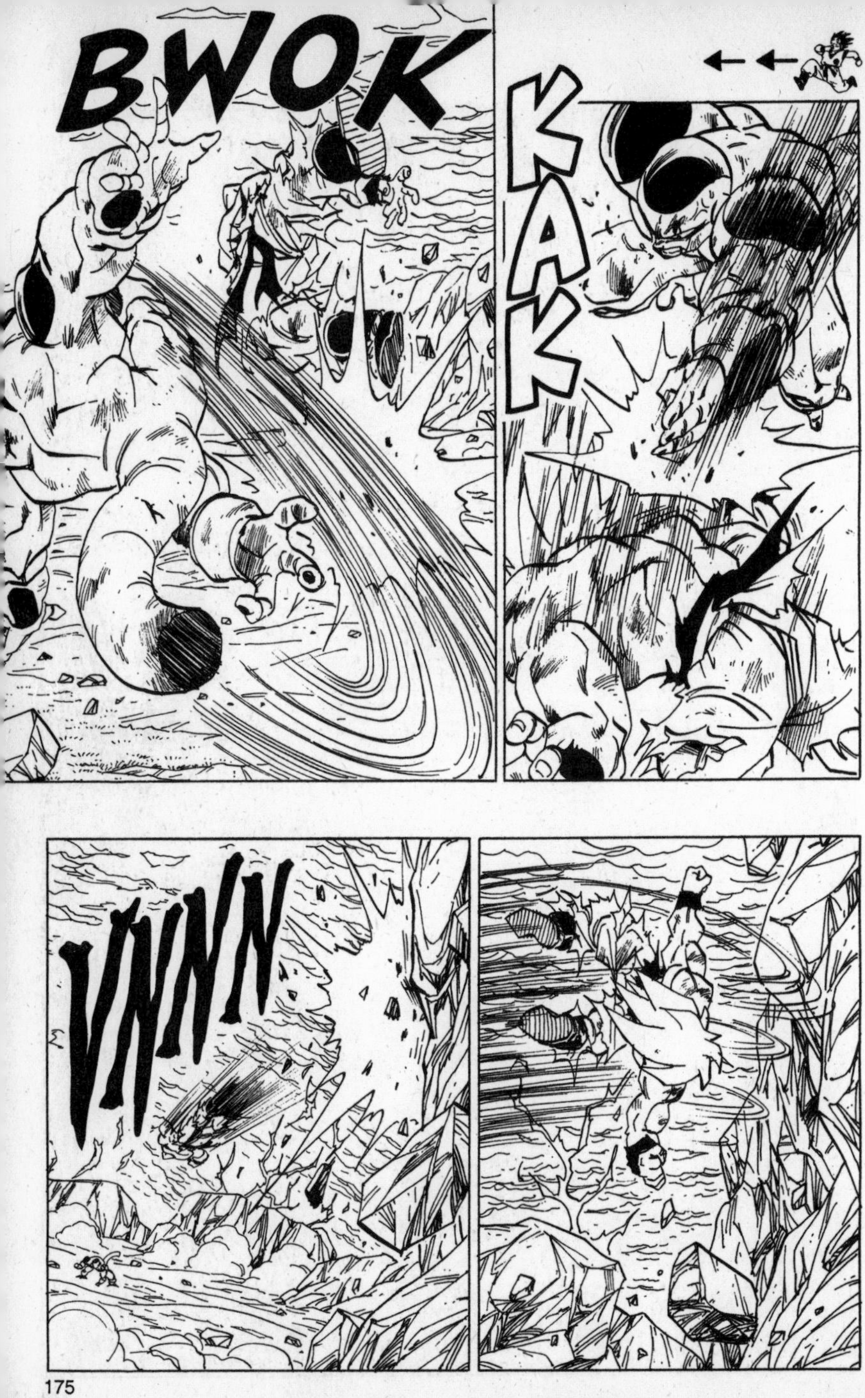
KAK
BWOK
VNNN

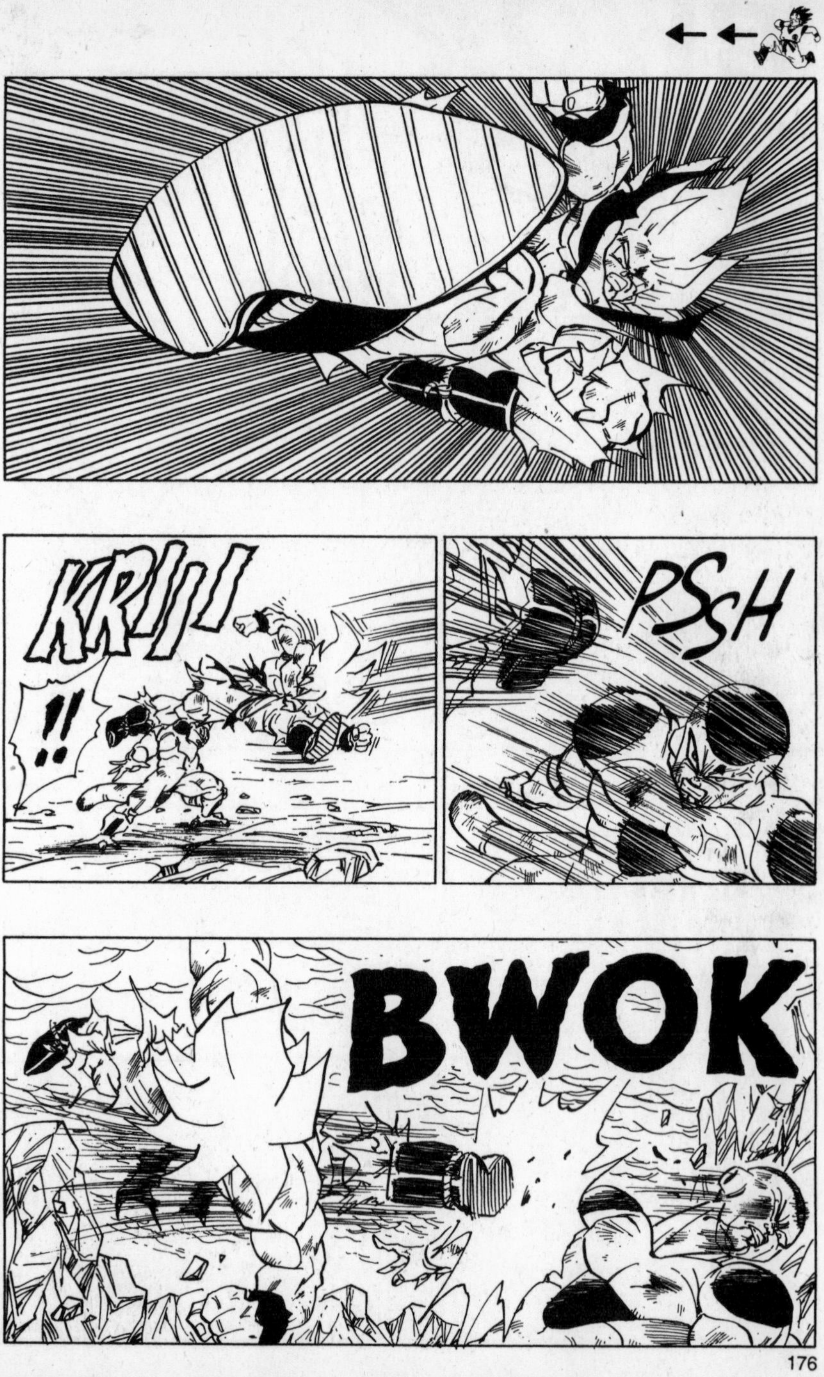
PSSH
KRIII
!!
BWOK

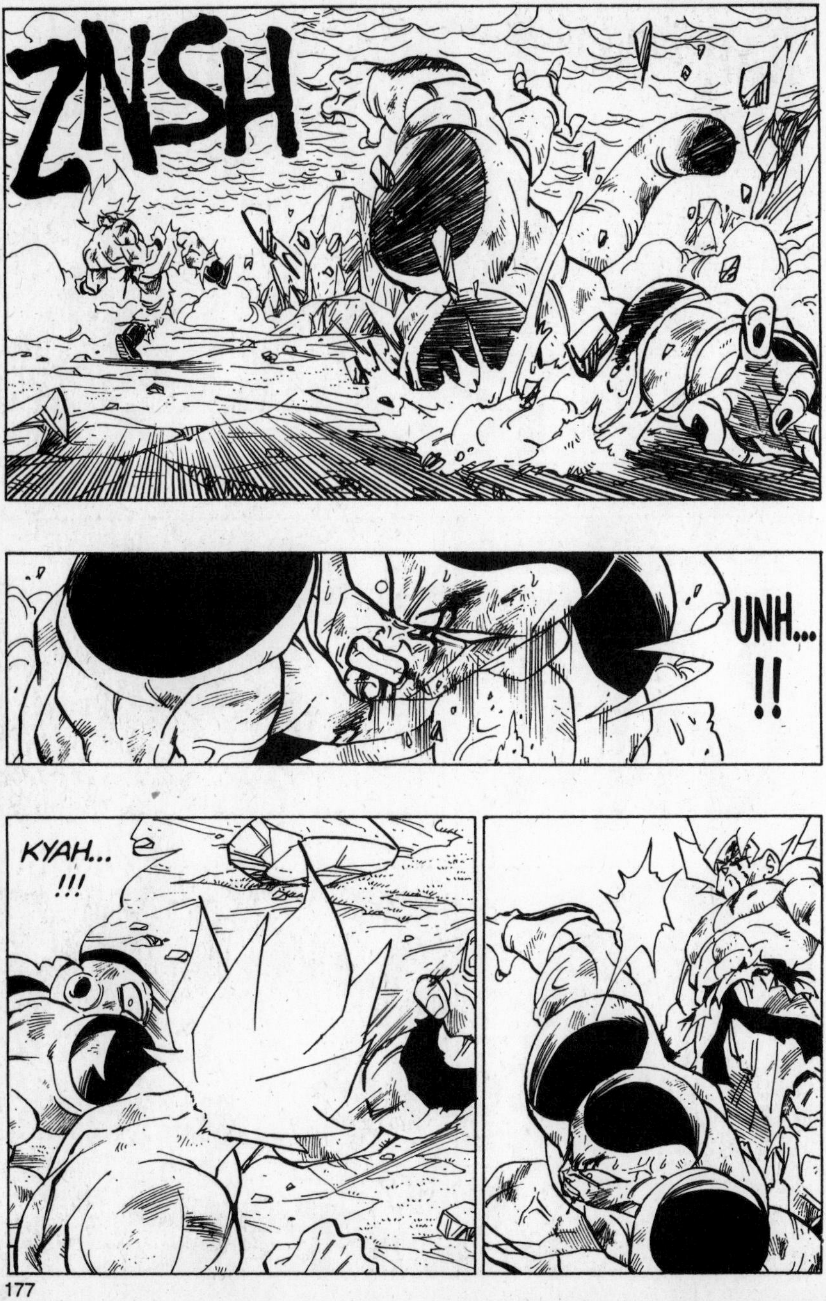
ZNSH
UNH... !!
KYAH... !!!

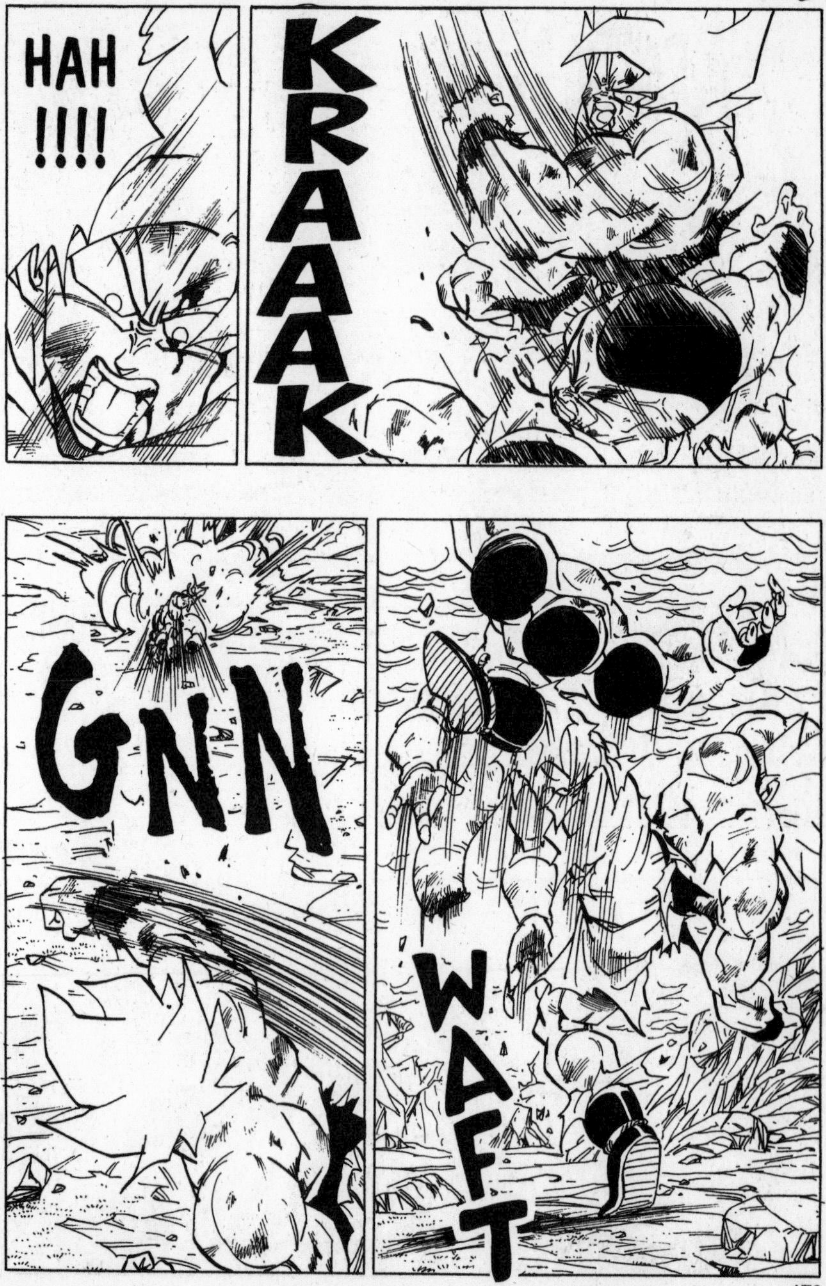
KRAAK
HAH !!!!
WAFT
GNN

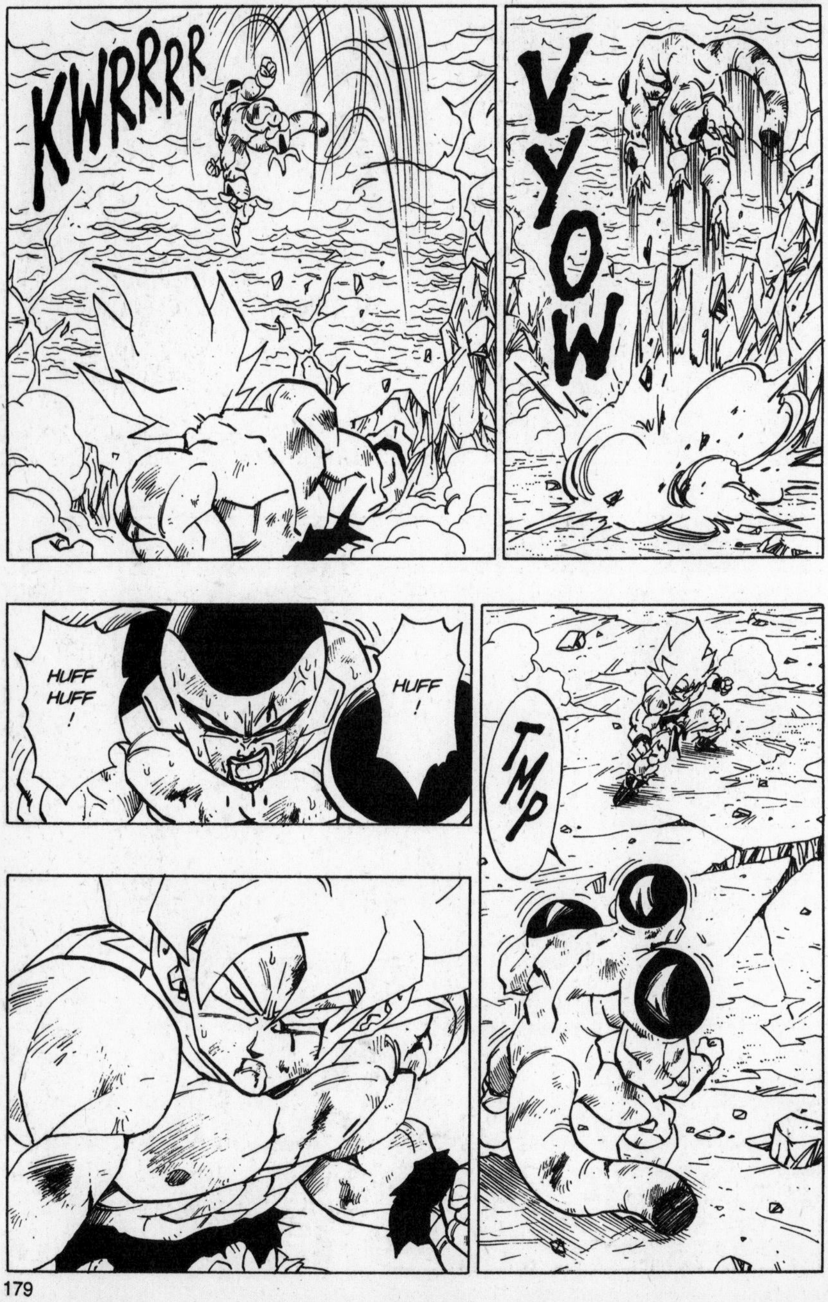
VYOW
KWRRRR
TMP
HUFF !
HUFF HUFF !

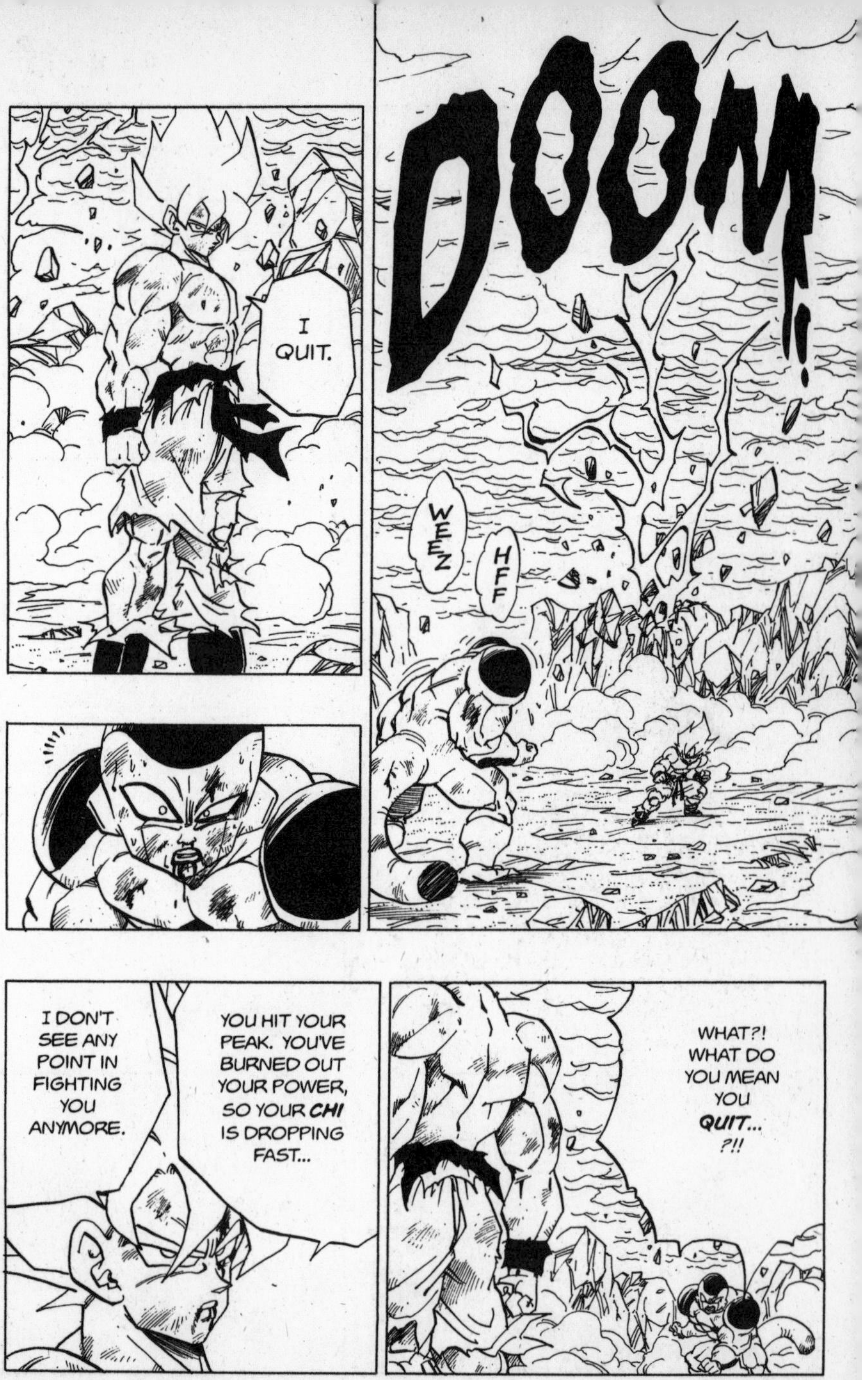
DOOM!!
WEEZ
HFF
I QUIT.
WHAT?! WHAT DO YOU MEAN YOU QUIT... ?!!
YOU HIT YOUR PEAK. YOU'VE BURNED OUT YOUR POWER, SO YOUR CHI IS DROPPING FAST...
I DON'T SEE ANY POINT IN FIGHTING YOU ANYMORE.

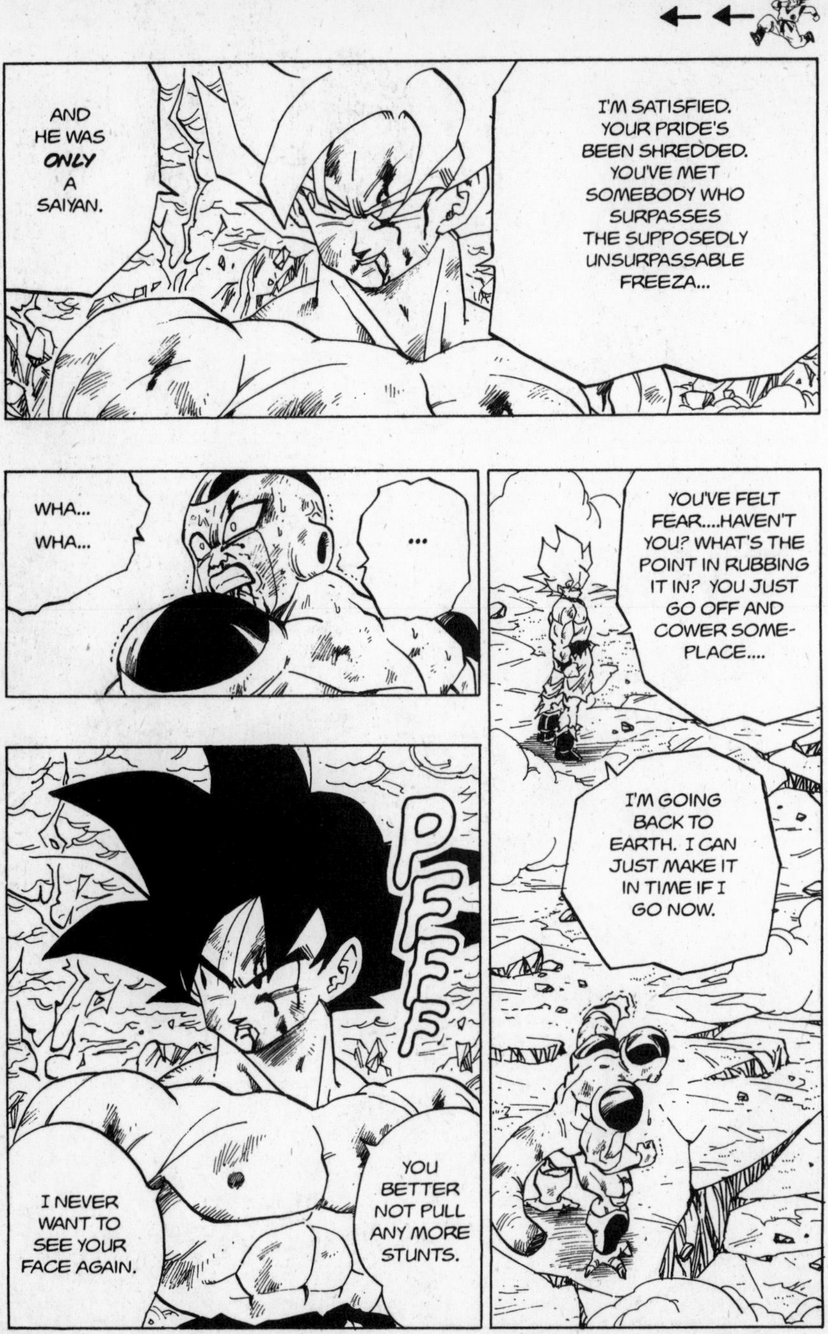
I'M SATISFIED. YOUR PRIDE'S BEEN SHREDDED. YOU'VE MET SOMEBODY WHO SURPASSES THE SUPPOSEDLY UNSURPASSABLE FREEZA...
AND HE WAS *ONLY* A SAIYAN.
YOU'VE FELT FEAR....HAVEN'T YOU? WHAT'S THE POINT IN RUBBING IT IN? YOU JUST GO OFF AND COWER SOME-PLACE....
I'M GOING BACK TO EARTH. I CAN JUST MAKE IT IN TIME IF I GO NOW.
...
WHA... WHA...
PFFF
YOU BETTER NOT PULL ANY MORE STUNTS.
I NEVER WANT TO SEE YOUR FACE AGAIN.

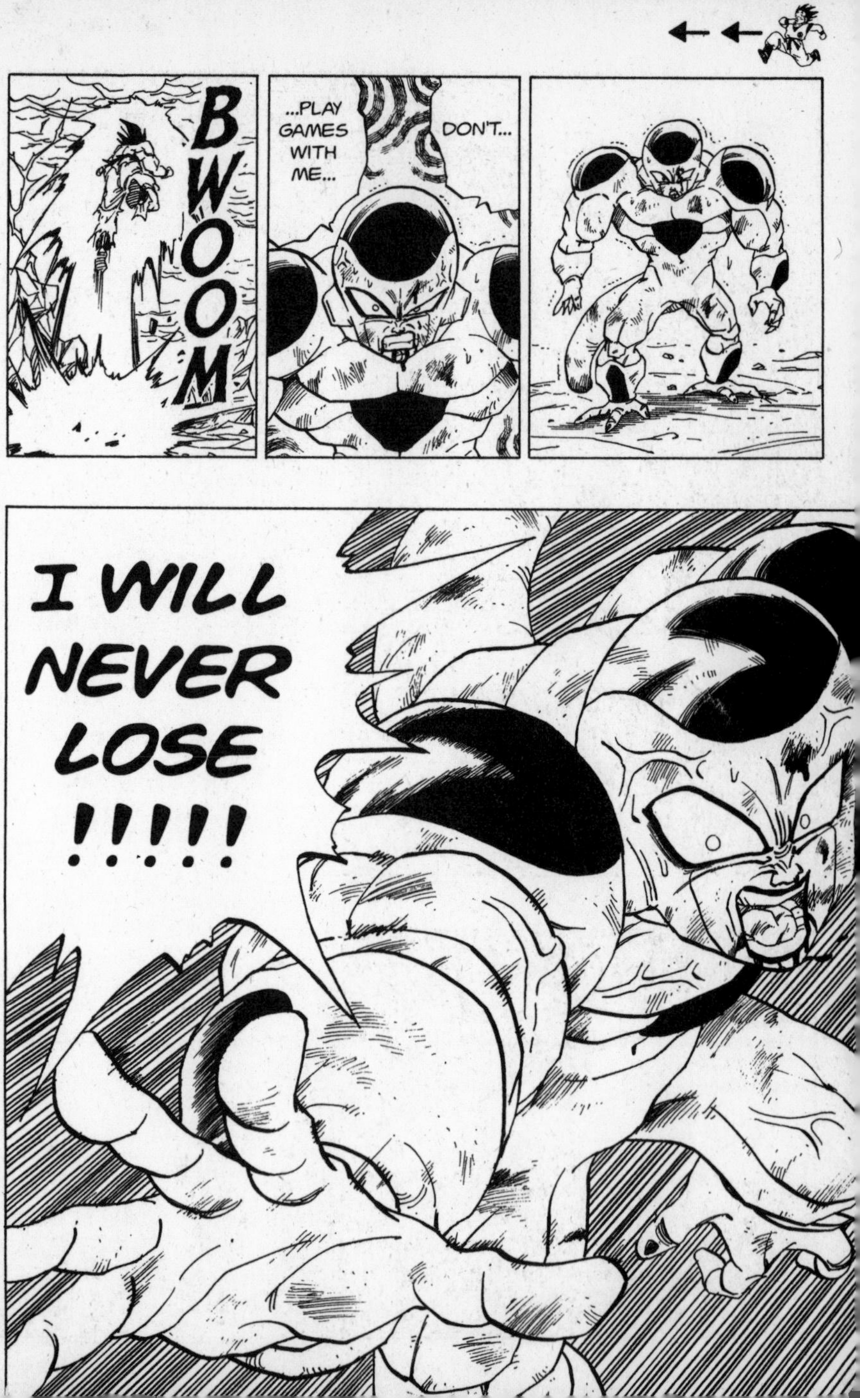
DON'T...
...PLAY GAMES WITH ME...
BWOOM
I WILL NEVER LOSE !!!!!

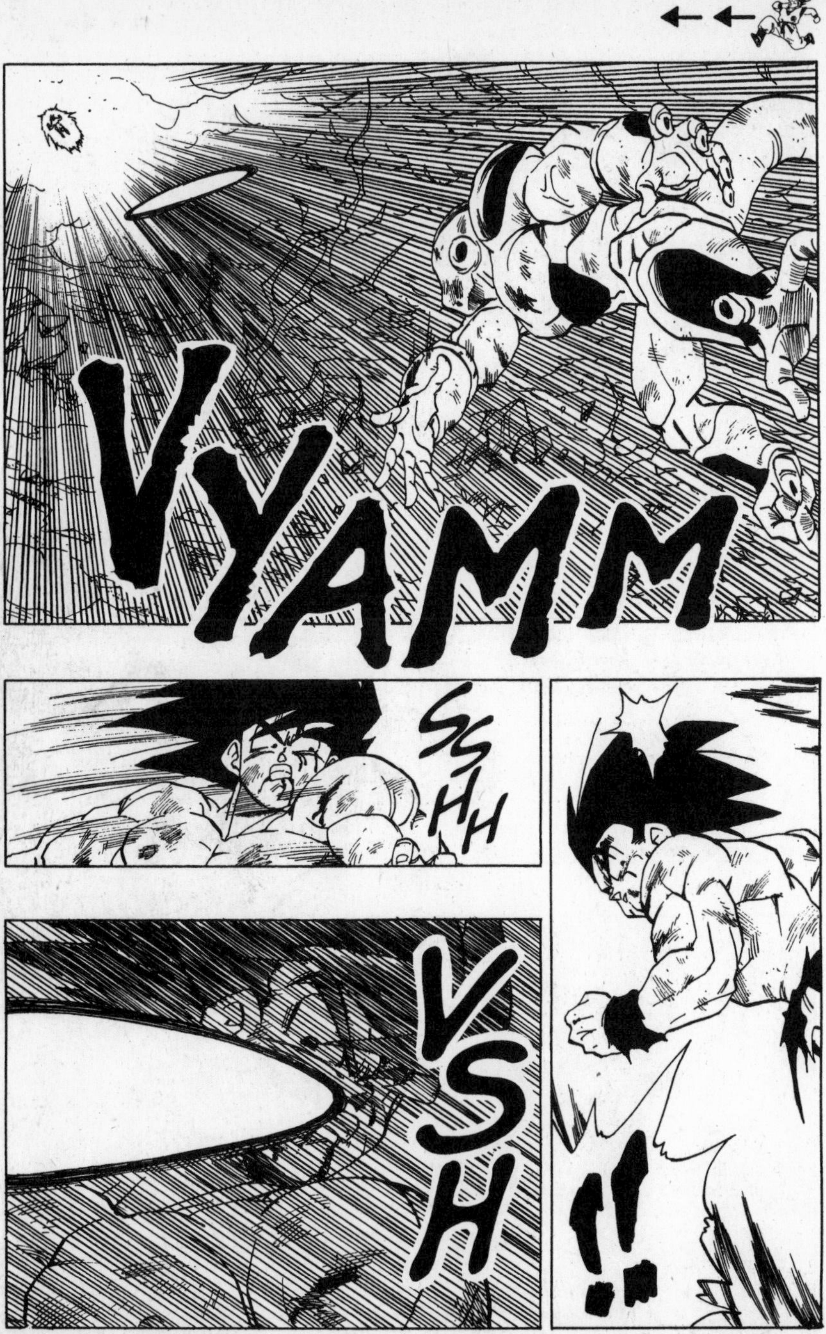
VYAMM
!!
SSHH
VSSH

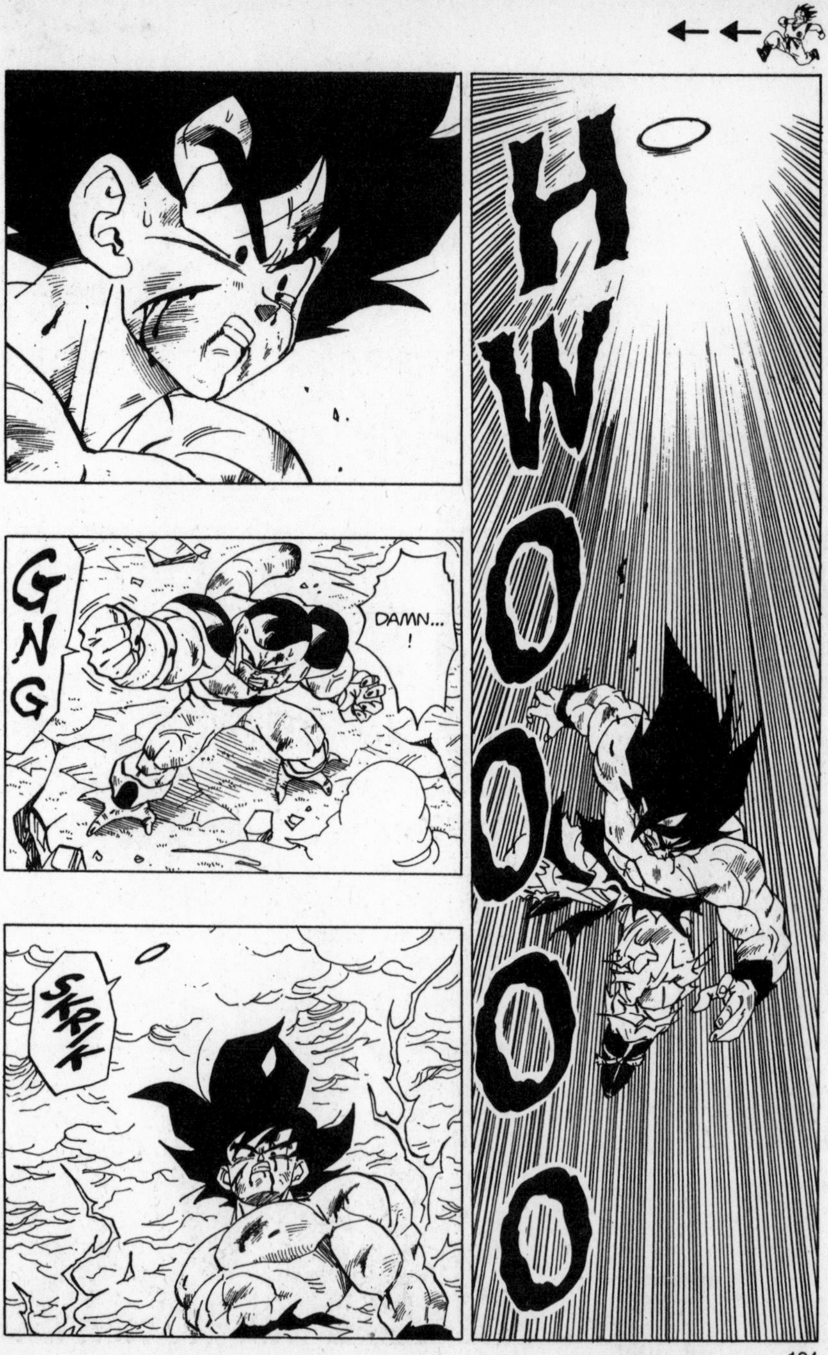
HWOOOO
GNG
DAMN... !
SKRIK

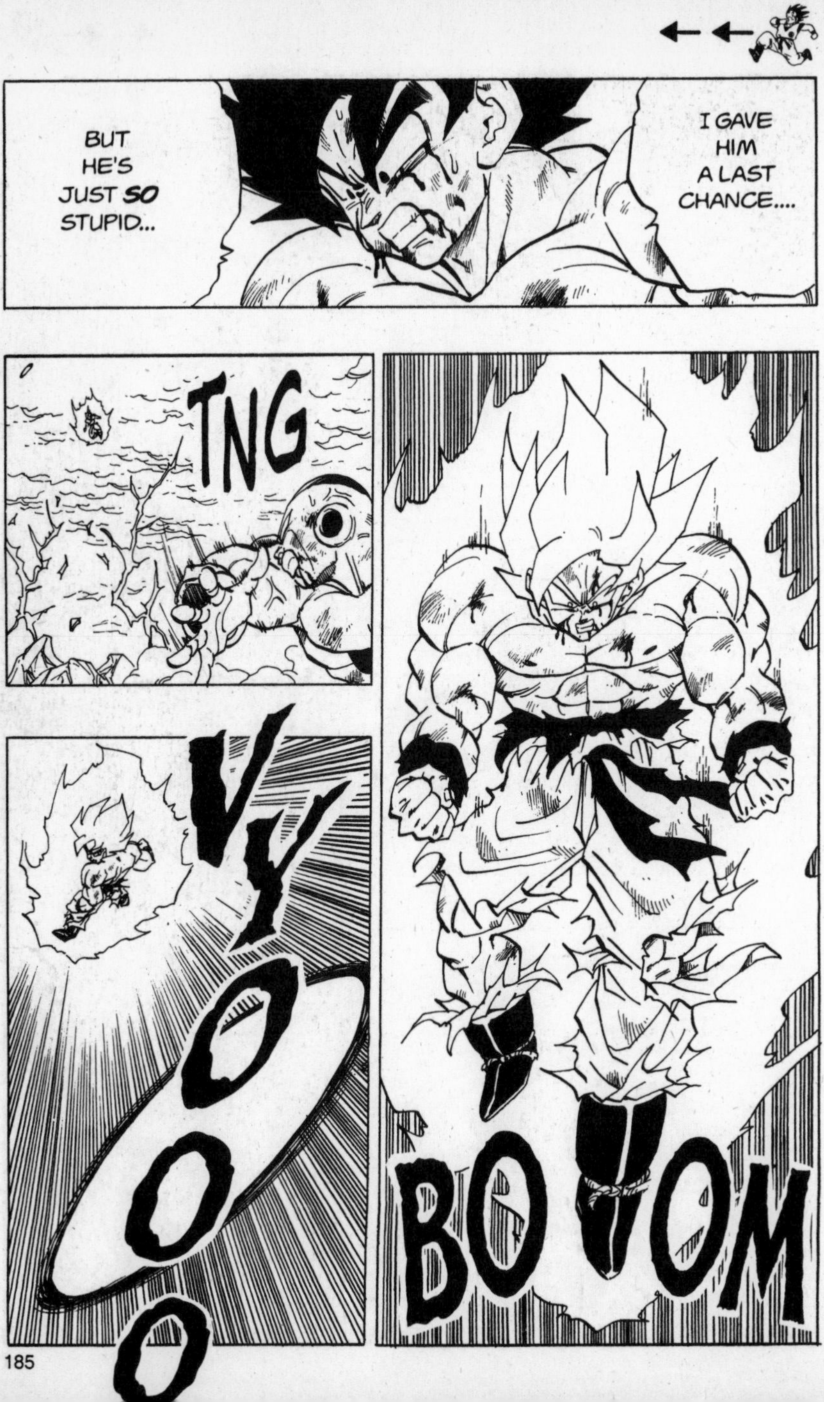
I GAVE HIM A LAST CHANCE....
BUT HE'S JUST SO STUPID...
BOOM
TNG
VOOO

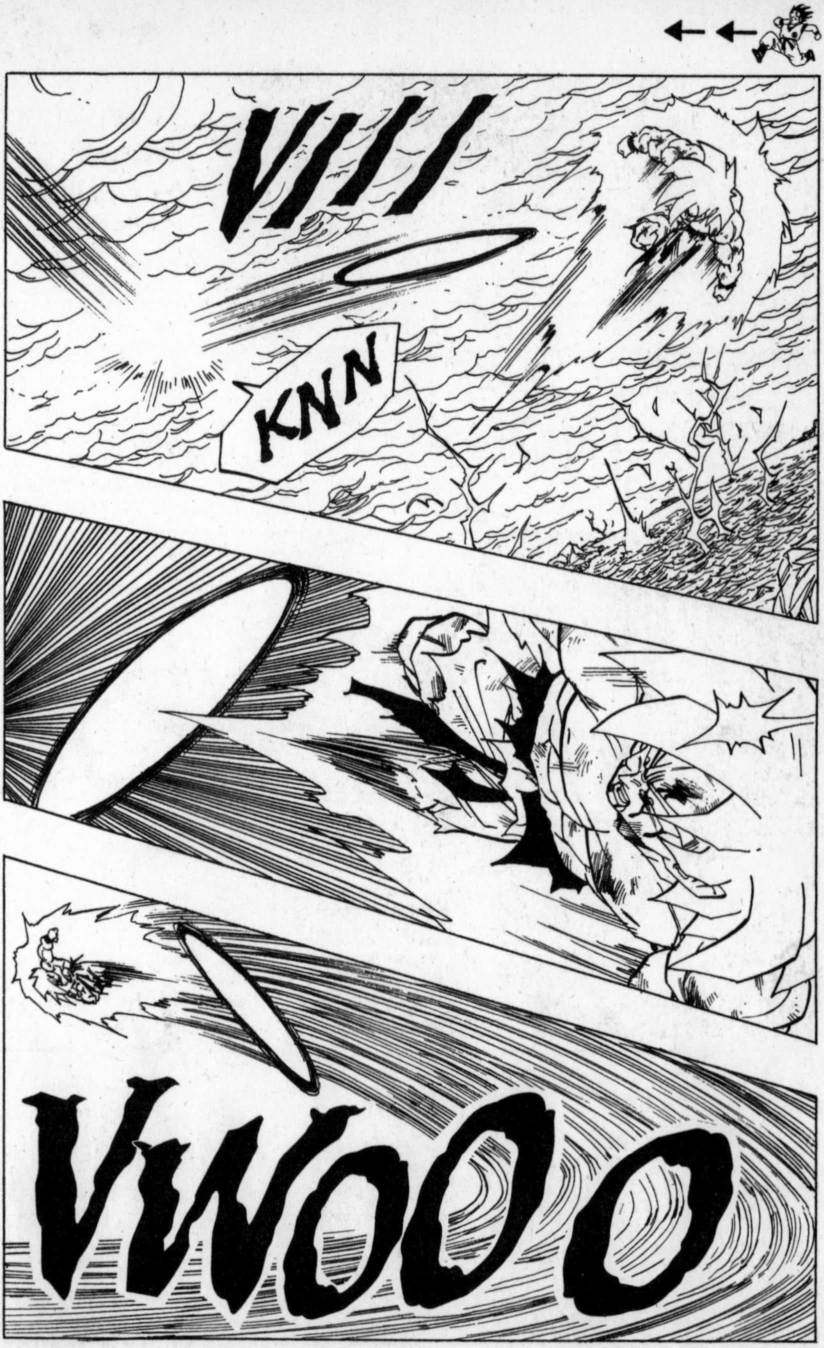
VIII
KNN
VWOOO

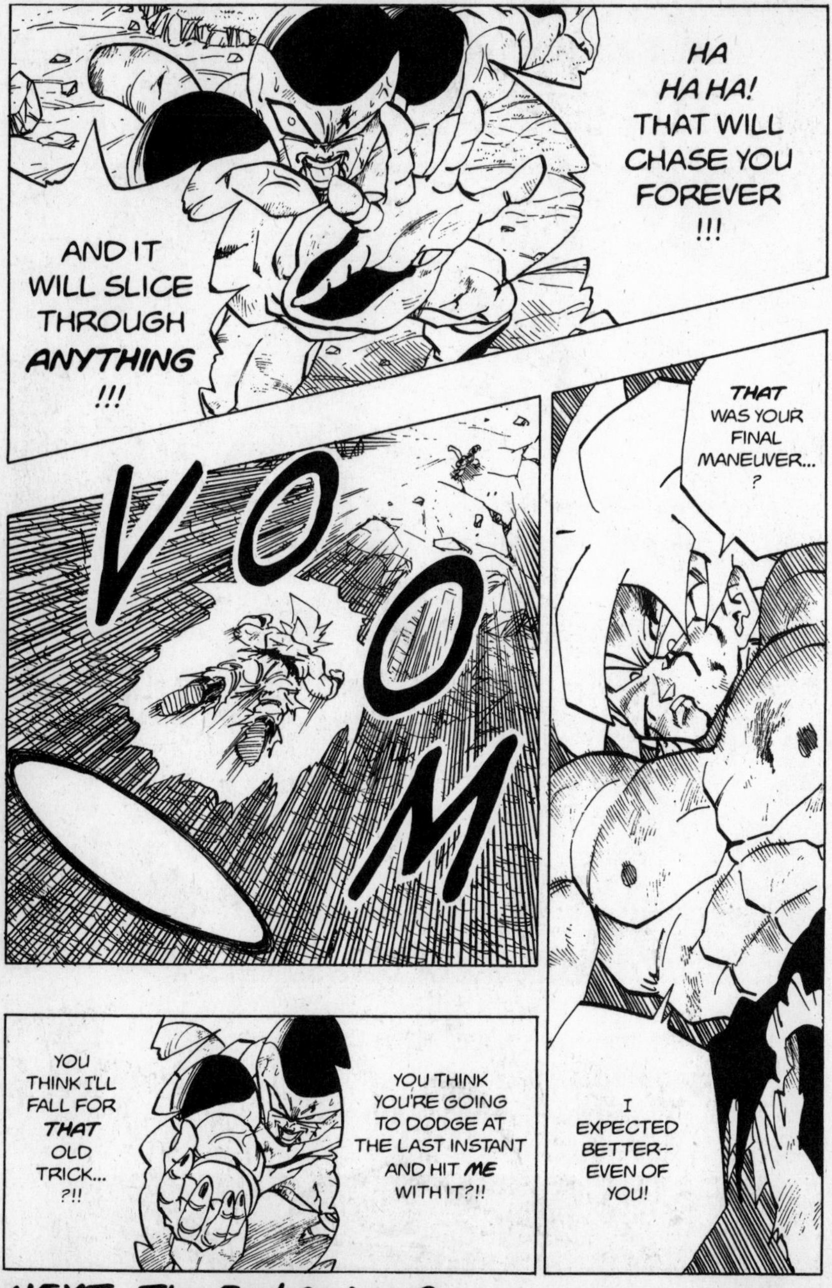
HA HA HA! THAT WILL CHASE YOU FOREVER !!!
AND IT WILL SLICE THROUGH ANYTHING !!!
THAT WAS YOUR FINAL MANEUVER... ?
I EXPECTED BETTER-- EVEN OF YOU!
VOOM
YOU THINK YOU'RE GOING TO DODGE AT THE LAST INSTANT AND HIT ME WITH IT?!!
YOU THINK I'LL FALL FOR THAT OLD TRICK... ?!!

NEXT: The End At Last?

TITLE PAGE GALLERY

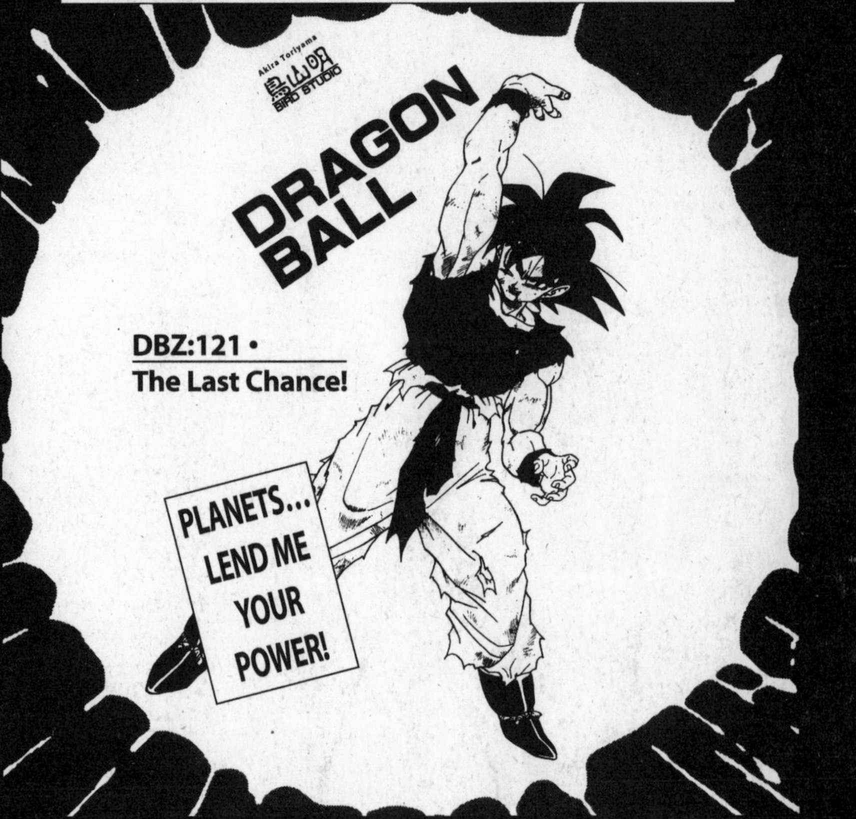
Akira Toriyama
鳥山明
BIRD STUDIO
DRAGON BALL
DBZ:121 •
The Last Chance!
PLANETS... LEND ME YOUR POWER!

This title page was used when these chapters of **Dragon Ball** were originally published in Japan in 1991 in **Weekly Shonen Jump** magazine.

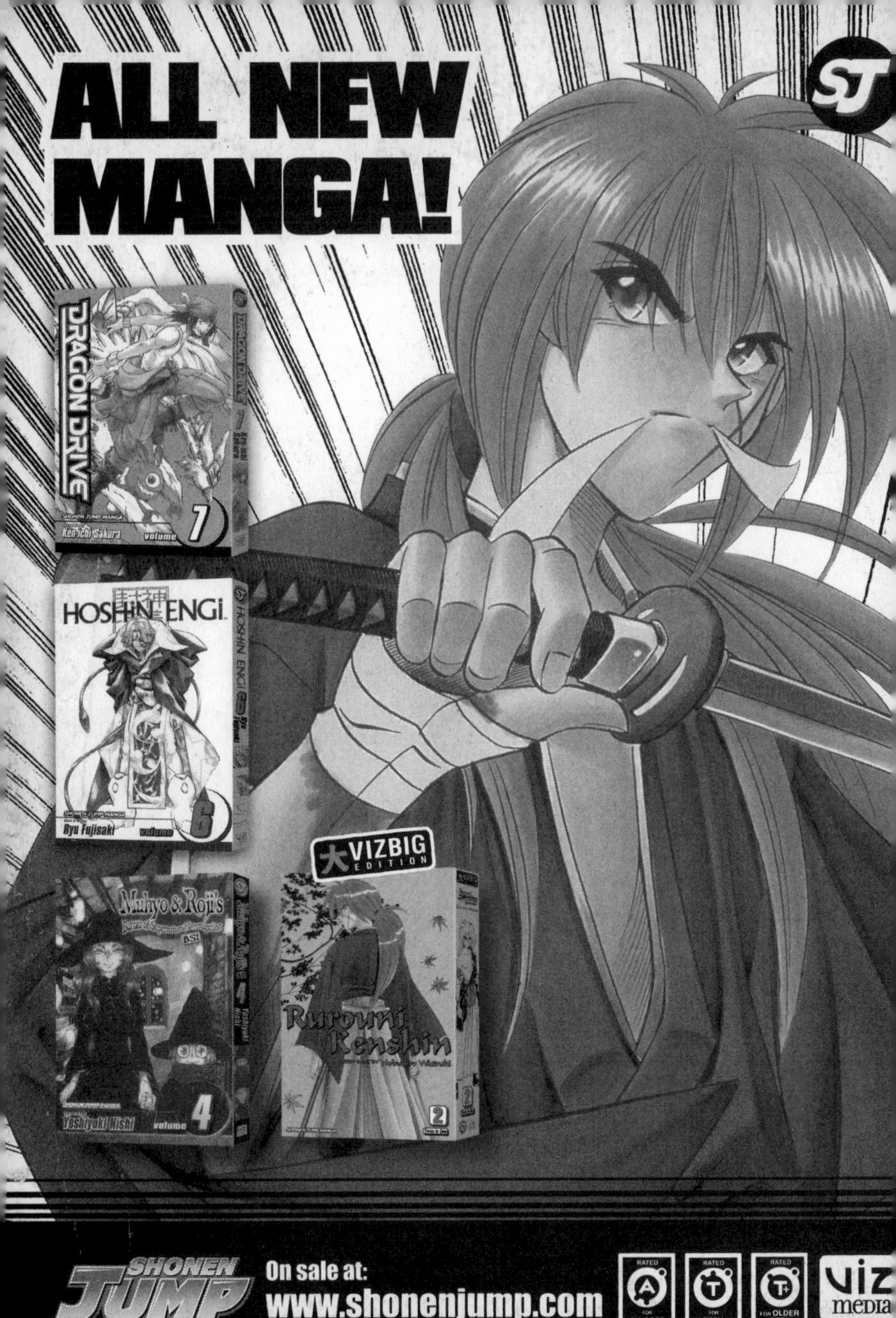
ALL NEW MANGA!
SJ
DRAGON DRIVE
SHONEN JUMP MANGA
Ken-ichi Sakura
volume 7
HOSHIN ENGI
Ryu Fujisaki
6
VIZBIG EDITION
Muhyo & Roji's
BSI
Yoshiyuki Nishi
volume 4
Rurouni Kenshin
2
SHONEN JUMP
THE WORLD'S MOST POPULAR MANGA
On sale at:
www.shonenjump.com
Also available at your local bookstore and comic store.
RATED A FOR ALL AGES ratings.viz.com
RATED T FOR TEEN ratings.viz.com
RATED T+ FOR OLDER TEEN ratings.viz.com
viz media
www.viz.co

Tell us what you think about SHONEN JUMP manga!

Our survey is now available online.
Go to: **www.SHONENJUMP.com/mangasurvey**

Help us make our product offering better!

Save **50% OFF** the cover price!

SHONEN JUMP
THE WORLD'S MOST POPULAR MANGA

Each issue of SHONEN JUMP contains the coolest manga available in the U.S., anime news, and info on video & card games, toys AND more!

☑ **YES!** Please enter my one-year subscription (12 HUGE issues) to **SHONEN JUMP** at the LOW SUBSCRIPTION RATE of **$29.95!**

NAME

ADDRESS

CITY   STATE   ZIP

E-MAIL ADDRESS   P7GNC1

☐ **MY CHECK IS ENCLOSED** (PAYABLE TO SHONEN JUMP)   ☐ **BILL ME LATER**

CREDIT CARD: ☐ **VISA**   ☐ **MASTERCARD**

ACCOUNT #   EXP. DATE

SIGNATURE

CLIP AND MAIL TO ➡

SHONEN JUMP
Subscriptions Service Dept.
P.O. Box 515
Mount Morris, IL 61054-0515

Make checks payable to: **SHONEN JUMP**. For 12 issues: $41.95 USD, including GST, HST and QST. US/CAN. 8 weeks for delivery.

BLEACH © 2001 by Tite Kubo/SHUEISHA Inc.
ONE PIECE © 1997 by Eiichiro Oda/SHUEISHA Inc.

RATED **T** FOR TEEN ratings.viz.com